VOLUME I.

THE Consultation Books for the years 1704 to 1710,
with an introductory account of the early history of the
English in Bengal, and addenda giving new extracts from
Thomas Pitt's correspondence, and new accounts of Bengal
in the seventeenth century.

THE EARLY ANNALS OF THE ENGLISH
IN BENGAL.

THE EARLY ANNALS OF THE ENGLISH IN BENGAL,

BEING

THE BENGAL PUBLIC CONSULTATIONS FOR THE FIRST HALF OF THE EIGHTEENTH CENTURY,

SUMMARISED, EXTRACTED, AND EDITED WITH INTRODUCTIONS AND ILLUSTRATIVE ADDENDA.

By
C. R. WILSON, M.A.,
OF THE BENGAL EDUCATION SERVICE.

LONDON:

W. THACKER & Co., 87, NEWGATE STREET.
CALCUTTA: THACKER, SPINK & Co.

1895.

PREFACE.

In the present volume, and in those which are to follow, I propose to do two things.

In the first place, I propose to publish extracts from the records preserved in the India Office which deal with the history of the English at Calcutta during the first half of the eighteenth century. This period is the dark age of British India. Thanks to the researches of Bruce, and still more recently of Sir Henry Yule, a considerable amount of information is available as to the history of the English in Bengal up to the first years of the eighteenth century. From this point hardly anything is known till we reach the year 1748, at which date Long began his selections from the records of the Government of Bengal. There is thus a gap in our knowledge of Calcutta history, which needs to be filled up.

In the second place, out of the new materials which I shall publish and the old which we already possess, I propose to construct the history of the English in Bengal.

It is the duty of the scientific enquirer to show the causes of every event. Is it not then strange that we are still without any adequate explanation of one of the greatest events of modern history, the English conquest of India? That conquest was the necessary result of a long series of changes which preceded it, but of this we have no demonstration. It remains not so much a subject of careful study as a matter for wonder, wonder the child of ignorance.

The history of British India has yet to be written. We have yet to understand why the English conquered India and not the Portuguese, French, or Dutch. We have yet to understand why it was from Bengal, not from Madras, or Bombay, that the English dominion took its rise. And we

have yet to understand the necessary connection between
the stages of the English advance into Bengal.

Undoubtedly a necessary connection does exist. Every
step is bound up with its antecedent and consequent steps
according to those invariable laws of development which the
genius of Hegel has discovered and explained.

The first period in this history lasts from 1633 to 1660,
during which the English take up a position in Bengal,
aiming at nothing more than commerce under the protection
of the Indian Government.

This moment in the development is of necessity followed
by its contradiction. In the period from 1661 to 1685
English industrialism finds itself opposed by militarism.
The English merchants are hampered by quarrels with the
native powers, by quarrels with interloping rivals, by quarrels
among themselves. At the end of this period we reach the
extreme antithesis of the first position taken up by the
English. Instead of trusting to their own peaceful intentions
and to the promises of the Indian Government, they resolve
to establish themselves in Bengal by force.

In the period lasting from 1685 to 1690 the English in
Bengal are in a state of flux. They wander from one policy
to another policy, and from one station to another station.
At last after repeated trials, they return to Bengal at the
invitation of the Nabob and form a fortified settlement at
Calcutta, thereby in a measure satisfying the claims both of
industrialism and of militarism.

In the fourth period, which begins from 1690, the settlement thus reached takes definite shape. English trade is
established in Bengal partly through the good-will of the
inhabitants and with the acquiescence of the native government, and partly by the powerful position which the English
had acquired. They command the sea, they dominate the
river traffic from Patna to Saugor, and behind the river they
are safely established at Calcutta.

Is it too much to say that these four stages are connected together in a necessary sequence? Is it fanciful to see in them the *sein, nichts, werden,* and *dasein* of English commerce in Bengal?

In this volume I publish summaries and extracts from the Bengal Public Consultations for the years 1704 to 1710, and in the introduction I have given the history of the English in Bengal up to and including the period covered by these records.

Resident as I am in India, only able to pay brief hurried visits to England, I have myself not been able to do more than read through the records in the India Office, indicate what extracts should be made, and verify my printed copy by comparison with the original. The actual copying out of the extracts was undertaken for me by my friend, Miss Stièvenard, who was good enough to devote many months to the work, and to whom consequently I can never be sufficiently thankful.

In writing the introduction I have received much assistance from Sir W. W. Hunter, from Mr. C. W. C. Oman, Fellow of All Souls College, Oxford, from Mr. J. Wells, Fellow of Wadham College, Oxford, and from Mr. E. M. Wheeler, Senior Tutor of Bishop's College, Calcutta, all of whom were so good as to read through my proofs and made many valuable suggestions.

I am also greatly indebted to Babu Gour Das Bysack for my knowledge of the Setts and the Bysacks, and of many other points in the local history of Calcutta.

For the sake of clearness I have illustrated my text with a number of rough explanatory maps and plans. The geography of Bengal is constantly changing, and there are no accurate maps of the country before those made by Rennell at the end of the eighteenth century. Under these circumstances it is obvious that plans of places in the sixteenth and seventeenth centuries must be to a certain extent conjectural. I have done my best to base my plans on the most reliable data, and here too I have been much helped by various friends in clearing up local topographical details.

Finally, my thanks are due to the Secretary of State for India in Council for allowing me to have access to the records in the India Office and to publish extracts from them, to the officials in charge of the records for courteous assistance of every kind, and to the Government of Bengal for giving me permission to use the Secretariat Press.

C. R. WILSON.

CALCUTTA, *November*, 1895.

CONTENTS.

CHAPTER IV.

CHAPTER V.

CHAPTER VI.

CHAPTER VII.

CHAPTER VIII.

CHRONOLOGY.

———◆———

1530 (circ.)	The Portuguese begin to frequent Bengal. Their ships anchor in Garden Reach at Betor.
1550 (circ.)	The Setts and Bysacks found Gobindpur and afterwards establish the Sūtānuṭī Hāt.
1575 (circ.)	The Portuguese settle at Hugli. The Thāna forts are built.

———

1620	Hughes and Parker are sent from Agra to Patna.
1632	The Portuguese are expelled from Hugli. Peter Mendy is sent from Agra to Patna and reports against trading there.
1633	The Governor of Orissa grants freedom of trade to Ralph Cartwright, who found English factories at Hariharapur and at Balasor. The Portuguese return to Hugli.
1636	The Portuguese are expelled from Hijili. Decay of Pipli.
1638	Grant to the English by Shāh Jahān.
1640	Foundation of Fort St. George.
1642	Thomas Day visits Balasor and advises its retention.
1645	Gabriel Boughton sent to Agra.
1651	Stephens and Bridgeman establish a factory at Hugli which becomes the chief station of the Bay with agencies at Balasor, Patna, Cassimbazar, and Rajmahal.
1652	Letters Patent granted to the English by Shāh Shujā'.
1653	Powle Walgrave, chief at Hugli.
1658	George Gawton, chief at Hugli. Reorganisation of the establishments in the Bay. Accession of Aurangzēb. Death of Shāh Shujā. Mīr Jamlah, Governor of Bengal. The English are forced to pay annually Rs. 3,000 in lieu of custom.
1658 Sept.	Jonathan Trevisa succeeds Gawton as Agent and Chief in the Bay.

———

1661	Trevisa seizes a native boat. Anger of Mīr Jumlah. The Mogul expedition to Assam.
1663	Death of Mīr Jumlah. Shāyista Khān, Viceroy of Bengal. Sir Edward Winter, Governor of Fort St. George. William Blake, Agent at Hugli. Winter's forward policy.
1665 Jan.	Winter superseded by Foxcroft.
1665 Sept.	Winter rebels and seizes Fort St. George.
1666	Shāyista Khān takes Chittagong.
1667	First grant to the English by Aurangzēb.

1668   Foxcroft restored. Stock for Bengal, £34,000. New factory at
            Dacca. Establishment of the Bengal Pilot Service.
1669   Shem Bridges, Agent in Bengal.
1670   Walter Clavell, Agent in Bengal. Bengal to supply all saltpetre.
1672   Sir W. Langhorne, President at Fort St. George. Order by
            Shāyista Khān freeing the English trade of all dues except the
            annual tribute of Rs. 3,000.
1673   The Court send skilled artisans to Bengal to improve the silk.
1675   Stock for Bengal, £85,000. Growth of the saltpetre trade.
1676   Streynsham Master sent to reform and regulate the establishments
            in the Bay. New Factory at Malda.
1677   Matthias Vincent, Agent in Bengal. The stock rises to £100,000.
            Shāyista Khān leaves.
1678   Letters Patent granted by Muḥammed A'zam, Viceroy of Bengal.
            The Rev. John Evans, first Bengal Chaplain reaches Hugli.
1679   Second visit of Master to the Bay. Captain Stafford makes the
            passage up the river to Hugli in the *Falcon*.
1680   Shāyista Khān returns. Ambiguous rescript of Aurangzēb. Stock
            for Bengal, £150,000.
1682   William Hedges, first English Governor of Bengal. Fruitless
            negotiations at Dacca.
1683   Mismanagement of Hedges.
1684   Hedges displaced. John Beard I, Agent under Fort St. George.
1685   Quarrel between Charnock and the Nabob. Death of John
            Beard I.

1686   Job Charnock, Agent at Hugli. Arrival of the fleet.
1686 Oct.   The skirmish at Hugli.
1686 Dec.   The English retire to Sūtānuṭī.
1687 Jan.   The Sūtānuṭī articles.
1687 Feb.   The English burn the King's salt houses, take the Thāna forts, seize
            Hijili, and sack Balasor.
1687 May   Arrival of the Mogul general at Hijili. His sudden attack on the
            English.
1687 June. Reinforcement under Captain Denham. The English withdraw to
            Ulubaria.
1687 July   First order from the Nabob.
1687 Aug.   Second order from the Nabob.
1687 Sept. Charnock returns to Sūtānuṭī.
1688   Eyre and Bradyll sent to Dacca to negotiate for Sūtānuṭī.
1688 Sept. Arrival of Captain Heath.
1688 Nov.   Heath and the English leave Sūtānuṭī. Attack on Balasor.
1688 Dec.   Heath starts for Chittagong.
1689 Jan.   The council of war decides not to attack Chittagong.
1689 Feb.   The English withdraw to Madras.

1690	Proclamation of Aurangzĕb.
1690 24 Aug.	Foundation of Calcutta.
1693	Death of Job Charnock. Aurangzĕb suspends all the privileges of the European traders. Sir John Goldsborough at Calcutta.
1694	Charles Eyre, Agent in Bengal. Loss of the *Royal James and Mary* in the Hugli.
1696	Rebellion of Çubha Singh. The English begin to build a fort at Calcutta.
1697	Building of the north-east bastion. 'Aẓīmu-sh-Shān, Viceroy of Bengal.
1698	Grant of the three villages by Prince 'Aẓīmu-sh-Shān. Foundation of the new English East India Company.
1699	John Beard II, Agent at Calcutta. Sir W. Norris, ambassador to the Mogul. Sir E. Littleton, representing the new Company, arrives in Bengal.
1700	Energetic efforts of the old Company. The Calcutta fort to be enlarged. Sir Charles Eyre, first President of Fort William in Bengal. Ralph Sheldon, first Collector of Calcutta. Benjamin Adams, second Bengal Chaplain.
1701	John Beard II, President. Building of the south-east bastion. Norris's fruitless negotiations with Aurangzĕb. Murshid Quli Khān, Treasurer.
1702	Aurangzĕb orders all the English goods to be seized. Ruin of the English Company in Bengal. Safety of Calcutta. " A fort better than an ambassador." Union of the rival Companies.
1703	Winding up the separate affairs of the rival Companies. Quarrels between the Prince and the Treasurer. Murshid Quli Khān made Deputy Governor as well as Treasurer.
1704 to 1707	Fruitless negotiations with Murshid Quli Khān.
1704	Installation of the Rotation Government. Benjamin Bowcher, Collector of Calcutta. Scheme for a church.
1705	Death of John Beard II at Madras.
1705 Oct.	John Cole, Collector.
1706 April	Arthur King, Collector.
1706 Oct.	John Maisters, Collector.
1707	Death of Aurangzĕb. Shāh 'Alam wins the race for Empire. Battle of Jājū. Building of the north-west and south-west bastions of Fort William. Building of the Hospital. Survey of the three villages. Death of Littleton.
1707 Feb.	Ab. Adams, Collector.
1707 Aug.	W. Bugden, Collector.
1708	Temporary alarm at Calcutta owing to the threats of the Governor of Hugli. Renewed efforts to secure a grant of privileges. Disputes with the Prince and the Treasurer. Death of Kām Bakhsh.
1708	Rapid growth of Calcutta.

1709   The Prince and Treasurer leave Bengal for Delhi. Sher Bulland Khān, the new Deputy Governor, grants the English an order for Rs. 45,000. At Madras Pitt proposes to send a present to the Emperor.

1709   Consecration of St. Anne's. Digging of the great pond or tank and completion of the riverside face of the fort. Death of Sheldon.

1709 Ap.   Sam. Blount, officiating Collector for W. Lloyd.

1709 Nov.   Sher Bulland Khān recalled. The new Treasurer tries to exact money from the English.

1710   The new Treasurer is murdered by the Naqdī horse. Murshid Quli returns as Treasurer and Deputy-Governor. Zaīnu-d-Dīn Khān, Governor of Hugli and Admiral in the Bay. Antony Weltden, President of Fort William.

1710 Jan.   Spencer, Collector.

1710 July.   J. Calvert, Collector.

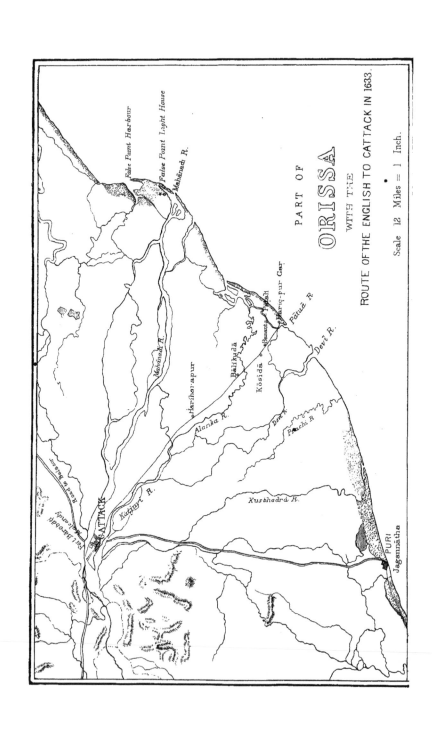

PART OF
ORISSA
WITH THE
ROUTE OF THE ENGLISH TO CATTACK IN 1633.

Scale   12 Miles = 1 Inch.

INTRODUCTORY ACCOUNT

OF THE

EARLY HISTORY OF THE ENGLISH IN BENGAL.

INTRODUCTORY ACCOUNT

OF

THE EARLY HISTORY OF THE ENGLISH IN BENGAL.

BOOK I.

HOW THE ENGLISH CAME TO BENGAL, FOR PURELY COM-
MERCIAL PURPOSES, RELYING ON THE GOOD-WILL AND
PROTECTION OF THE NATIVE GOVERNMENT.

CHAPTER I.

HOW THE ENGLISH CAME TO ORISSA IN 1633.

THE advance of the English from the Coromandel Coast up the
Bay of Bengal, like the recent advances of the Russians in Asia, was
primarily due to the enterprise of local officers. In March 1633, the
Company's Agent at Masulipatam, meeting with a growing scarcity
of cloth in that place, resolved on sending out an expedition to open
up trade with the fertile provinces at the mouth of the Ganges.
The party, which consisted of eight Englishmen, set sail in a country
boat such as may still be seen in many of the ports along the coast,
an odd-looking but serviceable craft, having a square sail, an oar-like
rudder, and a high poop, with a thatched house built on it for a cabin.

B

On reaching Harṣapur or Hariçpur, the modern Hariçpur Gaṛ, at the mouth of the Pātuā,[1] in Orissa, they transferred themselves and their merchandise to small boats, and so ascended the river some eight miles, as far as Kōṣīdā.   Here they took the high road to Cuttack which then, as now, passed through Bālikudā, the chief village of the fiscal division of Benāhār, and the important town of Jagatsiṁhapur, or, as it was till lately called, Hariharapur.[2]   From Cuttack the travellers repaired to the court of Malcandy, or Mukund Deo, in Fort Bārabāṭi, where they were received with great kindness by the reigning nabob.

To-day the journey may well seem commonplace, but it was then a wonderful and hazardous undertaking.[3]   Much, indeed, had the travellers heard of the countries to which they were going, but they knew little.   They distrusted the native inhabitants; they stood in awe of the high and mighty Mogul who had lately so terribly visited the Portuguese,[4] and above all they dreaded those very Portuguese whose jealousy could brook no rivals.   The history of this first coming of the English has therefore all the interest which attaches to new voyages of discovery and adventure.   Let William Bruton, of the parish of St. Saviour's, Southwark, quartermaster of the good ship *Hopewell*, and one of the founders of the English trade in Bengal, begin the story in his own words.[5]

---

[1] This river is called R. Pāṭali above, and R. Pātuā below, Basanta-Pāṭali, and at its mouth R. Bōita-kuliyā, ship-haven, a name significant of the former importance of the now sand-barred harbour of Hariçpur.

[2] Hariharapur, the city of the Tawny One and the Grasping One, *i.e.*, the city of Vishnu and Çiva combined.   Hariharapur is eleven miles from Bālikudā, and about twenty-five miles from Cuttack.   It was the capital of a parganā and a subdivision of Orissa.   Hariharapur and Jagatsiṁhapur, to the north of Hariharapur, are contiguous villages on the road from Kōṣīdā to Cuttack, from which they are distant some twenty-five miles.   Till the beginning of the nineteenth century Hariharapur was the principal village, and the place went by that name. To-day Jagatsiṁhapur has supplanted it.   The river at Hariharapur is the Alanka. Bruton's town of Hariharapur, six or seven miles in compass, must have included all the neighbouring villages.

[3] "The first thinge (of Note) that was Acted after our Cominge vnto this Coast." *Hedges' Diary*, III, 178.

[4] In 1632, by order of Shāh Jahān, Qāsim Khān destroyed the Portuguese settlement at Hūglī after an obstinate siege of more than three months.

[5] " NEWS from the EAST INDIES or a VOYAGE to BENGALLA.........WRITTEN BY WILLIAM BRUTON, now resident in the parish of *St. Saviour's, Southwark,*......... and now lately came Home in the good Ship called *The Hopewel* of London.......... Imprinted at London by I. Okes.........1638."   This voyage is reprinted in vol. viii. of a *Collection of Voyages and Travels* published by Osborne in 1752, and also in vol. v. of the enlarged edition of "Hakluyt" of 1809-12.   I have printed Bruton's account as it appears in the edition of 1752, without altering the punctuation or spelling.

"The twenty-second of *March*, 1632 [*i.e.*, 1633 N. S.], I being in the country of *Cormandell* with six *Englishman* more, at a place called *Massalupatam*, a town of merchandize, Mr. *John Norris*, the agent there, was resolved to send two merchants into *Bengalla* for the settling of a factory there: and these six *Englishmen* (of the which I was one) were to go with the merchants, and withal to carry a present from the agent to the *nabob*, or *king* of that country, to obtain the promises that formerly he had granted to the *English* for traffic, and to be custom-free in those of his dominions and ports. Wherefore a *junk* was hired at *Massalupatam*, to be our convoy; and the said *junk* did belong unto those parts, and the names of the *Englishmen*, that were appointed for that voyage, were Mr. *Ralph Cartwright*, merchant, Mr. *Thomas Colley* second, *William Bruton*, *John Dobson*, *Edward Peteforde*, *John Busby*, *John Ward*, and *William Withall*.

"Though we hired the aforesaid *junk*, *March* 22, yet it was the sixth of *April* following, before we could be fitted to depart from *Massalupatam*, and in much various weather with many difficulties and dangers (which to relate here would be tedious, and impertinent to my intended discourse); the twenty-first of *April*, being then *Easter-day*, we were at anchor in a bay before a town called *Harssapoore*: it is a place of good strength with whom our merchants hold commerce with correspondency. This twenty-first day in the morning Mr. *Ralph Cartwright* sent the money ashore to the governor of *Harssapoore* to take it into his safe keeping and protection until such time he came ashore himself. So presently there came a *Portugal* frigate fiercely in hostility towards us, but we made ready for their entertainment and fitted ourselves and the vessel for our best defences; but at last they steered off from us, and, upon our command, she came to an anchor somewhere near us, and the master of her came on board of us, who being examined whence he came and whither he was bound, to which demands he answered nothing worthy of belief as the sequel showed: for he seemed a friendly trader, but was indeed a false invader (where opportunity and power might help and prevail); for, on the 22nd day, Mr. *Cartwright* went ashore to the governor of *Harssapoore*; and on the twenty-fourth day, the said master of the frigate (with the assistance of some of the ribble-rabble rascals of the town) did set upon Mr. *Cartwright* and Mr. *Colley*, where our men (being oppressed by multitudes) had like to have been all slain or spoiled, but that (*Lucklip*) the *rogger* [1] (or vice-king there) rescued them with two hundred men.

---

[1] Lakshmīp the rājā.

"In this fray Mr. *Thomas Colley* was sore hurt in one of his hands, and one of our men much wounded in the leg and head; their *nockada*,[1] or *India* pilot, was stabbed in the groin twice, and much mischief was done and more intended: but by God's help all was pacified.

"The twenty-seventh day of *April* we took leave of the governor and town of *Harssapoore* (I mean three of us); namely, Mr. *Cartwright*, *William Bruton*, and *John Dobson*, leaving Mr. *Colley* and the four men with him, till news could be sent back to them from the *nabob's* court at *Cutteke* or *Malcander*,[2] of our success and proceedings there with our other goods; for he is no wise merchant, that ventures too much in one bottom, or that is too credulous to trust *Mahometans* or *Infidels*.

"And having laden our small boats with the goods which were gold, silver, cloth and spices (of which spices those parts of *India* are wanting), and they almost are as dear there as in *England*, we passed some two leagues and a half in water; and after that the said goods were carried by land in carts, till we came to a great town *Balkkada*, but it was more than three hours after sun-setting, or late before we came thither.

---

[1] *Nākhudā* (Pers.), a native skipper.

[2] Malcander, or Malcandy, seems to be a corrupt form for Makan Deo or Mukund Deo. Mukund Deo (Sanskrit, Mukunda Deva) was the last indigenous ruler of Orissa. He became king in 1550 A.D., six years before Akbar ascended the throne. In 1567 Sulaimān Shāh Kirānī, the Viceroy of Bengal, sent Kālāpahār, a fanatic Musulman, to conquer Orissa, and Mukund Deo fell in fight at Jājpur. Mukund Deo built a magnificent palace at Cuttack, which Bruton speaks of as the "Court of Malcandy."

"The city of Cuttack," says Abū-l Faẓl in the Āīn-i-Akbarī, "has a stone fort situated at the bifurcation of the two rivers, the Mahānadi, held in high veneration by the Hindus, and the Kātjurī. It is the residence of the Governor and contains some fine buildings. For five or six *kos* round the fort, during the rains, the country is under water. Rājā Mukund Deo built a palace here with nine courts [literally, 'of nine *ashianahs* or nests']." In giving the list of the mahals in the sarkār of Katak, Abū-l Faẓl again briefly notes that Katak Banāras is a suburban district with a city, having a stone fort of great strength, and a masonry palace within. The palace was in time abandoned by the Musalman Governors who preferred to live in the Lālbāgh, on the south side of the city. It is now a wilderness of stone pits.

The construction of Fort Bārabāti has been assigned to various monarchs with various dates. Sterling thinks it was built by Rājā Ananga Bhima Deva in the fourteenth century. The stone work has been taken by the Public Works Department to build lighthouses and hospitals, and to pave roads.

The ditch of the fort, however, still remains, and so does the gate, which is still approached by a causeway. The palace of Mukand Deo, like all eastern palaces, had a gathering of populace and artificers about it, and this is apparently what Bruton means by the "town of Malcandy."

" The twenty-eighth day of *April* in the morning, the governor of this town came and saluted our merchant, and promised him that whatsoever was in his power to do him any friendly courtesy he should command it : and indeed he was in every way as good as his word ; for he lent us horses to ride on and cowlers [1] (which are porters) to carry our goods ; for at this town the carts did leave us and our goods were carried on men's shoulders ; then we set forwards, being accompanied with the governor, with his music, which were shalms, and pipes of sundry forms, much after the forms of waits or hautboys, on which they played most delicately out of tune, time, and measure. In this manner the governor with a great number of people, did bring us about half an *English* mile out of the town, where he courteously took his leave of us, but yet he sent his servants with us as guides, and that they might bring his horses unto him that he lent us.

" This day at the hours of between eleven and twelve of the clock, it was so excessively hot, that we could not travel ; and the wind blew with such a sultry scalding heat, as if it had come forth of an oven or furnace ; such a suffocating fume did I never feel before or since : and here we were forced to stay near three hours, till the sun was declined, we having happily got under the shadow of the branches of a great tree all that time. Then we set forward for the town of *Harharrapoore :* which, in the space of two hours, or a little more, we drew near unto : so we staid awhile, till our carriages were come up together unto us ; which done, there met us a man, who told us that his master staid our coming : then we speedily prepared ourselves for the meeting of so high esteemed a person : and, when we came to the town's end, there met us at a great *pagodo* or *pagod,* [2] which is a famous and sumptuous temple or church for their idolatrous service and worship there used : and, just against that stately and magnificent building, we were entertained and welcomed by one of the king's greatest noblemen, and his most dear and chiefest favourite, who had a letter from the king his master, and was sent from him to meet us, and to conduct us to his court. The nobleman's name was *Mersymomeine ;* [3] he received us very kindly, and made us a very great feast, or costly collation, before supper ; which

---

[1] *Qulī,* the ordinary word used in India for hired labourers.

[2] Babu M. M. Chakravarti tells me that there still is at Hariharapur an old temple dedicated to Çiva, locally known as Somnāth. But he also argues that, if Mirzā Mōmin stopped in the *pagoda,* it could not have been a Hindu temple and may have been a pavilion erected for royal encampments, such as we find elsewhere in Orissa.

[3] *i.e.,* Mirzā Mōmin.

being done, we departed for our *surroy*,[1] or inn, where we lay all night with our goods; but *Mersymomeine* stayed with his followers and servants in his and their tents at the *pagod*.

"The twenty-ninth day of *April* we staid at *Harharrapoore*, and visited this great man; but the greatest cause of our staying was by reason of the *nockada*, or pilot, of the frigate, whose men affronted and hurt some of our men at *Harssapoore;* for which cause the frigate was staid there, and the pilot of her came to this great man, thinking by gifts to win him to clear his vessel; but he would not be allured by such rewards or promises; but told him that he must appear before the *nabob* and seek to clear himself there.

"The thirtieth day of *April*, we set forward in the morning in our way to the city of *Coteke* (it is a city of several miles in compass, and it standeth a mile from Malcandy, where the court is kept): but Mr. *Cartwright* staid behind, and came after us accompanied by the said nobleman: we went all the day on our journey, till the sun went down; and then we staid for our merchant, being eight *English* miles from *Coteke :* and about twelve or one of clock at night they came where we were: so we hasted, and suddenly got all our things in readiness, and went along with them; and about the time of three or four of clock in the morning, we came to the house of this *Mersymomeine* at *Coteke*, being *May-day*.

"Here we were very well entertained, and had a great variety of sundry sorts of meats, drinks, and fruits. About eight of the clock, *Mersymomeine* went to the court, and made known to the king that the *English* merchant was come to his house: then the king caused a great banquet to be speedily prepared, and to be sent to the house of *Mersymomeine*, which banquet was very good and costly. Then, about three or four of the clock in the afternoon, we were sent for to the court of *Malcandy*."

---

[1] *i.e., Sarāi*, an edifice, a palace, but in India a building for the accommodation of travellers.

CHAPTER II.

To the north of the city, at the bifurcation of the Mahānadī and the Kātjurī, stood the citadel of Cuttack, Fort Bārabāṭi, a spacious area, a mile and-a-half in circumference, defended by a broad ditch faced with masonry, by double walls of stone, and by square sloping bastions which clearly bespoke its indigenous origin. Fifty years before the coming of the English, Mukund Deo, the last Hindu ruler of Orissa, had built within it a castle of grey granite with nine lofty courts, but he had lost his kingdom to the Moslem, and Āghā Muḥammad Zamān of Tahrān, a Mogul viceroy, now abode in the stately palace of "Malcandy." The English travellers reached the place from the east, over a long narrow causeway, and were conducted through a labyrinth of buildings to the court of public audience.

Here Bruton and his companions awaited the coming of his Highness, and found themselves objects of much curiosity. At last the word came that the nabob was approaching. The place was forthwith spread with rich carpets, gold pillars being placed at the corners to hold them down, and in the middle a red velvet bolster for his Highness to recline against. Then, preceded by his brother, a comely man carrying a sword, accompanied by fifty grave looking courtiers, and greeted on all sides with low prostrations, came the

Mogul Governor, a fair and stately personage, leaning his arms upon two of his attendants. This was Āghā Muḥammad Zamān,[1] a Persian grandee, born in Tahrān, who was in high favour with the Emperor Shāh Jahān, and had recently been sent to Orissa to wage war against the king of Golkonda. He very affably inclined his head towards Mr. Cartwright, who was presented to him by Mirzā Mōmin, and, slipping off his sandal, offered "his foot to our merchant to kiss, which he twice refused to do, but at last he was fain to do it."

Then the nabob and the whole court sat down cross-legged. The English merchant brought forth his presents, and made his requests to the nabob for trading privileges. But, by the time he had reached the end of his story, the king's almoner gave the signal for prayers, and the whole company knelt down with their faces towards the setting sun. Prayers being ended, and business laid aside, the palace was soon

---

[1] Bruton does not tell us the name of the nabob, whom he saw in 1633, and who gave Cartwright the order for free trade in Orissa. All that we could infer from this narrative is that the nabob had recently succeeded Bāqir Khān, that he was a white man, and possibly that he was a Persian. But from a list of State papers found in the United Trade Consultations Book for 1704, under the date of the 19th February, we find that the name of Cartwright's nabob was Āghā Muḥammad Zamān. From other sources it appears that Āghā Muḥammad Zamān was a Persian, born in Tarhān, who was one of the high officials of Jahāngīr. He served in Bengal for a long time, and was Tuquldār and Faujdār of Sylhet. On the accession of Shāh Jahān, his allowance of two thousand rupees, and his command of one thousand horse were allowed to remain. According to the Pādshāh Nāmah, in 1040 H., i.e. 1630-31 A.D., he was serving in Bengal. The next year he was raised to a higher rank, that is his allowance and command were increased. In 1044 H., or 1634-5 A.D., he is mentioned as attending the court of Shāh Jahān, and presenting two elephants and nine horses brought from Bengal. In the same year he accompanied Islām Khān, who was sent to Bengal as governor. In 1047 H. he was sent by Islām Khān to carry on war in Kūch Hājar, and for the next few years fought with some success again-t the Assamese. For these services he was raised to a still higher rank. In 1051 H. Shāh Jahān having given the province of Orissa to Shāh Shujā', directed him to send Muḥammad Zamān Tahrānī to govern that province. In 1055 H. Mu'taqid Khān succeeded him, and Muḥammad Zamān was sent to Balkh to serve under Prince Aurangzēb.

There is thus no mention of his being governor of Orissa in 1633 A.D. On the contrary the Pādshāh Nāmah says that Bāqir Khān, who was nabob of Orissa at the succession of Shāh Jahān, was succeeded by Mu'taqid Khān in 1041 H., or 1631-2 A.D., who was succeeded by Nawāz Khān in 1049 H., or 1639-40 A.D. Muḥammad Zamān was made governor of Orissa and displaced Nawāz Khān in 1050 H.

In the face of the evidence of the English records there can be no doubt that the Persian authorities are in error here as they often are. Bāqir Khān was succeeded by Muḥammad Zamān in 1631-32 A.D., who was succeeded by Mu'taqid Khān in 1044 H., or 1634-5 A.D. Thus Muḥammad Zamān was twice governor of Orissa, and was twice succeeded by Mu'taqid Khān.

ablaze with countless wax tapers which the attendants lighted up with great ceremony. Between eight and nine o'clock the English returned to Cuttack.

"The second day we came in the afternoon again to the court before the *nabob*, which being set, there met us at the *derbar* [1] (or council house) our old enemy, the *nockada* of the frigate, who made a great complaint against us, that we had fought to make prize of his vessel, and to take his goods by force: he had likewise given a great gift to a nobleman, to stand his friend, and speak in his behalf.

"Our merchant pleaded likewise, that all such vessels as did trade on the coast and had not a pass either from the *English*, *Danes*, or *Dutch*, were lawful prize. He answered that he had a pass. Our merchant told him to produce the same before the *nabob*, and he would clear him; to which the *nabob* and the whole council agreed; but he could shew no pass from any of the aforenamed three nations, but he shewed two passes from or of the *Portugals*, which they call by the name of *fringes* [2]; and thus was he cast, and we had the better of him before the king and council.

"But then stood up the nobleman to whom he had given a reward (who had also a little knowledge or insight in sea affairs), and said, What stranger, seeking a free trade, could make prize of any vessel within any of the sounds, seas, roads or harbours of his majesty's dominions? This he spoke not so much for the good of the king, but thinking and hoping, that the vessel, by this means, should have been clear'd with all her goods, and the *nockada* (or pilot) acquitted; that so, by those means, he might have gained the more and greater rewards; but he was quite deceived in his vain expectation; for the *nabob* perceiving that she belonged to *Pipely*, a port-town of the *Portugals*, whom the *nabob* affects not, where the *Portugals* were resident, and that she was not bound for any of his ports, he made short work with the matter, and put us all out of strife presently; for he confiscated both vessel and goods all to himself, whereby the nobleman was put by his hopes, who was indeed a governor of a great sea-town, where to much shipping belonged, and many ships and other vessels built. Our merchant seeing that he could not make prize of the vessel or the goods, nor have any satisfaction for the wrongs which he and our men had received, he rose up in great anger,

---

[1] *i.e., darbār*, a court or levee.

[2] *Farangī*, a Frank. The term is used in India, as here, to denote the Indian-born Portuguese.

and departed, saying, that if he could not have right here, he would have it in another place; and so went his way, not taking his leave of the *nabob*, nor of any other: at which abrupt departure they all admired.

"The third day in the morning the king sent for our merchant by the lord comptroller of his court, who went with him accompanied with *Merssymomeine* and others to the *Derbar*, where there was a very grave assembly set: then come the king, who, being set, he smiled upon our merchant, and (by an interpreter) demanded the cause why he went away the last evening (or overnight) in such an anger? To whom he answered boldly, and with a stern undaunted countenance, that he had done his masters of the honourable company wrong, and, by his might and power, had taken their rights from them, which would not be so endured or put up. The king, hearing this, demanded of the assembly, which were as well merchants as nobles, in the *Persian* tongue, of what strength and force our shipping were, their number, burthen, and force; where our chief place of residence was for trading: he likewise sent for *Persian* merchants and diligently enquired of them the same demands and questions: who answered, that we had great trading on the coast of *Cormandel, India*[1] and *Persia*; and likewise in the south seas, as *Bantam, Japaro, Janbee*, and *Mocossor*.[2] They further told the *nabob* that our shipping was great, and of great force withal; and likewise if his pleasure was such as to be at odds with us, there neither could, would, or should any vessel, great or small, that did belong to these parts, stir out of any havens, ports, or harbours, of his majesty's dominions, but they would take them, for they were not able to withstand their force. At these words the king said but little, but what he thought is beyond my knowledge to tell you.

"Then the King turned to our merchant, and told him, in *Moors* language (the which he could very well understand), that he should grant the *English* free trade upon these conditions following:—

"That if the *English* ship or ships should at any time see any ship or ships, *junk* or *junks*, or any other vessel of the *nabob's*, or any of his subjects, in distress, either by foul weather, or in danger of enemies, or

---

[1] *i.e.*, the Malabar Coast.

[2] Bantam is on the west and Japara on the north coast of Java. Jambi is the name of a Malay State on the north-eastern side of Sumatra. Macassar used to be the name of a people of Celebes inhabiting the extreme end of its south-western peninsula. Captain Lancaster established a factory at Bantam in 1603. In 1613 a ship was sent for the first time to Jambi, "hitherto not discovered by any Christians." In 1626 a factory was established at Japara.

in any other extremity, that we (the *English*) should help, aid, and assist them, to our powers; or, if it happened they were in want of cables, anchors, water, victuals, or any other necessaries whatsoever, that did belong to them, that we, the said *English*, should help them as we were able; likewise that we, the said *English*, should not make prize of any vessel belonging to any of the dominions of the said *nabob;* and that we, the said *English*, should not make prize of any ship, vessel or vessels, within the ports, rivers, roads, or havens of the *nabob*, though they were our enemies; but at the sea we might make prize of them, if we could. To this all our merchants agreed. Then the king caused articles on his part to be drawn and published in this manner following :—

" ' Here I, the said *nabob*, vice-king and governor of the country of *Woodia*,[1] under the great and mighty prince *Pedesha Shassallem*,[2] do give and grant free licence to the aforesaid *Ralph Cartwright*, merchant, to trade, buy, sell, export, and transport, by shipping, either off or upon the shore, not paying any *junken* or custom, nor any under me to cause them to pay any : likewise, that if they do convey goods by shore between factory and factory, or any other place, for their better advantage of gain, within these his dominions, I strictly charge and command, that no governor, custom-gatherer, or other officer whatsoever, shall make or cause them to pay any *junken*[3] or customs; but shall suffer them to pass free, without lett, hindrance, molestation, or interruption of stayage, but shall (I say) help and further them in anything that shall be the furtherance of their business. Moreover, I do grant to the *English* merchants to take ground, and to build houses fitting for their employments, and where they shall see convenient for their best utility and profits, without lett or hindrance of any of my loving subjects.

" ' And further, I do give and grant to the *English* merchants free license to build shipping, small or great, or any other vessel they think best and fittest for their occasions and uses; they paying no more than the custom of the country to the workmen; and likewise to repair shipping, if any such occasion be to require it.

" ' Likewise I the *nabob* do command, that no governor or officer whatsoever under me shall do the *English* any wrong, or cause any

---

[1] This is Odiya or Oḍāon, *i.e.*, Orissa. All these forms are corruptions of the Sanskrit Odra-deca, which means the country of the Oḍras or Uḍras, but who the Oḍras were is not known.

[2] That is, Pādshāh Shāh Jahān.

[3] This word *junken* comes from the Tamil *chungam*, meaning customs.

to be done unto them, as they shall answer it at their perils, wheresoever they are resident: neither shall any wrong be done to any servant of theirs, that doth belong unto them.

"'And again, if any controversy should be betwixt the *English* and the people of the country if the matter be of any moment, then the said cause shall be brought before me the *nabob*, at the court at *Malcandy*, and at the *derbar* I will decide the matter, because the *English* may have no wrong (behaving themselves as merchants ought to do).'

"This licence formed and given at the royal court of *Malcandy*, the third day of *May* 1633, but not sealed till the fifth day of *May* following, at night.

"The fourth day of *May* the king sent a great banquet to the house of *Merssymomeine*, to our merchant; and there came to this feast the great man that spake on the *nockada's* side against us, at the *derbar*, about the frigate aforesaid: he brought with him to our merchant for a present, a bale of sugar, a bottle of wine, and some sweetmeats, saying, he was sorry for the things done before and past, but if anything lay in him to do the company and him any good, he and they should be sure of it. This man was governor of a town called *Bollasorye*,[1] a sea-town where shipping was built, as is aforesaid; his name was Mercossom,[2] and understanding that the merchant was minded to travel that way, he promised him to do him all the courtesies that could be.

"The fifth day of *May*, in the afternoon, we were before the king again at the *derbar*; at our coming he called for our *perwan*[3] (which was our warrant or licence), and then he added to it the free leave of coining moneys, and sealed it with his own signet himself, and so all things were strongly confirmed and ratified for our free trade in his territories and dominions."[4]

---

[1] *i.e.*, Balasor.
[2] *i.e.*, Mīr Qāsim.
[3] That is *parwāna*, an order. It technically denotes a grant signed by the nabob.
[4] The initiation of the trade with Bengal is usually ascribed to a farmān supposed to have been granted to the English by Shāh Jahān on the 2nd February 1634, allowing them liberty to trade in Bengal, but confining them to Pipli. I have taken no notice of this story for the following reasons.—The only evidence produced to prove that there ever was such a farmān is a letter from the Council of Surat, dated the 21st February 1634, in which they state that on the 2nd of that month they received a farmān of this description, but they go on to say, somewhat incredulously, that they had received "no English letter or syllable,

On the 6th of May the nabob gave a great feast to the English at the court under a canopy of velvet of four colours, and invested Cartwright with a dress of honour. On the 8th of May they again went to the court to get a free pass and a safe convoy, and found the nabob busy with his war preparations. The next day they finally took leave of the court.

"Thus have I," says Bruton, "plainly and truly related the occurrences that happened at the court of *Malcandy :* but although the palace of the *nabob* be so large in extent, and so magnificent in structure, yet he himself will not lodge in it, but every night he lodgeth in tents, with his most trusty servants and guards about him; for it is an abomination to the *Moguls* (which are white men), to rest or sleep under the roof of a house that another man hath built for his own honour. And therefore he was building a palace, which he purposed should be a fabric of a rest, and future remembrance of his renown : he likewise keepeth three hundred women, who are all of them the daughters of the best and ablest subjects that he hath."

---

private or public, directly or indirectly, concerning this or any other business." I may add that from that day to this no one has ever heard or seen one English letter or syllable, private or public, directly or indirectly, concerning this farmān, and that there is no evidence that the English in Bengal ever went to Pipli, or ever heard that they had been permitted to do so. I may also point out that if the farmān was granted at Agra on the 2nd of February, it could not have arrived at Surat on that same day. The farmān of course originated in the imagination of the native interpreter, who was employed to translate the despatch from Agra, and who did his best to please his masters according to his lights. Such farmāns and rumours of farmāns were common enough in those days, and we see that they did not put much faith in the story at Surat; yet it has been solemnly repeated as history ever since.

According to the legend, the English established factories at Pipli in 1634, at Hugli in 1640, and at Balasor in 1642. The truth is that the English never had any factory at Pipli except in the imagination of the historians. Sir Henry Yule, who has examined all the records extant relating to this period, has not been able to find any evidence whatever of any such thing. Bruton gives us the authentic account of the origin of the English factory at Balasor. It was established there by Ralph Cartwright in 1633 A.D. in response to an invitation from the governor, Mīr Qāsim. Even without Bruton's circumstantial account of the origin of the English factories at Haribarapur and Balasor in 1633, I should have thought that Day's letter would have shown our historians that the Balasor factory was established some years before 1642. Day says :—" Do not abandon Balasor after all your trouble and expense." This implies that the English had already come there, yet the historians perversely argue that the English came to Balasor in 1642. In the next chapter but one I shall give the true account of the establishment of the Hugli factory in 1650 A.D.

CHAPTER III.

THE ENGLISH FACTORIES AT BALASOR AND HARIHARAPUR IN ORISSA.

LEAVING the court of the nabob, the English proceeded to found a factory at Hariharapur. "The ninth of *May*, we gathered together all our things, and at night we departed from *Coteke*. The tenth, at the hour of two in the afternoon, we came to the town of *Harharrapoore*, and hosted in the house of our interpreter. The eleventh day we went to the governor of the town and shewed him our *fermand*,[1] or commission from the king: the governor made a great *salame*, or court'sy, in reverence unto it, and promised his best assistance and help in anything that he could do; and there the said governor had a small present given to him. The twelfth day of *May* Mr. *Thomas Colley* came to us at *Harharrapoore*, and the rest of the Englishmen with him, with all the goods; then we hired a house for the present, till such time as ours might be built, for our further occasions to the company's use.

"This town of *Harharrapoore* is very full of people, and it is in bounds six or seven miles in compass; there are many merchants in it and great plenty of all things: here is also cloth of all sorts, great store, for there do belong to this town at least three thousand weavers, that are housekeepers, besides all other that do work, being bound or hired.

"The fourteenth day, the two merchants went abroad, and found out a plot of land fitting to build upon; then they laid the king's *deroy*[2] on it and seized upon it for the company's use; and there was no man that did or durst gainsay them for doing the same.

---

[1] That is *furmān*, an order. It is used incorrectly here, as it properly denotes a grant signed by the Mogul.

[2] Mar. *durāhi* or Tel. *durāi*: "a prohibition in the King's name for anyone to have anything to do with them till that be taken off."

"The fifteenth day they hired workmen and labourers to measure the ground and to square out the foundation of the house, and likewise for the wall, which was one hundred conets [1] square, which is fifty yards, every conet being half a yard or a foot and a half; and it behoved us to make haste for the time of the great rains was at hand.

"The sixteenth day they laid the foundation of the walls, being nine feet thick: much haste was made and many workmen about it; but this our first work was but labour lost and cast away, for it came to nothing.

"For on the eighteenth day the rains began with such force and violence that it beat down all our work to the ground and washed it away as if there had not been anything done: this storm continued without ceasing (day and night), more or less, three weeks complete.

"The sixteenth day of *June* Mr. *Ralph Cartwright* took his journey for *Ballazary*, and two *Englishmen* with him who were *Edward Peteford* and *William Withall*, and from thence he was minded to travel further into the country of *Bengalla*." [2]

Meanwhile the Council at Masulipatam had not forgotten their mission to Orissa. The good ship *Swan*, under the command of Edward Austin, had recently arrived from England; and by a consultation held on the 27th June, it was decided that she and all her cargo, with Mr. Bannister and Mr. Littler, two new factors, should be sent on to Bengal to discover the condition and prospects of the trade in those parts, and to effect a permanent settlement. There were many reasons to be given for this decision. "Ffirst,[3] for the trade 'twixt that and this place [Masulipatam], in Rice, Sugar, Butter, and divers other sorts of Provisions and course Commodities. Secondly, it affords Store of white cloths at Cheape Prices, such as is Suitable for England, Persia, and the Southwards............Besides it yealdes good Store of exceeding good powder Sugar [4], which Costs not there above two pence halfe penny the English pound, with all charges aboard. As

---

[1] This seems to be a misprint for *covet* or *covid*, a corruption of the Portuguese *covado*, a cubit or ell.

[2] Bruton's voyage in Osborne's *Collection of Voyages and Travels*, volume VIII, p. 276, edition of 1752.

[3] *Diary of William Hedges*, edited for the Hakluyt Society by Colonel Henry Yule, volume III, pages 178, 179, edition of 1889. Bruce in his *Annals of the East India Company* altogether misunderstands this letter. See *op. cit.* I, p. 327. edition of 1810.

[4] They do not appear to have thought so highly of this commodity at home. In September 1660, the Court gave orders not to purchase any more Bengal sugars for the future.

much of this Commodity as may be got timely enough for Persia, we intend for that place by the *Discovery*. Gumlacke [1] vppon stickes is there to be had very Cheape, and is much required, as well for Macassar and Persia as for England............Silke may there be Bought likewise yearely to a great Summe at 4 *in* 5 *fanams* [2] the English pound. ....Divers other things it affords for Persia, as *Shashes*, Stuffes, *Allyjahs*, [3] fine Chite Cloths, and the like. Some whereof is now in Action for that place, and our Better experience will doubtless Bringe the rest Also within the compass of our future investments."

On the 22nd of July, the *Swan* anchored off Hariçpur and fired three guns; but as the English were all inland at Hariharapur, she got no answer. Having waited all night, they weighed anchor in the morning and went on to Balasor, where they met Mr. Cartwright. [4]

So far all had gone well with the English. But difficulties now began to arise in various directions. The new-comers were quite ignorant of the commercial needs of the people of Bengal. The goods brought out by the *Swan* were not of the right sort. She was chiefly laden with broadcloth and lead, but there was no demand for these commodities in Bengal, and so the whole of the cargo lay at Balasor for nearly a year without being sold. [5] Neither the merchants nor the common sailors understood the necessity for severe self-restraint and temperance in these Eastern regions. The place abounded with fruit and arrack, [6] and these when taken in excess produced the most lamentable consequences. [7] On the 25th of August, in the morning, Mr. Thomas Colley died of fever at Hariharapore, [8] and on the 17th October, John Poule, purser of the *Swan*, who had been sent from Balasor to take poor Colley's place, writes to Cartwright in the

---

[1] *Lac* is a resinous incrustation produced on certain trees by the puncture of the *lac* insect. The material in its crude form is called stick *lac*. It contains some 10 per cent. of dark red dye, and some 60 or 70 per cent. of resinous lac.

[2] *Fanam* denominates a small coin long in use in South India. It was anciently of gold, but latterly of silver. The Madas *fanam* was worth about two pence.

[3] It is not possible now to discover the peculiarities of all the different sorts of Indian piece-goods. The *alleja*, we are told, came from Turkistan, and was a silk cloth, five yards long, with a wavy line pattern running in length on either side. A *shāsh* is a turban cloth, hence our "sash." *Chittā* means white.

[4] Bruton's voyage as above.

[5] *Hedges' Diary* as above, vol. III, page 179.

[6] Arrack is derived from the Arabic *'arak*, meaning properly perspiration, and so the sap of the date-palm. In India the word denotes common spirit, especially that distilled from the fermented sap of palms.

[7] *Ib.*, vol. III, p. 180.

[8] Bruton's voyage as above.

following depressed strain : [1] "Your opinion of sending a man to
Gugernat *Et setera* places, there to procure cloth would very well
become our implyment had we but on home [2] we might truste in that
bissines but you well know the fallsity and desaytfullness of our new
implyed servants is such that we Durst not depose confidence in them to
the vallew of 10 *roopees*. Our servant Nirana cannot be well spared from
this place. I doo therfore, my Sellfe intend so farr as I can gett
musters of *Cussayes* [3] which are now A making to Leave the oversight
of this place vnto William Bruton and the broker, and A dress my Sealfe
for the greate pogodo, [4] there soposing Likewise to put ofe part such
Marchandise as heere Lyeth ded on our hands. The market of Saylls
in Harrapore seimes at present as if there were no marchantes in the
Contry............Those Portingalls whilome exspelied from Hvgly have
found greate favor with Shawgahan and reentered that place to
the number of 20 persones hows Cavidall [5] for their commensing A
new investment is the third part of there goods [6] formerly cessed
on which with Large priveliges and *tashareefes* [7] with honor, the
kinge hath bestowed on them so that our expectation of Hugly
is frustrayt and I feare likewise Pippely will be [not?] obtained
beeing A convenient Randyvoes of theirs wherefor som parsones have
Latly complained to this Nabob of our seeking to put them from that
porte; have Answered we entended no Svch mater but only for Bolla-
sary or Harssapoore, so with good *delassa* [8] they were dismissed."

Altogether, in 1633, five of the six factors of the Bay fell victims
to the climate. A large number of the *Swan's* men were visited with
sickness, and the *Thomas*, which was sent on after her, buried four
men, and returned with the greater portion of her crew dangerously
ill.[9] The place scon acquired a bad name amongst the English,
and its unhealthiness was one of the most serious obstacles in
the way of their progress. The hand of man was also against
them. The Aracanese pirates haunted the Bay, and, when the
Swan was in Bengal in 1633, some of them suddenly attacked

---

[1] *Hedges' Diary*, vol. III, p. 177.
[2] *i.e.* on whom.
[3] *Khāṣa*, a kind of fine muslin.
[4] *i.e.* the temple of Jagannath.
[5] *i.e.* "whose capital."
[6] *i.e.* "seized."
[7] Arabic *tashríf*, honouring, hence a complimentary present here.
[8] *Dilāsā*, heart-hope.
[9] *Hedges' Diary*, III, 180.

her boat as it was being sent ashore for water, killed three of her men and carried off the rest to Pipli.[1] The English also had to meet the opposition of the Portuguese, who in spite of recent reverses still retained a hold on the trade of the country, and the still worse opposition of the Dutch, who claimed sovereignty over the places within their limits, and excluded the English even from stations recognized as belonging to them by existing treaties. Owing to these various difficulties, Cartwright was unable to do more than make settlements at Hariharapur and Balasor. All hope of fresh establishments at Jagannāth or Pipli had to be abandoned. Even the factory, which Cartwright had established at Hariharapur, fell into decay, for as the river where the vessels used to lie gradually silted up, it became unsafe for ships to ride there and difficult to send goods by sea that way.[2]

The expulsion of the Portuguese from Hijili in 1636, and the consequent ruin of Pipli, offered fresh opportunities for developing the trade of the Bay; but the English were not at the moment in a position to avail themselves of them. It had been more than once pointed out to the Court that, if it wished to succeed in Bengal, it must send out an additional number of properly qualified factors and writers, and secure two or three small pinnaces as coasters, such as the Dutch had, of 80 or 120 tons, drawing little water, and carrying twelve or fourteen guns apiece.[3] But in spite of urgent appeals neither men nor boats ever came. Indeed the Company's affairs were too much embarrassed to allow them to attend to such matters. In India, on the Coromandel Coast, in spite of specious promises and golden firmans, their trade was hampered and restricted in every direction by the jealous rivalry of the Dutch and the vexatious oppression of the officers of the King of Golkonda. At home they had to struggle for very life with an Association formed in 1635 under the immediate patronage of Charles I., by Sir William Courten, for fitting out ships and sending merchandise to the East Indies. It was not till 1639 that the King was induced to revoke Courten's license on the condition that a fourth joint stock should be formed, and that greater efforts should be made to prosecute and develop the Eastern trade. For this purpose it was absolutely necessary that some station should

---

[1] *Hedges' Diary*, III, 180.
[2] *Ib.*, III, 181.
    Ib., III, 179.

be found on the Coromandel Coast, better situated than Armagon, to protect the trade, and Mr. Francis Day, one of the Council of Masulipatam, having been sent to examine the country near the Portuguese settlement of St. Thomé, reported strongly in favour of Madrasapatam. Accordingly, in 1640, the English here laid the foundation of Fort St. George, and established their first independent station in India.

A new impetus was given to the Company's trade. In 1641 Bengal seemed of so little consequence that the ship *Dyamond* was sent thither to pay off debts and fetch away the factors;[1] but in the very next year this policy of withdrawal was reversed. Francis Day came to Balasor in the autumn on a visit of inspection. He found the factory at Hariharapur on the point of dissolution. Only a few " Cassaes " and " Sannoes " were in preparation. Of the three factors then in the Bay, Yard and Trauell intended to return to Europe. Only Hatch would remain, and he was much discontented, as his contracted time had expired and he expected to get but little employment.[2] But the quick insight which had selected Madras for the head-quarters of the coast trade, here too enabled Day to discern the commercial advantages of a station at Balasor. Thanks probably to Mīr Qāsim, the English settlement occupied an excellent situation. The factory was built in the principal quarter of the new town and was easily defensible, commanding the river and a convenient careening creek, and having ready access to the native markets. The port had rapidly improved during the past eight years. The bar at the mouth of the river had opened, and the river itself proved much better than had been supposed; the road was safe, and the Hariharapur cloth could be easily transported thither by land.[3] Day, therefore, was strongly in favour of retaining the station at Balasor and of supporting it by ample supplies of men, money and goods. " Accordinge to that small time of my being heer," he wrote, " and that little observation that I have taken, I think Ballasara with the Adjacent places is not to bee totally left, for it is no such dispisable place as is voted, it being an opulent Kingdome and you haveing bin already at great charges in gaininge the free Custome of all Sorts of Goods, beleive it if you had but an Active man, two or three in these parts, you would find it very

---

[1] *Hedges' Diary*, III, 181.
[2] *Ib.*, III, 182.
[3] *Ib.*, III, 181.

profitable provided you double Stocke [1] the Coast, without which it is impossible to comply to your desires. Since I have knowen these parts, for the most parte you have had servants and little or noe meanes to imploy them, if you should inlarge your trade, you may happely have meanes and noe servants, especially such that should know how to imploy it to best advantage." [2] Day's recommendation was, no doubt, carried into effect, and the Company's servants, including the faithful Nārāyaṇ, concentrated at Balasor, for we find that in 1644 there were in those regions three factors, Henry Olton, William Gurney and William Netlam, of whom Olton was the chief. [3] Yet the English had little faith in Day's judgment. They shook their heads when they thought of the future of " Bengala," and referred the whole matter to the Court in London for decision. [4]

---

[1] *i.e.* not only funds sufficient to purchase the investment for the season, but funds sufficient to procure a stock to be ready on the arrival of the ships in the subsequent year. Such a resource would enable him to purchase coast cloths and Coromandel goods when they could be had cheap, and with most advantage to the Company.

[2] *Hedges' Diary*, III, 182.

[3] *Ib.*, III, 182.

[4] Bruce's *Annals of the East India Company*, vol. I, p. 402, edition of 1810.

CHAPTER IV.

HOW THE ENGLISH ADVANCED FROM BALASOR TO HUGLI.

WHILE, however, the Company's servants were discussing the utility
of a station at Balasor, and waiting for a despatch from home to
decide whether they should go on with the trade in Bengal or not,
events were coming to pass which answered the question for them in
the affirmative. For several years the districts in the vicinity of
Madras and Masulipatam had suffered from famines and desultory wars
between the local kings. The trade of the Coromandel Coast was in
consequence almost ruined, and the agent and factors at Fort
St. George were forced to look abroad in the hope of discovering
new openings for commercial enterprise.[1]

In Bengal the signs were encouraging. Here was Gabriel Boughton,
formerly surgeon of the *Hopewell*, who had been sent across from
Surat to Agra in 1645 at the special request of Aṣālat Khān, and
had by his professional services acquired great influence at Court. He
had in fact become a prime favourite with Shāh Shujā', the Prince

---

[1] Bruce's *Annals*, I, pp. 410, 424, 430.

Governor of Bengal, and was residing with his patron at Rajmahal.[1]
The doctor would naturally use all his influence in favour of his countrymen and would interfere to free their trade from all vexatious imposts and customs. Urged by the necessities of the time, and trusting
to the good-will of the Bengal Government, the English Court of
Committees resolved to follow the example of the Dutch, and establish
a factory inland up the Ganges. In 1650 the *Lyoness* was despatched
to Bengal for this very purpose. The ship was under the command of
Captain John Brookhaven, and had on board three factors, named
Robert Spavin, James Bridgeman, and William Fairfax, and a large
cargo of moneys and goods all destined for Hugli.[2]

The *Lyoness* arrived at Madras on the 22nd of August, and the
agent and factors, who had been eagerly expecting her, at once set
about debating the best manner of carrying out their honorable masters'
wishes. With the Dutch cruisers scouring the Bay of Bengal, the
enterprise seemed at best precarious, and in any case many of the
details must be altered. Spavin had died on the voyage. Fairfax
was set aside as unfit. The management of the whole business was
therefore committed to Captain Brookhaven, with James Bridgeman
and Edward Stephens to assist him. For local knowledge, Brookhaven
was directed to use the advice and experience of Richard Potter, who
would be found somewhere about Balasor. William Netlam, who had
been some eight years or more stationed in the Bay, though he was at
his own request allowed to return thither, had fallen under suspicion,
and was not to be trusted.

So far the Madras merchants were prepared to go, but they boggled
at the idea of sending the *Lyoness* up the Ganges to Hugli. With

---

[1] *Hedges' Diary*, vol. III, pp. 182 and 185. According to our historians,
Boughton was sent for in consequence of a sad accident which had occurred at
the Mogul Court. The princess Jahān-Ārā was the eldest and best beloved
daughter of Shāh Jahān. "Returning one night from visiting her father to
her own apartments in the haram, she unfortunately brushed with her clothes one
of the lamps which stood in the passage. Her clothes caught fire, and as her
modesty, being within hearing of men, would not permit her to call for assistance,
she rushed into the haram in flames; and there was no hope of her life." It
was to attend the poor burnt princess that Boughton was summoned to Agra,
say our historians, and it was through his skill that she recovered. Sir Henry
Yule has not been able to find any confirmation of this story in the records.
The accident happened in 1643-4. Boughton was sent, it appears, at the beginning
of 1645, in which case he must surely have arrived too late. Besides the native
historian who tells us of the accident, also tells us that a famous physician was
brought express from Lahore to treat the case.

[2] *Hedges' Diary*, III, 186.

one consent they resolved to avoid so great a hazard and to stay the ship in the Balasor road. The factors designed for Hugli were to make their way thither as best they could upon some other freighted vessel.[1]

The consequence was that when the *Lyoness* reached Balasor her Captain determined to stay with her and to send up Bridgeman to Hugli as chief, with Stephens as his second and Blake and Tayler as assistants.[2] The paper of instructions which he drew up for their guidance before parting from them in December is still extant, and gives a picture of the position of the English in Bengal at this period.[3]

The tone of the opening paragraph is markedly devout. "Principally and above all things," it begins, "you are to endeavoar with the best of your might and power the advancement of the glory of God, which you will best doe, by walking holily, righteously, prudently, and Christianly, in this present world that soe the Religion, which you professe, may not be evil spoken of and you may enjoy the quiet, and peace of a good conscience towards God and man and may alwayes bee ready to render an accompt in a better world, where God Shall be Judge of all."

After this we come to more mundane matters. "Whereas it is the designe of our Masters the honoble: Company to advance, and encrease the trade in these parts of Orexea and Bengal, you are by all possible meanes to endeavour more and more to informe yourselves how best and most profitably to carry out the trade thereof, especially for Saltpeter, Silke and Sugers. To this ende, that you endeavour the sale of those goods remaining in the ffactories to the most advantage, therebye assoone as may bee, to gett moneys into your hands that soe you may proceed to invest the same in the best time of buying the aforesaid goods."

Particular directions about the investments in saltpetre, silk, and sugar follow, commending the example of the Dutch for imitation. "Patenna being on all Sides concluded the best place for procureing Peter, desire you therefore to make a tryall how you can procure the same from thence, wherein you may make vse of W. B.,[4] who you know is able to informe you. You must soe order that business as hee may have proffitt thereby and may bee encouraged, by which meanes you

---

[1] *Hedges' Diary*, III, 186, 187, and 197, 198.

[2] Perhaps Waldegrave, William Pitts, and William Netlam were left at Balasor.

[3] *Hedges' Diary*, III, 184 to 186.

[4] Perhaps William Blake.

will soonest arrive to our desire. In this commodity invest at least one halfe of your Stock, and endeavour the refineing of the same at Hukely. In case you runne into debt, lett it bee for this commodity yet I dare not advise you soe to do, vntill you receive order from the Agent, and Councell, the Interest being (as you know) soe exceeding high.

"In silke you know what great matters are to be done, therefore it doth import the Company much, that you strive both by relation and your own experience to know how, and where best to carry on the Manufacture thereof, where the best Silkes are procured, and where the best conveniences are for fitting and preparing the Same for the Sale, of Europe, that soe if the Company shall require large quantities you may bee in a posture to fitt them all at the first hand. I suppose the order of the Dutch is very good, and will be freest from adulteration, the properest way will bee to make three sorts, as Head, Belly, and ffoote, each apart by them Selves. You may also make an experience of washing thereof at Hukely or elsewhere, and Send the Company a maund of each Sort apart by the next Shipping for a Sample, with an exact accompt of the losse in washing, and charge of the same. In this commodity you may invest neare three eight parts of your remaines.

"As for Sugers, you know they are procured in many places, you may make a small tryall in each. Herein I suppose you need but inquire secretely into the order of the Dutch, how, where, and when they proceed to buy the said Commodity, and how the seasons doe fall for bringing the same out of the Countrey, or downe the Rivers. I am informed that the quantity they last bought at Patenna is well approved of, therefore I desire also that you procure some from thence by the same way or Instruments that you make use of to obtayne the Peter."

The instructions go on to speak of Gabriel Boughton, from whom the Company expected such great services. "You know how necessary it will bee for the better carrying on the trade of these parts to have the Prince's *ffirman*, and that Mr. Gabriel Boughton, Chirurgeon to the Prince, promises concerning the same. To putt matters out of doubt it is necessary that you forthwith after our departure, and the settlement of the business here, and at Hukley, proceed to Rajamall with one Englishman to accompany you; where being come consult with Mr. Boughton about the busines, who hath the whole contents of the Dutches last *ffirman*, and together endeavour (if possible) that according to Mr. Boughton's promise) the Company may have such a *ffirman* granted, as may outstrip the Dutch in point of Privilege and freedome, that soe they may not have cause any longer to boast of theirs. You know what I have written to Mr. Boughton about it, who (without doubt) will be very faithfull in the busines and strive that the same may bee procured, with as little charge as may bee to the Company, knowing that the lesse the charge is the more will bee the reputation, according to his owne advice in his last vnto me: what you shall present, or expend in the busines I cannot advise, however what you doe, lett it bee done with joint consent, and I pray you bee as spareing as may bee in a busines of this Import."

Directions are also given on various matters of minor importance. The two assistants, Blake and Tayler, are each to have a salary of £5 or £6 a year; Nārāyaṇ, the Company's broker, who had been on the Bengal establishment since 1633, was to be kept on in spite of the accusations made against him; the trade of Balasor is to be carried on in "*Rupees Morees*";[1] friendly relations are to be cultivated with the governors of Balasor and Hugli; all matters of concern to the Company are to be declared to their servants, so that in case of sickness, "which doth often happen in this part," their successors may always know how, what, and where the Company's interests are; and lastly, land is to be procured for building additional houses for the Company at Balasor, but in this, as in everything, they are to have a special regard not to put the Company to unnecessary expense.

Such were the excellent intentions and edifying admonitions with which the Company sent forth Bridgeman and Stephens in 1651 to establish a new factory at Hugli; and for a time all seems to have gone well. Gabriel Boughton was not unmindful of his promises. In 1652 we hear that for so trifling a sum as Rs. 3,000 the English have obtained letters patent granting them freedom of trade in Bengal without payment of customs or dues. An indefinite quantity of saltpetre could be purchased there, particularly at Balasor and Hugli.[2]

---

[1] Yule suggests *muhri, i.e.,* round rupees.

[2] Bruce's, *Annals,* I, 463, 464. It is very doubtful, however, whether Boughton ever secured any grant at all for the English. In 1650, when we last hear of him, he is still promising, but not performing. In 1651-2 Bruce and Stuart tell us that the English in Bengal obtained a *nishān* from Shāh Shujā'. If it could be shown that they did get a *nishān* in this year, and that Boughton was then living, we might conjecture that his influence had something to do with it. But neither of these conditions can be established. There is nothing to show that Boughton was still living and influencing Shāh Shujā' in 1651-2, and there are considerable doubts as to whether any *nishān* was granted by the prince in that

Later on accounts grow much less favourable. The Madras Council complain that the sums which the Bengal factors have paid to be exempted from dues and customs will counterbalance the profits of the trade, and will be rather a benefit to their own private trade than to the Company's investments.[1] Gabriel Boughton is dead, his widow married again, and she and her husband are making claims on the Company on account of Boughton's services. In fact Bridgeman and his friends were acting irregularly and dishonestly.[2] When called to account, two of them, Bridgeman and Blake, deserted the Company's service without vouchsafing any explanation;[3] another, Waldegrave, in his journey to Madras overland, managed to lose all the Company's accounts and papers, among them, apparently, the letters patent granted by Shāh Shujā'.[4]

As for Madras itself, although it had just been raised to the dignity of a separate Presidency, its real power was greatly crippled by a

---

year. A copy of the *nishān* of Shāh Shujā' exists, but it is said to have been given "at the request of Thomas Billedge, in the sixth month, in 1066 H., in the 28th year of Shāh Jahān's reign, *i.e.*, in April 1656 A.D." This would be conclusive against the whole story about Boughton if we could trust the copy; but we cannot. In spite of the date, 1656 A.D., given in 'the copy, Stuart assigns the *nishān* to the year 1651-2; and he tells us in 1703 that forty (? fifty) years before, *i.e.*, in 1663 (? 1653), the original *nishān* was lost. Writing on the 31st December 1657, the Court refer to the fact that Waldegrave has lost all their papers, *farmāns*, and the like. This looks as if the *nishān* was granted earlier than 1656, otherwise the losing of the *nishān*, the reporting of its loss to London, and the considering of the business by the Court, followed the granting of it in April 1656 with unexampled rapidity. Again, in the list of Government papers that I have found in the United Trade Consultation Book of 1704, the copy of this *nishān* is dated 1652, although it is said to have been given in the 28th year of Shāh Jahān's reign. Once more I may point out that, if the *nishān* was granted in the 28th year of Shāh Jahān's reign, it was not granted in 1066 H., or 1656 A.D., which was the 30th year of the reign. The 28th year of the reign was 1064 H., or 1654-5 A.D. Hence the existing copy must be incorrect, as it is not consistent with itself. I am on the whole inclined to accept the date given by Bruce and Stuart, and to believe that the original *nishān* was granted in the 25th year of Shāh Jahān in 1061 H., or 1651-2, and that it was lost in 1653 or 1654 by Waldegrave on his journey to Madras. In consequence of the loss of the original the English had to rely on a rough copy or note of the contents of the *nishān*, and in this way the 25th year was altered to the 28th year. This would account for the entry in the Consultation Book of 1704. After the regnal year had been altered, some other wise person took it into his head to correct the Hejira year.

[1] Bruce's *Annals*, I, 485.

[2] *Hedges' Diary*, III, 187, 188.

[3] Bridgeman seems to have left sometime in 1653. See Danvers' *Bengal, its Chiefs, Agents*, and *Governors*, p. 7, edition of 1888. Edward Stephens died in Cassimbazar in 1654 much in debt. See *Hedges' Diary*, III, 194.

[4] *Hedges' Diary*, III, 188.

variety of circumstances. Inland trade on the Coromandel Coast had become impracticable, owing to the convulsed state of the country; the coasting trade was hazardous from the superior force of the Dutch, with whom England was openly at war from 1652 to 1654; and lastly the merchant adventurers, who had obtained a charter from Cromwell in 1655, competed with their countrymen in every direction. In 1657, the year in which Sivaji first invaded the Carnatic, the Madras Council seem to have "despaired of the republic." Once more they resolved to withdraw from Bengal.[1]

---

[1] Bruce's *Annals*, vol. I, pp. 499, 525, and 526, edition of 1810.

CHAPTER V.

HOW THE ENGLISH RE-ORGANISED THE HUGLI AGENCY.

THAT the English, who boast of a special faculty for organising foreign establishments, should thus without encountering serious external opposition twice fail to effect a settlement in Bengal will probably excite surprise. We were not prepared for this repeated failure; yet we should remember that repeated failure is the road to success. Like nature, man does nothing great at a bound. He makes a hundred attempts which come to nothing before he hits upon the one true expedient. Such has been the history of most of the achievements of genius: such is the history of the settlements of the English in India. They bought their experience. Schooled by repeated failure, they advanced from the Spice Islands to the mainland, from the Coast to the Bay, from Balasor to Hugli, from Hugli to Calcutta. At each step they made mistakes; at each step they learnt lessons which led them to further and wiser efforts. Let us look again at the two steps which they have just taken.

The English did well to come to Balasor in 1633; for the provinces at the head of the Bay were far richer and far easier of access to western merchants than the Carnatic and the Coast of Coromandel, and it was from Bengal that a maritime empire of India must of necessity begin. Yet the settlements made by Cartwright languished as soon as he left them. No one cared about them; they were distant, unhealthy, dangerous.

Then the English found out their mistake. They had been too timid; they now went to the opposite extreme and became too rash. Confiding implicitly in the promises of the Indian Government and in the good-will of its subordinates, the Court of Committees transferred the head-quarters of the trade in the Bay from Balasor to Hugli.[1] This too was a step in the right direction. It was right to adopt a forward policy; it was right to advance further into the country than Balasor; but the English now advanced too far.

Some of the inconveniences of making Hugli their head-quarters appeared at the very outset. In commerce, as in war, sustained operations cannot be conducted without a secure starting point. Such a starting point could not be Hugli, where the English were surrounded by rivals and possible enemies, and separated from the sea by more than a hundred miles of a difficult and dangerous river. The refusal of the Council of Fort St. George to allow the *Lyoness* to proceed further than Balasor was indeed a bad omen for the new factory.

Another mistake soon showed itself. The number of the Englishmen in Bengal was so small that their *morale* quickly degenerated. Right conduct is largely supported by public opinion, and an Englishman in India, placed in the midst of new and bewildering circumstances, needs all the moral support that can be given him. He needs to be in constant contact with those who may help him with their criticism, their advice, their sympathy. The Court at home could not understand this. They sent out a young man of eighteen or twenty on a salary of five pounds a year to a lonely post of difficulty and danger; and when he proved an unprofitable and unfaithful servant, they marvelled.

But they did not despair. In 1657, the very year that the Madras Council was thinking of withdrawing from Bengal, the company of merchant adventurers had been amalgamated with the original Company. At a general meeting of proprietors the rights of the respective stock-holders were satisfactorily adjusted. The Company's charter was renewed, and Cromwell was petitioned to protect their settlements against the depredations of the Dutch, and to vindicate the honour of the English in India. Having settled their charter and exclusive rights in England, the Court turned their attention to the re-arrangement of their factories abroad. A commission was appointed in Bengal to

---

[1] Danvers, *op. cit.*, p. 7, says that Balasor was at first the head-quarters of the Company's Bengal factories, and apparently thinks it was so in 1651. But it appears that Bridgeman was always at Hugli.

inquire into the misdemeanours and corrupt practices which had been going on there; and, to prevent further irregularities, private trade[1] on the part of the Company's servants was prohibited and their pay increased. Before drawing their enhanced salaries they were to sign security bonds or covenants to specified amounts to observe this condition. They were also directed to keep diaries of their proceedings and transmit copies of them annually to the Court. All the Company's factories were to be subordinate to the Presidency of Surat, besides which there were four agencies, at Bantam, at Madras, in Persia, and in Bengal. Inferior agencies were established at Balasor, Cassimbazar and Patna, in subordination to the agency at Hugli.[2]

A despatch, dated the 27th February, 1658, gives an almost complete list of the Councils established in Bengal. It appoints George Gawton, Chief Agent at Hugli, with a salary of a hundred pounds a year. His second is not named. The other members of the Council are Mathias Halstead, William Ragdale, and Thomas Davies. Hopkins is made agent at Balasor, Kenn at Cassimbazar, Chamberlain at Patna. To each of these agents three coadjutors are assigned; among them the celebrated Job Charnock, who is appointed fourth at Cassimbazar.[3] By a subsequent despatch the Court appointed Jonathan Trevisa to fill the vacant post of second at Hugli, and, failing Gawton, to succeed to the agency itself. This he did in September, 1658.[4]

By these arrangements the number of the Company's servants in Bengal was more than doubled. For the first time in that distant land there was an English society. Its character may be gathered from the private correspondence still extant. They often had to come to terms with the climate in matters of dress and cut short the flowing locks of the cavalier. But they consoled themselves with drinking-bouts and bowls of clear arrack punch. A more respectable solace was the reading of books such as the *Eikon Basilike* or *Religio Medici*. The latter seems to have been especially popular, and they amused themselves by corresponding with each other in good Brownese. We may laugh at the Latin saws which stuff these Ciceronian epistles, the elaborate compliments, the invocations for Heliconian

---

[1] They were not to trade privately in any of the Company's commodities, but they were not forbidden to trade in other commodities.

[2] Bruce's *Annals*, vol. I, p. 532.

[3] *Hedges' Diary*, III, 189.

[4] Danvers' *Bengal, its Chiefs, Agents, and Governors*, p. 8, edition of 1888.

irrigations to sublimate the writer's thoughts; but they are more to our taste than the ill-penned, ill-spelt, ill-constructed scrawls which do the duty of letters in the earlier period.[1]

The Court had certainly succeeded in raising the moral tone of the Bengal establishment, but it had done nothing to add to its security. At first all seemed to go well with the Company's servants. "Bengal," they wrote home, "is a rich province. Raw silk is abundant. The taffaties are various and fine. The saltpetre is cheap and of the best quality. The bullion and pagodas you have sent have had an immediate and most favourable effect on the trade; the goods have been sold at great advantage. Our operations are growing so extensive that we shall be obliged to build new and large warehouses."[2]

But, in the meanwhile, changes had taken place in the native government of India and of Bengal. On the 8th September, 1657, Shāh Jahān fell seriously ill at Delhi, and a fratricidal war broke out between his children. In the end Prince Aurangzēb, the third son, succeeded in defeating his brothers and in seizing the person of his sick father. On the 22nd July, 1658, he took his seat on the throne of Hindustan. A few months later Shāh Shujā' was barbarously murdered in Arakān, whither he had fled, defeated and heart-broken, and Mīr Jumlah, the imperial general, was nabob of Bengal.

Under the new Government, the English began to see the folly of trusting to the promises and good-will of a power so arbitrary and variable as the Mogul government. In 1658 the governor of Hugli, considering that the deposition of Shāh Jahān rendered all Imperial grants null and void, had insisted on an annual payment of three thousand rupees in lieu of custom. In 1659, the governor of Balasor began to make exorbitant charges for anchorage. The Hugli was infested with pirates, and to send up goods in small craft without a convoy was no longer safe.[3] At Rajmahal all the English boats as they came down the Ganges from Patna laden with saltpetre were stopped by Mīr Jumlah. On every side the English found themselves oppressed and the trade vexatiously hampered.[4] At last in 1661 the agent at Hugli lost patience and seized a native vessel as security for the recovery of debts. Mīr Jumlah was greatly incensed. He demanded immediate reparation of the offence, and threatened to

---

[1] *Hedges' Diary*, III, 192 to 194.
[2] Bruce's *Annals*, vol. I, pp. 544, 550, 560.
[3] *Hedges' Diary*, III, 198.
[4] Stewart's *History of Bengal*, p. 180.

destroy the out-agencies, to seize the factory at Hugli, and expel the English from the country. Alarmed at this danger, the agent wrote to Madras for instructions, and was directed to restore the boat, and to apologise to Mīr Jumlah. Trevisa accordingly submitted and was forgiven, but the viceroy continued to exact the annual payment of the three thousand rupees.[1]

Fortunately for the English, Mīr Jumlah's attention was soon engaged with much more serious matters. Rebellions had taken place in Kooh Bihār and Assam, and the Mogul general had to conduct a great expedition against those distant provinces to reduce them to submission. From the hardships of these campaigns he returned to die near Dacca on the 30th March, 1663.

He was succeeded in the Government of Bengal by Shāyista Khān, the Premier Prince of the Empire.

---

[1] Bruce's *Annals*, vol. I, pp. 560, 561. Stewart's *Bengal*, pp. 180, 181.

BOOK II.

HOW THROUGH OPPOSITION AND OPPRESSION THE ENGLISH
LEARNT THAT THEY MUST PROTECT THEMSELVES BY
FORCE.

CHAPTER I.

HOW SIR EDWARD WINTER FIRST ADVOCATED A POLICY OF RETALIATION,
AND HOW HE REBELLED AGAINST THE COURT.

In 1651 the English had come to Hugli full of confidence in the
good-will and good order of the Mogul empire. In less than ten years
that confidence had been utterly destroyed. They had seen their friend
and patron driven to his death in Burmah; they had seen India torn
with fratricidal wars; they had seen how little control the central
government could exercise over the arbitrary proceedings of its
subordinates. They were, therefore, forced to consider in what way
they could best protect themselves and their trade against the oppressions
of the local officers. The seizure of the Bengali boat and the
consequent dispute with Mīr Jumlah marks the beginning of a new
period in the history of the English in Bengal—a period of growing
anxiety and danger.

This second period is the antithesis, the contradiction, of the first. In it industrialism is checked, and at last overcome, by militarism. Provoked by the vexatious exactions of the local rulers, the English are led to abandon their peaceful attitude and seek to establish their trade by force. The men who in 1661 apologised for seizing a small boat, in 1685 waged open war upon the Mogul, capturing his ships and burning his ports.

Is this antithesis, this contradiction, accidental? On the contrary it is necessary. In the first period English industry simply takes its place in Bengal. Its aims, its limits, its resources, are vague and indefinite. It is therefore at once exposed to opposition. As the Hegelian would say, *sein* at once negates itself and becomes *nichts*.

Of this inevitable opposition the Court at home had no prevision. The prospects of the Company seemed fair. The restoration of Charles II. terminated all hostilities with Spain and Holland, and placed the government of England in the hands of friends. On the 3rd of April, 1661, a new charter was conferred on the Company, granting them the whole trade with the East Indies for ever, and declaring that no person should trade thither without their license. They were empowered to seize unlicensed persons, to erect fortifications, to raise troops, and to make war with non-Christians. The king also gave the Governor and Council of the several settlements authority "to judge all persons belonging to the said Governor and Company or that should live under them, in all causes, whether civil or criminal, according to the laws of the kingdom, and to execute judgment accordingly." In effect the charter for the first time introduced British law into India.[1]

Armed with these powers the Court proceeded to set in order their establishments in Madras and Bengal. Trevisa was superseded by William Blake, who was directed to call all their servants "to account for all actions which hath passed since their being in the Bay."[2] At the same time Sir Edward Winter was appointed President at Fort St. George, and the whole of the Bengal establishment was made subordinate to his government.[3] The Court gave orders that the fort should be strengthened, but the new President had been told to discharge the Portuguese soldiers, to reduce the number of out-agencies,

[1] Bruce's *Annals*, I, 556 to 558. Morley's *Administration of Justice in British India*, p. 5, edition of 1858. Stephen's *Nuncomar and Impey*, vol. II, p. 29, edition of 1885.

[2] Danvers, *op. cit.*, p. 8.

[3] Bruce's *Annals*, II, 109.

to suppress private trade, to avoid quarrels with the local governors, and to devote himself to the buying of saltpetre and taffaties.[1]

It was Winter who first saw that the English trade in Bengal had entered upon a new phase. A year's residence in India convinced him that this policy of peace and retrenchment was impossible. How could he provide for the investment if the factories were withdrawn? Of what avail was it to complain to Indian princes of the arbitrary dues exacted by their tax-gatherers or the depredations committed by their followers on goods passing to Madras? He had complained to one of them; and how had he been answered? "When the English horns and teeth are grown," said the prince, "then I will free your goods from the duty."[2]

Winter, therefore, wrote to the Court, explaining that he intended to follow the policy of the Dutch, whose large capital and naval power gave them their trade and kept the native powers in awe. He required increased sums of money in order to furnish a double stock.[3] He refused to discharge his Portuguese soldiers, and directed all his efforts to making retaliation on the vessels of the petty chiefs on the Coromandel Coast. We needed to convince them that we were as powerful at sea as they with their armies were on shore. The same policy should be pursued in Bengal. Here it was quite impossible to withdraw the out-agencies. The plan of inducing weavers to come to Hugli had failed. Part of the money in the treasury must be applied to building and maintaining boats on the river to bring saltpetre from Patna and silks and muslins from Cassimbazar.[4]

But this bold course of action did not commend itself to the Court at home. They did not understand it, and consequently they became very uneasy and began to suspect that their spirited agent was engaged in private trade for his separate interests. In June, 1665, a ship arrived at Fort St. George, bringing out Mr. George Foxcroft, and his son Nathaniel, and a letter from the Court, informing Winter that his measures had not met with approval, and that Mr. George Foxcroft was appointed agent in his stead. He might, however, continue to rank as second in the Madras Council till his departure.[5]

The change of government seems to have been unpopular with the settlement. They probably sympathised with Winter in his forward

[1] Bruce's *Annals*, II, 121, 131, 139.
[2] *Ib.*, II, 147, 159, 160.
[3] See *ante*, note on p. 32.
[4] Bruce's *Annals*, II, 147, 159, 160, 161.
[5] *Ib.*, II, 179, 180.

policy and looked coldly on the man who had been sent out to reverse it. Moreover, Foxcroft was something of a Puritan and came near to being thought a heretic and a traitor. His son was a dabbler in philosophy, who held strange views about the relations between king and people. During the hot weeks of August, as the servants of the Company met together at their mid-day dinner within the fort, violent bickerings arose on matters political. Amongst other things the Foxcrofts maintained that no king had any right to his throne except might, and that a man's private interest came first, before that of the Sovereign.[1]

The enemies of Foxcroft began to plot. A little while before, Sir Edward Winter had of his own accord asked to be allowed to return to England; he now resolved to stay and become President once more. On Thursday, the 14th September, he accused Foxcroft of treason against the King and produced the chaplain, Simon Smythes, as a witness. The charge was formally made before two members of the Council, Jeremy Samebrooke and William Dawes, but they refused to entertain it. They even went so far as to affirm that the Company's Agent at Fort St. George was not liable to such charges. Simon Smythes was ordered to keep to his room and was not allowed to leave the fort.[2]

Winter determined to gain his end by force. Chuseman, the captain of the garrison, was his friend. The agent was defenceless. On Saturday the blow was struck.[3] At the time of morning prayer, just as the agent was going to church, he learnt that the soldiers were in arms against him. Drawing his rapier, the only weapon ordinarily worn in the fort, he hurried down the stairs which led from his rooms to the quadrangle below, followed by Samebrooke and Dawes. At the foot of the stairs the agent beheld an ominous sight. There stood the whole garrison fully armed. Their swords were drawn; their pistols cocked; at their head was Captain Chuseman. On seeing Foxcroft and his friends the cry arose "*For the King! For the King! Knock them down! Fire!*" The agent advanced to ask for an explanation, but Chuseman answered by discharging his pistol and rushing at him with his sword. He closed with the agent, and flung him to the ground.

This was the signal to the rest to fire. With modern weapons of precision the whole of Foxcroft's party would have fallen riddled through and through with shot discharged in so confined a space. But the seventeenth century pistol, a kind of miniature arquebus with

---

[1] *Hedges' Diary*, II, 278 to 280.

[2] *Ib.*, also Bruce's *Annals*, II, 180.

[3] The account which follows will be found in *Hedges' Diary*, II, 280, 281

a barrel two feet long, only carried forty paces, and was by no means sure at that. The result of the volley was that no one was mortally wounded except Dawes, who had halted on the stairs. Samebrooke, who rushed forward to help the fallen agent, escaped unhurt; but, closing with Chuseman, he was set upon by the soldiers and knocked down. Nathaniel Foxcroft, a brisk man in a broil, contrived to get his pistols from his room on the ground floor; yet he was seized before he could do any execution.

In a few minutes the affray was over. George Foxcroft was clapped up in a rubbish hole, and Sir Edward Winter resumed the government of Fort St. George. On the 19th September he made a solemn declaration that he had accepted the office of Chief Director in consequence of the exigencies of the Company's affairs and upon the unanimous request of the Company's factors, servants, and officers, until it should be ordered otherwise either by the plurality of the Council or by the Court.[1]

It remained for Winter to vindicate his conduct, if possible, to the authorities at home. He at once wrote to the Court giving them an account of the seditious and traitorous conduct of the Foxcrofts, and forwarding the attestations of his witnesses. He assured his masters that he would do his best to preserve their rights and provide for their investments. In obedience to their orders he would withdraw the out-agencies on the Coromandel Coast, but it would ruin the English prestige, and contrast very badly with the proceedings of the Dutch, who took every opportunity to add to their out-agencies. Similar evils would follow in Bengal, and therefore he had left the matter to the discretion of Blake and his Council. The fort was well enough and he would maintain it, but two or three armed cruisers would produce more effect in the minds of the natives than many forts. We were now once again at war with the Dutch, and he dreaded their numerous ships, ready to seize on those of the Company bringing Bengal produce to Madras.[2]

It would have been well had Winter stopped here. But besides justifying himself to the Court, he took upon him to write directly to the Archbishop of Canterbury, to the King, and to the King's officer in charge of the royal fort at Bombay. Foxcroft too wrote from his place of captivity to Masulipatam, giving his account of the

---

[1] *Hedges' Diary*, II, 277, 278.
[2] Bruce's *Annals*, II, 181, 182, 183.

matter and applying for assistance. At Surat Sir Edward's professions met with utter disbelief, and it was feared that he would give up the fort either to the Portuguese Viceroy of Goa or to the Dutch Governor of Ceylon.[1]

All this would have aroused the suspicions of a less suspicious body of men than the Court. In their alarm they applied to the King to interpose his authority. Mr. Clavell was vested with extraordinary powers by King and Company, and directed to proceed at once to Surat. Here he was to consult with the Company's agent. If Sir Edward should still be in possession of Fort St. George, Clavell was to make his way to Masulipatam, and thence by messenger announce his mission and authority, demand the release of Foxcroft and the delivery of the fort into his hands. A proclamation from the King, dated the 28th of January, 1667, offered pardon to Winter and his adherents on condition of their returning to their duty.[2]

These measures produced little effect, for, although the King had done his best to support the Company, his officers in India were at variance with the agent at Surat. Captain Henry Gary, who was Governor of Bombay during the latter half of 1667, openly aided and abetted Sir Edward Winter, and proclaimed Foxcroft and his party rebels and traitors against the King. Thus encouraged, Sir Edward Winter and his Council treated Clavell's orders as gross forgeries.[3]

Next year the Court resolved on more vigorous measures. The treaty of Breda had put an end to the Dutch war, and the King had made over to them the island of Bombay. They were therefore in a strong position to assert their authority and extend their commerce. A royal commission gave them full power to reduce the rebel government to the obedience of the Company. Five ships, with five companies composed of sailors and soldiers, were despatched to Madras, and were ordered to blockade it, if necessary, by land and sea.[4]

On the 21st of May, 1668, the *Rainbow* and the *Loyal Merchant* anchored in Madras road. Two representatives from the rebels came on board. They were detained prisoners. The commissioners informed Sir Edward Winter by letter that they had the orders of the King and the Company to take possession of the fort in His Majesty's name. Winter saw that the end had come. He only asked for

---

[1] Bruce's *Annals*, II, 180, 181.
[2] *Ib.*, II, 187, 188.
[3] *Ib*, II, 217, 218. Also *Hedges' Diary*, II, 323 to 325.
[4] *Ib.*, II, 203 to 206.

personal safety and protection of property. The commissioners agreed. On the 22nd of August they landed, took possession of the fort, and released Foxcroft from his three-years' captivity.[1]

The re-instated agent acted with great moderation. Chuseman and Smythes were allowed to return quietly to England. Winter was forbidden to remain within the fort, but was otherwise left at perfect liberty to live in Madras, Masulipatam, or elsewhere, if he chose, waiting the decision of the Privy Council, to whom the whole case had been referred.[2]

The result of their deliberations was communicated to Madras in a letter from the Court, dated the 7th December, 1669. Nathaniel Foxcroft was ordered to return at once; his father was permitted to remain at the head of the government of Fort St. George for one year more. Sir Edward Winter was also permitted to stay on for a short time to dispose of his property and recover his debts. He was to be treated with respect and to have a passage given him to England. A commission was appointed to investigate the whole transaction and take evidence on the spot. At the head of it was Sir William Langhorne, who was to succeed Foxcroft in the government of Madras.[3] Its investigations, however, do not seem to have been very successful. After spending about eighteen months in vain attempts to adjust the disputes between Winter and Foxcroft, the whole case had again to be referred home. On the 26th October, Nathaniel Foxcroft died in Madras at the age of thirty-five.[4] George Foxcroft embarked in January, 1672, leaving Sir William Langhorne agent at Fort St. George. At the same time Winter sailed on another vessel for England. His offence had been practically condoned.[5]

Such is the unsatisfactory conclusion of this unsatisfactory and somewhat unintelligible episode. It is difficult to determine the rights of the matter. It is clear that the charter of 1661 constituted the Madras Council a Court of Justice, having power to judge the Company's servants in all causes, whether civil or criminal, and it was not proper for Samebrooke and Dawes to refuse to entertain a charge of treason against Foxcroft when duly made before them by Winter. Samebrooke was quite wrong if he said that the agent at Fort St. George was not

---

[1] Bruce's *Annals*, II, 245 to 248.
[2] *Ib.*, II, 245 to 248.
[3] *Hedges' Diary*, II, 281. Also Bruce's *Annals*, II, 256 to 258.
[4] See his tombstone in the Fort Church, Madras.
[5] Bruce's *Annals*, II, 307.

liable to a charge of treason and above the reach of the English law. On the other hand, these improprieties do not excuse Winter's violence. In his declaration he seeks to justify it by insinuating that Foxcroft was the aggressor. Foxcroft wantonly attacked the innocent soldiers, who were compelled to fire in self-defence. Few will believe this.

It does not follow, however, that Winter was altogether dishonest in his professions. On the contrary, it must appear that in his general views Winter was more far-sighted than his critics, and we shall see in the sequel how they were gradually led to adopt his policy of retaliation. Finally, whatever doubts may be felt as to the details of the case, there can be no doubt as to its real significance. It is the first struggle between the earlier policy of peace and the new policy of force.

CHAPTER II.

WHILE industrialism and militarism are thus fighting out their battle, the history of the Bengal establishments to a certain extent hangs fire, and waits upon the course of events in Madras. Blake, who remained for many years in office at Hugli, at last requested leave to return to England, and in 1668, when the Court despatched their armada of five ships to Madras, they sent out orders appointing Shem Bridges in the place of Blake. This appointment was not for long. In the letters from the Court of the 7th December, 1669, which announced the decision of the Privy Council, Bridges was informed that he might come home according to his wish, and that Mr. Henry Powell would succeed him. In 1650 or 1651 Walter Clavell became chief in the Bay.[1]

These changes are not of much interest or importance. It is more interesting to note the brightening prospects of the trade, which steadily increased owing partly to the Company's resolution to enlarge their operations on the east coast, and partly to the growing demand for Bengal goods. In 1668, the stock furnished for Bengal was valued at £34,000;[2] in 1675, its value rose to £65,000, and the factors were authorised to take up £20,000 in addition at interest.[3] In 1668 permission was granted to form a new establishment in Dacca, then the capital of Bengal, celebrated for the fineness of its muslins and the beauty of its woven stuffs.[4] The Court were never weary of asking for saltpetre

---

[1] Danvers, *op. cit.*, p. 9. It does not appear that Powell actually succeeded. See below, p. 381.

[2] Bruce's *Annals*, II, 228.

[3] *Ib.*, II, p. 361.

[4] *Hedges' Diary*, III, 195.

from Patna, where it could be had so good and cheap that the contract for it was discontinued on the west coast in 1668,[1] and at Masulipatam in 1670.[2] In 1674 the agent at Hugli received orders to keep the salt-petre-men constantly employed, so as to have a stock always ready for shipment.[3]

The demand for Bengal silk would have been equally urgent had it not been for defects in the native manner of preparing it. The Court objected to the vicious practice of dyeing it " in the gum," and as early as 1663 asked that the taffetas should be bought " in an ungummed state, as they could receive this improvement in England in a superior manner, a successful experiment having been tried, which made the Bengal silks pass in the market as Italian."[4] In 1671 they desired that, besides taffetas and muslins for home consumption, £5,000 should be annually invested in silk for Japan.[5] Two years later, finding that the taffetas were still defective in colour, especially the shades of green and black, they sent out a number of skilled artisans, who were to endeavour to improve the silk manufac-tures, but to keep their art secret from the natives.[6] So great were the quantities of silk imported to England round the Cape of Good Hope, that in 1680 the Turkey merchants, who before this had monopolised the trade, made a formal complaint to the King. " We export woollen manufactures," they said, " and other English wares, and import raw silk, drugs, cotton, and the like, which are all manufactured in England, and afford bread and employment to the poor. But this East India Company is sending away precious metal out of the kingdom in return for a deceitful kind of raw silk which will destroy the Turkey trade. Besides, they have sent to India throwsters, weavers, and dyers, and have set up a manufacture of silk, which, by instructing Indians in these manufactures and by importing them so made, tends to impoverish the working people of England." In the infancy of economic science the East India Company could only reply to these objections by pointing to the fact that, since they had begun their importations, the silk manufactures of England had increased fourfold. Like all other commodities, Indian silks varied in quality, some being good, some bad, some indifferent. They had only sent one or two dyers to Bengal, and

---

[1] Bruce's *Annals*, II, 207.
[2] *Ib.*, II, 259.
[3] *Ib.*, II, 332.
[4] *Ib.*, II, 121.
[5] *Ib.*, II, 297.
[6] *Ib.*, II, 314.

this was for the advantage of the nation as well as the Company, as the plain black silks thus made and imported were again exported.[1]

As Winter had foreseen, these extended operations necessitated additions to the factories on the east coast. Under pressure of the wars with Holland,[2] the rivalry of the new French Company,[3] and the difficulties which from time to time arose with the natives, the Company found itself compelled to send recruits, ordinance, and small arms to strengthen Fort St. George, and to issue orders that the inhabitants of the town and such natives as could be trusted should be embodied as troops. In 1668 they determined to obtain an equality with the Dutch. All idea of withdrawing out-agencies was abandoned. Sixteen factors and eight writers were at once sent out to augment the Madras establishment.[4]

The same year witnessed the inauguration of the Bengal Pilot Service.[5] The Court had all along desired that their ships should be taken to Hugli, but at first it was considered too dangerous. In 1662 Captain Elliott offered to venture up the river with his vessel, and would have done so had he not been forbidden by Agent Trevisa, to the intense chagrin of the Court. The captain then left a written memorandum at Hugli stating that the passage up was hazardless. The Dutch had ships of 600 tons which tided it up thither, and it was proposed that the English vessels should in future go direct to Hugli, that Balasor should be abandoned, and "our business in the Bay brought into some decorum."[6] The Court supported the proposal by offering to defray all expenses for pilotage and to give the shipowners ten shillings a ton extraordinary for all goods conveyed "within the bar of Ganges."[7] But these offers came to nothing. The native pilots were too expensive, and the owners refused to risk their ships without proper pilots and proper charts pointing out depths and soundings. Accordingly, in 1667, the Court had built a small vessel called the *Diligence*, and directed that she should be employed in the river and should take soundings, note shoals and channels, and make a chart of them.[8] In 1668 the Court reiterated and completed their

---

[1] Watt's *Dictionary of Economic Products of India*. Article, "Silk." Vol. VI, pt. III, pp. 184, 185, edition of 1893.

[2] In 1665—67 and in 1672—74.

[3] Founded in 1666.

[4] Bruce's *Annals*, II, 206.

[5] *Ib.*, II, 228-29.

[6] *Hedges' Diary*, III, 198.

[7] *Ib.*, III, 198-99.

[8] *Ib.*, III, 199.

instructions. They renewed their proffered bonus; they ordered the
commanders of their vessels in the Hugli " to put all persons, from
the youngest to the eldest, upon taking depths, shoals, setting of tides
and currents, distances and buoys, and making drafts of the river or
what else needful for the enabling them in this affair." In order to
secure a supply of young men to be trained up in the work, they
"entertained as apprentices for seven years, George Herron, James
White, Thomas Massen, James Ferborne, John Floyd, and Thomas
Bateman, the first three years at £6, the next two years at £7, and the
last two years at £8 per annum ; the whole to be paid there by you for
their provision of clothes."[1] The labours of these six apprentices bore
fruit in a more accurate knowledge of the navigation and topography
of the Hugli ; and to Herron in particular is due not only the earliest
detailed instructions in print for piloting ships up the river, but probably
also the earliest chart of any pretension to scientific accuracy.[2]

But although the Court had thus abandoned all thoughts of retrenchment, they still clung to their peace policy, and still trusted the safety
of their factories in Bengal to the good-will of the local governors.
And certainly, if Imperial rescripts could have protected them, they were
abundantly safe. In the time of Shāh Jahān they had received letters
patent from the Emperor himself in 1638, together with the oft-
quoted grant of the unfortunate Prince Shujā' in 1652, or 1656.
Already Aurangzēb had granted letters patent in 1667.[3] In 1672
Shāyista Khān, who like Mīr Jumlah exacted an annual offering of
three thousand rupees, issued an order confirming all the privileges
of the English Company, and warning all the local officers in Bengal
and Orissa to govern themselves according to the Imperial patents.
" And whatsoever goods the said Company shall import from Balasor,
or any other place near the sea-side, up to Hugli, Cassimbazar, Patna,
or any other place in these two kingdoms, as also what saltpetre, or
any other goods, they shall export from Patna, or any other place,
to Balasor, or any other port to the sea, that you let them pass
custom-free, without any let, impediment, or demands whatsoever.
And wherever they have factories or warehouses, that you help their
factors in getting in their due debts from any weavers, merchants,
and the like, that really appear to be indebted to them, without giving

---

[1] *Hedges' Diary*, III, 199.

[2] *Ib.*, IiI, 201.

[3] For these grants see the list of Government papers in the *Summaries*,
p. 241, § 54.

protection to any such person so indebted whereby they may anyways be wronged. And whatsoever boats and the like, whether their own or freighted, let them not be stopped on any pretence whatsoever, but suffered to pass without molestation. And notwithstanding I have lately, by reason of a great outrage committed by the Dutch, absolutely forbidden them any trade in these kingdoms aforesaid, so that governors and other officers have taken occasion to stop and hinder the English trade, which I have not interdicted, with that of the Dutch, which I have strictly forbidden, I do declare that the English never committed any offence of so high a nature that their trade should be hindered. And therefore I resolve and order, as before that according to the above-mentioned order, and as their trade has for so many years quietly and without impediment gone on in these kingdoms aforesaid, that it now also be not hindered, but that whatever their factors and other servants shall buy or sell as aforesaid be no ways letted or impeded. And that I may hear no more complaints from the English in this matter see that this my order be strictly observed." [1]

In spite of all these rescripts, the evils complained of by the English recurred again and again, and nothing seems to have been done by Shāyista Khān to check the vexatious proceedings of the local underlings. The country, however, and its commerce were indebted to him for one great benefit. At the beginning of his government he rooted out the pirate hordes which for more than a century had infested the Bay of Bengal. In 1665 a numerous army and fleet were assembled at Dacca, and rigorous measures were resolved on. To the Portuguese desperadoes at Chittagong and in the service of the king of Arakān, Shāyista Khān sent threats. He told them that mighty forces had been got together, and that it was the Emperor's fixed determination to destroy the power of Arakān. They too would be spoiled and ruined if they continued in their evil ways. If they were wise they would enter the service of the Mogul. These threats took instant effect. The Portuguese came over in a body, and were settled near Dacca. Chittagong was taken in 1666, and the name of the city was changed to Islāmābād. [2]

---

[1] Stewart's *History of Bengal*, edition of 1847, Appendix, p. iii.
[2] *Ib.*, 187 to 189.

E

CHAPTER III.

HOW STREYNSHAM MASTER TWICE VISITED THE BAY AND INTRODUCED REFORMS.

IT was not long before the Court relapsed into its chronic state of anxiety as to the good order of its factories on the east side of India. Under Sir William Langhorne the affairs of the Company were at once laxly and injudiciously administered. The express orders of the Company were not seldom neglected or set aside, while the Agents and Councils of the different stations spent their time in disputing with one another or with the government at Fort St. George. To remedy these evils, the Court directed its attention to the formation of a more regular system of administration. The rank of their servants was in future to be fixed on the principle of making seniority the rule of succession to offices of trust, and the civil and military services were connected in such a manner as to give the chief authority to the former and render the latter subservient to the preservation of the settlements and promotion of trade. "For the advancement of our apprentices," said the new regulations, "we direct that after they have served the first five years they shall have £10 per annum for the last two years; and having served those two years to be entertained one year longer as writers and have writer's salary; and having served that year to enter into the degree of factors, which otherwise would have been ten years. And knowing that a distinction of titles is, in many respects, necessary, we do order that when the apprentices have served their times they be styled writers; and when the writers have served their times they be styled factors; and the factors having served their times be styled merchants; and the merchants having served their times to be styled

E 2

senior merchants." [1] All civil servants were directed to apply themselves to the acquisition of the knowledge of military discipline, so that in event of any sudden emergency, or of being found better qualified for military than for civil duties, they might receive commissions. For the purpose of introducing the new system of administration at Hugli and its dependencies, and enforcing the subordination of these distant stations to Fort St. George, a special commissioner was appointed, who was to succeed Sir William Langhorne when his term of office should expire.[2]

The man selected for discharging these important duties was Streynsham Master, who had already done good service to the Company in Western India, and had received a gold medal in remembrance of the gallantry and skill with which he had held the factory at Surat when it was attacked by Sivaji in 1670. He was undoubtedly a fit person to introduce order and decorum into the factories of the day. Worthy, religious, and methodical, he treated others with kindness and liberality. He writes like a gentleman, and, notwithstanding that he came to India before he was sixteen years old, his papers show that he was decidedly better educated than the majority of his contemporaries in the Company's service.[3] His instructions were to inspect all the books and accounts and reduce them to the plain and clear method of the Presidency of Surat, to find out the best methods of disposing of imports to India and of providing exports for England, especially raw silk and taffetas, to investigate the characters and qualifications of the Company's servants, and to inquire into the causes of dissensions and quarrels amongst them, and to exhort to peaceable and quiet living. He was also to inquire into the business of Raghu Podar, "who was beaten by the house broker of Cassimbazar, and died presently after." [4] With this commission Streynsham Master left England on the 8th of January, 1676, and, arriving at Fort St. George after a voyage of seven months, left again in the *Eagle* for the Bay on the 31st July. The original manuscript of the diary, which he kept during the voyage, is preserved among the Indian records. It gives a minute account of his proceedings, and is our most authentic record of the condition of the English in Bengal at this time.[5]

---

[1] Bruce's *Annals*, II, 374, 375 and 378.
[2] *Ib.*, II, 375, 378.
[3] *Hedges' Diary*, II, 222 to 230.
[4] *Ib.*, II, 231-32.
[5] *Ib.*, II, 232.

There were then three most important English establishments in the Bay, Hugli and Cassimbazar, where they made their principal sales and investments, and Balasor, where they loaded and unloaded the "Europe" ships.[1] After them came the outlying factories at Patna and Singhiya[2] and at Dacca. At Rajmahal there was a small agency in connection with the Mogul mint, to which the English had to send all their treasure to be coined into rupees.[3]

At Balasor the voyager left his ship which had brought him all the way round the Cape from Europe, and went on board a smaller sloop. The entrance to the Hugli was then, as now, obstructed by a number of sand banks called "the Braces." Sailing cautiously over them, and entering the river, Master came to anchor off Saugor Island. It was early morning, and boats came round the voyagers, offering fish for sale. They were fresh and cheap. A single anna bought enough to feed ten men.[4] Oysters were also abundant.[5] This was the eastern channel; on the other side was the western channel by the island of Hijili, where the Mogul had built a small fort to protect his salt works, a "direful place," destined in a few years to be the grave of many a stout-hearted Englishman.[6] From his sloop Master could see the pits and places to boil brine; and swarms of bees flew humming over the deck. The whole river-side was studded with manufactures of wax and salt, which were royal monopolies. The deep channel running eastwards was "Rogues River," the favourite haunt of the Aracanese pirates before the days of Shāyista Khān.[7] By the evening Master came to that awkward corner, Hugli Point. Below, the stream was eighteen or nineteen fathoms deep; above, only eight or nine. This caused such a whirling, especially at the first of the flood and the last of the ebb, that your sloop went twisting round and round with the current, and sometimes was shot past the channel of the Hugli into the Rūpnārāyaṇ. But coming near upon

---

[1] *Hedges' Diary*, II, 236.

[2] Singhiya, or Lalganj, on the left bank of the Gandak river, about fifteen miles north of Patna, is frequently mentioned in the early records of the Company as *Singee* or *Singe*. It was not a healthy place, being mostly saltpetre ground; but the English kept an establishment there because it was close to the saltpetre and removed from the interference of the nabob of Bihār and his subordinates. They had at this time no factory of their own at Patna where they lived and hired houses. The Chief of the Bihār establishment usually lived at Singhiya.

[3] See *Hedges' Diary*, vol. I, *passim*, e.g. pp. 57, 69, 70, 75, 97, 98, &c.

[4] *Ib.*, I, 68.

[5] *Ib.*, II, 232.

[6] *Ib.*, II, 237.

[7] *Ib.*, II, 232.

high-water, Master made the point without any accident. Then they cast anchor again, for the freshes would not allow them to go any higher that night.[1]

Next day they found themselves opposite Betor, in Garden Reach, where the Portuguese ships used to ride over a hundred years ago, when Cæsar Fredrick came that way. The place was now called Great Thānā, and you could see the mud walls of the old forts built here on each side of the river to prevent piratical incursions.[2] The people would still tell stories of how, ten or twelve years ago, before the strong hand of the viceroy had completely crushed Arakān, no one dared to dwell lower down the river beyond the protection of the old fort, and how the people by the bank used to flee into the jungle from the grasp of the spoilers, who carried them off captive to sell them into slavery at Pipli.[3] Opposite, to the right, was the village of Govindpur, where the Setts and Bysacks had cleared away the dense jungle and built homes for their families. Running off to the south of the village was the "Old Ganges," and a little further along it stood the shrine of Kālī. Above Govindpur was Calcutta, but there was little to show its future greatness.[4]

Master could see only the signs of the commercial prosperity of Holland. Early next day he passed Bārnagar, with its Dutch establishment for killing and salting hogs. Two miles short of Hugli he came to the Dutch garden at Chandannagar, and a little further was a deserted place which the French had intended for their factory. The gate had not yet fallen into ruin, but the place was now in possession of their neighbours.

At Chinsurah he saw the Dutch factory, standing by itself like an English country seat. About seven o'clock in the evening he landed at Gholghāt, where he was welcomed to the English Company's house.[5]

On a Monday evening Master set forward again to the Company's garden, two miles north of the town. In two days he reached Nadia, the time-honoured seat of Sanskrit learning. And so he made his way up the river, sometimes meeting the state barge of a rich Indian noble, and sometimes the cargo boats laden with the Company's saltpetre from Singhiya and Patna, till at length in five more days

---

[1] *Hedges' Diary*, II, 233.

[2] One stood where the house of the Superintendent of the Sibpur Botanical Garden now is; the other was placed on the opposite side of the river at Maṭṭiya-Burj.

[3] *Hedges' Diary*, II, 237.

[4] The history of these places will be given subsequently in Book III, chapter IV.

[5] *Hedges' Diary*, II, 233-34.

he reached his destination.[1] Cassimbazar was the head-quarters of the silk trade and was almost equal in importance to Hugli. It was an ordinary Indian town, about two miles long, with streets so narrow in some places where markets were kept, that there was barely room for a single palanquin to pass.[2] The houses, as everywhere in Bengal, were all made of mud dug out of the ground, so that every house had a holeful of water standing by it, a good reason why the country should be unwholesome.[3] The loose, fat soil was exceedingly fertile; yet firewood was scarce, and timber dear and bad. All the district round was planted with mulberry trees, the young leaves being in great request for feeding the silkworms.[4] The silk itself was yellow, like most crude silks, but the people of Cassimbazar knew how to bleach it with a lye made of the ashes of the plantain tree, which made it as white as the silk of Palestine.[5]

Streynsham Master reached Balasor at the end of August, and leaving it again on the 5th September, was in Hugli eight days later. On the 25th the governor of Maqṣūdābād was informed that Master had arrived at Cassimbazar.[6] Here he remained for upwards of six weeks.

Three important questions awaited his decision. In the first place he had to settle a number of disputes between the Company's servants and inquire into the case of Raghu Podar, the Company's cash-keeper. This man had been put into custody by order of Vincent, then chief of the Cassimbazar factory, in order to extract payment from him of sums due to the Company; and while Vincent was away in the country, Anantarāma, the Company's broker, who had charge of the prisoner, had ordered him to be severely beaten, and Raghu Podar had died that same night. This had naturally caused great excitement amongst the native community and had led to trouble with the Mogul government. The matter had only been hushed up by the payment of thirteen thousand rupees. Streynsham Master held an inquiry into the whole affair, which lasted for upwards of a fortnight, and also investigated a number of other charges and counter-charges brought by the members of the Council against one another. An utter stranger, coming to the

---

[1] Hedges' Diary, II, 234.

[2] Ib., II, 236.

[3] Ib., II, 238.

[4] Ib., II, 236.

[5] Tavernier's Voyages, vol. II, p. 261, Paris edition of 1677.

[6] Hedges' Diary, II, 232 to 234.

factories of Bengal for the first time in his life, he could not, we may be sure, succeed in ascertaining the real rights of the cases upon which he was called upon to decide.[1] All that he could do was to try and prevent further scandals, here and elsewhere, by new modelling the consultations, assigning particular duties to each of the Company's servants, and ordering regular records to be made of the whole of their proceedings and transmitted first to Fort St. George and thence to England, together with translations of all letters and grants from the Indian government.[2]

In the second place, Master took steps which led to the founding of a new factory at Malda, a town on the other side of the Ganges, a day's journey from Rajmahal. On the 14th October it was resolved to invest a sum of four or five hundred rupees in various coarse stuffs to be procured there, and a sixth centre of English commerce was formed in Bengal.[3]

Lastly, on the 1st November, the Cassimbazar Council "haveing taken into consideration and debate which of the two places, Hugli or Balasor, might be most proper and convenient for the residence of the Chiefe and Councell in the Bay, did resolve and conclude that Hugli was the most fitting place notwithstanding the Europe ships doe Unloade and take in their ladeing in Balasor roade, Hugli being the Key or Scale of Bengala, where all goods pass in and out to and from all parts, and being near the center of the Companys business is more commodious for receiving of advices from and issuing of orders to all subordinate ffactoryes.

" Wherefore it is thought Convenient that the Chiefe and Councell of the Bay doe reside at Hugli, and upon the dispatch of the Europe ships the Chiefe and the Councell, or some of them (as shall be thought Convenient) doe yearly goe down to Balasor, soe well to expedite the dispatch of the ships as to make inspection into the affairs of Balasor ffactory. And the Councell did likewise Conclude that it was requisite a like inspection should be yearly made in the ffactory at Cassambazar the Honble Companys principal concernes of sales and investments in the Bay lyeing in those two places, and the expence of such visitation will be very small, by reason of Conveniency of travelling in these Countreys by land or water." [4] The day of Calcutta was not yet.

---

[1] *Hedges' Diary*, II, 234-35.
[2] Bruce's *Annals*, II, 403.
[3] *Hedges' Diary*, II, 235.
[4] *Ib.*, II, 236.

On the 8th of November Streynsham Master left Cassimbazar and on the 29th Hugli. On the 17th January, 1677, he arrived at Madras.[1]

Within a year of this visitation Clavell, the chief of the Bengal factories, died, and on the 7th September, 1677, Matthias Vincent reigned in his stead.[2] The new agent, who has already been noticed as concerned in the affair of Raghu Podar, seems to have never been liked or trusted by his honourable masters. They accused him of homicide, "diabolical arts with Bramminees" exercising charms, using poison, and worse.[3] For of all crimes under the sun which a man could commit, the two most heinous in the Court's eyes were for a private merchant to infringe their monopoly by coming to India to trade without their license in their commodities, and for a covenanted servant of theirs to encourage, protect, and share in such criminal proceedings. At this time there was in those parts a notable private trader and interloper, Thomas Pitt, destined in after years to be Governor of Fort St. George, discoverer of the finest diamond in the world, and progenitor of two of England's greatest statesmen; but as yet only "a young beginner," trading in his own account between Persia and Bengal.[4] Somewhere about the end of 1678 or the beginning of 1679, Pitt married Jane Innes, one of whose aunts was Vincent's wife. The agent at Hugli looked upon himself as the uncle of "the pirate" Pitt, and always wrote to him and treated him as his nephew. He was thus clearly guilty of "the treacherous and unpardonable sin of compliance with interlopers."[5]

We cannot say whether the Court ever knew the whole of this dreadful story. They were, however, always suspecting Vincent of such iniquities, and attempted to exercise a jealous supervision over the establishment in Bengal through the governor of Fort St. George.[6] In 1679, Streynsham Master found it again necessary to visit the Bay. He went in state as Governor of Madras, taking with him Mr. Mohun, one of the Madras Council, a chaplain, the Rev. Richard Elliott, a secretary, two writers, an ensign, and thirteen soldiers, besides orderlies and palanquin boys. They set sail on the 1st of August, reached Balasor

---

[1] *Hedges' Diary*, II, 236 to 238.
[2] Danvers, *op. cit.*, p. 10.
[3] *Hedges' Diary*, II, 284, 290-91.
[4] *Ib.*, III, 1 to 9.
[5] *Ib.*, III, 28.
[6] *Ib.*, II, 290 to 292.

on the 17th and Hugli a month later, and did not return to Madras till
the 26th January, 1680.[1]

Streynsham Master this time exercised his authority more decisively
and vigorously than he had done three years earlier. He did not
displace Vincent, but he did what he could to improve the discipline
and moral tone of the agencies. He had the wretched huts in use
replaced in many cases by brick buildings, he drew up a number of
disciplinary regulations, settled the order of precedence and succession
among the Company's servants, and suggested that their salaries should
be increased. These things did not please the Court. They were ready
enough to find fault with their servants, but slow to do anything to
improve them; and while they expected every one to sacrifice his
interests to theirs, they grudged to spend a few pounds in return for the
benefit of others.[2]

Under Vincent, in spite of his misdoings, the Bengal trade continued to make rapid progress. In 1675 the factors, besides the £65,000
of stock, were authorised to take up £20,000 at interest, and with this
sum to buy principally silks and taffetas of a finer quality and six hundred
tons of saltpetre, and after that white sugar, cotton-yarn, turmeric, and
bees-wax to fill up any spare tonnage in the ships.[3] Two years later the
sales of Dacca and Malda goods in England turned out so profitably, that
the Court raised the stock to £100,000.[4] The result was that the investment despatched from the east coast in the next year consisted almost
entirely of exports from Bengal, and was on the whole greater than "it
had been in any other period of the Company's commerce."[5] Fort St.
George was ordered to store up annually five hundred tons of saltpetre
ready for despatch.[6] In 1680 as much as £150,000 was appropriated
to the factories of the Bay. In this year £20,000 was assigned to
Balasor alone, which became a purchasing as well as a shipping
centre.[7]

The measures which the Court had taken to improve the navigation of the river had at last succeeded. In 1679 Captain Stafford made
the passage up with the *Falcon*, and for the first time Mother Ganges bore

---

[1] *Hedges' Diary*, II, 243.
[2] *Ib*, II, 247.
[3] Bruce's *Annals*, II, 361.
[4] *Ib*., II, 409.
[5] *Ib*., II, 430.
[6] *Ib*., II, 425.
[7] *Ib*., II, 451, 453.

on her tide a British ship.[1] A curious recollection of the event still survives in Calcutta. The story is told that, while lying in Garden Reach, at all times a favourite anchorage, Stafford sent over to Govindpur to ask the Setts and Bysacks for a *dobhāsh*,[2] meaning an interpreter or broker. The simple villagers mistook the word *dobhāsh* for *dhoba*, a washerman, and accordingly sent one, named Ratan Sarkar. Luckily the man could understand a little English, and was so intelligent, that his new employers were quite satisfied with him, and thus the quondam washerman was promoted to the dignity of being the English interpreter in Bengal.

---

[1] *Hedges' Diary*, III, 200.

[2] In Bengali *dobhāshiyā* means interpreter, and *dhobā* a washerman. *Dobhāsh* is the common word in Madras for broker; in Bengal the word used is *banyan*. Hence the mistake.

CHAPTER IV.

THE visits of Streynsham Master to Bengal afford a convenient opportunity for pausing in our history, and attempting to form some idea of the condition of the English in the Bay before the foundation of Fort William, and at the time when their commercial operations all came to a head at Hugli. Here, or near here, had been for centuries the chief mart of Western Bengal. From the parts all about came silk, sugar, and opium, rice and wheat, oil and butter, coarse hemp and jute; and in the neighbourhood lived large numbers of weavers of cotton cloth and tasar silk of various sorts. In the town of Hugli itself the Portuguese were numerous, but their trade was inconsiderable. Reduced to a low and mean condition, their chief subsistence was to take service as soldiers under the local government. As a centre for the English trade the place had many defects which could not be remedied by any improvements in the pilotage of ships. It was separated from the Bay by a long and dangerous river, and was therefore hard to defend from the sea : it stood on the west bank, and was therefore easy to attack from the land. And the founders of the Hugli factory had done their best to add to these faults. The large, badly-built Indian town, with its narrow lanes, stretched for about two miles along the river-side. North of it was Bandel, the ill-fated colony of the Portuguese; south was the Dutch settlement of Chinsurah.

---

[1] See also the contemporary account given below p. 375 *et seq.*

Near the middle of the town, for the space of about three hundred yards, a small indentation occurred in the bank, forming a diminutive whirlpool, whence the Bengalis called it Gholghāṭ. It was this spot, hemmed in on all sides by closely-packed houses, hard by the residence of the Mogul governor which the English, with short-sighted rashness, chose as the site of their factory.[1]

To the eyes of one accustomed to the house at Surat, with its ample rooms and fair oratory, its warehouses and cellars, its baths and ponds of clear water, the establishment at Gholghāṭ seemed a poor place of eastern residence. It afforded no accommodation at all to the married servants of the Company, who had to live outside in the native town, neither had it any proper quay with lodgings for the captains and pilots. In 1676 Streynsham Master gave instructions for rebuilding and enlarging the factory. Besides improving and adding to the main building, he had that part of the precinct which was near the river repaired and enclosed, and " hovels" set up for the use of the English employed on the ships and sloops. It was ordered that those who were living outside in houses of their own should by degrees be brought into the factory precinct, and allowed to build such accommodation as they desired, if married. All persons so living were to be under the inspection of the purser marine and to live under such orders as they might receive from the Council.[2]

As elsewhere, the governing body at Hugli consisted of four members, the agent, who was chief of the factories in the Bay, the accountant, the storekeeper, and the purser marine. Next in order of succession was the secretary, who attended all the meetings of the Council and kept a diary of their consultations, a copy of which was sent home every year, together with a general letter reviewing their proceedings; the chaplain, when there was one, ranked as third after the accountant; the surgeon came between the purser marine and the secretary; the eighth in order of precedence was the steward. After these dignities came the general body of merchants, factors, writers, and apprentices. The pay of the agent was originally £100 a year, but it must have been gradually raised, till in 1682 it was £200 a year and £100 gratuity. The chaplain, too, was paid £100, the factors received from £20 to £40, and the writers only £10 a year. These rates of salary were merely nominal: what the real incomes of the various ranks were it is impossible to say, for, besides what they gained by private trade,

---

[1] *Hedges' Diary,* II, 238 to 240.
[2] *Ib.,* II, 236 and 237.

they drew considerable sums from the public funds as allowances for various purposes. Every servant of the Company had a right to free quarters in the factory, dinner and supper at the public table, lights and attendants. The senior officers, who were married, and desired "to diet apart," were given their diet money, servants' wages, free candles, and other additions.[1] To enforce his authority, the Chief had under him a force of thirty or forty native orderlies, to which was added in 1682 a corporal and twenty European soldiers.[2]

The usual intermediary between the English and the local producers and consumers was the Indian broker, who was sent out into the districts round the factory to buy on the Company's behalf in the cheapest markets. He had to give a security, and was rewarded by a brokerage of three per cent. on all transactions. Another way was to invite the merchants living in the town by the factory to send samples, and buy through them. But in whichever way the purchases were made, passes were given to the broker or merchant in the English Company's name, so that the goods might be freely conveyed to their destination; and in the same way, whatever the Company sold, whether for ready money or on account, they gave with it a free pass, so that the buyer might not have to pay duty.

No one could live outside the factory unless he received permission to do so.[3] Within, life was regulated after the fashion of a college. The hours of work were from nine or ten till twelve in the morning, and again in the afternoon till about four if work was pressing. Ordinarily there was not so much to do, but during the shipping time the place was filled with busy hum of men. At midday they all dined together in the common hall, seated strictly in order of seniority. The table was loaded with every sort of meat and dish which the country could afford, prepared by Indian, Portuguese, English, and even French cooks. There was a plentiful supply of plate. A silver ewer and basin were used at the beginning and end of the meal for washing the hands. They drank arrack punch and Shiraz wine. European wine and bottled beer were great luxuries. On Sundays and holidays they had game to eat, and drank the healths of King and Company and of every one at table, down to the youngest writer. The drinking of tea every day

---

[1] See *Hedges' Diary*, II, pp. 10 and 11, Hyde's *First Bengal Chaplain*, pp. 3 and 5, published in the *Indian Church Quarterly Review*, January 1890. Compare also Ovington's *Voyage to Surat*, pp. 389 to 391, edition of 1696.

[2] Ovington's *Voyage*, pp. 391-92: Bruce's *Annals*, II, 467-68.

[3] *Hedges' Diary*, II, 237. Ovington's *Voyage*, 393.

at their ordinary social meetings was even then in fashion, and was common all over India.[1] The second meal taken together in the hall was supper.[2] At nine o'clock the factory gates were shut.

Their pleasures and amusements were few indeed. Sometimes they entertained, or were entertained by their Dutch neighbours.[3] Occasionally they might go out into the country around to shoot, or hunt in company with some local grandee,[4] or see such antiquities as Bengal possessed.[5] But as a rule their excursions were limited to the English garden two miles north of the factory,[6] whither they would go, morning and evening to breathe the fresh air and to walk underneath the shady trees and bathe in the cool ponds of water.[7] Their exercise was shooting at the butts; their refreshment a bottle of wine and a cold collation of fruits and preserves, which they brought with them.[8] The chief and second had a palanquin each when they went abroad, and the rest of the Council with the chaplain were allowed to have large umbrellas borne above them in solemn state, but this protection against the sun's rays was rigidly denied to the rest of the Company's servants.[9] No one, however, could stir without being attended by a number of orderlies.[10]

On high days the governor went to the garden in a procession which, according to native ideas, must have been most magnificent and imposing.[11] First came two men carrying swallow-tailed silk flags displaying the broad red cross of St. George fastened to a silver partisan;[12] next the musicians sounding their trumpets, and the chief's Persian horses[13] of state led before him gallantly equipped in rich trappings. The chief and his wife reclined in palanquins borne by

---

[1] See Mandelslo's *Voyage*, in Wheeler's *Early Record's Voyage of British India*, edition of 1878, p. 22.

[2] Ovington's *Voyage*, 394 to 398. At Surat it was the custom for the Chief and Council to have supper together alone "for the maintenance of a friendly correspondence and to discourse of the Company's business."

[3] Tavernier's *Voyage*, II, 81. *Hedges' Diary*, I, 56.

[4] *Hedges' Diary*, I, 66.

[5] *Ib.*, I, 88.

[6] *Ib.*, I, 34, 35, II, 234, and constantly in our authorities.

[7] Ovington's *Voyage*, 400.

[8] Mandelslo's *Voyage*, as above, p. 22.

[9] Hyde, *op. cit.*, p. 5.

[10] Ovington's *Voyage*, 392.

[11] For this procession, see Ovington's *Voyage*, 399, 400. Compare *Hedges' Diary*, I, 123, quoted below, p. 74.

[12] The English flag was also displayed at the factory and at the garden.

[13] *Hedges' Diary*, II, 237.

four orderlies, with two others to relieve them, and were escorted by the whole body of orderlies in scarlet coats on foot. After the chief came the other members of council in large coaches, ornamented with silver knobs, drawn by oxen. The rest of the factors followed, some on horses and some in carriages. If their wives were with them, the carriages, in accordance with native etiquette, were closed. Otherwise they were open, so that the people might behold and admire their fine clothes.

Of course they imitated the European changes of mode, but at a respectful distance, for in those times "the butterfly passion" took many years to flit across to India. In 1658 a good cloth coat with large silver lace was all the fashion, and was considered to be the badge of an Englishman. Without it, or something like it, a man got no esteem or regard.[1] Perukes, I expect, were not generally adopted in India till long after their introduction into Europe. No doubt great personages, like Streynsham Master or His Reverence the Chaplain, came out wearing the ample wig,[2] but those who consulted comfort cut the hair short and condescended "to enter into the Moor's fashion."[3] What the English ladies wore I cannot imagine, but I dare say they took care to be less old-fashioned than the men. Unfortunately there were few of them, the hardships and dangers of the long voyage being very great, and a large number of the Company's servants had to find their wives in the country.

I find it difficult to give a fair and impartial account of the English in Bengal at this period. The pictures we have of them, like all pictures of societies, dwell upon the darker aspects of the scene. In those days of greatest isolation the tendency to gravitate towards the local ways of living and acting was very strong. They took their meals when away from the factory lying on carpets;[4] they wore the Indian dress; they married Indian wives.

But besides these practices, which, if we consider the circumstances, are at least excusable, the English in Bengal developed other characteristics, which gained for their establishments the reputation of being the laxest and worst disciplined in India, just as the Surat factory was reputed the godliest. It was the general belief that their

---

[1] *Hedges' Diary*, II, 347.
[2] Hyde, *op. cit.*, p. 5.
[3] *Hedges' Diary*, III, 194.
[4] Ovington's *Voyage*, 401.

F

untimely deaths were due rather to gross intemperance than to the climate. "It cannot be denied," writes Bernier[1] in 1666, "that the air is not so healthy there, especially near the sea, and when the English and Hollanders first came to settle there many of them died. I have seen in Balasor two very fine English ships, which, having been obliged by reason of the war with the Hollanders to stay there above a year, were not able to go to sea, because most of their men were lost. Yet since the time that they have taken care and given orders, as well as the Hollanders, that their seamen shall not drink so much bowl-punch, nor go so often ashore to visit the sellers of arrack and tobacco and the Indian women, and since they have found that a little Bordeaux, Canary, or Shiraz wine is a marvellous antidote against the ill air, there is not so much sickness among them. Bowl-punch is a certain beverage made of arrack, that is of strong water, black sugar with the juice of lemon, water, and a little muscadine squeezed upon it. It is pleasant enough to the taste, but the plague of the body and health." In spite of all this the habit of drinking did not die out so soon. When Master first came to Bengal he found a punch-house within the Balasor factory; and in 1678 the youthful Pitt writes: "There is a general complaint that we drink a damnable deal of wine this year."[2]

The English in Bengal were equally notorious for their quarrels, the natural outcome of the prevailing eagerness to make money and the spirit of espionage fostered by their masters, who were pleased that their servants should tell tales of one another. The old viceroy Shāyista Khān called them "a company of base, quarrelling people and foul dealers;" and our great modern authority will not gainsay that the nabob had good grounds for his assertion. The impression of the moral and social tone of the Company's servants in the Bay which has been left on the mind of Sir Henry Yule by his exhaustive study of the records of the time is "certainly a dismal one," and he has found it "hard to augur from their prevalent character at this time the ultimate emergence among the servants of the Company of such men as Elphinstone, Munro, and Malcolm, Henry and John Lawrence, Martyn and Heber," or a host of other noble souls who lived their days without regret in India, studious alike of its good and of the good of their own nation.[3]

---

[1] Amsterdam edition of 1724, vol. II, p. 334.
[2] *Hedges' Diary*, III, 5.
[3] *Ib.*, II, 29, 30.

But men do not gather grapes of thorns, or figs of thistles. Surely, knowing the brighter future, we may make reply :

> " You make our faults too gross.
> At times the small black fly upon the pane
> May seem the black ox of the distant plain."

We must not allow the noisy riot of a few callow boys new to the country, or the excesses of a ship's crew set loose after a tedious voyage, to silence the quiet but eloquent testimony of hundreds of lives spent in serving the Company faithfully, soberly, hopefully, honestly. There is another account to be given of early English life in Bengal. The native inhabitants, shrewd judges of character, saw matters in a very different light from the nabob. They saw, on the one hand, the viceroy of Dacca and his officers throughout the country oppressing the people, demanding bribes and presents upon a thousand petty pretexts, monopolising every useful article, down to the very grass for their cattle and wood for their fire, harassing trade, obliging the Hindu merchants to buy goods at unfairly enhanced prices, urging them to borrow money at exorbitant rates of interest, and requiring them to repay principal and interest before they become due.[1] They saw, on the other hand, the English careful to discharge all their obligations, anxious to defend their servants, and to do justice. "Never," says the Court in 1693, "never any native of India lost a penny debt by this Company from the time of the first institution thereof in Queen Elizabeth's days till this time;"[2] and the faithfulness of the Hindu merchants to the Company's interest was a commonplace with the Court. Where is the evidence to justify the belief in the general corruption of this period? It is easy to turn history into melodrama, and people the stage with villains, in the midst of which some favourite hero shall move as an angel from another world. But the fact is that the English at Hugli were for the most part not so very different from their successors of to-day, sincere, manly, and earnest, happy in their work, proud of their position, anxious for the good name of their religion and their country, anxious to leave the place of their sojourn a little better than they found it.

To minister to such a flock came in 1678 the Rev. John Evans, the first Bengal Chaplain.[3] Born of the stock of an ancient family in North Wales, educated at Jesus College, Oxford, he was, while still the

---

[1] *Hedges' Diary*, II, 238 and 239.
[2] *Ib.*, III, 17.
[3] For the details about Evans see Hyde, *op. cit.*

F 2

curate of Thistleworth, on the recommendation of Sir Joseph Ashe, elected
by the Court to be their chaplain in the Bay. Though married, he was
still a young man in his twenty-eighth year, with handsome features
and a fine stature. He was eager to go forth to his work. Twenty
pounds were given him for his outfit, and in December, 1677, only a
month after his formal appointment, he embarked with his wife at
Gravesend. On the 23rd of June following he arrived at Hugli,
and for a year or more was busied in visiting the out-agencies and
providing a chapel for the factory. His youth, his impetuous zeal, and
his liberal opinions prejudiced him in the eyes of some of the older
men. It is clear that he sympathised with the interlopers, and that, in
common with the other members of the factory, but with more than
ordinary aptitude and vigour, he accommodated himself to the necessity
of trading to eke out his salary. For all this he incurred the censure
of the Court. Still we cannot doubt the good influence of one who " ever
had greatly at heart to fulfil the ministry which he had received in the
Lord." His character, in fact, presented the rare combination of
gentleness and strength. Even the " Gentiles," it is said, revered
him. "He drew men by his sweet words, moulded them by his grave
looks, led them by the example of his strict life."

In 1679, when the governor of Madras paid his second visit to
Bengal, accompanied by his chaplain, Elliott, the three men took counsel
together as to the best means of propagating in Bengal the godly
discipline of Surat. On the 12th December a number of regulations
were issued " for advancing the glory of God, upholding the honour of
the English nation, and preventing of disorders," and were ordered
to be observed by all persons employed in the Company's service in
the factories of the Bay. The voice of Streynsham Master, the great
disciplinarian, may be heard throughout plainly enough. He begins
with admonition, he ends with threats of condign punishment. The
preamble declares that persons of all professions ought to hallow God's
name, attend His services, and seek His blessing by daily prayers,
and warns every servant of the Company "to abandon lying, swearing,
cursing, drunkenness, uncleanness, profanation of the Lord's Day, and
all other sinful practices, and not to be out of the house or from their
lodgings late at nights, or absent from, or neglect, morning or evening
prayer, or do any other thing to the dishonour of Almighty God,
the corruption of good manners, or against the peace of the Government." Should any still refuse to hear the voice of the preacher, he will
have recourse to the judicial powers committed to him by the Royal

Charter. If any one is found absent from the house after nine o'clock at night he will have to pay ten rupees for the use of the poor. Any one guilty of profane swearing must pay twelve pence for each oath. Drunkenness is to be punished by a fine of five shillings for each offence. One shilling is the fine for neglecting to attend public prayers morning and evening on the Lord's day. If these sums are not paid on demand, they will be levied by distress and sale of the offender's goods; failing this the offender will have to sit in the stocks. Whoever is guilty of lying will pay twelve pence to the poor for every such offence. Any Protestant staying in the Company's house and absenting himself without lawful excuse from the public prayers morning and evening, will also pay twelve pence to the poor for every such default, or be confined a whole week within the house. "If any, by those penalties, will not be reclaimed from their vices, or any shall be found guilty of adultery, fornication, uncleanness, or any such crimes, or shall disturb the peace of the factory by quarrelling or fighting, and will not be reclaimed, then they shall be sent to Fort St. Geogre, there to receive condign punishment." And "these orders shall be read publicly to the factory twice in a year, that is, upon the Sunday next after Christmas Day and upon the Sunday next after Midsummer Day, in the forenoon, after Divine service, that none may pretend ignorance thereof." Lastly, "one of the factors or writers shall be monthly appointed by the respective chiefs to note and collect the forfeiture, and to pay the same to the chief who is every year to send it to the chief at Hugli, and they are to remit the whole collections every year to the agent at the Fort,[1] there to be paid to the overseers of the poor.[2]

And thus Christian observance and Christian order were introduced amongst these hitherto neglected members of the Church. Morning and evening the English at Hugli joined again in that princely liturgy, whose very words have a strange charm, like the melody of far-off bells, to draw the soul Godwards. Day by day was offered up the appointed prayer for the Divine blessing upon the Company and their servants. "O Almighty and most merciful God, who art the sovereign protector

---

[1] The Fort, of course, means Fort St. George, Madras. Mr. Hyde seems to take it as meaning Hugli. (See I. Q. R., vol. iii, p. 78, Gervase Bellamy, p. 5.)

[2] These regulations occur in the Hugli Diary of 1679, in the India Office Records. They are given by Mr. Hyde, op. cit. They are also given in extenso in a MS. account of Bengal in the British Museum, Add. MSS. 34, 123.

of all that trust in Thee, and the author of all spiritual and temporal blessings, we, Thy unworthy creatures, do most humbly implore Thy goodness for a plentiful effusion of Thy grace upon our employers, Thy servants, the Right Honourable East India Company of England. Prosper them in all their undertakings, and make them famous and successful in all their governments, colonies, and commerce, both by sea and land, so that they may prove a public blessing, by the increase of honour, wealth, and power to our native country, as well as to themselves. Continue Thy favour towards them, and inspire their Generals, Presidents, Agents, and Councils, in these remote parts of the world, and all others that are entrusted with any authority under them, with piety towards Thee our God, and with wisdom, fidelity, and circumspection in their several stations, that we may all discharge our respective duties faithfully and live virtuously, in due obedience to our superiors, and in love, peace, and charity towards one another. That these Indian nations, among whom we dwell, seeing our sober and righteous conversation, may be induced to have a just esteem for our most holy profession of the Gospel of our Lord and Saviour Jesus Christ, to whom be honour, praise, and glory, now and for ever. Amen." [1]

---

[1] Ovington's *Voyage*, 408, 409.

CHAPTER V.

HOW WILLIAM HEDGES, FIRST ENGLISH GOVERNOR OF BENGAL, WAS SENT
TO DESTROY THE INTERLOPERS, AND FAILED.

THE Court at home had learnt two lessons: first, that the trade of
Bengal was of the greatest importance; secondly, that the regulation of
the factories in that distant region was extremely difficult. The control
exercised by their agent at Madras was uncertain and unsatisfactory;
and, in spite of his well-meaning zeal, they were far from contented with
Streynsham Master. They complained of delay in despatching the
shipping and of the bad quality of the goods sent. They rebuked him
for the haughty tone of his letters. They were indignant at the
expenses which he had incurred in his "progress" in Bengal with his
"princely retinue," costing them far more than it was worth. Above
all, they were angry at what they considered to be a wanton disregard
of their orders in his treatment of their favourite servant. In 1679
Job Charnock, who was then at Patna, was appointed by the Court to be
chief of the Cassimbazar factory and second of the Council of the Bay;
and in November, when Streynsham Master was on his second visitation of the Bengal factories, Charnock was ordered to send off the

Company's saltpetre cargoes from Patna and to come down at once to join his new appointment. Charnock, however, made various excuses, and delayed leaving Patna. At length, on the 10th December, Streynsham Master wrote to Charnock, censuring him for his disobedience and the inconvenience he had caused, and transferring him from Cassimbazar to Hugli, where he was to be second. This action of their agent, which was surely not so very unreasonable, drew down upon him the fulness of the Court's displeasure. They were weary, they said, of long discourses concerning "the succession," which "made doctrine more intricate than the text," and ended with a " use shamefully contradicting both." Their old servant had the right of succession. He had served them faithfully for twenty years, and had never been a "prowler for himself." He had stayed on at Patna to despatch their saltpetre simply out of a sense of duty and care for their service. Besides, they had given clear orders that he was to be chief at Cassimbazar, and so it should be.[1] As for Master, his five-years term of service expired in July, 1681, and he was dismissed their employment, and William Gifford nominated to supersede him as Agent and Governor of St. George.[2] To Vincent also the Court meted out the same measure, but with more justice. Besides "his odious infidelity in countenancing interlopers," he shared with Master the guilt of injuring Charnock and retarding the shipping. He had connived at the base sorting of the goods, sent no invoices, kept back the accounts, neglected orders. He displayed gross partiality and favouritism in his management of the factories, and set an evil example by his riotous and evil way of living. He sacrificed the Company's interests to his own private trade by giving passes to the natives and by the ungodly taking of bribes.[3] To prevent such irregularities from again arising in the establishments of the Bay, the Court determined that the agency at Hugli should be distinct and separate from Fort St. George, and that they might act with certain knowledge, they appointed William Hedges, one of their number, with special powers to be Agent and Governor of their affairs and factories in the Bay of Bengal.[4] The new agent's instructions are dated the 14th November, 1681. They rehearse the various abuses, frauds, and malpractices, prevailing in the Bay, which are the occasion of the electing and sending of William Hedges, who is to correct and remove

---

[1] *Hedges' Diary*, II, 47-48.
[2] *Ib.*, II, 246.
[3] *Ib.*, II, 13.
[4] *Bruce's Annals*, II, 466 to 468.

them as speedily as possible. Vincent was to be seized and sent home a prisoner. Vigorous proceedings were directed against the interlopers, who had now grown so bold that with the assistance of the Turkey merchants [1] they were attempting to found a rival East India Company.[2]

On the 28th January, 1682, the *Defence*, commanded by Captain William Heath, and the *Resolution*, under Captain Francis Wilshaw sailed out of the Downs with a fair wind. On board the *Defence*, with his wife and family, was Governor Hedges, the Company's chosen reformer of abuses and destroyer of interlopers.[3] About the 20th February, William Pitt, the arch-interloper, set sail for Bengal in Captain Dorrel's ship, the *Crown*, together with three or four other vessels chartered by him or his principals.[4] The Court had tried to stop Pitt in vain, but they made no doubt that Hedges, who had with him a corporal and twenty soldiers, would be able to arrest Vincent, Pitt, and their partners, before they could do any mischief. The Court were, in fact, fully confident of the "wreck of the interlopers," which they said would be "a just judgment of God upon their disloyal and unjust proceedings," and would "have such an effect upon all men's minds here, as to convince the deluded world of the vanity and folly of those persons." [5]

In these expectations the Court were sadly disappointed. The *Crown* was a fast sailer. In less than two months she overhauled and passed the *Defence* and the *Resolution*, and on the 8th July arrived at Balasor eleven days before Hedges.[6] Consequently the new governor found the interlopers well prepared for him and quite able to take care of themselves. Pitt, on his arrival, had given out that the Company was on the point of expiring, and that a new Company had been formed, of which he was the agent. Vincent, the late chief at Hugli, at once removed to safer quarters. On the 24th July he received Hedges at the Dutch Garden, guarded by thirty-five Portuguese firelocks, fifty Rajputs, and a number of other native soldiers. On being served with a subpœna out of Chancery and summoned to answer it, he most politely declined, saying he would answer in England. Pitt

---

[1] *Hedges' Diary*, III, 9. For the opposition of the Turkey merchants to the East India Company, see *ante*, p. 46.
[2] *Hedges' Diary*, II, 15 to 17.
[3] *Ib.*, I, 15.
[4] *Ib.*, III, 9, 10.
[5] *Ib.*, III, 12.
[6] *Ib.*, III, 1 and 10.

also went about attended by red-coated Portuguese and native soldiers and trumpeters. He sailed up to Hugli in three ships, landed with great pomp and circumstance, and took up his quarters at Chinsurah. Here he was joined by Vincent, and with the assistance of the Dutch and the Bengali merchants began to build warehouses and start a new trade. He treated with the native governor of Hugli as an agent, and obtained an order from him, under the title of the New English Company, giving him commercial privileges and liberty to build a factory.[1]

Governor Hedges did not arrest Pitt. After much tedious negotiation with the nabob of Dacca, an order was issued to the customs officer, Balchandra, and to the governor of Hugli, directing them to seize Pitt and Dorrell, but it was never executed. The interlopers readily agreed to pay the Mogul his dues, and no arguments or bribes availed against them.[2]

A year later the interlopers and their friends openly defied the agent. In September, 1683, at the very time when Hedges was making a last fruitless attempt to assert his authority, Captain Alley, a notorious interloper, audaciously came up to Hugli in a barge rowed by English mariners in coats with badges and with four musicians. On his arrival he went to visit the governor "in a splendid equipage, habited in scarlet richly laced. Ten Englishmen in blue caps and coats edged with red, all armed with blunderbusses, went before his palanquin, eighty peons before them, and four musicians playing on the waits with two flags before him like an agent."[3]

A few weeks afterwards on he went with like pomp to Balchandra. "He agreed to pay three and-a-half per cent. custom on all goods imported and exported: upon which they parted good friends."[4] The interloper was also on the best of terms with the factors at Hugli. "Captain Alley, Captain Smith and that gang," says Hedges, "are frequently visited, to our shame and the Company's discredit, by every considerable person in this factory, except myself. They and our Captains caress one another daily. Thus they send adventures home by them."[5] On the 13th November 1683, Alley actually dined with Captain Lake on board the *Prudent Mary*, one of the Company's ships, together with Honor, Clerk, and other interlopers, "making great mirth and jollity by firing

---

[1] *Hedges' Diary*, III, 11.
[2] *Ib.*, I, 55, 130.
[3] *Ib.*, I, 118, 123.
[4] *Ib.*, I, 130.
[5] *Ib.*, I, 130.

guns all the afternoon." [1] Hedges indeed succeeded in procuring an order
from Shāyista Khān to the governor of Hugli, ordering him to arrest
the interloping captains and send them to Dacca, but Balchandra came
to their rescue promising to be himself responsible for them. It was
represented to the nabob that the "Old Company" wanted to have a
monopoly of the trade, whereas the "New Company" were merchants
as well as the others and were willing to pay even five per cent.
custom, and that hence it would be foolish to hinder their trade.
"Hereupon the old doting nabob replied that they should trade freely,
so that now the business being thus determined by the nabob, there is
no possibility of rooting out or doing any prejudice to the interlopers."

---

[1] *Hedges' Diary,* I, 137-38.
[2] *Ib.,* I, 131, 136, 142.

CHAPTER VI.

It was not altogether the fault of Hedges that he failed to suppress the interlopers. On arriving in Bengal his attention was almost
immediately drawn to other matters of greater urgency. He had to
face another difficulty, which, though it was the characteristic difficulty
of the time and of the situation, had not been mentioned in his instructions, the growing exactions of the native rulers and their subordinates.
This difficulty, signalised at the beginning of the period by Sir Edward
Winter, but ignored by the Court, had not on that account disappeared.
On the contrary it had become more urgent.[1]

It was, as has been seen, one of the congenital defects of the
system instituted by the Court in 1651 that the security of the trade
and of its chief centre at Hugli depended entirely upon the good-will
of the natives of the country. The Court supposed that they would
not interfere unnecessarily or without reason. And yet nothing was
more probable. Although the Mogul had at first granted the most
liberal terms to the Company, his orders were often disregarded by
his subordinates, and all the privileges conceded might be revoked at
pleasure. By the letters patent of Shāh Shujā', the English in Bengal
were granted perfect freedom of trade, and this privilege was confirmed

---

[1] For instance see Stewart's *Bengal*, p. 190.

by an order made by the nabob Shāyista Khān in 1672 at the suit of Walter Clavell. But the order was very little observed, and, when Shāyista Khān left Bengal in 1677, the new nabob Fedai Khān and the King's officer Haji Sufi Khān altogether disregarded it. Fortunately in the very next year Fedāi Khān died at Dacca and was succeeded by Prince Muḥammad A'zam, from whom Vincent in 1678 procured fresh letters patent freeing their trade.[1] The Court, however, were not content with this. They found it very expensive and troublesome to procure a fresh order for freedom of trade from every succeeding governor. They desired the higher authority of a mandate from the Emperor. They had therefore sent with Shāyista Khān, when he left Bengal, an agent to solicit an imperial grant to settle the matter for ever.

In 1680 they had their desire. The following rescript was issued by Aurangzēb, and was received at Hugli with much feasting and rejoicing, processions marching and guns [2] firing on the most lavish scale :—"In the name of GOD, Amen. To all present and future rulers in *Surat* that remain in hopes of the Emperor's favour. Be it known that at this happy time it is agreed of the English nation besides their usual custom of two per cent. for their goods, more one and a half per cent. *jizyah*, or poll-money, shall be taken. Wherefore it is commanded *that in the said place*, from the first day of Shawwal, in the twenty-third year of our reign of the said people, three and a half per cent. of all their goods, on account of custom or poll-money, *be taken for the future. And at all other places*, upon this account, let no one molest them for custom, *rāh-dāri*, *pesh-kash*, *farmāish* [3] and other matters by the Emperor's Court forbidden, nor make any demands in these particulars. Observe. Written on the twenty-third day of the month Çafar, in the twenty-third year." [4]

This document is an historical example of the difficulties and dangers which arise from uncertain punctuation. Read as above, with a full stop after "*future*," it would appear that Aurangzēb demanded three and a half per cent. on account of custom and poll-tax only from the English at Surat, and that in all other places their trade was to

---

[1] Stewart's *Bengal*, pp. 190-91.

[2] *Ib.*, pp. 194, 195.

[3] *Rāh-dāri*—from rāh-dār, road-keeper, means transit duty. *Pesh-kash*, first fruits, came to mean an offering or tribute. *Farmāish*, means commission for goods.

[4] Stewart's *Bengal*, Appendix, p. 4.

be absolutely free. This was the English punctuation, but the Indian officials did not "stand upon points." If the full stop be removed, and placed after *and at all other places*, the sense is altered. At Surat and at all other places a tax of three and a half per cent. is to be levied on the English. This is how the Indian officials understood the matter, and they lost no time in acting according to their understanding. Shāyista Khān, who returned to Bengal in this very year, at once demanded the payment of the poll-tax.[1]

When Hedges reached Hugli in 1682 he found that the general trade there was almost at a standstill. On the 9th October, "the several affronts, insolences, and abuses dayly put upon us by Boolchund, our chief Customer[2] (causing a general stop of our trade), being grown insufferable, ye Agent and Councell for ye Hon'ble E. India Company's affairs at Hugly resolved upon and made use of divers expedients for redress of their grievances; but all means proving ineffectual 'twas agreed and concluded in consultation that the only expedient now left was for the Agent to go himself in person to the Nabob and Duan at Decca, as well to make some settled adjustment concerning ye customs, as to endeavor the preventing Interlopers trading in these parts for ye future; in order to which preparations were caused to be made. Mr. Richard Trenchfield and Mr. William Johnson were appointed to go along with ye Agent to Dacca. 'Twas also thought convenient to go by ye way of Merdadpore,[3] a towne within 4 or 5 hours travell of Cassumbazar, to have ye opportunity to speak and consult with Mr. Charnock, and some others of ye Councell there, what course is best to be taken in this exigency."[4]

This resolution to appeal to the nabob at Dacca led to a characteristic altercation between Hedges and Parameçvar Dās, the local collector of customs. Ostensibly Parameçvar Dās permitted the English to start for Dacca. Two barges and a number of small boats with provisions were made ready, and the agent, escorted by twenty-three Englishmen in soldier's garb and by fifteen Rajputs and footmen, proceeded on the evening of the 10th October to the English garden to the north of Hugli. But Parameçvar Dās had secretly

---

[1] *Hedges' Diary*, I, 100.

[2] Bal Chandra Ray, the Superintendent of Customs at Hugli.

[3] Probably Mirzāpur.

[4] *Hedges' Diary*, I, 33.

sent armed parties to seize the English boats; and so the quarrel
began. The English lost two boats and tried to recover them by force.
The myrmidons of Parameçvar Dās set upon the English, who were
afraid to fire their pistols. Both sides negotiated, argued, protested.
Parameçvar offered liberty to any slaves who should run away from
the English. He beat and imprisoned as many of the Company's
footmen and boatmen as he could catch; or, if he could not catch the
men themselves, he beat and imprisoned their relations. Hedges went
on board his sloop to go to Dacca by the route through the Sundar-
buns, and then on second thoughts returned to his barge.[1]

After five days spent in disputing, he was reduced to the undignified
expedient of running away from Hugli by night. On the 14th October,
"resolving now to be abused no more in this manner, I sent all ye laden
boats before, with Mr. Johnson, to see them make all the haste that
might be, and not to stop all night. Next to them went the Souldiers
with ye other Budgero.[2] I followed that, and 2 stout fellows, an
Englishman and a Spaniard, in a light boat came last of all. About
2 hours within night a boat full of armed men came up very near to
the Spaniard, who speaking ye language demanded who they were,
and commanded them to stand; but those in the boat returning no
answer, nor regarding what he said, he fired his Musket in the Water,
at which they fell astern. About an hour after, when we were got up
as far as Trippany,[3] the armed boat came up with ye Spaniard again,
who commanded them to keep off, otherwise he would now shoot
amongst them, though he shot at random the time before; so the boat
fell astern, and, perceiving that we resolved not to stay at that place,
we saw them no more."[4]

Hedges followed what was then the usual route to Dacca up the
Hugli and the Jellinghi into the broad stream of the Ganges, and

---

[1] *Hedges' Diary*, I, 34 to 37.

[2] A word of uncertain derivation denoting a lumbering keel-less barge in use
on the Gangetic rivers.

[3] Triveni, three-fold braid. The name properly belongs to Allahabad, where
the three holy rivers, the Ganges, the unseen Sarasvati, and the Jamunā, unite.
Here it denotes the village a little way above the town of Hugli, where the local
Sarasvatī and Jamunā of lower Bengal unite with the river Hugli or Ganges.
This Triveni has long been a centre of trade and a celebrated place of pilgrimage
and of Sanskrit learning. South of the village is the mosque of Zafar Khan;
north of it is a magnificent flight of steps said to have been built by Mukund
Deo, the great king of Orissa.

[4] *Hedges' Diary*, I, 38-39.

thence by various cross cuts into the Burīgangā. In July and August, during the time of the great rains, these eastern districts are more than half submerged, the familiar land marks disappear, the rivers become tempestuous seas over which the boatmen labour, often in doubt, sometimes in danger. But in October, when Hedges started for Dacca, the rivers, though much deeper than at present, had shrunk to their normal size. With clear skies and cool breezes the voyage was pleasant enough. The barges in which Hedges and Johnson travelled were of the sort commonly in use on the Gangetic rivers, lumbering and clumsy to look at, but roomy and comfortable. Two-thirds of their length aft was occupied by cabins with Venetian windows in which the traveller could sit or recline at ease and watch the varied life of the river, the craft plying up and down the stream, the fishers dragging their nets, the water-side folk bathing, arguing, chatting, praying. At noon they landed and ate their dinner beneath the shade of tamarind trees, the home of the peacock and the spotted deer. Then, after resting a few hours, they rowed on. In the evening came supper, and all night long they were "tracked" or towed from the bank, while the boatmen chanted in a minor key weird songs invoking the favour of the water-spirits.[1]

On the 20th October Hedges was not far from the junction of the Jellinghi with the Ganges. At Kālkāpur he was met by Charnock and the local Council, with whom he had a short consultation.[2]

On the 25th October he reached Dacca.[3] The English factory stood in the quarter now occupied by the English officials. It was some way from the river, and what were then the chief centres of business and power in Dacca. Shāyista Khān held his court two miles away in the Lāl Bāgh, a large red brick fort built to command the river which once washed its south face but has since receded some distance from it.[4] The only old buildings now standing within the enclosure are a ruined mosque and the white marble tomb of Bibi Peri, the daughter of Shāyista Khān, and niece of the lady of the Taj. But from the traces which remain, we may well believe that a palace once faced the visitor as he entered under the great north portal. Hither came Agent Hedges

---

[1] *Hedges' Diary*, I, 39 to 42.
[2] *Ib.*, I, 41.
[3] *Ib.*, I, 42.
[4] *Ib.*, I, 43, 44.

full of hope, to ask that the interlopers might be expelled from the country; that the vexatious proceedings of the Mogul underlings might be stopped; that the Company's servants might no longer be forced to pay customs and duties, or that at least they might be exempted for seven months while they laid their case before the Emperor. It seemed that all difficulties were now nearly at an end. Hedges was well acquainted with Turkish and Arabic, but he had no knowledge of the delays of Indian diplomacy.

After a month and a half spent in negotiation, Hedges returned to Hugli completely satisfied with the results of his mission. "My going to Decca," he said, " has in ye first place got 7 months' time for procuring a Phirmaund ; 2ndly, taken off wholly ye Pretence of 5 per cent. Custome on all Treasure imported this and ye three ˑpreceeding years, besides 1½ per cent. of what [was] usually paid, at ye mint for some years past; 3rdly, procured ye general stop to be taken off all our trade, our Goods now passing as freely as ever they did formerly ; 4thly, got a command to turn Permesuradass out of his place, and restore ye money forced from us ; 5thly, and last, prevailed with ye Nabob to undertake ye procuring a Phirmaund for us from ye King.......If God gives me life to get this Phirmaund into my possession ye Hon'ble Company shall never more be troubled with Interlopers. I bless God for this great success I have had, beyond all men's expectations, in my voyage to Dacca.".[1]

Such were the bright hopes entertained by Agent Hedges. It would be cruel to dwell on the story of his disillusionment. Suffice it to say that his voyage to Dacca had practically effected nothing. The quarrel between the English and the native officials continued. Again and again Balchandra made every profession of respect and good-will, and then through his subordinate, Parameçvar Dãs stopped the Company's boats and seized their goods.[2] Nothing could be done without bribes, and yet it was in vain that Hedges offered large sums of money to be excused payment of the custom. The Mogul government refused to waive its claims, and in the end Hedges' successor had to admit them.[3]

---

[1] *Hedges' Diary*, I, 62.

[2] For instance see *Hedges' Diary*, I, 59, 60, and 63.

[3] *Hedges' Diary*, I, 172.

CHAPTER VII.

MEANWHILE Hedges returned to Hugli, elated with his supposed successes, and proceeded to reform the Bengal establishments in a way which led to the confusion of everything and everybody, including himself. The Commission which made Hedges Governor, associated six others with him in the Council of the Bay, Job Charnock, John Beard, John Richards, Francis Ellis, Joseph Dodd, and William Johnson. A wise and judicious Governor on coming out to Bengal would have done his best to conciliate the other members of the Council, and above all to gain the co-operation of Job Charnock, the second in the Council, who represented the traditions and experience of the place. With a little tact Hedges might have made a friend of Charnock, for, as will be seen, they agreed on many important points. But Hedges did nothing of the sort. Far from consulting with the senior merchants associated with him in the Council of the Bay, he regarded them with distrust, and lent a willing ear to the stories of informers, whose interest it was to foment disputes between the English. While at Dacca he had listened to scandal about Job Charnock's private character,[1] and he returned to Hugli full of suspicions. He had actually stooped to employ young Mr. Johnson as a kind of spy, and directed him to mix with the interlopers and find out their associates. In this way he

---

[1] *Hedges' Diary*, I, 52.

hoped to detect the Company's enemies. What he really did was to set all the English in Bengal against himself. From the lowest to the highest every one complained of the proceedings of the agent, and they took care that their complaints should reach the ears of the Court. In January, 1683, Hedges went to Balasor to despatch the *Defence* and the *Society* to England. Each ship carried a bundle of letters against the agent. One of them, written by Beard, was somehow seen by the spy Johnson, who "communicated" it to his chief.[1] The letter, it seems, contained a virulent attack on the Agent and his wife. "It is stuffed up," says Hedges, "with such notorious falsities that I stand amazed that such a professor of religion and honesty[2] should be the author of it, having played the hypocrite and dissembled so handsomely with me, professing so great kindness, respect, and affection to me that I can scarce believe my own eyes when I read it. I see he has written against me by the *Williamson* and *Nathaniel* on the 20th ultimo. Let the event of it be what it will, I cannot help it. God's will be done. I see the Company are apt to believe and credit every rascal upon his own bare information. God knows I have never had the least quarrel or difference with Mr. Beard in all my life. Nor has there been any conspiring or caballing against him, as he has declared. I cannot run through every particular, not having time to give it an answer. But, God willing, when your son [*i.e.*, William Johnson] and I return to Hugly we will call Mr. Beard to a public examination, and make no question but he will most readily and willingly acknowledge his fault and make a public recantation. *And therefore I am of opinion 'tis not good to deliver the letter till we send home his recantation or our proceedings upon it.*"[3]

In other words, Hedges took upon himself to detain a private letter written by the third member of the Council to Sir Josiah Child, the Governor of the Company. The act was foolish, if not dishonest; but Hedges was hard-pressed, and, like many others before him, justified his action on the ground of public utility.

The only step which Hedges could now take to put himself right in the eyes of his fellow-men was to carry out his resolution to openly tax Beard with his letter, and call upon him to retract his accusations. But Hedges had not the strength to adhere to his resolution. On his return to Hugli, instead of attacking Beard, he turned upon Ellis.

---

[1] *Hedges' Diary*, II, 18-19, 43-44.

[2] John Beard, senior, was a Presbyterian.

[3] *Hedges' Diary*, II, 42, 43.

On the 26th March, "information," says the diary, " was brought in against Mr. Francis Ellis by most of the Merchants in Hugly ; that he, the said Ellis, had taken bribes to the value of four thousand rupees or thereabouts, to pass the Hon'ble Company's goods in the Shipping, part of which was positively proved against him, and nine hundred rupees being confessed by him, it was thereupon ordered that he be dismissed the Hon'ble Company's Service, and that Mr. Joseph Dodd forthwith take the charge of the warehouse upon him, and that the money which shall be proved to be taken by the said Ellis to pass the Hon'ble Company's goods shall be endeavoured to be secured for the Hon'ble Company's use." [1]

A fortnight after this Hedges' zeal for reform took him on a second visit to Cassimbazar. William Johnson had informed Hedges that the principal factor of the interlopers for procuring their raw silk and taffetas at Cassimbazar was Mr. Naylor, a dyer in the employ of the Company, and that it was more than probable that Job Charnock was a confederate. On the 16th April Hedges "called a consultation and accused Mr. Naylor of trading with interlopers, which being proved by three letters under his own hand, he was judged guilty by all present. His person, his papers and goods [were] ordered to be seized to see whether we could find further testimony out of his own books and writings." [2]

On the next day Hedges dealt out justice to James Harding. The man had come out to India as as a writer in 1671, but had been subsequently dismissed from the Company's service. He was now in the private service of Job Charnock. The members of the factory complained against him as a person notoriously scandalous in life and conversation, and Hedges "ordered him not to eat at the Company's table, and reproved Mr. Charnock for entertaining so vicious a person." To which Charnock said little or nothing. " I was also informed," says Hedges, "of one Ananta Ram, [3] the same person who slippered the merchant who poisoned himself in the time of Mr. Vincent, being employed by Mr. Charnock in all the Company's affairs. Which Mr. Charnock positively denying, I brought the said Ananta Ram to confess and affirm he had done all the business of concernment in the factory ever since the first month after Mr. Charnock's coming to be chief." [4]

---

[1] *Hedges' Diary*, I, 72.
[2] *Ib.*, I, 77.
[3] For Anantarām, see *ante*, page 55.
[4] *Hedges' Diary*, I, 78.

The next persons to fall under suspicion with Hedges were Richard Barker and John Threder, the second and third of the Council of Cassimbazar. A great number of silk merchants and weavers complained that they "took from them four or five tolahs upon a seer overweight on all their silk brought into the warehouse, besides one or two of the best skeins of silk that was weighed in every draught. Which amounting to a very considerable sum of money, they demanded satisfaction. Threder and Barker positively denying the overweight, the merchants proved it by their books; but the skein out of every draught was confessed and claimed as their due, having always been their custom."[1] In consequence of these suspicions, Barker and Threder desired to be removed from Cassimbazar to some other factory. Their request was granted, but they remained at Cassimbazar.[2] In fact, Hedges seems to have been afraid to take measures against them.

Much less did he dare to attack Charnock and Beard, the second and third in the Council of the Bay. Page after page of his diary is filled with secret complaints and innuendoes, but he never ventures to bring any formal accusation against them. At the same time, he wondered why Mr. Charnock was so cross with him, thwarting everything he proposed or did, and he was exceedingly troubled that the Company's servants in the several factories were all in general so unkind and disrespectful to him, more than to Agent Master, who was nothing near so respectful and civil to them.[3]

In attempting to suspend another of the Company's servants at Casimbazar, Hedges came to an open rupture with the Council of the Bay. James Watson was a quarrelsome man, who had been warned that he might chance to be sent for by the Agent and Council at Hugli to answer for his abusive language. In a moment of passion he had replied "that if he were sent for he questioned whether he should come down or not, for he had no dependence on them, he being placed there by the Company as much as the Agent and Council in Hugli and so [it was] not in their power to remove him." For this heinous crime Hedges wished that Watson should be suspended from the Company's service till such time as answer should be sent out from England.[4]

This was more than the other merchants could bear. The Council at Cassimbazar told the Agent that Ellis, being one of the Hugli Council,

---

[1] *Hedges' Diary*, I, 83.
[2] *Ib.*, I, 84-85, 93.
[3] *Ib.*, I, 102, 107.
[4] *Ib.*, I, 108 to 115.

could not be dismissed, but only suspended; and that to suspend
Mr. Watson was altogether opposed to the Company's orders. The
government of the establishment in Bengal belonged to the Council of
the Bay, "which ought to be annually called, as hath been the custom
of former chiefs till now of late, which consists of all chiefs of the
subordinate factories or as many of them as can be spared, and this used
to be in the most commodious season, which is just after the departure
of the shipping."[1]

Hedges had now lost all control over his subordinates. Good order
and good discipline were at an end. Throughout all the establishments in Bengal no one feared Hedges, and hardly any liked him.
Ellis, who had been dismissed by the agent from the Company's
service, went about openly bragging of his influence with the Court
at home. "You shall see," he said, "what a man I shall be in
nine months' time. I shall be above them all."[2] Another talked
mysteriously of his private instructions from the Company and
some great men of the Committee, and protested that he regarded nothing that was written him from Hugli.[3] Above all, Job
Charnock was Hedges' bitter opponent. He boasted constantly that no
chief had ever been able to contend against him, and confidently
declared at the beginning of 1684 that the obnoxious agent would be
given his *mittimus* by that year's shipping.[4] And Job Charnock was
right. On the 17th July, Hedges was advised by Mr. How, the commander of the Company's ship *Thomas*, newly returned from Fort St.
George, that he was dismissed the Company's service, that Mr. Beard
was made agent in his place, and that Gifford was to be President of
the coast of Coromandel and the Bay.[5] Thus Bengal was again made
subordinate to Madras.

On the 30th August President Gifford reached Hugli. He was a
narrow-minded man and a fit instrument of the Court at home. He
had already been used to displace Streynsham Master at Madras and
undo his work. He was now sent to degrade poor Hedges. He lost
no time in setting about the business. "About half an hour after the
President's arrival in Hugli Factory," says Hedges, "he called me,
Mr. Beard, Mr. Francis Ellis, Mr. Richard Trenchfield, Mr. Thomas Ley,

[1] *Hedges' Diary*, I, 111, 124 to 127.
[2] *Ib.*, I, 107.
[3] *Ib.*, I, 129.
[4] *Ib.*, I, 146.
[5] *Ib.*, I, 152.

and Mr. Richard Gough into the counting house to hear his commission read. Which being done by John Stables, his Secretary, I wished His Honour much joy with the rest of the Company, assuring them I did readily and willingly submit to the Company's pleasure. To which the President made no other reply but, ''Twas very well.' The Secretary showed me the seal to the commission, telling me 'twas the Company's. I replied 'I made no doubt of it.' " [1]

Gifford was not fit to do anything except undo other men's work. He paid a visit to Cassimbazar in October and, after spending altogether about three months in Bengal, left matters in a worse state of confusion than he found them.[2] Agent Beard, under whose direction the affairs of the Bay now passed, was a feeble man, no better able to cope with the growing difficulties of the time. It is said that the troubles and disputes between the local officials and the English, which reached an acute stage in 1685, brought on a fatal illness. On the 28th August John Beard died at Hugli, crushed beneath the load of anxiety and responsibility which he had rashly taken upon him, but was quite unable to support.[3]

The story of Hedges's agency has been written for us in great detail in the pages of his diary from which we gain a contemporary picture of the establishments in the Bay, together with a self-painted portrait of an honest but weak-minded man. Though most of his efforts failed, he may fairly lay claim to one great success. He may fairly claim to have convinced the Court that a fortified settlement was necessary in Bengal.

Hedges seems to me typical in the development of his views. Like his countrymen he came to Bengal as a simple merchant anxious to protect the English trade beneath official treaties and agreements. Experience soon showed that treaties and agreements were of no avail against the lawlessness of the local officials. Threats and demonstrations of force were useless. It was not that the Mogul government would not protect the foreign merchants against oppression

---

[1] *Hedges' Diary*, I, 157-58.
[2] *Ib.*, I, 171.
[3] *Ib.*, II, 103-104.

and wrong. It could not. Whatever control it had, it was gradually losing. Like Shāyista Khān, it was in its old age. Hedges was thus forced to the inevitable conclusion. We must protect ourselves; we must break with the Indian government; we must seize some convenient post and fortify it.

This idea entered Hedges's mind a few months after his arrival. He explained it to the Company at home He repeats it more than once in his diary. Custom, he says, must not be paid. The Company's affairs will never be better, but always grow worse and worse with continual patching. We must resolve to quarrel with these people, and build a fort on the island Saugor at the mouth of the river, and run the hazard of losing one year's trade in the Bay, in a quarter of which time there is no fear of bringing these people to our conditions.[1]

Later on it appears that these opinions are shared by Gifford and Charnock, who discussed the whole question at Cassimbazar in October, 1684. "But," according to our diarist, "Mr. Beard, Mr. Ellis, Mr. Trenchfield,' and Mr. Ley for their own private interest and regard, to carry on their little trade in the country, being persuaded to this opinion by Mr. Evans, the Minister, declared themselves of a contrary judgment and would not consent to it."[2]

At first the Court were not prepared to accept the idea. In the despatches of the 21st December, 1683, in which they ordered the dismissal of Hedges, they discussed at length the view of "our late agent and some of our captains, that there is no way to mend our condition but by seizing and fortifying one of those pleasant islands in the Ganges about the Braces." To this proposal they had many objections. It would be too expensive. It would enrage the Mogul, who would be assisted by the Dutch. It would be better to attack the Mogul from Bombay, or, if you must begin a war in Bengal, then why not take Chittagong? Not that the Court could encourage such a project, though they were not quite sure that it would not be proper to seize Balchandra and Parameçvar Dass, to stop the Mogul's salt-vessels, and make an armed demonstration. But in spite of all objections, the idea gradually took hold of the English mind at home as in Bengal; and year after year the Court recurred to the scheme of getting possession of Chittagong.[3]

---

[1] *Hedges' Diary*, I, 117, 121, 133, 139.
[2] *Ib.*, I, 161, 165.
[3] *Ib.*, II, 22 to 24.

In the end the Court resolved to break with the Mogul. They obtained from James II. permission to retaliate their injuries and reimburse themselves for the loss of their privileges by hostilities against Shāyista Khān and Aurangzēb; and in 1686 commenced a vigorous attack upon both sides of the Indian peninsula. Orders were sent to the Governor of Bombay to withdraw from Surat and the other ports on the west coast, and to direct his cruisers to seize every Mogul ship and vessel that could be met with. To commence hostilities in the Bay of Bengal, they sent thither the largest force which they had yet displayed in Indian seas. The fleet was to sail to Balasor, and there take on board the agent and the principal men of the Council of the Bay. An ultimatum was to be sent to the nabob at Dacca, and if, as was probable, no satisfactory answer was received, the bulk of the force was to proceed to Chittagong. Here, "after summons, if the Fort, Town, and Territory thereunto belonging be not forthwith delivered to our Lieutenant-Colonel Job Charnock, we would have our forces land, seize and take the said Town, Fort, and Territory by force of arms." The place, when captured, is to be made "as the art and invention of man can extend to," and Job Charnock was to be " Governor of our Fort, Town, and Territory of Chyttegam." [1]

---

[1] *Hedges' Diary*, II, 51 to 53.

BOOK III.

HOW AFTER MUCH FIGHTING AND WANDERING THE ENGLISH
FOUND IN CALCUTTA THE PLACE FOR THEIR FORTIFIED
TRADE CENTRE.

CHAPTER I.

OCTOBER 1686 TO FEBRUARY 1687.

HOW THE ENGLISH RANSACKED HUGLI, AND CAME TO SUTANUTI.

WE have now reached the third stage of the English advance into
Bengal. It is the necessary outcome of the first two. The first
period put forward the policy of entirely peaceful industry. The
second exhibited the opposition between this policy and the policy of
force and retaliation. The third period gives us their reconciliation.

Already a policy has been found in which both militarism and
industrialism are combined. The Court in its last despatches has
decided to establish a fortified station in Bengal to maintain its trade
there. The question at issue is the site of this station. Industrialism would have been content to remain at Hugli, militarism demanded

the violent seizure of Chittagong, the former seat of piratical hordes, and now an important Mogul city. But the English have to find a place where both principles may be satisfied.

Convinced that a fortified settlement is their only adequate safeguard, they have to fix on the best site for it. This they do, not by any immediate intuition, nor by mere haphazard as fancy strikes them, but, after many experiments, many attempts to settle at different points on the river Hugli. The man who conducted them through their strange experiences safe to the goal, and to whom consequently belongs the glory of having laid the foundation-stone of British India, was Job Charnock, one of whom historians and biographers have been slow to take notice, but who, as the father of Calcutta, certainly deserves better treatment.

Job Charnock came out to India in 1655 or 1656.[1] He first appears in the records as Junior Member of the Council of Cassimbazar. We read in a nominal roll of that factory entered in the Court Books under the date 12th—13th January, 1658 : *Job Charnock, Fourth, Salary* 20£. From Cassimbazar he was transferred to Patna. His original engagement was for five years, and a memorial of his, dated the 23rd February, 1664, shows that he had intended to return to England at the expiration of the covenanted period, but was willing to remain if appointed chief of the Patna factory. The appointment was given him, and in it he continued till 1680.[2]

It was at Patna that Charnock learned to understand the Indian ways of thought and action, and to estimate the forces with which he had subsequently to contend. He married an Indian wife, adopted many of the local manners and customs; he is even said to have adopted some of the local superstitions and to have been in the habit of worshipping the Five Saints with the sacrifice of a cock after the manner of the

---

[1] Nothing has yet been discovered regarding the birth, parentage, and early life of Job Charnock. Of his Indian wife we have various gossiping stories. He is said to have rescued her from the funeral pyre, and married her before, or about, 1678. The Charnock mausoleum is still standing in St. John's Churchyard. It was built about 1697, by Charles Eyre. (See Hyde in the *Proceedings of the Asiatic Society of Bengal*, March 1893.) In it Charnock and his wife are said to have been buried, but the inscription on the original tombstone only mentions Job. Lower down on the same stone is an inscription to the memory of Mary, eldest daughter of Charnock, and wife of Eyre, who died 1697. On another stone in the mausoleum is an inscription to Job's youngest daughter, Catherine, wife of Jonathan White, who died in 1701, and, as appears from White's will, was buried in the mausoleum. A third daughter of Job, Elizabeth, survived in Calcutta till 1753. She married William Bowridge, who died in 1724. (See Hyde on the *Bengal Chaplaincy* in the *Indian Church Quarterly Review* for 1892.)

[2] *Hedges' Diary*, II, 45, 46.

people of Bihar.[1] He had ample experience of the exactions of the local officials when left to do as they liked, uncontrolled by their superiors. In 1672, owing to the supineness of a bookish Nabob, one Ibrāhīm Khān, the saltpetre trade at Patna was almost ruined.[2] He knew the futility of negotiations with the Court of Delhi, for he had sent political agents there to little purpose. As early as 1678 he had discovered that an Imperial grant would be after all no protection to the English trade. Had Shāh Jahān been king, he said, an agreement with him would have had great force. But it was otherwise with Aurangzēb. His orders were little accounted of by the local governors.[3] Thus when others were still impressed with the seeming greatness of the Mogul Empire, Charnock had already discerned its weakness.

The ability of the man could not be overlooked by his employers, and they seem to have greatly relied on him in their dealings with the Indian Government. In 1671 an order of the Court increases his salary to £40 a year. In 1675 they give him an additional £20 a year as a gratuity. In 1680, after giving repeated orders on the subject, the Court established Charnock as chief of the Cassimbazar factory and second in the Council of the Bay, with the right of succeeding Vincent as chief of the Bay. Nevertheless Charnock did not succeed Vincent, but was twice superseded, first by Hedges and then by Beard.[4]

---

[1] *Hedges' Diary*, II, 90, 91.—The story is told by Alexander Hamilton, who says that Charnock, instead of converting his wife to Christianity, was converted by her to Paganism. " The only part of Christianity that was remarkable in him was burying her decently ; and he built a tomb over her, where all his life after her death he kept the anniversary day by sacrificing a cock on her tomb, after the Pagan manner." This story, told by an enemy of the Company and its servants, should be taken with many grains of salt. It is rejected altogether by Sir H. Yule, because the sacrifice of a cock is not Hindu. But Dr. Wise (*Journal of the Asiatic Society of Bengal*, Volume LXIII, Part III, No. 1, 1894) tells us that the sacrifice of a cock is part of the worship of the *Pānch Pīr*, or Five Saints, in Bihar, a cult, which though primarily confined to low-class Muhammadans, is also there adopted by Hindus. Who the *Pānch Pīr* are no one exactly knows, but they are powerful protectors of their devotees. Dr. Wise tells us a very interesting story of an Englishman in East Bengal who was known as the *Pānch Pīriyā Çāhib*, "it being said that his parents losing one child after another were advised by a favourite servant to consecrate the next to the *Pānch Pīr*, and by so doing preserve him. They followed this advice, and were gratified to find their son grow up strong and healthy. Hindus always quote this as an instance of the benefits accruing to those who believe in the *Pānch Pīr*."

[2] *Hedges' Diary*, II, 45.

[3] *Ib.*, II, 46.

[4] *Ib.*, II, 46 to 49.

While at Cassimbazar Charnock learnt a second lesson. He had seen that treaties could not protect the English trade; he now saw that a fortified station would. Charnock, Hedges, and Gifford, in spite of many differences, agreed in this. The idea was not the discovery of an individual mind; it was the common thought of the English in Bengal.[1]

As in Patna, so in Cassimbazar, Charnock at length came into conflict with the local government. Even before Hedges had left Bengal, it appears from his diary that the native merchants and dealers employed in the business of the Cassimbazar factory had made a large claim against Charnock and his colleagues there, which the judge of the place had decided against the English to the amount of Rs. 43,000. The judgment was supported by Shāyista Khān, who, in default of payment, formally summoned Charnock to appear before him at Dacca. Charnock refused, and many attempts were made, both at Cassimbazar and at Dacca, to get the decision modified. It was little short of open war between Charnock and the nabob. All communications with the Cassimbazar factory were cut off, and at the time of Agent Beard's death the place was watched by troops to prevent Charnock's escape. In April, 1686, however, he managed to give his enemies the slip, and reached Hugli, where he at once assumed the chief direction of the English affairs. Here he received the news that the Court had resolved on war, and had despatched a great expeditionary force against the Mogul.[2]

The squadron designed for Bengal had consisted of six ships, carrying as many companies of soldiers: but only half that number reached their destination. They were the *Beaufort*, with seventy guns and three hundred seamen, commanded by John Nicholson; the *Nathaniel*, with fifty guns and a hundred and fifty seamen, commanded by John Mason; and the *Rochester*, with sixty-five guns. To each of these men-of-war was attached a frigate or light-vessel built for speed, armed with twelve guns and manned with twenty seamen. Besides these, the Company already had in the Ganges a number of sloops and river-craft, and orders had been given that all the vessels available at Madras should be sent on to Bengal. Nicholson was appointed Admiral, and Mason Vice-Admiral.[3]

---

[1] See above p. 89.
[2] *Hedges' Diary*, II, 53.
[3] *Ib.*, II, 52.

The land forces placed at the disposal of Charnock were, like the fleet, very miscellaneous. The men ordinarily employed at this time to defend the Company's factories and trade were Rajputs or other natives of India, who retained their own dress and customs, organisation, and officers. But the English could not rely on them in an attack upon the Mogul. Other soldiers were Native Christians or Portuguese, whom the English thought "very sorry fellows." They dressed like Europeans, and had learnt the manual exercise and the parade drill of European troops. Lastly, there were the English soldiers sent out by the Court. Usually they were very few in number, and were consequently united with the Portuguese in the same company. But on the present occasion their numbers had been greatly increased, and, although one of the ships sent was lost and two others were not able to make their passage, at least three, if not four, companies of English soldiers must have in the end reached Bengal.[1] According to custom, the Court sent out with the troops Lieutenants, Ensigns, and inferior officers. But, the commanding officers were to be the Company's servants in Bengal, Agent Charnock becoming Colonel, the second in the Bay Lieutenant-Colonel, the third Major, and so on.[2] In fact the Court appear to have anticipated the views of Lord Wolseley, and to have fully understood "that no one can conduct a campaign or administer an army successfully who is not a thoroughly good man of business."

The English troops reached Bengal by driblets towards the end of the year 1686. The *Rochester* and her frigate, having been despatched earlier than the rest, were also the first to arrive. They brought a company of a hundred and eight men, who were sent up the river in

---

[1] *Hedges' Diary*, II, 54, 58.—These English and Portuguese companies were presumably formed after the model of the troops of James II. Each company numbered from one hundred and ten to one hundred and twenty men. The uniform of the soldiers was red, trimmed with blue; their arms were the sword and the firelock gun. Over the left shoulder they wore the bandoleer, a leather belt on which were suspended the bullet bag, the primer and a number of little copper cylinders, each containing one charge. Some of the men, or perhaps all, may have been furnished with the great knife or bayonet, which was then coming into use, and which was attached to a wooden haft and screwed into the muzzle of your gun, so that you could never fire when your bayonet was fixed. The sergeants carried a halberd ; the officers a half-pike seven feet long. The men were ranged in four ranks, with an interval of twelve feet between them in open order. The officers took post according to seniority in front of the line ; but before the charge was given or received they retired among the men of the first rank, and the interval between the ranks was reduced to three feet.

[2] *Ib.*, II, 52.

small vessels. The *Beaufort* and her frigate arrived later with some
two hundred men. The total number of the Company's soldiers at
Hugli—Indian, Portuguese, and English all told—amounted to less
than four hundred men.[1] They were quartered, some in the town, and
some at Chandannagar, three miles lower down the river.[2]

These preparations, though not very extensive, were enough to alarm
the country. By order of the Nabob, three thousand foot and three
hundred horse were concentrated at Hugli to guard the town. Under
their protection, the governor, 'Abdu-l Gani, became more and more
threatening. He raised a battery of eleven guns to command the English
shipping in the "hole" or harbour. He refused all necessaries for trade.
He even forbad the English to buy victuals in the market, and
prohibited the soldiers from resorting thither. This last order brought
on the skirmish at Hugli.[3]

On the 28th October three English soldiers, going in the morning
as usual into the market, were not only refused victuals, but were
violently set upon by the Governor's guards, beaten, cut, bound, and
carried away prisoners to 'Abdu-l Gani. The news flew apace through
the town, and it was reported that two Englishmen were lying desperately wounded in the highway. On this Captain Leslie was ordered to
sally out from the factory with a company of soldiers and bring back the
bodies, dead or alive. The attempted rescue was actively opposed. The
enemy fell at once upon the advancing company with horse and foot,
and, when forced to retire with the loss of seven men, killed or wounded,
invoked the aid of the fiery element itself to destroy the foreigners, or
at least bar their further progress. In a short time all the thatched
hovels which surrounded the English quarters were in a blaze, and
the factory was encircled with a broad band of flame. At the same
time the newly raised battery opened fire on the ships in the "hole."[4]

Matters now began to look serious. The English troops quartered
at Chandannagar were immediately ordered up to Hugli. Meanwhile a detachment under Captain Richardson was sent out to
attack the battery, but unable to face the hot fire of the enemy, they
were compelled to fall back with loss. Luckily by this time the reinforcements from Chandannagar had arrived, and Captain Arbuthnot,
advancing at the head of a fresh body of troops, assaulted the battery,

---

[1] *Hedges' Diary*, II, 54. 58.
[2] *Ib.*, II, 55.
[3] *Ib.*, II. 54.
[4] *Ib.*, II, 54.

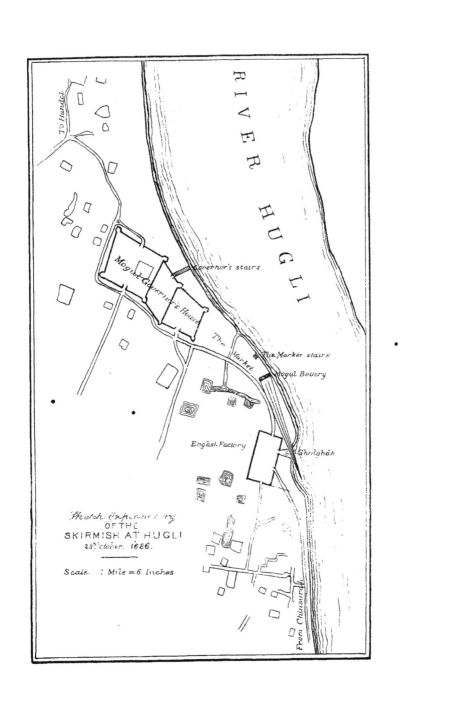

RIVER HUGLI

To Handel

Governor's stairs

Mogul Governor's House

The Market

The Market stairs

Mogul Batery

English Factory

Ghaighat

Sketch Explanatory
OF THE
SKIRMISH AT HUGLI
28th October 1686.

Scale. 1 Mile = 6 Inches

From Chinsurah

took it, and spiked and dismounted all the guns. So fierce was his onset, that he carried the battle on beyond the governor's house, burning and driving all before him. The governor himself, it is said, fled in disguise by water, leaving Hugli panic-stricken. To complete the enemy's discomfiture, the river-craft were ordered to open fire on the town, but the wind and tide being contrary, caused delay. Towards evening, however, the ketches and sloops came abreast of the place, took a ship of the Mogul's, "and kept firing and battering most part of that night and next day, and making frequent sallies on shore, burning and plundering all they met with."[1]

The skirmish was over, and the advantage remained decidedly with the English. Captain Arbuthnot was the hero of the fight, and it is pleasant to find that the gallant soldier received from the Court a gold chain and medal in recognition of his services.[2] The English loss was trifling. One man had been killed and a good many wounded in the first attempt on the battery, and one of the men first attacked in the market died within three days. The old factory, with some of the Company's saltpetre and a good deal of private property, had been consumed in the conflagration. The enemy on their side lost about sixty men killed, including three men of note, and a great number wounded. Four or five hundred of their houses had been burnt down, together with a great number of barges, lighters, and boats.[3]

Under these circumstances the governor of Hugli, through the intervention of the Dutch, entered into negotiations for peace. He was alarmed at the vigour and success of the English and wished to gain time. He therefore demanded a cessation of arms. To Charnock the proposal was most opportune. For the past six months he had been preparing to quit Hugli, but owing to the difficulty of bringing away the Company's saltpetre, besides all the Company's servants and large stores of goods of all kinds, had not yet been able to carry out his intentions. He had been more than once disappointed in his efforts to secure ships for the cargo. Some of the local vessels were lost; others proved to be worm-eaten. Of the ships sent out from England, the *Beaufort* was the next to arrive after the *Rochester*; but she was so leaky, that Admiral Nicholson had to take her into the Hijili river to be careened. Of the rest of the squadron Charnock had

---

[1] *Hedges' Diary*, II, 55.
[2] *Ib.*, II, 295.
[3] *Ib.*, II, 55.

H

received no tidings. The English therefore agreed to the cessation of arms proposed by the governor, on condition that he would allow them to supply themselves with victuals, servants, and labourers as usual, and for the present, while the saltpetre was being packed, they strove to be peaceable. This did not, however, prevent them from seizing a ship of the nabob's at the mouth of the river and sending Nicholson down with orders to seize three more in the Balasor road. Nor did it prevent them from entering into negotiations with a local magnate, the owner of the country adjoining the island of Hijili at the mouth of the Hugli, who was in open war with the Muhammadan government, and who offered to provide them with men, provisions, and all things necessary to establish a fort and factories in his territory. Hither they intended to retire as soon as the saltpetre was shipped, after first making an armed demonstration and seizing some of the chief citizens of Hugli for the ransom of the Company's servants left in the outstations in Bengal.[1]

So the English proposed, but the nabob had very different purposes. Whatever Charnock might think, Shāyista Khān was not a man to be trifled with. As soon as he heard of the skirmish at Hugli, he sent to Patna to seize on all the Company's property there and imprison their servants. At Dacca he would have also imprisoned Watts, but that Baramāl, a friendly Hindu, interposed. Large detachments of horse were ordered to Hugli. The nabob was resolved to crush the English and force them to submit to his wishes. Meanwhile the Dutch, who had been at variance with the local government, were reinstated at Barānagar.[2]

For nearly two months after the "eruption" did the English remain at Hugli, packing saltpetre, negotiating with the governor, and hoping to procure an Imperial rescript or at least an order from the nabob redressing their grievances. It was not till the 20th December that they withdrew from the place, bringing off all the Company's concerns and their own. Their coming off was peaceable, and in their opinion "no less honorable, having continued the cessation of arms on both sides hitherto, for conveniency of getting off the Right Hon'ble Company's estate, and not without hope of some accommodation of the differences."[3]

---

[1] *Hedges' Diary*, II, 55 to 58.
[2] *Ib.*, II, 55 to 58.
[3] *Ib.*, II, 59, 60.

And, now, what was Charnock going to do after leaving Hugli? Would he follow the plan of action laid down for him by the Court? Would he assemble his armament at Balasor, arrest all the Mogul's vessels, and then proceed to Chittagong to take it by storm? Or would he carry out his professed intentions? Would he stop at Hijili and join forces with the local magnate there? He did neither. On his way down the river he halted at Sūtānuṭī, a village which has since grown into the northern quarter of Calcutta, and there spent the Christmas of 1686. He still hoped for peace; he still negotiated. By the end of December, Watts, accompanied by Baṛamāl arrived at Sūtānuṭī from Dacca. Baṛamāl had powers to accommodate, and through him Charnock sent up his demands to Shāyista Khān. He asked that the English should have a sufficient quantity of ground to build a fort on, that they might there have a mint, and be henceforth allowed to trade custom-free. He asked that the nabob should rebuild the factory at Malda, which had been destroyed, restore all the money which he had taken, and help the English to recover their debts. The nabob in reply appointed as his commissioners Baṛamāl and two others, and allowed them to treat for peace. In three days they agreed upon twelve articles formulating the English demands. On the 11th January the articles were signed and sealed, and transmitted to the nabob for confirmation. Charnock also required that they should be ratified by Aurangzēb himself, and on the 28th January he was actually told that the nabob approved of the articles and had sent them to the King for confirmation.

It is difficult to know whether the old agent had so forgotten his political experiences at Patna as to seriously believe in all these fair speeches. If he did, he greatly overestimated the strength of his position. Shāyista Khān was not in the least frightened by the skirmish at Hugli. He merely wished to gain time. After waiting more than three weeks, he returned the articles unsigned, threatened the English for daring to make such demands and the commissioners for listening to them, and issued orders to the subordinate governors throughout the province to levy all the forces they could get together and drive the English out of Bengal never to return.

On all sides the country was in arms. The time for negotiation was past. Nothing remained but to fight. On the 9th February the English burnt down the King's salt-houses. On the 11th they assaulted and took the forts at Thānā, or Garden Reach, "with the loss only of one man's leg and some wounded." The forts were considered

H 2

too far up the country to be tenable; and so, while Charnock was demolishing them, Captain Nicholson was sent down the river with half the fleet and forces to take possession of the island of Hijili.[1]

When historical personages or historical events strike the popular imagination, it is never content to hand down to posterity the bare truth about them. It magnifies every detail and adds wonders of its own creation. The person becomes a national hero; the event a national calamity, supernatural powers being introduced to aid in its progress. That Priam, Agamemnon, and the swift-footed Achilles were real men, who lived in some dim prehistoric age, is highly probable. That in this age a war took place in Asia Minor, and that one of the incidents of the war was the siege of some strong town in the Troad, built either at Hissarlik or on the Bali Dagh above Bunārbashi, is certain. But the siege became legend, and the legend poetry, and now all the labours of an Euhemerus and a Thucydides, of a Curtius and a Schliemann, will never recover the substratum of truth underlying the glorious fiction of Homer. For us Achilles will ever be the son of a divine mother, the hero mighty for good or evil; Agamemnon will ever be the stately ruler, swaying all the hosts of the Greeks with a God-given sceptre; Priam the old kind father, whose length of days and abundance of children were turned from blessings into curses. For us there can be no other Troy than the familiar windy city, with broad streets and beetling acropolis, whose walls were built by Apollo and Poseidon. So, too, the personality and career of the great Emperor Charles have passed into the regions of legend and romance, although fortunately in his case written records remain which leave no doubt as to the actual history. We know from Eginhard that the Emperor conducted a victorious expedition into Spain. We know that on his return the difficulties which he experienced in recrossing the Pyrenees led him to unduly prolong his line of march. We know that on the 15th August 778, when the rear guard was entangled in the valley of Roncesvalles, too far from the van to be succoured in time, the mountaineers rushing from their ambushes fell upon the Franks, who were all put to the sword,

---

[1] *Hedges' Diary*, II, 60 to 65.

including Hruodlandus, the Prefect of the Britannic march. Such are the bare facts. But the death of Roland, it would seem, moved the chords of popular sympathy, and it straightway became transmuted by the alchemy of fancy into the most celebrated romance of the middle ages. The love of Roland for Oliver's sister, the fighting with the giant Ferracute, the treachery of Ganelon, the wonderful sword and horn, the last prayer of the hero, his death, and Charles's vengeance, these are added touches which have given such life and power to the original story, that, like the mystic sounds, which reached Charlemagne across the Pyrenees at a distance of thirty leagues from the valley of Roncesvalles, the song of Roland has gone forth into all lands, and "makes itself heard across nine centuries in the refined ears of our own times."

The career of Job Charnock and the ransack of Hugli seem to have exercised a similar fascination over the minds of the Indian people to whom the story first came, for we find that they very soon began to embellish the facts with fabulous additions. According to the legend, when Chanak was chief of the English, a flood arose and destroyed their house at Hugli. Then they cut down trees and began to build them a new house two and three storeys high. But the Moslem nobles and great ones came to the governor and said: "These strange dogs of Englishmen are making their dwelling so high that they may spy into our homes and look upon our wives and daughters. Such a dishonour must not be permitted." So the governor sent and forbad all the masons and carpenters to carry on the work. Wherefore Chanak made ready to fight. For the Moguls came together in great multitudes, and Chanak had only a few men and one ship. But with a burning-glass he caught the sun's fires and burnt the river face of the city as far as Chandannagar. Then the governor took two great iron chains. Each chain had many links, and each link weighed twenty-two pounds. These chains he stretched across the Hugli. But Chanak cut the chain with his sword and went on his way to the Deccan. Having thus defeated the malice of his foes he went to the court of King Aurangzēb, who was at this time fighting against the Kings of the Deccan. Chanak was brought into the presence of the King, and stood before him with folded arms. Then one came and whispered to the King that the provisions of the Mogul army were all gone ; and the King's countenance fell and his thoughts troubled him. Now Chanak perceived that the King was troubled, and knew that it was because he had no food left. He therefore ordered his servants to carry in secret all sorts of meat and drink to the King's army. This act of generosity won the heart of the King, and he said to Chanak : "Ask what you will, and I will give it you." But Chanak said : "First bid me defeat your enemies, and then I will take somewhat of you." So Chanak, having obtained orders from the King, marched against the enemy and put his armies to flight. Then he came again and stood before the King and asked that the English might be given the village of Calcutta. And the King consented, and departed to Delhi, but Chanak returned and founded Fort William in Bengal.[1]

Such are some of the traditions which at a very early date gathered round the events of 1686 and the following years. In them the reader may easily discern hints and adumbrations of the Chanakiad which should have been. Had there been no English conquest of Bengal, had there been no consequent introduction of western culture and western refinements of criticism, the Company's old agent would by this time have been transformed into a warrior-hero as bold as the wielder of Durandal, as terrible in wrath as the avenger of Patroclus. The ransack of Hugli might have become an epic poem which critics and *savants* might have analysed and quarrelled over, some maintaining that it arose from the corruption of a Sanskrit root, and others that it was a solar myth symbolising the struggle between light and darkness which takes place at the dawning of the day.

---

[1] *Hedges' Diary*, II, 97 to 99.

CHAPTER II.

HOW THE ENGLISH ATTEMPTED TO OCCUPY FIRST HIJILI AND THEN ULUBARIA, BUT AGAIN RETURNED TO SŪTĀNUTĪ.

AN Indian river in its old age is a thing full of caprice. It approaches its end rich with spoils gathered during a long and prosperous life, but uncertain where to leave them. Torn in a hundred different directions, it reaches the sea through an ever-varying number of ever-varying distributaries. Now the stream eats away its right bank, now its left. It oscillates in wide sweeping circles, depositing silt on either side, and again breaks through the curves thus formed and takes a more direct course. Sometimes it spills over its banks and completely abandons its old channel. From these vagaries of an Indian river the Ganges is by no means exempt, and its great western distributary shares in them, though in a lesser degree. A tidal river, the Hugli has not during the last three or four hundred years much changed its course, but the alterations which have taken place in its confluents and in its banks have been so many and so considerable, that an enquirer into its topography in the days of Job Charnock will often find the greatest difficulty in tracing out many localities which were at that time well known and conspicuous. In such a case our only resource is to begin with the present which we know, and thence work back to the unknown past.

The course of the Hugli below Calcutta may be divided into four sections. From Fort William to Ulubaria the stream runs for some twenty miles in a south-westerly direction. For the next twenty miles it continues almost due south. Then at Hugli Point begins a wide semi-circular sweep of about twenty-five miles, in which is situated Diamond Harbour. In the last section the river enters the sea, flowing south with the island of Sāgar as its left bank. On its right side it receives during the whole of this course four confluents, the Dāmodar, the Rupnārāyaṇ, the Haldi, and the Rasulpur river. Of these, the largest and the most important is the Rupnārāyaṇ, which joins the main stream at Hugli Point. Here occurs the most critical turn in the whole navigation of the river, for here lies the James and Mary sand, which for the past two centuries has been the dread of all ships making their way to Calcutta. In the seventeenth century the Hugli was considered to begin at this point, and although we do not hear of the fatal sand, yet we find that the place was noted for its dangerous eddies and currents. Lower down at the junction of the Rasulpur river with the Hugli, just opposite the centre of the modern island of Sāgar, is situated the old fort of Hijili in the district of Qasbā Hijili; seven and-a-half miles above this on the great river is the town of Khejiri. The Cowcolly light-house stands about half-way between the two places, and to the north of Khejiri a slender water-course, known as the Kunjapur Khāl, runs back from the Hugli to the Rasulpur river, thus forming the base of an inverted triangle of which the apex is Hijili.

At the present day Qasbā Hijili is rather an out-of-the-way corner of the world. To get to it by land you must leave the grand trunk road, which runs through Midnapore to Orissa, and strike off to the south-west by the way from Belda to Kānthi, a distance of some thirty-five miles. From Kānthi the more ancient and more direct route runs over the sand-hills to Dariāpur at the mouth of the Rasulpur river, whence you may cross straight over to the old town of Hijili. But the post road passes in a north-easterly direction to Rasulpur, where the river is crossed by a ferry, and from thence continues in a direction almost parallel to the Kunjapur Khāl, but a mile and-a-half to the south of it, till it reaches Khejiri, while a more circuitous path diverging to the right from the ferry, leads to the same place past the old town of Hijili, Pāchuriya, and the Cowcolly light-house.

Nij Qasbā Hijili, all that now remains of the old town, is a somewhat large collection of hovels standing at the junction of the two rivers. Five hundred yards to the west on the Rasulpur river is a

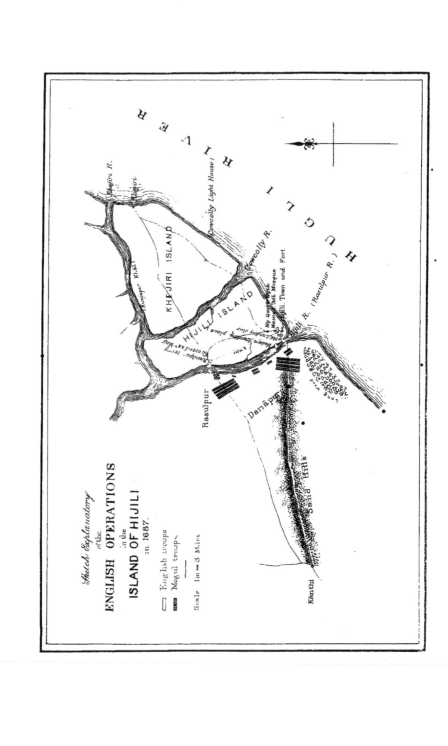

Sketch Explanatory
of the
ENGLISH OPERATIONS
in the
ISLAND OF HIJILI
in 1687.

English troops.
Mogul troops.

Scale 1in = 3 Miles

HUGLI RIVER

Khejiri R.

KHEJIRI ISLAND

Kunspur Khal.

Cowcolly Light House

Cowcolly R.

HIJILI ISLAND

Khejiri R.

Khossed As May

Rasulpur ferry

Nijh's Landing place

Raja's Landing place

Raja's Mosque

Hijili. Town and Fort

Hijili R. (Rasulpur R.)

Rasulpur

Damapur

Long Sand Palm woods

Sand Hills

Kauthi

landing place with a bazar. Between this and the village rises the white tower of a mosque, conspicuous for miles away; and by the mosque stands the shrine of Masnad 'Alī Shāh, the first Musulman ruler of the place, whose memory is still held in veneration by Hindus and Mahomedans alike. Masnad 'Alī held rule in the first half of the sixteenth century; but when his warrior brother, the Mighty Wrestler, was dead, and he heard that the Mogul was sending an army to attack him, the holy man buried himself alive, and left his son Bahādur Khān to make peace with the emperor, and hold his land as a feudatory of the Court of Delhi.[1]

Further down to the south, almost completely covered by the water of the river, lie the ruined walls of the old fort. Behind for some distance up in the apex of the triangle of land included between the Hugli and the Rasulpur river rise a number of small sand-hills thickly covered with prickly bamboos and the ever-green Indian oak, from which Hijili is said to take its name. All round beside the rivers and away towards Khejiri and the Kunjapur Khāl the land lies low, a great dyke encircling it like the wall of a Roman camp, preventing the influx of the adjacent salt waters and allowing it to be cultivated. Two hundred years ago the land unprotected by any embankment was for the most part swamp. So fatally malarious was the spot that the difference between going to Hijili and returning thence passed into a Hindustani proverb.

It was, however, a place of the greatest importance, an accessible frontier, a land rich in grain, the seat of the salt manufacture, the private domain of the Mogul who had the monopoly of the precious mineral extracted from these low-lying swamps by the easy process of filtration and by boiling the brine. The Kunjapur Khāl was then a deep, broad stream, which completely cut off both Khejiri and Hijili from the main land, and these again were divided into two distinct islands by the river Cowcolly, of which the channel has now completely vanished. Both places were considered "exceeding pleasant and fruitful, having great store of wild hogs, deer, wild buffaloes, and tigers." It was an amusing and interesting trip in those days to take a boat at the town of Khejiri and row all round the two islands into the Rusulpur river, and so back to the Hugli, noting the busy scenes which met you on your way.[2]

---

[1] Hunter's *Statistical Account of Bengal*, edition of 1876, III, 199, 200.
[2] *Hedges' Diary*, I, 68, 172, 175.

Such was the "pleasant island in the Ganges" to which the English in 1687 were persuaded to entrust all their fortunes. On the approach of Nicholson, Malik Qāsim, the Mogul commandant, deserted the place and surrendered all its forts and batteries, all its guns and ammunition, without striking a blow. The island was full of inhabitants and well stocked with cattle. By the 27th February, Charnock had established himself in the town and collected the bulk of his forces round him. They consisted of four hundred and twenty soldiers, the *Beaufort* with her frigate, and nearly all the Company's sloops, except one, which had been left at Hugli Point, to guard the passage of the river, and another which remained at Balasor with the *Rochester* and the *Nathaniel*. But the English knew that what had been so easily won might also be as easily lost, unless they took steps to secure their position. Sloops were therefore placed all round the island wherever it was thought likely that a landing might be effected, and the long-boats and pinnaces were ordered to keep cruising all night to prevent the people from crossing over to the mainland with their cattle. The so-called fort at Hijili was a small house surrounded by a thin wall with two or three armed points. It stood in the midst of a grove of trees, and was hemmed in on all sides by a thick town of mud houses. The landing to the west on the Rasulpur river was at least five hundred yards distant, and had to be defended by a separate battery. The English began to look back with regret to their old factory at the Gholghāṭ in Hugli, and to think that they might have made a much better fight there.[1]

The first blow was struck by the ships at Balasor. The port is situated on the Burā-balung, a sinuous river doubling back upon itself in numerous loops, with an awkward bar a little more than two miles from its mouth. Some way up the stream occurs a projecting promontory, which frequently appears in the records of Charnock's time under the name of the *Point of Sand.* The point commands the river for miles, and was armed by the Mogul rulers with a fort and batteries. West of it stood the old town of Balasor; beyond this, still further up the stream, was the rapidly growing new town where the Europeans had established their factories. The hostile measures of Charnock had alarmed the whole country round. New Balasor was alive with horses-soldiers and foot-soldiers, and every

---

[1] *Hedges' Diary,* II, 65.

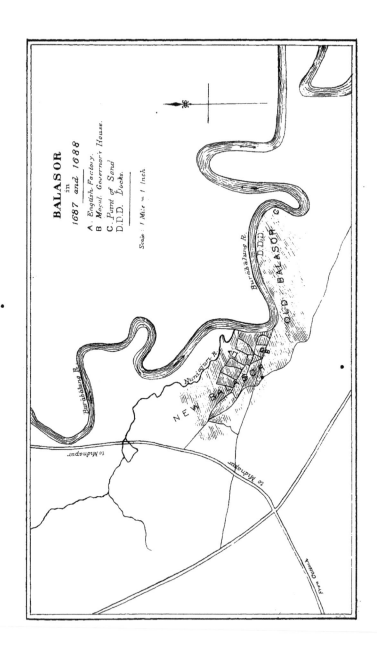

BALASOR
in
1687 and 1688

A. English Factory.
B. Mocul. Governor's House.
C. Point of Sand
D.D.D. Docks.

Scale : 1 Mile = 1 Inch

Mogul's house was turned into an improvised fortification. The ships were drawn up in dry docks of mud under the protection of the *Point of Sand*. The batteries were armed to the teeth with guns taken out of the vessels. But these preparations were of no avail to stay the attack of one hundred and seventy British soldiers and sailors. In a single night the fort was taken with small loss. On the following day, the river being clear of hostile ships, the English easily marched up to the new town, and after a short struggle made themselves masters of the whole place, burning and destroying all before them. For two days new Balasor was given over to the spoilers. They broke into the king's custom house; they plundered the private merchants; and, returning to the old town, burnt all the shipping as it lay in the docks. Two vessels arriving at the mouth of the river, one belonging to the Prince, and the other to the nabob, with four elephants on her, were seized and made prizes. Satisfied that enough had been done to vindicate their honour in the eyes of the people of Balasor, the English determined to leave, but they were not allowed to get off scot free. While waiting at the mouth of the river for a favourable wind, a long boat with a crew of seventeen men, was surprised two miles up the country, and all the men taken except one. The heads of three of the prisoners were cut off and stuck up at Hugli. Meanwhile the *Rochester*, the *Nathaniel* and the *Samuel* sailed to join Charnock, and in their stead the sloop *Good Hope* was sent down to keep watch in the Bay.[1]

Charnock had commenced his operations with vigour. He had ransacked Hugli, attacked the Thānā forts, destroyed Balasor, seized Hijili. To him these things seemed ample demonstrations of power, and he, no doubt, expected matters to come to a crisis at once. But to the rulers of India they seemed very minor incidents. Aurangzēb was at this time intent upon the taking of Haidarabad. He did not hear of the proceedings of the English till the beginning of March, and then contented himself with calling for the map and ascertaining where such obscure places as Hugli and Balasor were situated.[2] Shāyista Khān was almost equally unconcerned. He had ordered adequate forces of horse and foot to advance against Hijili, and he had no doubt that they would reach the place in due course and drive the rash invaders into the sea. At the same time, it was satisfactory to reflect

---

[1] *Hedges' Diary*, II, 65, 66.
[2] *Ib.*, II, 63, 64.

that they had chosen to coop themselves up in the most pestilential
swamp in all lower Bengal, so that they might almost be safely
left to stew in their own juice.

March and April must have been trying months for the English
at Hijili. Day by day the tropical heat grew fiercer ; day by day their
forces dwindled away, while the numbers of their enemies increased
and multiplied. By the beginning of May the supplies of provisions
had run very short. Nothing was to be had in the island, but beef
and a little fish, a diet scarcely suited to the season of the year. Both
ashore and on board the ships, great numbers died daily, the number
of soldiers sick being never less than a hundred and eighty. The inhabitants, who had at first been friendly, and with whose assistance
alone the necessary fortifications could be completed, either through fear
or for want of rice, had begun to leave the island. The local magnate,
who had offered to co-operate with Charnock, refused to give any help.
The island was closely beset by the Mogul troops. On the other side of
the Rasulpur river, opposite Hijili, Malik Qāsim had raised a battery
which commanded the river, the landing place, and even the fort.

The English were thus forced to resume the offensive. In one
sally on to the mainland they carried off fifteen thousand maunds of
rice ; in another they took the battery, split the great guns, and brought
away the small ones, with a large quantity of powder and ammunition.
But the respite thus gained was short. The enemy soon returned in
increased numbers, erected a larger and more powerful battery than
before, beat the ships from their anchorage, and even flung shot into
the fort of Hijili.

By the middle of May, 'Abdu-s Samad, the nabob's general, arrived
at Hijili. His forces were considerable, amounting to twelve thousand
men, and he was entrusted with ample powers to deal with the English
as he thought best. He resolved on decisive measures. More batteries
along the river wherever it was narrowest, and a furious cannonade
opened upon the shipping. Every shot told. The English forces were
completely disorganized. On the 28th May, in the afternoon, a detachment of seven hundred Mogul cavalry and two hundred gunners, filled
with enthusiasm and bhang, crossed the Rasulpur river at the ferry three
miles above the town, and surprised an unfinished battery of four field
pieces. The men in charge hastened at once to give notice of the attack,
but so vehement was the onset of the enemy that 'Abdu-s Samad's horsemen arrived as soon as the news, seized the town, and set it on fire.
One of the English officers was cut to pieces as he lay sick in his house,

and his wife and child were carried off prisoners. The stables which contained the English horses and the four elephants lately taken in the nabob's ship, fell an easy prey to the enemy. Already they had lodged themselves within the trenches, but the English, hurrying together after a desperate fight which lasted all the evening, succeeded in saving the fort.

Charnock's position now seemed altogether desperate. Two hundred of his men he had buried. Scarcely one hundred soldiers, weak with repeated attacks of fever and ague, remained to hold the fort. Out of forty officers only one lieutenant and four sergeants were alive and able to do duty. The *Beaufort* had sprung another great leak, and Nicholson had been compelled to empty her of her guns, ammunition, provisions, and goods, and order her away to careen. None of the ships were more than half manned ; and it was evident that unless the fort could be held, and the passage to the landing place kept open, all would be lost.

Fortunately for the English, there stood half-way between the fort and the river a masonry building which Charnock had converted into a battery by placing on it two guns and a guard, while the landing stage itself was similarly protected. As long as these posts could be maintained, Charnock's connection with his base was safe. The next day most of the small craft that had hitherto kept guard round the island were brought into the broad river, the most valuable of the Company's goods placed on ship-board, and more provisions and troops conveyed into the fort. With these men Charnock drove the enemy out of his lines, and for four days maintained his position against overwhelming odds. The courage of the Mogul warriors "went out with their bang ;" and though a great many more were landed in the island, and the English were besieged three quarters round, yet the fort and the two batteries which secured the passage to the shipping were still untaken, when, on the first of June, a most welcome relief arrived in the shape of seventy men fresh from Europe under the command of Captain Denham.

The tide of war had turned ; the timely reinforcement saved Charnock. The new troops were full of life and spirit. The day after their arrival Denham sallied out of the fort, beat the enemy from their guns, burnt their houses, and returned having lost only one man. A bright idea occurred to Charnock. Seeing what a strong effect the arrival of the reinforcements had produced upon the minds of the enemy, he determined to repeat it. Accordingly, he quietly dropped his sailors by one or two at a time out of the fort, and sent them down to the landing place, whence the whole body was ostentatiously marched up again in all the panoply of war, flags flying, drums beating, trumpets sounding, and the men huzzaing loudly as they had done on the first day of their arrival. "In war," as the great Napoleon used to say, "the moral is to the physical force as three parts to one." The effect of Charnock's device was instantaneous. The enemy, supposing that the English were somehow supplied with a constant succession of recruits, began to despair of shaking their position. On the 4th June, in the morning, they held out a flag of truce, and Charnock was informed that 'Abdu-s Samad wished to treat for peace.

A cessation of arms was agreed upon ; and Charnock, having duly received a hostage from the enemy, sent over Richard Trenchfield, who seems to have been on more friendly terms with the Indian officials than the other servants of the Company, to open the negotiations. On the 6th June Macrith and Jolland were united with Trenchfield in a commission which was entrusted with full powers to conclude peace, two more hostages were taken from the enemy, and the three men were sent over to 'Abdu-s Samad. They were instructed to insist as much as possible on the ratification of the twelve articles drawn up at Sūtānutī and on the surrender of those who infringed the Company's monopoly, but in any case to conclude a peace as best they could. In three days the terms were settled and ratified. On the 10th June the Mogul commander entered the fort, and the next day the English, taking with them all their ammunition and artillery, marched out of the place which they had so gallantly held for more than three months, with drums beating and colours flying.[1]

On leaving Hijili, Charnock went up the river to Ulubaria, where he remained for the next three months. 'Abdu-s Samad had promised to give him passes to allow the English to go further up the river above the Thānā forts, but the passes never came. Neither were 'Abdu-s Samad's other promises any better observed. He had agreed to procure from the nabob the confirmation of the Sūtānutī articles, but the nabob did nothing of the sort. On the 2nd July and again on the 16th August orders were signed and despatched from Dacca, in which, after dwelling upon the mischief which had been done, and declaring that the Mogul would never pardon such offences should he hear of them, his Highness was understood to accord his gracious

---

[1] *Hedges' Diary*, II, 66 to 69.

permission to the English to secure themselves at Ulubaria and re-main in their factories at Hugli, carrying on their trade with the merchants. But as regarded their demands for compensation, for exemption from taxation, and for the establishment of a mint, Shāyista Khān could say nothing definite. He had referred every-thing to the King, his master. Charnock perceived "that the war was not yet at an end or like to be suddenly." The first order he had indignantly returned to Dacca; but on receiving the second order at the beginning of September, he determined to accept it so far as to go up to Sūtānutī with all his ships, " as well for a recruit of provisions as for the spinning out of this monsoon, with a firm resolution not to settle no trade till he [*i.e.* the nabob] confirms these last articles and gives us some security against any demands of damages that arise against us hereafter." [1]

---

[1] *Hedges' Diary*, II, 69 to 70.

CHAPTER III.

NOW THE ENGLISH AFTER WANDERING OVER THE BAY OF BENGAL, AND
SOJOURNING AT MADRAS, RETURNED ONCE AGAIN TO SŪTĀNUTĪ.

IN spite of their professed regard for their old servant, Charnock's honourable masters at home were not slow to criticise his late military and political exploits. • The letters from the Court to Bengal at this time are a curious mixture of cupidity, patriotism, bravado, piety, and acrimonious abuse. "We know," say they, "your interest leads you to return as soon as you can to your trades and getting of money, and so, it may be, our interest prompts us; but when the honour of our King and country is at stake, we scorn more petty considerations, and so should you."[1] "When we perused," say they in another letter, "your Hugli diary, commencing September 1685, and concluding November 1686, wherein we observe the manifold, insupportable, and heinous abuses offered to you by the natives of Bengal, to the robbing of us of almost half our stock, it provokes us as well to indignation as to admiration, at your insensible patience that you should let them pass with so easy a correction after you had them at your mercy in Hugli, and much more, that you should be yourselves, and suppose us to be, such weak and unthinking men as to venture our estates

---

[1] *Hedges' Diary,* II, 73.

I

again into the hands of such false and rapacious villains, without a
strong fort at hand to revenge the injuries they may hereafter do us;
which we are so far from intending, that we are peremptorily resolved
never to send any of our estate again into Bengal until we know you
are well settled and fortified in some strong place of our own, with an
English garrison, and it is for that purpose principally that we have
been and are at so vast a charge in sending out so many strong ships
last year, and so many soldiers as we have sent this last and this present
year; though we are not without great fear that your backwardness and
hankering after your profitable easy old habitations, as the Israelites
did after the onions and garlick of Egypt, may deprive us of the fruit
of all our cost."[1]   In a third letter they write:—"It is of vanity to
fancy that your prudence or subtlety procured at last those good terms
you obtained of Abdul Samad, when you and your forces were by your
errors aforesaid reduced to that low condition you were in upon the
island of Hijili. It was not your wit or contrivance, but God
Almighty's good providence, which hath always graciously superin-
tended the affairs of this Company, particularly by the success he was
pleased to give our general on the Surat side.   This fatal disappointment of the whole trade of India caused insurrections, and an universal
lamentation and cry, not only of the natives, but of the other nations
aforesaid, *Peace with the English, or we must all starve ;* and this caused
the Mogul only of his known humane, benign disposition and love
to mankind to send *Cossids* and *Dogchuckys*[2] in haste to Bengal and
all places to make up the breach, and one of his great Princes to Surat
in such manner, and with such express instructions, that the English
should remain contented."[3]

The Court did not stop at criticism. They went on to draw out a
definite plan of campaign, and to supersede Charnock in favour of a
new and untried commander. The most consummate general of modern
times has told us that " it is not permitted at the distance of three
hundred leagues, and without even an account of the condition of the
army, to direct what should be done ;" yet a committee of English
traders in London at a distance of fifteen thousand miles from Bengal
felt quite competent to direct military operations against a mighty
empire. These sapient tacticians had somehow arrived at the conclusion
that all would be well in the Bay if they could seize upon Chittagong.

---

[1] *Hedges' Diary,* II, 74.
[2] *i.e.,* couriers and posts.   *Qāṣid* is a courier, and *dāk-chauki,* a post.
[3] *Hedges' Diary,* II, 74.

They did not very well know where Chittagong was, and appear to have thought it would be found some way up the Ganges,[1] but they were sure it was the right place for the English settlement in Bengal. They also believed that they had found the right man to take it, Captain William Heath, of the *Defence*, a hot-headed skipper, by no means deficient in the art of navigating and managing a ship, but with pride and obstinacy enough to spoil any abilities and ruin any enterprise. He had, however, so impressed the Court with his swaggering and boasting, that without more ado they placed him in command of a fleet of ten or eleven ships,[2] and sent him off to the Bay at the beginning of the year 1688 to take over the management of all their affairs in those parts and put them in possession of the post they coveted.[3]

What is the meaning of these new orders? It is the earlier policy of violence criticising the new policy of a fortified settlement. Ideas at this time were necessarily slow in travelling outwards to India and homewards to England. The Court which was the last to abandon its confidence in the native rulers was also the last to understand that a policy of simple retaliation was not the best method of defending the English trade in Bengal.

---

[1] *Hedges' Diary*, II, 78.

[2] See the fragment of a diary which is found in the Egerton Collection, No. 283, entitled "Voyage from Bengal to Madras, 1688 until 1690," and which has been printed by Mr. Long in 1871 as an "Historical Notice concerning Calcutta in the Days of Job Charnock."

When Captain Heath left Sūtānuṭī on the 8th November 1688, he was in command of the following fleet [see page 4 of the *Notice*]:—

    (1) Ship *Resolution*, Captain William Sharp, Commander, Captain Heath being thereon;

    (2) Ship *Williamson*, Captain Stephen Ashby, Commander;

    (3) „ *Diamond*, Captain George Herron, Commander;

    (4) „ *Recovery*, Captain John Hampton, Commander;

    (5) „ *Success*, Captain Thomas Walthrop, Commander;

    (6) Ketch *Samuel*, Edward Tench, Master;

    (7) „ *Thomas*, John Gorbold, Master;

    (8) Sloop *Beaufort*, Edward Hussey, Master;

    (9) Ship *Resistance*, John Blunt, Master;

    (10) „ *Cumneer Merchant*, Anthony Pennislon, Master;

    (11) „ *Retriever*, George Paulin, Master;

Some way down the river they fell in with—

    (12) Ship *James*, Captain Abraham Roberts, Commander, and (13) Ship *Madapollam*.

In Balasor road they found waiting for them—

    (14) Ship *Defence*, and (15) Ship *Princess of Denmark*.

While in the road they took two French ships, the *Energie* and the *Lorette*, and on the 26th November were joined by the ship *Frances* from Madras.

[3] *Hedges' Diary*, II, 76, 77.

2

To Charnock these designs against Chittagong must have seemed madness. He knew Chittagong, and knew where it was. He had grave doubts whether it could be taken at all by the English, and still graver doubts whether it could be retained ; and he was sure that even if it could be taken and retained it was too distant from the northern and western parts of Bengal to be a fit centre of the English trade there. For this purpose some spot on the Hugli was needed, and the question to be settled was, which spot. Charnock, as I have said, was not a genius to divine by intuition what should be done, but he was a shrewd, clever man, who quickly profited by experience. He had tried three places on the right side of the river, Hugli, Ulubaria, Hijili. The first two were completely exposed to the attack of an enemy advancing from the west, and it was therefore impossible for the English to remain at either of them if the Mogul Government attacked in sufficient force. Hijili, being an island, seemed suitable enough at first sight, but it was not really more defensible, for the river, which cut it off from the mainland, was so narrow that it could be easily swept by the enemy's guns. It was besides a malarious swamp. The fourth place which Charnock had tried was Sūtānutī, a position as secure for a naval power as the others were insecure. It could only be approached on one side. To attack it the Mogul troops must cross the river higher up and march down upon it from the north. But if the river were crossed while the English ships still dominated it, the attacking force was exposed to swift and certain destruction. The English sending their troops up the stream could land and assail the enemy on his march to Calcutta, cut him off from his base, force him to form front parallel to his line of communication, and so place him in the most dangerous predicament in which an army can find itself. It is not pretended that Charnock grasped all these military advantages when he came to Sūtānutī, neither is it pretended that they were the only advantages which the place had to offer; but it is surely not too much to believe that when Charnock returned to Sūtānutī a second time, it was because he had found out that it was strategically safe, and that for this reason among others he fully intended to stay there.

At any rate there he stayed for more than twelve months, during which time the Company's civil servants and soldiers were compelled to live in huts till proper brick houses could be erected. The operations at Surat which were the cause of so much pious thankfulness at the India House must have excited very different feelings in the breast of Charnock, for the nabob learning that the war on the Malabar Coast had broken out afresh, felt himself no longer bound by the terms he had recently made with the English, and at once set about annoying them in every possible way. He ordered them to return to Hugli, prohibited them from building in brick or stone at Sūtānuţī, demanded large sums as compensation for the war, and finally gave his soldiers full permission to plunder the English trade and property. Charnock, determined at all costs to remain at Sūtānuţi, had recourse to negotiation. Eyre and Braddyll, two members of the Council, were despatched to Dacca to request permission to remain at Sūtānuţī and to be allowed to purchase from the native owners sufficient ground for a factory. At Hugli, they were to urge, the English had no convenient anchorage for their large ships, and were so closely entangled with the native town that disputes were sure to arise. By settling at Calcutta these difficulties would be for the future avoided.[1]

But while Charnock was thus straining every nerve to establish himself at Calcutta, Captain Heath was hastening on his way from England to supersede the old Agent, and unsettle everything which had been done for the last fifty years. The instructions sent with him to Madras were admittedly drawn up in the dark. The Court confessed that it had no certain knowledge of the state of affairs in Bengal, and could not guess whether Charnock had made peace or not. If he had made peace and had settled and fortified himself in any place which would at all answer the purpose, Heath was to wait at Madras and await further orders. In any other case Heath was to sail at once against Chittagong and take it, and thence send for Charnock and his companions.[2]

These were wild instructions. The proceedings of the wrong-headed swash-buckler intrusted with their execution were wilder still. Arriving at Calcutta on the 20th September, he immediately called a council of war, and communicated the Court's orders to the assembled merchants and captains. The matter of discussion was serious and the debate protracted, each member recording his opinion separately in writing.[3]

We do not know what their arguments were, but we can guess at some of them. Heath, it seems, began by quoting his orders which he considered left them no alternative but to pack up and be off to Chittagong. But instructions drawn up for the conduct of a distant

---

[1] Stewart's *Bengal*, p. 201. *Hedges' Diary*, II, 72. Long's *Notice*, 19 to 21.
[2] *Hedges' Diary*, II, 77-78.
[3] *Ib.*, II, 79, 81.

campaign must always leave some measure of latitude to the commander. Absurd as were as the orders of Court, they were not so absurd as to leave no alternative. The authorities at home, trusting in the fidelity and discretion of their old Agent, had sanctioned the settlement at Calcutta. The letter which went with Heath expressly says:—"If the place Mr. Charnock may have already settled and fortified upon will in any measure answer our known purpose, in such case, since we can't now help it, we would have you proceed to strengthen that place already settled and to forbear proceeding against Chittagong until you receive further orders from us." [1] In another letter written three weeks later the Court pronounces still more decidedly in favour of remaining at Calcutta:—"We have no manner of doubt," they say, "of the continuance of our peace in all the Mogul's dominions, and therefore we think the sooner our Agent Charnock resettles the factories at Cassimbazar and Malda, from whence we used to have our best returns, the better it will be for the Company; and since he likes Sūtānutī so well, we are content he should build a factory there, but with as much frugality as may be, and we hope he will so continue that business as to the duties of the town being to be the Company's by the Bengal articles." [2] It may, however, be urged that the settlement was not fortified. Certainly there were no brick bastions or walls to defend it. Yet nature had planted morasses on its eastern and southern sides, and had placed between it and its enemies a broad river on which the English ships could come and go as they liked. But Captain Heath, though no stranger to the locality, had never studied it as a general. We cannot therefore be surprised that he failed to understand its strategic advantages. Clive saw them at a glance, but Clive was a genius.

The other arguments which may have been used in favour of staying at Calcutta are of a more obvious nature. Heath had been told to consult with the Agent and Council, and the majority were in favour of peace. They had had enough of fighting for the present. They were contented to stay at Sūtānutī, where they had found many advantages and had already begun to establish a certain amount of trade. Shāyista Khān, the great enemy of the English, had left Bengal, and in his stead Bahādur Khān was acting as nabob. They were not without hopes that the new vice-nabob would after all give way and grant their demands, especially now that they had received such large reinforcements from Europe. These arguments Heath had little .

[1] *Hedges' Diary*, II, 77.
[2] *Ib.*, II, 75.

difficulty in overruling. He informed the Council that he had the sole
management of the Company's affairs, and that he saw no prospect
of their ever coming to an agreement with the Indian government.
He gave them till the 10th of November to make what investment they
could and wind up their affairs. By that time his vessels would
be repaired, fitted, provisioned, and ready for sea, and he would
then proceed with the whole of the establishment to Chittagong.
Quick work this for men habituated to Indian methods of procrastina-
tion and delay; but Captain Heath was rapid in everything, even
in changing his mind. In less than three weeks the impetuous
seaman had gone off on quite another tack. He understood that
Bahādur Khān, the new ruler at Dacca, was intending to send an
expedition against the King of Arakān, and hastily wrote off to offer
his help, provided that the nabob should confirm all the old privileges
of the English in Bengal and immediately send an order, under his
hand and seal, for building a fortified place which might secure the
Company's servants and their trade from the villainies of every petty
governor. "Otherwise," said he, "we design in a few days to depart
this country peaceably, our positive orders being to stay no longer here
to trade in fenceless factories." [1]

An offer made in such insulting terms would have been regarded
by Bahādur Khān rather as an ultimatum than as a friendly overture,
and perhaps it was so meant. But the two English plenipotentiaries at
Dacca, with the help of their native friends, took care to make their
requests in a much more respectful manner, and were so successful that
at the beginning of November they were in immediate expectation of a
favourable order from his Highness, who had in fact despatched Malik
Barkhwurdar to Hugli to arrange matters. [2] But Captain Heath had by
this time veered round to his former opinion. He was not going to stay
for Malik Barkhwurdar, who was an inveterate enemy of the English
and the chief contriver of the sham articles signed at Sūtānuti.
Although the time he had originally fixed had not yet expired, he bade
the Company's servants pack and be gone, and on the 8th November
the English, taking with them all their belongings, once more started
on their wanderings in search of a secure centre for their trade.
Eyre and Braddyll and the rest of the factors in different parts of the
country were abandoned to their fate. Malik Barkhwurdar, astonished

[1] *Hedges' Diary*, II, 79, 81. Also Long's *Notice*, 2.
[2] Long's *Notice*, 3.

beyond measure at this sudden departure, sent repeated messages after the retreating ships, but without any result.[1]

Charnock and Heath arrived in Balasor road on the 16th November. Besides the *Defence* and the *Princess of Denmark*, which had been sent out from Europe, they had some thirteen or fourteen smaller vessels, and shortly after their arrival had the good fortune to capture two French frigates, the *Energie* and the *Loretto*.[2] The number of soldiers amounted to about three hundred, of whom more than half were Portuguese. The Mogul governor of Balasor was living, with his retinue in tents pitched on the Point of Sand where the fortifications had been greatly strengthened. He was daily expecting news and instructions from Dacca, and in the meantime refused to allow the English at Balasor to leave the place or to send off any of their goods, and prohibited the English in the ships from buying provisions ashore.[3]

At this juncture Captain Heath, who began to find difficulty in procuring food for so large a number of persons as were now under his care, returned to his pacific mood. Instead of immediately landing his forces and marching wide of the fortifications on the Point of Sand so as to surprise the town of new Balasor, and, if possible, bring off the English with their goods, he hung about in the Bay and kept sending envoys ashore to the Mogul governor to ask if any news had arrived from Dacca, to demand the surrender of the Company's servants and property, and finally to warn the governor that the sole blame would lie on him if he took no heed and refused to prevent a breach of the eace.[4] On the 28th November, finding that his negotiations were proceeding too slowly, he placed the bulk of his troops on small sloops and ascended the Burā-balung. The next day between eight and nine in the morning Charnock and those with him in the ships could hear the rattle of the English musketry answered by the booming of the enemy's pieces of ordnance. In less than three hours the great guns were silenced, and flames and smoke were seen rising up inland. Boats bringing back news of the fight soon followed. The English had landed under the cover of some clumps of cocoa-palms, dispersed a body of horse and foot, and with a rush carried the great battery which guarded the river and the Point of

---

[1] *Hedges' Diary*, II, 79, 81.
[2] Long's *Notice*, 13.
[3] *Hedges' Diary*, II, 80, 82.
[4] *Ib.* Also Long's *Notice*, 10 to 15.

Sand on which they had hoisted the king's flag. All the artillery and stores had fallen into their hands, and they were already shipping off the ammunition. The victors were resting on the Point, and intended to march up to new Balasor that night. Their loss was only one killed and six wounded.[1]

In the attack on the town which took place next day the soldiers, according to the peace party, committed great excesses. They made no difference between friends and foes, Christians and non-Christians, men and women, but ill-treated all alike. They failed, moreover, to rescue their countrymen, for the Governor on hearing of their approach burnt the English factory, and carried off the factors up the country.[2] On the 4th December Heath again returned to the ships and to the policy of negotiation. On the very day that the soldiers were attacking Balasor letters had arrived from Eyre and Braddyll at Dacca, holding out hopes that Bahādur Khān would even now grant the requests of the English if Charnock would write and confirm the offers made in October. For a second time Heath called a council of war. It met in the great cabin of the *Defence*. The letters received from Dacca were read and discussed, and to all appearances the Captain was willing to make his peace with the nabob. Agent Charnock was allowed to write and confirm the offers, and envoys once more passed to and fro between the shipping and the town. But in reality Captain Heath, so far from intending peace, had returned to the design of taking Chittagong. On the 23rd December, having already sent two vessels to the King of Arakān and two more to explore the mouths of the Chittagong river, he sailed away from Balasor, leaving one of his English envoys behind him.[3]

Arriving at Chittagong about the 18th January, he sent parties of men with a flag of truce in a pinnace up the river to the town to find out its strength, and to intimate to the Governor that the English had come according to agreement to help the Mogul against the King of Arakān.[4] On the 21st January Heath called his third council of war, and asked them whether they would advise him to attack the town. The absurdity of the whole project was now manifest. A city like Chittagong defended by some ten thousand men was not to be "taken by the collar," nor could it have

[1] Long's *Notice*, 16, 17.
[2] *Hedges' Diary*, II, 82.
[3] *Ib.*, II, 80 and 83.
[4] *Ib.*, II, 80 and 83.

been kept if taken. The council, therefore, advised Heath to adhere to his offer of help to the Mogul, and to wait for a definite answer.[1] But waiting was intolerable to the lively sea-captain. He declared that "there was nothing but lies wrote on both sides," that it was never his intention to transport the nabob's soldiers to Arakān, and that he did not intend to stay for an answer. After this outburst of passion Heath, as was his wont, permitted communications to be opened with the governor of Chittagong, which continued till nearly the end of the month, when he suddenly weighed anchor and sailed away to offer his services to the King of Arakān.[2] But the King, instead of rushing to meet the English with open arms, received their overtures and presents very coldly. This last rebuff completely disgusted Captain Heath with the whole expedition, and, after making a futile attempt to stir up a rebellion against the King, he determined to return to Madras, as usual abandoning an unfortunate English envoy who had been sent off on one of his strange errands.[3] "So," says our captain, "when [we] found that [we] could not persuade those foolish people from the present ruin and destruction which is just upon them, we watered our ships and refreshed our men, which were much distempered with the scurvy. So on the seventeenth February [we] sailed directly for this place, Fort St. George, giving orders for every ship to make the best of her way, that no more time might be lost, and that perchance, if any Moor's ship were in those seas we might by being scattered meet with them."[4]

The story of how Captain Heath with the whole of the Company's establishment in Bengal for six whole months went "tripping from port to port," is so extraordinary that we could hardly credit it were it not recorded in three different original documents, one of them drawn up by the captain himself. But the results of his foolish proceedings, conjoined with the defiant attitude of the settlements at Madras and Bombay, are almost equally surprising. At first Aurangzēb had been greatly incensed at the audacity of the English, and in an outburst of anger had ordered his servants to extirpate these infidels from his dominions and to seize or destroy all their goods. But his anger, it is said, cooled on reflection. The commerce carried on by the Company enriched his treasuries, and he could not well afford to lose it. Yet he could not

---

[1] *Hedges' Diary*, II, 85.
[2] *Ib.*, II, 83-84, 34.
[3] *Ib.*, II, 80, 81, 84.
[4] *Ib.*, II, 81.

help thinking from the violent and unusual conduct of Captain Heath
that he had somehow driven the English to desperation, and that
they intended to altogether abandon Bengal. Besides, their power,
though insignificant by land, was formidable by sea. Their ships
might interrupt the trade with Arabia, and hinder the faithful in
their yearly pilgrimages to the house of God at Mecca. He forced
himself, therefore, to swallow his resentment and retrace his steps.[1]
"You must understand," he wrote to the nabob of Bengal, "that
it has been the good fortune of the English to repent them of their
irregular past proceedings, and their not being in their former greatness, have by their attorneys, petitioned for their lives, and a pardon
for their faults, which, out of my extraordinary favour towards them,
have accordingly granted. Therefore upon receipt here of my order
you must not create them any further trouble, but let them trade in
your government as formerly, and this order I expect you see strictly
observed."[2]

Had Shāyista Khān been still in power when this order came
from the emperor, it is possible that some means would have been found
for evading it. But, as has been said, he had resigned his office, and,
after a decent interval, during which Bahādur Khān, "armed with a
little brief authority," had done his best to please the Mogul by seizing
the English property and imprisoning the English factors, Ibrāhīm
Khān, the old bookworm, who had before given rise to so much trouble
at Patna, had come to be ruler of Bengal. The new nabob was a man of
peace. Without military abilities, he desired to administer justice with
strict impartiality and to encourage agriculture and commerce. The
policy of the emperor was quite in accordance with his natural disposition. He at once set at liberty the Company's agents who were
confined at Dacca, and wrote letters to Charnock at Madras inviting
him to return to Bengal. At first Charnock hesitated. He had not
forgotten his experiences at Patna. He knew that even if the nabob
himself was sincere, there was still a host of subordinates ready to
harass the English as in the old days before the war. He demanded a
specific warrant clearly stating terms on which trade would be resumed.
The nabob applied to the emperor, but at the same time pointed out
to Charnock that the granting of such a warrant must take many
months, and pressed him to come without further delay.[3] The English

---

[1] Stewart's *Bengal*, 203-205.
[2] *Ib.*, Appendix, p. iv.
[3] *Ib.*, 204-205.

resolved to trust these promises of friendship and protection. In
August, Charnock, with his Council and factors, escorted by thirty
soldiers, arrived in the Bay, and sent forward Stanley and Mackrith to
occupy Hugli. On Sunday, the 24th, at noon, the wanderers found
themselves once more at Sūtānutī. Ibrāhīm Khān, whom the English
now styled " the most famously just and good nabob," was true to his
word. The restored merchants were received with respect by the
commander of the Thānā fort and the governor of Hugli.[1] On the
10th February 1691, an Imperial order was issued under the seal of

---

[1] *Hedges' Diary*, II, 86-87.
The account of the third occupation of Sūtānutī and the foundation of
Calcutta is given in the " *Diary and Consultation Book for affairs of the Rt.
Hon'ble English East India Company, kept by the Rt. Worshipful the Agent and
Council, beginning 16th July* 1690." From it we learn that the Bengal Council
returned from Madras on the *Princess*. At Balasor they left the *Princess* and
went on board the ketch *Madapollam*. The *Diary* records :—

"*August* 24*th*—[Sunday] This day at Sankraul ordered Captain Brooke
to come up with his vessel to Chutanuttee, where we arrived about noon ; but
found the place in a deplorable condition, nothing being left for our present
accommodation and the rain falling day and night. We are forced to betake
ourselves to boats, which, considering the season of the year, is unhealthy ;
Mellick Burcoordar and the country people at our leaving this place (in October
1688) burning and carrying away what they could. On our arrival here the
Governor of Tana sent his servant with a compliment."

" *Thursday, the* 28*th August*—At a consultation—

Present :

The Rt. Worshipful Agent Charnock.
Mr. Francis Ellis.
Mr. Jere [miah] Peachie.

"Resolved that a letter be sent to Mr. Stanley, &c., to come from Hugli
and bring with them what Englishmen are there, that the war with the French
may be proclaimed, and also that commissions be given to all command [ers] of
ships in order to the prosecution of the same.

" In consideration that all the former buildings here are destroyed, it is resolved that such places be built as necessity requires and as cheap as possible,
viz.—

" (1) A warehouse.
" (2) A dining-room.
" (3) The Secretary's office to be repaired.
" (4) A room to sort cloth in.
" (5) A cook-room with its conveniences.
" (6) An apartment for the Company's servants.
" (7) The Agent's and Mr. Peachie's house to be repaired, which were past
standing, and a house to be built for Mr. Ellis, the latter being
totally demolished.
" (8) The guard-house.

"These to be done with mudd walls and thatched till we can get ground
whereon to build a factory.

Asad Khān, allowing the English to "contentedly continue their trade" in Bengal on payment of Rs. 3,000 yearly in lieu of all dues.[1] A large number of Armenians and Portuguese soon gathered round the English, who assigned each nation its quarter in the growing town and a piece of land to build a church on.[2]

"Resolved that 2,000 maunds of wheat and 200 maunds horse grain be bought at Malda, that being the cheapest place, and here to be provided 6,000 maunds rice and 200 maunds butter and 200 maunds oyle (and 200 maunds oyle) [*sic*] to be sent to Fort George.

[1] Stewart's *Bengal*, Appendix, p. vi.

[2] Relations were established between the English and the Armenians in 1688 through Khojah Phanoos Khalanthar, a native of Julfa in Ispahan, who entered into negotiations with the Company on behalf of the Armenian merchants in Bengal and elsewhere. The Court made a treaty and issued the following orders :—

"Whenever forty or more of the Armenian nation shall become inhabitants of any garrison cities or towns belonging to the Company in the East Indies, the said Armenians shall not only enjoy the free use and exercise of their religion, but there shall also be allotted to them a parcel of ground to erect a church thereon for worship and service of God in their own way. And that we also will, at our own charge, cause a convenient church to be built of timber, which afterwards the said Armenians may alter and build with stone or other solid materials to their own good liking. And the said Governor and Company will also allow fifty pounds per annum, during the space of seven years, for the maintenance of such priest or minister as they shall choose to officiate therein. Given under the Company's large seal, June 22nd, 1688."

Armenians were, moreover, at liberty to sail at all times in any of the Company's ships for the Southern sea, China, and Manilla, paying the same fares and duties as the English.

As a mark of their esteem for Khojah Phanoos Khalanthar, the Court of Directors conferred on him an important personal privilege, whereby they granted him the monopoly of the "Amethyst" trade in India, and after him to his children and descendants, on which he had to pay only 10 per cent. duty.

It appears from a letter of Pitt to Khojah Sarhad that Sarhad was the nephew of Khalanthar. Pitt met them several times at Mr. Ongley's at the time, I suppose, of the negotiations with the Court, *i.e.*, in 1688. (See below p. 369)

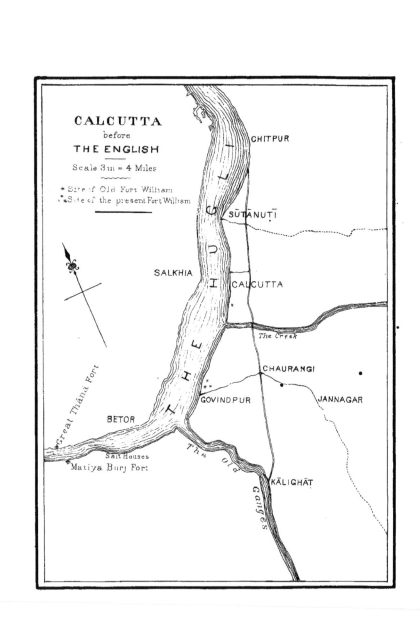

CALCUTTA
before
THE ENGLISH

Scale 3in = 4 Miles

* Site of Old Fort William
*. Site of the present Fort William

CHITPUR

SŪTĀNUTĪ

SALKHIA

CALCUTTA

The Creek

CHAURANGI

GOVINDPUR

JANNAGAR

BETOR

The Old Ganges

Salt Houses
Matiya Burj Fort

KĀLIGHĀT

Great Thānā Fort

CHAPTER IV.

THE foregoing pages will have been written in vain if they have not convinced the reader that the site of Calcutta was chosen by Charnock, not out of a mere whim, but after careful consideration. The experience of more than half a century had convinced the English that their trade in Bengal would never prosper without a fortified settlement as its centre. In 1686 they set about the discovering of a spot suitable for such a fortification. *After repeated trials Charnock came to the conclusion that the required spot was Sūtānuṭī, and here out of deference to his views and in spite of much adverse criticism, the foundation-stone of the British Empire in India was at last laid. And Charnock chose not only deliberately, but also wisely. Calcutta was the fit place for the English purposes from two distinct points of view. Not only was it strategically safe, but it was also an excellent commercial centre. The military advantages have been sufficiently dwelt upon; what were the other advantages, will appear from the history of the place previous to the arrival of the English.

The capital of British India did not, as some seem to think, spring up, like Jonah's gourd, in a single night. Calcutta, or at any rate that portion of the Hugli where Calcutta now stands, has a history, and the city is the growth of many centuries. At first the place was merely a group of villages to all appearance, not distinguishable in any way from hundreds of other riverside places. There was, however, this difference, that at the point where these villages stood in the 16th century, the stream became much shallower and less accessible to sea-going vessels. As long as the local trade was carried on in small boats, this was of little importance, and Sātgāon, on the Sarasvatī, near the modern Hugli, was the great centre of commerce. But when the Portuguese began to frequent the river, about 1530, this difference made itself felt. The foreigners did not care to risk their galliasses in the shallow waters, but sent their goods on to Sātgāon in small boats. Meanwhile their ships lay at anchor in Garden Reach, and an important market sprang up on the west side of the river at Betor, close to Sibpur. This foreign market attracted native traders and merchants to the spot, and in particular, four families of Bysacks and one of Setts, leaving the then rapidly declining city of Sātgāon, came and founded the settlement of Govindpur on the site of the present Fort William, and established the Sūtānutī market, on the north side of Calcutta, where they did business with the Portuguese. Soon after this the Portuguese themselves going higher up the river abandoned Betor, and the whole of the trade was thus transferred to the east side of the river, from Betor to Sūtānutī. Thus the settling of the chief Bengal factory at Calcutta by the English was only the third stage in the early growth of the city, the two previous stages being the establishment of a commercial centre at Betor by the Portuguese, and the transference of this trade from Betor to Sūtānutī, the market of the Setts and the Bysacks. It is the history of these first two stages that we have now to consider.

Like other cities Calcutta has its legend. Long, long ago, in the "age of truth," Daksha, one of the Hindu patriarchs, made a sacrifice to obtain a son, but he omitted to invite the god Çiva to come to it. Now Satī, the daughter of Daksha, was married to Çiva, and she was indignant that so great an insult should be offered to her divine husband, and deeply grieved that such a slight should have been passed upon him through her kindred. In vain did she expostulate with her father. "Why," she asked, " is my husband not invited ? why are no offerings to be made to him ?" "Thy husband," was the reply, " wears a neck-lace of skulls; how can he be invited to a sacrifice ?" Then, in grief and indignation, and shrieking out—"This father of mine is a villain; what profit have I then in this carcase sprung from him ?" she put an end to her life;[1] and Çiva, "drunk with loss," transfixed her dead body on the point of his trident and rushed hither and thither like a madman

---

[1] According to some authorities she burnt herself; others say that she ended her life by means of *Yoga*.

through the realms of creation. The whole world was threatened with destruction; but Vishnu, the preserver, came to the rescue. He flung his discus at the body of Satī, and broke it into pieces, which fell scattered over the earth. Every place where any of these pieces, or any of the ornaments of Satī fell, became a sanctuary, a sacred spot full of the divine spirit of Satī. The names of these spots are preserved in the *garlands of sanctuaries*. Some of them are well-known places of pilgrimage; others are obscure and forgotten; but to-day the most celebrated of them all is Calcutta, or rather Kālighāt, the spot which received the toes of the right foot of Satī, that is of Kālī.[1]

Such then appears to be the mythical origin of Calcutta, but, historically, the English capital of India has grown up out of the union of a cluster of riverside places. The three hitherto recognised members of this cluster are Calcutta, Sūtānutī, and Govindpur; but, besides these, we must reckon among the elementary constituents of the city, Chitpur and Sālkhia, the sanctuary of Kālighāt, and as the original focus of the trade, Betor, on the west bank of the river, close to the modern Sibpur. As regards two of these places, Sūtānutī and Govindpur, we are able to confidently say when and how they arose; as regards four of the others we may affirm with equal confidence that their origin is completely lost, for the villages of Sālkhia, Chitpur, Calcutta, and Betor are all mentioned by the fifteenth and sixteenth century Bengali poets, and the *parganā* of "Kalkātā" is found in earliest survey of the country; as regards the origin of Kālighāt, we can state nothing definitely, but we have a tradition which may as well be given here, for what it is worth. According to this, the founder of Kālighāt was an ascetic, named Jangal Gir, who lived somewhere about the 15th century. In those days the fashionable quarter of Calcutta, now known as Chowringee, was covered with forest and tropical vegetation, and Jangal Gir was living there as a hermit of the woods. One evening he was performing his devotions by the bank of the Adi-Gangā, which was then a great stream flowing south of Calcutta, when suddenly a bright light shone round about him,[2] and that same night, when he had gone

---

[1] Babu G. D. Bysack's *Kalighat and Calcutta*, in the *Calcutta Review*, April 1891, p. 306. Kālighāt and Calcutta are, as a matter of fact, totally different places. The names even are not connected, "Calcutta" being probably derived from some aboriginal language.

[2] This is the tradition according to Babu Surjakumar Chatterji. Babu Gour Das Bysack gives a different account.

to sleep, the goddess Kāli appeared to him in a dream, and told him that the spot was one of those holy places which had once received a portion of her severed body. The next day he dug up the ground, and proved the truth of his vision. The sacred emblems thus miraculously found were set up for worship in a small wooden house on the bank of the Adi-Gangā, but for a long while the sanctuary of Kālighāṭ was unknown and unfrequented.[1]

A poem in praise of the Serpent-goddess written by an obscure Bengali author named Bipradās in the year 1495 A.D., when Husain Shāh was the reigning sultan of Bengal, gives us our first authentic picture of Calcutta, Betor, and Kālighāṭ.[2] The hero of the story, Chānd Sadāgar, a hater of the Serpent-goddess, goes on a voyage from Bhagalpur to the sea, and so gives occasion to the poet to describe the banks of the river as he knew them in his day. Chānd Sadāgar's small fleet of seven ships after passing Rājghāṭ and Indraghāṭ, Nadiya and Ambua, comes at last to Trivenī, the famous junction of the Ganges, the Sarasvatī, and the Jamunā. Here Chānd the merchant landed on the bank to see the great city of Saptagrām. "This is the home of the seven saints. Here all the gods reside. Here is the abode of all bliss, and no sorrow or misery enters. The saints and blessed ones have no troubled thoughts, but undisturbed perform their austerities and tell their beads without intermission. Here are found the Gangā and the Jamunā, and the wide flowing Sarasvatī, and Umā Maheçvari presides over all. Overjoyed at the sight of the Ganges at Trivenī, Prince Chānd stayed his boat *Madupara* by the bank. Glad at heart, the king performed the ceremonies befitting a place of pilgrimage, and with devotion worshipped the god Maheçvari. Then, having finished his devotions, the king with joyful heart repaired to the city and compassed it round about. After staying there two days the king returned to his fleet. The boat reached Kumārhāṭ. Hugli was passed on the right, and on the left Bhātpārā. Boro stood on west bank, and on the east Kānkinārā. Rapidly they passed Mulājor and Gāñruliā on the east, while Paikpārā and Bhadreçvar remained on the west; Chāmpdānī was passed on the right and Ichāpur on the left. Often and often the king cried, *Row on! Row on!* and cherrily did they row, with Bānkibāzār on their left. Having passed Chāmpdāni, the king came into the place where

[1] G. D. Bysack, *op. cit* , pp. 311 to 313.
[2] See on article on Bipradās by Paṇḍit H. P. Çāstrī in the *Proceedings of the Asiatic Society of Bengal*, 1892, p. 1893.

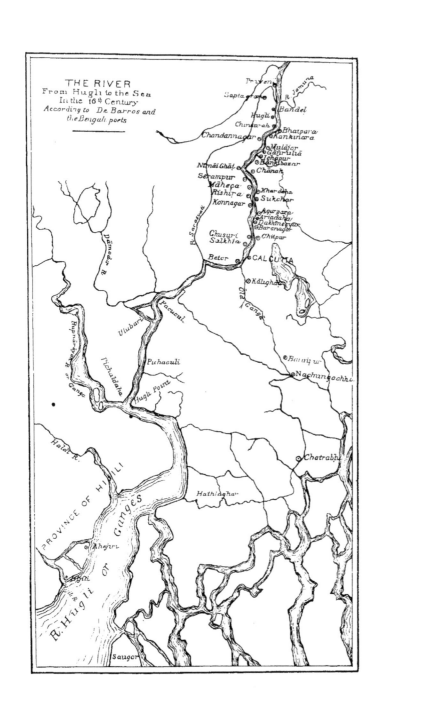

THE RIVER
From Hugli to the Sea
In the 16th Century
According to De Barros and
the Bengali ports

Prizen
Saptagram
R. Jamuna
Bandel
Hugli
Chinsurah
Bhatpara
Chandannagar
Kankinara
Mulajor
Garulia
Ichapur
Bankibazar
Nimai Ghāt
Chanak
Serampur
Māheça
Khardaha
Rishira
Sukchar
Konnagar
Agurpara
Ariadaha
Bakhmerpur
Barrnagar
Chusuri
Chitpur
Salkhia
R. Sarassti
Betor
CALCUTTA
Kālighat
Old Ganga
Damoda R.
Facucuti
Uluburi
Barug ur
Puhaculi
Nachingachhi
Hugli Point
Pichaldaha
Halai R.
Chatrabhi
Hugli or Ganga
Saugor
Hathiagha
Khejiri
PROVINCE OF HIGLI
R. Hugli or Ganges

two streams met. In order due they paid their worship to the holy place of Nimai by the water side, where they found the *Nīm* tree with the China roses blooming on it. Away they went to the flood country, leaving behind them Chānak. Thence they rowed past Rāmnān, Aknā, and Māheça. Having prostrated himself at Khardaha, the abode of the blest, the king proceeded. Again and again he cried out, *Row on ! Row on !* Rishira was passed on the right and Sukchar on the left. With delight the king sped by Konnagar. Kotrang was passed on the right and Kāmārhāti on the left; Āriadaha was on the east and Ghusuri on the west. At Chitpur the king worshipped the goddess Sarvamangalā. Day and night the boat sped on ; they never neglected their duty. Rowing by the eastern bank the great and heroic Chānd passed by Calcutta and arrived at Betor. The pious Chānd Datta worshipped Betai Chāndi, the presiding deity of Betor. In the boat the king's servants sang a song of delight. Various dainties they cooked and ate, and quickly passed Dhalandā. King Chānd having worshipped Kālikā at Kālighāṭ, passed by Churāghāṭ and Jayadhāli. Passing by Dhanasthān with great curiosity they reached Bāruipur." Here was a great whirlpool sacred to Kāli, and here the serpent-goddess put the Prince to great difficulty, raising a storm and sending an army of serpents. But overcoming all difficulties he entered the Huniā, reached Chhatrabhog, and so passing through Hatiagar made his way to the sea.

Such is the story of Bipradās, a Bengali Brahmin, who was doubtless well acquainted with the localities of which he here writes ; for the description contains indisputable marks of veracity, and, even if the author were unknown, would deserve acceptance on its own internal merits. It presents us with a picture which is in itself probable, and which agrees with what is to be learned from other sources. The time described is the end of the fifteenth century. Sātgāon, not Hugli, is the great port; lower down the river, Betor, on the right bank, is a large market town, where the voyagers stop to buy provisions and to worship the goddess Chandī. Chitpur and Calcutta are neighbouring villages which were passed just before reaching Betor. Govindpur and Sūtānuṭī do not exist. Kālighāṭ is a small sanctuary claiming just a bare notice.

With the beginning of the sixteenth century we leave the dim twilight of legend and poem and reach the broad daylight of ascertained fact. The real history of Calcutta begins with the coming of the Europeans. On the 22nd November, 1497, Vasco da Gama

K 2

doubled the Cape of Good Hope, and the Indian Ocean was opened to
Western trade. In 1510, Albuquerque took Goa. By the year
1530 the Portuguese began to frequent Bengal, and for the next
century they remained the sole and undisputed masters of its
foreign trade. It is under their commercial supremacy that the place
which we now know by the name of Calcutta first began to have
any importance, and it is to them that we are chiefly indebted
for our first reliable information about the Hugli and its markets.
The accounts of the river given us by contemporary native poets cannot
be relied on unless they are supported by writers such as De Barros or
Cæsar Frederick; but by comparing the various native and foreign
statements, we may gain a large measure of historical certainty.[1]

When the Portuguese first came to Bengal, the two great centres
of trade were Chittagong in the east, and in the west Saptagram, or
Sātgāon.[2] The former, on account of the convenience of its harbour for
shipping of every kind, was distinguished as the Great Haven, or Porto
Grande, and under favourable circumstances it might have retained
its mercantile importance; but in an evil hour it became, as we shall
see, the rendezvous of Feringi outlaws and pirates. The latter, which
has now dwindled down to an insignificant group of huts in the neighbourhood of the modern town of Hugli, had been for centuries a
great and celebrated commercial emporium, and was known as the Little
Haven, or Porto Piqueno. Hither came merchants, bringing wares to
sell, from every part of Northern India. The bazars were filled with
the busy hum of men, the river was crowded with boats. Hard by was
Trivenī, the resort of thousands of pilgrims eager to bathe in the all-
cleansing stream, for at this sacred spot, the Ganges, the Jamunā, and
the Sarasvatī mingled their waters.[3] Between Sātgāon and the sea,
the main stream of the Ganges flowed along much the same course as
does the Hugli of to-day; but it had a good many important
tributaries which have since either greatly diminished, or altogether
disappeared. The Jamunā was a considerable river, branching off to
the east at Trivenī, and so was the Sarasvatī, which, flowing on the
west of the Ganges, rejoined it lower down. Further on, at Ulubāria,
was the threefold mouth of the Dāmodar. And to the south of this
again, the Rūpnārāyaṇ entered the Ganges, or Hugli, between

---

[1] I have already dealt with the topography of the Hugli in an article in the
Journal of the Asiatic Society of Bengal, Vol. LXI, Part I, pp. 109 to 117.
[2] Van Linschoten, Hakluyt Society's edition of 1885, Vol. I, p. 95.
[3] This is told us by all the early travellers and the early Bengali poets.

Pichhalda and Hijili, or, as the Portuguese called it, "Angeli." On the left side of the Hugli, opposite the Haven of Angels, was the Rogues' River coming from Arakān, the lurking-place of the pirate devils, who hid themselves in the deep channels watching their opportunity to plunder the unwary voyager. Higher up, on the eastern side, another large tributary formed the northern boundary of the island and district of Pacuculi, and twenty miles higher still was the Adi-Gangā, then a large river leading south-eastwards to the sea, but now a poor shrunken nulla, which owes its continued existence to the enterprise of Colonel Tolly. It is by this stream that Bipradās conducts Chand to the sea, not, as some might suppose, because it was then the main channel, but rather because being shallow it was safer for small boats.[1]

So far the river was easily navigable by sea-going ships, but beyond this it was considered too shallow for any but country boats. Here then in Garden Reach was the great anchoring place of the Portuguese; and at Betor, on the western bank, near Sibpur, every year, when the ships arrived from Goa, innumerable thatched houses were erected, markets were opened, and all sorts of provisions and stores brought to the waterside. An immense number of galliasses lay at anchor in the deep water waiting, while the small budgerows made their way up the river past Barānagar, Dakshineçvar, and Agrapārā, to the Porto Piqueno at Sātgāon, and returned filled with silks and muslin, lac, sugar, and rice. During these months the banks on both sides of the river were alive with people, and a brisk trade was carried on. But no sooner was the last boat come back from Sātgāon, and her cargo safely shipped aboard the galliasses, than they set fire to the temporary houses and improvised markets of bamboo and straw, and the place vanished almost as suddenly as Aladdin's palace when carried off by the Jinnee. Away sailed the Portuguese back to Goa, leaving apparently no traces of their coming except burnt straw and ruined huts.[2] And yet a careful observer might have noticed more important results, for here we can see being formed the nucleus of the future city of Calcutta. Attracted towards Betor by the magnetism of the Portuguese trade, the various forces and influences which combined to produce the capital of India are seen assembling themselves together gradually, quietly, surely. Chitpur and Sālkhia are filling with people: markets and landing-stairs are

---

[1] See my article on the Hugli and the map of DeBarros.
[2] Cæsar Frederick in Hakluyt, edition of 1598, I, 230.

built at Kuchiṇān and Calcutta. Religious enthusiasm conspires
with commercial ardour. Betor is a sanctuary of the goddess Chandī;
and just across the river, on the banks of the Adi-Gangā, there are
preserved in a small wooden shrine the petrified toes of the great Kali,
which fell from heaven in the far-off age of truth, and which have been
discovered at this spot by a holy recluse of the woods.

To complete the picture of the river at this time, one more circumstance remains to be mentioned. The coming of the Portuguese had
its dark side. During the 16th century Chittagong was a place of
retreat for fugitives and outlaws from Goa and its dependencies. Some
of them became adventurers, and hired themselves out as soldiers to the
native powers; but the majority were neither more or less than pirates.
"These people," says Bernier,[1] "were Christians only in name. The
lives led by them in Arakān were most detestable, massacring or
poisoning one another without compunction or remorse. They scoured
the neighbouring seas in light gallies, called galliasses, entered the
numerous arms and canals of the Ganges, ravaged the islands of Lower
Bengal, and often penetrating forty or fifty leagues up the country,
surprised and carried away the entire population of villages on market
days, and at times when the inhabitants were assembled for the celebra-
tion of a marriage, or some other festival. The marauders made slaves
of their unhappy captives and burnt whatever could not be removed.
It is owing to these repeated depredations that we see so many fine
islands in the mouth of the Ganges, formerly thickly peopled, now
entirely deserted by human beings, and become the desolate receptacles
of tigers and other wild beasts."

During the 16th century we reach the second period in the history
of the growth of Calcutta. Two events happened which greatly
affected the fortunes of the river and its markets, the one being due
to the enlightened policy of Akbar, the other to the blind working
of nature. The existence of any great city standing by the waterside,
"where Ganges rolls its widest wave," must always be precarious.
For centuries perhaps it flourishes in continued wealth and importance. Then the river by some freak of nature changes its course,
and the place is soon abandoned to the jackals. Such has been the fate
of Gaur and many another once famed city. Such was the fate of
Sātgāon. From the beginning of the century its river had been gradually silting up. In the year 1540 its harbour was becoming difficult

---

[1] Amsterdam edition of 1724, 1723, Vol. I, pp. 233, 234.

of access for ships. In 1565 it was still "a reasonable fair city" abounding with all things.[1] But its commercial importance was visibly doomed. Its merchant princes, who had been wont to boast that they sat at home and grew rich while all the world came to them to trade, were one after another forced to take ship and seek elsewhere for their livelihood. The great majority removed only a short distance and settled down at Hugli. Others, more adventurous, made their way further down the river determined to profit by the growing trade of Betor. Amongst these were four families of Bysacks and one of Setts, who colonised the east bank of the Hugli, just above its junction with the Adi-Gangá, and founded the village of Govindpur. They cleared the jungle, excavated tanks, and built houses for themselves, and a shrine for their tutelary deity, Govindji, in whose honour they had named their settlement; and in a short space of time they opened, on the north side of Calcutta, a place for the sale of cloth which was soon to become celebrated as Sutánutí Hát, the Cotton Bale Market.[2] The descendants of these five pilgrim fathers have carefully preserved the genealogies of their families. They now reckon some fifteen or seventeen generations from the founders, so that their migration must have occurred towards the middle of the sixteenth century.[3]

In thus establishing themselves at Govindpur there can be no doubt that the Setts and Bysacks were attracted by the foreign trade at Betor, and we are told that the first settlers did business with the Portuguese.[4] Great then must have been their dismay, when, not long after they had settled down, they found that the Portuguese themselves were going higher up the river, having been invited by the liberality of the emperor Akbar to form a permanent settlement at Hugli. The emperor, it is said, had heard strange stories about these Western strangers who came year after year to Bengal, and was anxious to see one of their number. Accordingly, Captain Tavarez was sent up to the court at Agra, and was there received by Akbar with great favour. Permission was given him to select any spot he liked near Hugli, and

---

[1] Cæsar Frederick, in Hakluyt, I, 230.

[2] The name of this place is *not* properly spelt "Chatánatí." It is properly spelt "Sútánutí" and means Cotton-bale. "Sútánutí" is pronounced by Bengalis "Shútánutí," and this is transliterated in the old records Chutanuttee, just as "Sháh" is transliterated "Cha" and "Sháyista" "Cha-Est." The "ch" was of course meant to be pronounced soft as in *Romance languages*, the transliteration being in fact borrowed from the Portuguese.

[3] G. D. Bysack, *op. cit.*, pp. 314, 315.

[4] *Ib.*

there erect a permanent town, so that the Portuguese might settle there, and no longer come from year to year to live for a few months in temporary bamboo sheds. Full liberty was granted to build churches, and preach the gospel; but, in return for this, the emperor demanded that the Portuguese should put a stop to the outrages and barbarities committed by their piratical countrymen.[1] In pursuance of this arrangement the Portuguese established themselves at Hugli; and here Fitch[2] found them permanently settled, when he came to Bengal in 1586. But the country was full of thieves, and so Fitch was compelled to go through the wilderness, and gives us no account of the river from Hugli to the sea. In 1599 the Portuguese ventured for the first time to build a fort and a church at Hugli, and effected new settlements in Dacca, Pipli, and other places.

The character, however, of the foreign traders must have seriously hampered the whole commerce of the place, for the Portuguese were at the best dangerous people to deal with, and there was not so much difference between the merchants of Hugli and the pirates of Chittagong. "The Portuguese in Bengal," says Van Linschoten,[3] writing in 1595, "live like wild men and untamed horses. Every man doth there what he will, and every man is lord and master. They pay no regard to justice, and in this way certain Portuguese dwell among them, some here, some there, and are for the most part such as dare not stay in India [i.e., Goa] for some wickedness by them committed. Nevertheless there is great traffic used in those parts by divers ships and merchants."

But the days of the Portuguese, both for evil and for good, were rapidly drawing to a close. The merchants at Hugli had engaged to keep the gulf of Bengal clear of pirates, but they shamefully neglected their engagement. At length Shāh Jahān determined to make a terrible example of these infidel thieves, who provoked him beyond measure by the encouragement they gave to violence and robbery, and by their refusal to release the numerous slaves in their service, though they were all of them his subjects. "He first exacted, by threats or persuasion, large sums of money from the Portuguese, and when they refused to comply with his ultimate demands, he besieged and took possession of their town, and commanded that the whole population should be transferred as slaves to Agra."[4]

---

[1] Hugh Murray's *Discoveries and Travels in Asia*, II, 98, 99, edition of 1820.
[2] In Hakluyt, edition of 1598, I, 257.
[3] Hakluyt Society's edition of 1885, I, 95.
[4] Bernier, I, 236.

The fall of Hugli took place in 1632. Seven years previously the Dutch had made their way to Bengal, and they at once stepped into the place of the fallen Portuguese and established themselves at Pipli and Chinsurah. As we have seen, the English, reaching the Bay a year later, did not at first venture to dispute with the Dutch or even the Portuguese.[1] They contented themselves with Hariharapur and Balasor. It was not till the days of the great Protector Oliver that they ventured up the river to Hugli.

Meanwhile the fortunes of Calcutta were slowly but steadily rising. In the Āīn-i-Akbarī the place is noticed as a district in the government of Sātgāon, which, together with the districts of Barbakpur and Bakuya, paid into the imperial exchequer the annual sum of Rs. 23,405. Somewhere about the end of the sixteenth century forts were built at Betor and on the opposite bank to protect the upper part of the river from pirates and sea-rovers.[2] The strategic importance of the place was thus greatly increased, but its trade had now passed to the other side of the river and was in the hands of the Setts and Bysacks. In the seventeenth century Betor disappeared from history; its name changed into the village of great Thānā, its foreign market was transferred to Sūtānutī.[3] Here the Setts and Bysacks gradually built up a European connection, particularly with the English, to whom they seem to have been especially friendly. Whether the Bengali merchants ever invited the English to come and settle near them, we cannot say; but the advantages of doing so must have been manifest, and it is clear that Garden Reach was always a favourite anchorage for the Company's ships. It is therefore not surprising that Charnock, when forced to leave Hugli, should have turned almost instinctively to Sūtānutī as the place for the destined fortified settlement of the English.

[1] The Portuguese were soon restored to favour. (See above page 18). The Emperor presented them with an assignment of land at Bandel, above Hugli. They never, however, regained their old power.

[2] *Hedges' Diary*, II, 237.

[3] In the Armenian Churchyard, Calcutta, there is a tombstone dated the 11th July 1630. This has been taken as showing that the Armenians were established in Calcutta as early as 1630. The inference, however, does not seem valid. 1. The instance is isolated. No other tombstones in the churchyard are dated earlier than the eighteenth century. It is suggested that there may be other equally early tombstones beneath the floor of the church, but I do not see any reason to suppose this. 2. There is nothing to show that the stone is *in situ*. It may well have been brought to Calcutta from elsewhere. An inscribed stone has recently been found in St. John's Churchyard which must somehow have come there from China. 3. Even if the stone is *in situ*, it does not prove the existence of an Armenian colony. In India a person must be buried where he dies. If an Armenian voyager died in a ship near Calcutta, it would be necessary to bury the body there. (See *Hedges' Diary*, II, 233.)

BOOK IV.

HOW THE ENGLISH SETTLED AT CALCUTTA AND BUILT FORT WILLIAM.

CHAPTER I.

THE ENGLISH ESTABLISH THEMSELVES AT SŪTĀNUTĪ, AND BEGIN TO BUILD THEIR FORT.

1690 TO 1698.

THE foundation of Calcutta marks the beginning of the fourth period in the history of the English in Bengal, the period in which their trade is established on a fixed basis and their policy of armed industrialism definitely formulated. We shall here be concerned with the first twenty years of this settling down.

Now that the right commercial policy had been adopted and the right commercial centre found, though the old difficulties recurred, they rather helped than hindered the English purposes. They quarrelled among themselves as of old, with the result that their numbers were doubled. The rebellion of Çubha Singha was the occasion of the foundation of Fort William. Their disputes with Aurangzēb and

Murshid Quli only served to convince them of the strength of their position on the Hugli.

In spite of the favour shown them by the nabob Ibrahim, the situation of the English at Calcutta was at first miserable in the extreme. As the result of the policy pursued by William III., they found themselves immediately involved in an attack upon the commercial interests of the French,[1] and on September 5th, 1690, they were compelled to proclaim at Sūtānutī a war, of which they could only remain passive spectators, while rival fleets carried on a desultory struggle in Indian waters. Far from being fit to take part in offensive operations, they had hardly any means of defence, or even subsistence. The buildings which they had occupied two years previously had been plundered and burnt. Only three ruined mud huts remained. The rain fell incessantly day and night, forcing them to take refuge in sloops and country boats, and there wait till the commonest necessaries of life could be sent them from Hugli. Nor did their position improve for many months. So late as May 1691, we are told that "they could dispose of little, nor have they safe godowns to secure them from damage, and the truth is they live in a wild unsettled condition at Chuttinuttee, neither fortifyed houses nor goedowns, only tents, hutts and boats, with the strange charge of near 100 soldiers, guardship, &c."[2]

The many hardships he had undergone during his long sojourn in India now seem to have taken effect upon Job Charnock. His health gave way, habits of indolence crept over him, his spirit failed him, his temper grew moody and savage, the reins of government slipped from his relaxing fingers. On the 10th January 1693 he died, leaving the management of the struggling settlement to Francis Ellis, the man who ten years before had been dismissed from the service by Agent Hedges for corrupt dealings, but who had been reinstated by President Gyfford.[3]

Under him things went from bad to worse, the difficulties of the English being greatly increased by the action of Aurangzēb. The late war had shown that a naval power could best wound the Indian Empire by attacking the ships sailing between the West Coast and Arabia, and in consequence of this knowledge adventurers had established themselves in the Red Sea for the purpose of plundering the Mogul vessels. These pirates, for such they were, had nothing to

---

[1] The French had settled at Chandannagar in 1688 under an edict of Aurangzeb.
[2] *Hedges' Diary*, II, 87, 88.
[3] *Ib.*, II, 92, 93.

do with the English Company, who looked upon them as a new species
of interlopers, but Aurangzēb in his anger held all Europeans alike
responsible for the outrages thus committed, and was provoked to
suspend their privileges. Fortunately for Calcutta the English there
suffered less than might have been expected, owing to the friendly
disposition of the local authorities. Still their operations were
retarded, and their trade could only be carried on secretly.[1]

On the 12th August, Sir John Goldsborough, Commissary-General
and Chief Governor of the Company's settlements, arrived at Sūtānutī
intent upon reforming its growing abuses. The worthy Captain has
left us an unfavourable estimate of Charnock's character and a melancholy picture of the state of the things prevailing in 1693. Charnock
had contracted for an investment far in excess of what he could possibly
pay for. He had marked out no place for the factory, but allowed
every one to enclose lands, dig tanks, and build houses where and how
they pleased. "He was poisoned with the expectation of a new Company; which Mr. Braddyl upon some occasion had the confidence to tell
him; in a little time he would not be his 'worship,' but 'Mr. Charnock,'
and then he would require satisfaction of him. This affront Mr.
Charnock swallowed very patiently, as fearing it would be so, and the
law courts at Madras scared him exceedingly, so that he was afraid to
think of medling with anybody." Yet at the same time we are told
that "he loved everybody should be at difference, and supported a
serjeant that set them to duelling." The whole settlement was in the
hands of Hill, the Secretary and Captain of the soldiers, a dissolute
fellow who had opened a house for the entertainment of strangers of all
sorts, and "was allowed to keep a punch house and billiard table gratis
while others paid for it." [2]

Such is the unfavourable account which Goldsborough gives of the
father of Calcutta, and later critics have been content to echo it. Charnock's talent and services, we are told, were greatly overrated. The man
was honest, no doubt, but withal indolent and indecisive, timid and obse-
quious, with a low trick of casting the blame of his own failure upon the
shoulders of others. We must, however, remember that Goldsborough's
adverse opinion, though given in all honesty, was founded upon the
reports of detractors and the bad impression produced by the few last
years of Charnock's weakness. The charges of indolence, irresolution,

---

[1] Stewart's *Bengal*, p. 206.
[2] *Hedges' Diary*, II, 92, 93.

and disorderliness will not lie against Charnock's earlier life. He was no doubt sometimes disposed to take life easily and to side with his friends in their private quarrels, but not more so than his contemporaries. On the contrary, at the crisis of his life, when Hedges was dismissed from the agency, we see Charnock taking the right side, and preferring vigorous action and self-sacrifice. When others wished to temporise and thought of their selfish interests, he was for breaking with the native powers, and thus deliberately gave his adhesion to the policy of the man who was his private enemy. But, it is said, he was pusillanimous in the war which followed. On this point let the actual story of the struggle decide. The man who, without waiting for all his forces to assemble, attacked the Mogul troops at Hugli, seized Sūtānuṭī, held out in the face of tremendous odds at Hijili, and in the end succeeded in outwitting his opponents, would seem to deserve blame rather for rashness than for cowardice. But he did not seize Chittagong. Charnock was not a military genius; and even if he had been, it is doubtful whether Chittagong could have been taken with the forces at his disposal. In fact, Charnock had the wisdom to see that a settlement on the banks of the Hugli would be more suitable to the requirements of the English trade. Accordingly, after trying Hijili and finding it too unhealthy, he fixed upon Sūtānuṭī as the best place available. In what way he would have used the forces which reached Bengal in 1688 for the purposes of fortifying and securing his position we cannot tell. He was superseded by Captain Heath, and the opportunity never returned. The building of *Fort William was reserved for other hands. But the fact remains that Charnock, and Charnock alone, founded Calcutta. Many of his contemporaries failed to see the need of such a measure ; others saw it, but the Court would not trust them, or give them the necessary means. In Charnock the Court reposed an almost unwavering confidence. He wished to make a fortified settlement at Sūtānuṭī, and in the end the settlement was made. In short, Charnock possessed the one rare but absolutely needful virtue of disinterested honesty,—a virtue which must have been at this time difficult to retain ; a virtue which must have raised up against him scores of secret enemies; a virtue which makes us slow to believe evil of one who, in spite of all petty detraction, will always occupy a place amongst those who have the sovereign honour of being founders of states and commonwealths. Coarse and wilful he may well have been, for he seems to have been imperfectly educated ; and he passed an unprecedented length of years in Indian service. But for my part I prefer to forget the minor blemishes, and to remember only his resolute determination, his clear sighted wisdom, his honest self-devotion, and so leave him to sleep on in the heart of the city which he founded, looking for a blessed resurrection and the coming of Him by Whom alone he ought to be judged.

The worthy Commissary-General, Sir John Goldsborough, lost no time in setting about his work of reform. He found that Ellis, who had been appointed to succeed Charnock, was a man of little character or ability, his weakness being so well-known that he had lost the respect of Europeans and Natives alike. The only one of the Company's servants in Bengal who appeared to be at all fit to be chief of the settlement was Charles Eyre, of whom there was little to complain, except that he was much addicted to the country habits and customs. He was accordingly summoned to Sūtānuṭī to replace the incompetent Ellis.[1] As for Captain Hill, the Commissary-General dismissed him summarily from all but the Company's service, and ordered him to Madras.[2] The military establishment was cut down to two sergeants, two corporals, a drummer and twenty men, and the paymaster was told that the soldiers were to have only Rs. 4 each a month, which, considering the plentifulness and cheapness of food, was great wages. By this and other similar reforms Goldsborough effected a retrenchment of nearly Rs. 4,000 a year in the expenses of the settlement.[3] He also did what he could to provide proper buildings for the Company's business. He ordered a piece of ground to be inclosed with a mud wall whereon to build a factory as soon as the native government should allow of it, and he intended to add four upper rooms to the house which had been bought for the Company, so that the accountants and secretaries might be brought within a brick house with their books and papers which were then lying scattered about in thatched houses liable to catch fire every day.[4] Neither was Goldsborough pleased with the religious condition of the place. He found that the merchants and factors were marrying black wives who were Roman Catholics, and in his opinion their husbands were too much under the influence of the Augustinian Friars. Without more ado, he turned the Roman priests out of Sūtānuṭī, and pulled down their Mass house.[5] But in the midst of these plans and hopes the

---

[1] *Hedges' Diary*, II, 93.

[2] *Ib.*, II, 92.

[3] *Ib.*, II, 92, 93.

[4] *Ib.*, II, 94.

[5] Hyde's *Bengal Chaplaincy in the reigns of William and Mary and Anne, Indian Church Quarterly*, Vol. V.

worthy man was overtaken by a fatal sickness, and before November was
ended the disorders of Sūtānutī had ceased to trouble him.[1]

It is significant of the distrust with which Goldsborough regarded
Ellis and the merchants at Sūtānūtī that he took the precaution
of keeping the intended change of government a profound secret.
It was not till two months after his death, when the ships had
received their despatches and Eyre had reached Calcutta, that the orders
which had been left in the hands of Captain Robert Dorrill, were made
public and put into execution. "On the 25th January 1694, all the
Rt. Hon'ble Company's servants were summoned to appear to hear the
said orders read, which was accordingly done, and the charge of the
Agency taken from Mr. Francis Ellis and delivered to Mr. Charles
Eyre, and likewise the Rt. Hon'ble Company's papers, as bills of
debt, obligations, cash-book, &c., were demanded of said Mr. Francis
Ellis, which he promised to deliver up as soon as possible, his weakness
at present not permitting him to proceed therein any further than the
delivery up of the Rt. Hon'ble Company's cash, which amounts to
Rupees 22,748-3-8."[2] The subsequent conduct of the agent chosen
and appointed in this unusual manner, justified the expectations formed
of him. He did his best to maintain and promote the good order
which had been restored by the Commissary, and under his management
the situation of affairs in Bengal began to improve. He respected
the memory of the Father of Calcutta, whose daughter Mary he
married, and over whose remains he raised the massive octagonal
mausoleum, which still stands in St. John's Churchyard.[3]

During the year 1694 we get our last views of Tom Pitt, the
notorious interloper, just before he turns into the Governor of Madras,
and of Chaplain Evans, the merchandising parson, destined eventually
to become Bishop of Bangor. Evans had gone to Madras with
Charnock in March 1689, and while there had been dismissed for his
irregular commercial dealings. In June 1693 he had managed to
escape from the place on the Armenian Ship *St. Mark*, and reaching
Sūtānutī while Ellis was in power, had been allowed by that incompetent officer to go on to Hugli.[4] Pitt, now member of parliament for Old
Sarum, had reached Bengal on the *Seymour* in the October of 1693,

[1] *Hedges' Diary*, II, 96.

[2] *Ib.*, II, 94, 125.

[3] Hyde on the *Charnock Mausoleum, Proceedings of the Asiatic Society of
Bengal*, March 1893, pp. 79 to 81.

[4] Hyde's *First Bengal Chaplain*.

and Sir John Goldsborough had done his best to frustrate the "pyrott," and had directed Captain Dorrill [1] to arrest him and stop his trade. But it was all in vain. A little judicious bribery by the interloping Captain proved more efficacious than the most convincing arguments addressed by the Company's Commissary-General to the Nabob of Dacca. In spite of Goldsborough and his successor Eyre, the people of the country countenanced and encouraged the interlopers who had established themselves at Hugli and enjoyed every facility for buying and selling.[2] In February 1694, Parson Evans sailed from Sūtānuṭī for England on Dorrill's ship the *Charles II.*[3] The other interlopers continued their trading undisturbed. As a last resort Eyre had recourse to violence, hoping that by a display of force he might arouse the attention of the nabob and induce him to move against Pitt. For this purpose he sent up his sergeant and twenty men to Hugli with orders to arrest, not the interlopers, but a certain Messenger who had unlawfully taken possession of a house adjoining the interlopers and against whom a warrant had been received from Madras. The man and his goods were seized and a certain amount of bickering and fighting followed, but no substantial result was obtained. In the end Pitt gained the day; for the Court having received a new Charter from William III. had at this time resolved to come to terms with the interlopers, and wrote out to its agents to that effect. Wherefore at the beginning of 1695 Mr. Pitt left Bengal, returned to the Parliament and the India House in London, and though unrepentant was pardoned for the sin of interloping.[4]

The only other event worthy of record during the first year of Eyre's rule is a memorable catastrophe on the river, the loss of the *Royal James and Mary* on the fatal shoal which still bears the name. She had arrived from Sumatra in August with a cargo of behars, pepper, and redwood candy, which she took in at Madras; but coming up the river, on the 24th September, she struck upon the well-known sand, turned over immediately, broke her back, and was lost with four or five of her men. As soon as the news of the accident was received, the

---

[1] It is probable, but not absolutely certain, that this Captain Robert Dorrill, the confidant and righthand man of Sir John Goldsborough, is the same as Dorrell, the interloping Captain of the *Crown*, on which Pitt took his cargo in 1682. As Yule points out, the division between Company's servants and interlopers was not so very great, and their hostility to each other was official and perfunctory.

[2] *Hedges' Diary*, III, 18 to 22.

[3] Hydes' *First Bengal Chaplain.*

[4] *Hedges' Diary*, III, 22 to 24, 31, 32.

master of attendance, Captain Hampton, was ordered to go to the assistance of her crew with the *Mary Buoyer*, the "Europe" ship's long boats and seamen. Several boats from the shore, and as many lascars as could be spared from the different ships, were also sent off. But after many days' labour they found that they could do no more than save the guns and rigging and a small portion of her cargo. The ship herself was a total wreck, and was sold as she lay with the long boat for 1,500 rupees.[1]

The year 1695 is even less eventful than its predecessor. The diary of the year, which is extant, contains little else than accounts. Still even from these meagre resources a certain amount of information may be gleaned giving local colour to our picture of this time. The Council meets on Thursdays. It consists of four members, Charles Eyre, John Beard, Roger Braddyll, and Edward Cornell. The Secretary, who is not a member of the Council, is Jonathan White. The usual entries regularly occur. Money is invested, soldiers are sent every now and then up the river to rescue some unfortunate boat which has been stopped on its way to Calcutta, ships come and go, and the accounts of the settlement are duly brought in month by month. From them we learn that Samuel Shaw was allowed to keep a public house on payment of twenty rupees a month, and that Mrs. Domingo Ash was licensed to distil arrack. The revenues of Calcutta amount to some seventy or eighty rupees a month, being derived partly from the rent of shops, partly from fines and fees, and partly from duties levied on hemp, grain, salt, and other petty wares. The chief expenses connected with the town are for servants, most of whom are employed as police, and whose wages come to nearly seventy rupees a month. In November we have given us a list of all the Company's servants in Bengal. Besides the Council and the Doctor, Francis Simson, the establishment consists of six senior merchants, three merchants, seven factors, and four writers.[2]

Meanwhile the Court at home had been revolving great schemes for their new settlement. They directed that the revenues of the place should be carefully developed and the Madras plan gradually introduced. Interlopers were to be obstructed and driven away, but without violence. A thousand tons of saltpetre was always to be kept in store, and a large quantity of Bengal silk. For the better regulation

---

[1] *Hedges' Diary*, II, 133.
[2] *Chutanuttee Diary*, 1694-5. India Office Records.

of the settlement a court of judicature was to be established to take cognisance of disputes between the Company's servants.[1] Eyre was obliged to point out to the Court that these schemes were a little too large for the present. In obedience to their wishes the factories had been withdrawn from Dacca and Malda; the first thing to do was to re-establish them. It was premature to talk of establishing a court of judicature at Sūtānūṭī, seeing that the tenure of the English there was still precarious and the revenues only amounted to a hundred and sixty rupees a month. Nothing could be done without an imperial rescript defining the Company's right to a seat of trade, and with this purpose he had endeavoured to obtain the lease of two or three towns adjoining Sūtānuṭī at the rent of two or three thousand rupees a year.[2]

In the year 1696 events happened in Bengal which gave the English the very opportunity for which they had so long waited. A Hindu landowner in the district of Burdwan, named Çubha Singha, being dissatisfied with the government, broke out into rebellion and invited Rahīm Khān, an Afghan chief, to march from Orissa and join him in his attempt. The two malcontents, having united their forces, advanced to Burdwan, slew the rājā Krishṇa Rām in battle, and seized his family and property. His son Jagat Rāi alone escaped to Dacca, where he laid his complaints before the nabob. But his Highness was engaged with his books, and his Highness's commanders, intent upon making money, considered the matter of little importance. While they hesitated and delayed, the rebel force rapidly increased in numbers, marched upon Hugli, and took it. Still his Highness remained inactive. He could only repeat that civil war was a dreadful evil, and that the rebels, if let alone, would soon disperse. What was the use, then, of fighting? Why should he wantonly destroy the lives of God's creatures? Why could he not be left to read his *Gulistān* in peace? Such being the sentiments of the nabob, the three European settlements in Bengal perceived that they must shift for themselves, raised bodies of native troops without delay, and wrote to Dacca asking for permission to fortify their factories. The nabob in reply ordered them in general terms to defend themselves, and thus tacitly permitted the construction of the forts at Chinsura, Chandannagar, and Calcutta.

But the rebels were not suffered to have it all their own way. Seeing the whole country round him given up to plunder and hearing

---

[1] Bruce's *Annals*, III, 144.

[2] *Ib.*, III, 171 to 173. In reality the revenue was not hundred rupees a month.

daily the cries of the unhappy inhabitants who implored his protection, the Governor of the Dutch factory at Chinsurah fitted out two ships of war, anchored them opposite Hugli, and firing broadsides upon the marauders drove them out of the place. Then a blow was struck by the hand of a woman, the young daughter of the murdered Krishna Rām, whom Çubha Singha had carried off captive to Burdwan. Here was enacted once again the old, old story of man's brutality and woman's constancy. Çubha Singha, after flattering and entreating in vain, at last had recourse to violence. But the girl, driven to extremities, plucking from her dress a sharp knife, stabbed the wretch to death through his body and then plunged the point in her own heart. At Maqṣūdābād another heroic spirit showed itself in the person of Ni'amut Khān, a gallant officer in the Imperial service, who held a royal grant of lands, and who resolutely refused to espouse the cause of his master's enemies. Incensed at the opposition, Rahīm Khān, at the head of a band of Afghan horse, turned to destroy the faithful subject. As the rebels drew near the estate of Ni'amut, his nephew, well mounted and armed, advanced and challenged any of the Afghans to a single combat; but the whole body fell upon him and cut him to pieces. Then Ni'amut Khān, though dressed only in a thin vest of muslin, seized his sword, mounted his horse, and rushed forth to meet the foe. Singling out the rebel chief, he spurred up to him and struck him full on the head, but the blade fell shivered by the impenetrable helmet. With all the force of disappointed rage he flung the sword hilt at the Afghan and felled him from his horse; then dismounting he seized his enemy's dagger and tried to pierce his throat. Once more he failed. The chain armour stopped the point, and before he could stab again he was surrounded and slain.[1]

Such isolated acts of daring could do but little to check the flowing tide of anarchy and rebellion. Maqṣūdābād fell, and so too did Rajmahal and Malda. Cassimbazar yielded up itself without a struggle; the Thānā fort was closely beset. By March 1697 the Afghan held the whole of the land west of the Ganges.[2]

When the emperor learnt of these events through the ordinary public news-letter, his surprise and indignation were unbounded. He instantly recalled Ibrahīm Khān and appointed his grandson, 'Aẓīmu-sh-Shān, in his stead. In the meantime he ordered the nabob's son Zabardast Khān to take the field and extirpate the rebels. The

---

[1] Stewart's *Bengal*, pp. 207 to 209.
[2] *Ib.*, p. 210.

young general, who had beheld with impatience the apathy of his father, was nothing loth.[1] During the month of April he quickly got together his forces at Dacca and advanced to meet Rahīm Khān on the river Bhagwāngolā. His cavalry, sent on in advance, speedily recovered Rajmahal and Malda. In May, the whole army being come up with the rebels, he attacked them by land and by river, cannonaded them, routed them, and plundered their camp. Then, joined on all sides by the inhabitants, who had shaken off their fear of the enemy, he pursued the Afghans to Burdwan, and was hunting them from place to place, when he received an order from 'Aẕīmu-sh-Shān commanding him to stay further movements till the prince himself should arrive. Understanding the jealousy which prompted this order, Zabardast Khān, after paying his respects to the grandson of the emperor, withdrew from Bengal with his father. The prince, left to himself, after wasting much time in foolish negotiation, and so losing an envoy and his escort through treachery, had the glory of seeing an Arab officer throw Rahīm Khān from his horse and cut off his head. All that was left for 'Aẕīmu-sh-Shān to do was to distribute honours to his lieutenants and alms to the poor, and thank God he was rid of a knave.[2]

The part played by the English at Calcutta in these events was subordinate, but not unimportant. On the 23rd December 1696, finding that the rebels, who occupied the opposite bank of the river, were growing "abusive," they ordered the *Diamond* to ride at anchor off Sūtānutī Point and keep them from crossing the stream. They also had lent the *Thomas* to the governor of the Thānā fort to lie off it as a guardship. On receiving full instructions from Madras, they set to work to build walls and bastions round their factory, and in January 1697, reported that they were employed in fortifying themselves, but wanted proper guns for the points, and desired the people at Madras to send at least ten guns for present use. At the beginning of April, a neighbouring rajah secretly deposited the sum of forty-eight thousand rupees with the agent for safe custody, and a week or two afterwards the late governor of Hugli honoured Calcutta with a visit. In May, learning that the rebels were all dispersed, they got rid of the band of fifty native gunners which they had raised, but continued building their fort, and substituted a structure of brick and mud for the old thatched house which used to contain the Company's stores and

---

[1] Stewart's *Bengal*, p. 210.
[2] *Ib.*, pp. 211, 213, 214, 215, 216, 217.

provisions. In June they sent Khojah Sarhad, an influential Armenian merchant, with a present to the camp of Zabardast Khān to apply for help against interlopers, and to ask that the property of the English at Rajmahal and Malda, which had been recovered from the rebels, should be restored to its original owners.[1]

These negotiations produced very little result. Zabardast Khān refused to restore any of the goods, and the English had to turn to 'Aẓīmu-sh-Shān. Towards the end of the year Khojah Sarhad,[2] together with Mr. Stanley and Mr. Walsh, appeared in the camp of the Prince at Burdwan for the purpose of advocating the English claims. Here they met with better success. 'Aẓīmu-sh-Shān was lazy and covetous. He was ready to concede anything for a sufficient bribe. Accordingly, in July 1698, for the sum of sixteen thousand rupees, the English procured letters patent from the Prince allowing them to purchase from the existing holders the right of renting the three villages of Calcutta, Sūtānaṭī, and Govindpur. The grant, after some delay in order that it might be countersigned by the Treasurer, was carried into execution, and the security of Calcutta, which began with the permission to build a fort, was now completely assured, to the great satisfaction and credit of Eyre, under whose auspices these advantages had been gained. Nearly two years later the Prince also renewed the permission which the English had to trade free of custom, but at that time Eyre was no longer agent. His five years of rule came to an end on the 1st February 1699, when he delivered over charge to John Beard and departed for England.[3]

---

[1] *Chutanuttee Diary* for 1696-7. India Office Records.
[2] *Ib.*, 1696-7.
[3] Stewart's *Bengal*, p. 215.

CHAPTER II.

THE RIVAL COMPANIES,

1698 TO 1700.

THE Court had hardly succeeded in overcoming its various difficulties in India and in placing the trade in Bengal upon a sure footing,
when it found itself called upon to encounter a new danger in the
shape of a rival company. For years had they contended with all
their might and by every means in their power against interlopers.
Before the revolution they had invoked the authority of the Crown;
after the accession of William III. they applied to Parliament to
authorise their rights and privileges by a special Act. But for various
reasons Parliament demurred to their requests. Its attention was
occupied with the war against France. It wanted to raise money by a
Land Bank. The Court, therefore, understanding that the Government
were in urgent need of money offered to advance seven hundred thousand pounds, at four per cent. interest for the public service, provided
that their Charter should be confirmed by Act of Parliament, and
the Indian trade legally settled on them. In opposition to them, a
number of private merchants applied to Parliament against the old
Company's monopoly, and, on condition that they should have the
exclusive trade to India vested in them without being obliged to trade

on a Joint Stock, proposed to advance the nation no less than two millions, at eight per cent. interest. The larger offer carried the day. In spite of all the efforts of the old Company an Act was passed by the Legislature in the year 1698, " for raising a sum not exceeding two millions, upon a fund, for payment of annuities after the rate of eight pounds per cent., and for settling the trade to the East Indies."[1] On the 3rd September the King, in accordance with the provisions of Act, incorporated the subscribers to these two millions by a Royal Charter under the name of the *General Society trading to the East Indies*.[2] Two days afterwards it became necessary to incorporate the majority of the subscribers by another charter to be one exclusive company trading on a Joint Stock under the name of the *English Company trading to the East Indies*.[3] The old Company were now obliged to assume a less popular title, and henceforth were to be known as the *London Company*. They were to be allowed to trade to India till the 29th September 1701, but no longer.[4] But, though the voice of authority had thus complacently decided the speedy extinction of the London Company, the commercial spirit of the elder association, far from being depressed, was actually refreshed and invigorated.[5] The puny bantling of the Parliament was only kept alive with the greatest difficulty. Before the year had closed the English Company had quite lost confidence in their own speculation, and in March 1699 they actually proposed a coalition, which, however, was rejected as inadmissible by the London Company.[6] Disappointed in this project, as a last resort, they obtained permission from the King to send Sir William Norris as his ambassador to the Great Mogul, with the object, it would seem, of securing for themselves the favour of the Indian Government, or at any rate doing what they could to ruin their rivals.[7]

The old Company was accustomed to deal with Indian princes through commercial agents. Only once in the early days of its history had it made use of the services of a royal ambassador. In the time of James I., Sir Thomas Roe had spent many weary years at the Court of Jahāngīr trying to promote and safeguard his country's interests, and had returned disgusted at the smallness of the results achieved.

---

[1] *Bruce's Annals*, III, 252 to 255.
[2] *Ib.*, III, 257.
[3] *Ib.*, III, 258.
[4] *Ib.* III, 258.
[5] *Ib.*, III, 256.
[6] *Ib.*, III, 260.
[7] *Ib.*, III, 261.

" I had words enough," he remarked, " but such delays in effect that I am weary of flatteries as of ill-usage." [1] The English Company, however, was determined to avoid what it considered to be the error of the other, and to deal with Aurungzēb, not through paltry native attorneys, but through the dignified medium of an envoy duly accredited by William III.

But the experiences of Norris were no better than those of Sir Thomas Roe: rather worse. Arriving on the east coast of India at the end of 1699,[2] he spent a whole year fruitlessly in trying to make his way into the interior.[3] In December 1700, he reached Surat from Masulipatam, and by means of large bribes, managed to secure a public entry in state.[4] At the beginning of the next year, on the 26th January, he set out on his journey to the Mogul's camp with a retinue of sixty Europeans and three hundred natives. On the way he passed through Burhānpūr, where the Imperial vizier was staying, and desired to pay him a visit. But as the ambassador's dignity would not allow him to go without his drums and trumpets, and the vizier's dignity would not allow of his reception with these ceremonies, the meeting never took place.[5] In April he reached the court, and went to his audience with Aurungzēb in a procession such as his soul loved. First came the presents duly guarded, big carts with brass artillery, small carts with broadcloth, glassware and horses. These were followed by a varied display of ambassadorial pomp, the Union Jack, red flags, white flags, and blue flags, crests and coats of arms, state horses and state palanquins, music, trumpets, and kettle-drums, servants, soldiers and officers. Immediately in front of his Excellency's embroidered palanquin rode his Excellency's master of the horse, carrying the sword of state pointed up. On each side were two pages, and behind came his Excellency's two secretaries and his Excellency's treasurer, wearing a golden key.[6] The court of Aurungzēb were very glad, indeed, to hear of the rival company and to welcome such a rare bird as a royal ambassador ; and having in their usual way granted him all his requests and fed him fat with vain hopes, they proceeded to pluck his feathers. Just as the Emperor had given orders to make out

---

[1] *Hedges' Diary*, III, 173.
[2] Bruce's *Annals*, III, 321.
[3] *Ib.*, III, 345, 346, 374, 395 to 401.
[4] *Ib.*, III, 374, 375.
[5] *Ib.*, III, 404 to 406.
[6] *Ib.*, III, 462 to 464.

the necessary grants and patents, difficulties arose as to matters of detail. Officers sprang up who raised objections at every turn and expected to be bribed. His Excellency now awoke to the fact that the king, lords, and commons of England were held very cheap in India; that the favours of the Mogul, like those of parliament, would go to the men who offered most; and that as there were two companies the bidding was expected to be good.[1] Out of funds and out of temper the ambassador left the Court to return to Surat, but was some months placed by the vizier under arrest. It was not till the middle of 1702 that he could set sail for his native land, which, however, he was never to see again. The unfortunate man was seized with dysentery while on the voyage, and died at St. Helena.[2]

About the same time as Sir William Norris was started on his bootless errand to the Mogul, Sir Edward Littleton was sent out to be the New Company's president and agent in the Bay. The members nominated for his Council were Richard Trenchfield, Robert Hedges, and George Gay. Of this party three at least were discharged servants of the old Company. Littleton himself had first come to India as a factor in 1671 and had been dismissed for unfaithfulness by an order of the Court dated 25th January 1682.[3] And now rehabilitated, knighted, and armed by the King with consular powers, he arrived in July, 1699, at Balasor, from whence on the 29th he despatched to Agent Beard, and the Council at Calcutta, a letter in which threats and flattery are most curiously combined.

"The Generall herewith to your Self and those in Councill Employ or Commission with you is not in the least from any disrespect to your Self, for whom I have no mean esteem, nor to any of the rest who are known to mee only by name or employ, but intirely to represent unto you the true state of the case, being it may be supposed you have not had any full account thereof from your employers except by the *Antelope*, this affair of the Consulship being transacted, as I take it chiefly after the departure of your Ships, and to prevent any unhappy occurrence which might otherwise perhaps succeed, nor is there any design in the least, therein to embarrasse or obstruct the currency of your affaires, as in practice you will find, nor create any difference between us, but rather a firmer and stricter Friendship and correspondence, and will certainly prove so if no failure on your part

---

[1] Bruce's *Annals*, III, 464 to 468.
[2] *Ib.*, III, 469 to 473.
[3] *Hedges' Diary*, II, 205 .

which I will not suspect. I must confess an absolute ignorance of your Employers' orders or designes, but as a reall ffriend I do take upon mee to advise you that whereas upon the arrivall of Ships particular there hath been frequently applications made to the Government against them, and odious calumnies cast upon them, which probably may have caus'd recriminations, and have all tended not only the National prejudice, but even to [that of] Christianity itself. Wee are now come on Parliamentary Sanction, the greatest Authority our Nation affords, so may not expect any Such usage, however think it not amiss that you are warned thereof for the resentment of our Employers for Such Actions may be Such. as may cause theend to prove bitter, and possibly fatall to the Actors, nor can you think but wee shall be as vegorous on our part as you Shall be Vehement on yours nor will our hands wax weaker but Stronger Dayly.

The affaires of the Durbar with respect to the English Interest will center in the Consull, so to be foreborne by all others, also all Passes for Ships, so that you will do well to let Such know thereof least they bring them Selves under some disappointment.

You must needs know that at our first coming wee are to seek for needful things, especially Small vessels and Pilots. I am not for withdrawing any Mens Servants against their Masters consent, but yet rather our own Countrymen doe reap the benefit then aliens. So that if you think not fit to Spare any your Self yet it may not be imprudent not to hinder any others, but should be willing thereto. Know not how to Speak so plain in this matter as otherwise I might, being a stranger to your circumstances and directions, but am well assured nothing will be done of service to our Employers by any persons, but will Surely meet with very gratefull acceptance and remuneration.

I ad not more. Let not what is offered with the Right hand be received with the left." [1]

Had Sir Edward contented himself with claiming a right to carry on trade in Bengal and to open up negotiations with the Indian Government, he would not in all probability have met with any serious opposition from the Calcutta Council, and might have even been allowed to use the pilots and other necessaries which he required. But he had ordered them to suspend all applications to the Mogul and forbear issuing passes for their goods. And this from a parvenu

---

[1] *Hedges' Diary*, II, 206, 207. With reference to the concluding sentence, I may note that in India it is insulting to offer or take with the left hand.

without status or power to an agent of long experience who had a
defined position in the eyes of the natives, and whose authority to
exempt his Company's goods from all duties had been established by
a special imperial decree! Beard might well have been angry, but he
replied temperately, firmly, loyally. He had his duty to his own
masters. He should defend their rights and character, and maintain
their privileges which had been granted them by the English King
and the Great Mogul, and which even the omnipotent Parliament had
allowed to continue till 1701. The Calcutta Council had a better
position, and it was more proper for them to manage their master's
affairs than to address a stranger who would have to pay for his
footing before he could do anything. Beard, therefore, refused to
recognise the authority of the Consul to represent or control the
proceedings of the London Company, and turned a deaf ear to his
requisitions.[1] Sir Edward Littleton being thus left to his own devices
at Hugli, could do nothing but write an angry letter of complaint
to the Duke of Shrewsbury. The old company would take no notice
of His Gracious Majesty's character and would own no authority but
what came from their masters. "Upon my coming up to this place
I passed by their chiefe factory, and having His Majesty's flagg
at the top of our mast they were soe far from taking notice thereof
in the least that tho' it's usual for them to spread their colours
on the least vessels passing by, Yett now in meere affront to the
Consular dignity they not only forebore to spread any colours
themselves, but prevented all shipps of English there, of which there
were diverse, from taking any notice of the king's flagg always usual
heretofore, and they having at that time a servant of the new Company
in their factory, on his complaint I sent two of my company to demand
his liberty, which was not only refused, but on the 20th September,
being three days after, fixes a pestilent paper upon the gate of the
factory of very trayterous import,[2] a true copy whereof goes herewith
by which your Highness will perceive what sort of subjects the
English in the old Companies service are, and his Majesty will also
see how much his authority is here villified by those to whom on many
accounts he had been exceeding gracious, even to admiration."[3]

---

[1] *Hedges' Diary*, II, 208. Also Bruce's *Annals*, III, 323, 324.

[2] It enjoined all the English under the protection of the Calcutta Council
to refuse obedience to any order of Littleton.

[3] *Hedges' Diary*, II, 207, 208. Also Bruce's *Annals*, III, 349.

The weariness with which we follow the miserable details of the squabbles between the agents of the old and new Companies is at this time relieved by a comic incident in the history of Calcutta. When Mr. Charles Eyre returned home in 1699, the Court seems to have been much impressed with the value of his services and with the importance of the rights secured by the Prince's grant. The worthy agent was made a knight, and long consultations were held between him and his honourable masters as to what system of administration should be devised to suit the improved state of their possessions. The result of these deliberations was announced with great solemnity in a letter dated 20th December 1699. Beard and the Council at Calcutta were informed that Sir Charles Eyre had now recovered a good state of health, and "out of a just but unusual gratitude" had offered his services again in the Bay. Bengal was, therefore, constituted a separate Presidency, and Sir Charles Eyre its first President. Besides him there were to be four members of Council; namely, John Beard, second, and accountant; Nathaniel Halsey, third, and warehouse-keeper; Jonathan White, fourth, and purser marine; Ralph Sheldon, fifth, and receiver of revenues. The President was empowered to fill up vacancies, subject to the approbation of the Court, promotion being by seniority; and no servant was to be dismissed except by an order of the Court. Taxes were to be imposed and levied at Fort William according to the Madras system. Eyre was also instructed to enlarge and complete the fortifications begun in 1696, or, if he thought good, he might construct a new fort in the shape of a pentagon. If that were not possible, then the present factory was to be made strong, particularly in its timbers. At the angles additional buildings like warehouses were to be erected to serve as bastions; the windows might be used as loop-holes. In compliment to his Majesty the fort was to be called Fort William. With enhanced dignity Sir Charles Eyre arrived in Bengal and resumed office on the 26th May 1700. What steps he took to carry out his commission it is impossible to say owing to a curious hiatus in the records. But it seems that he took little interest in brick fortresses, whether four-cornered or five-cornered, and cared only for the three-cornered fortress of a lady's heart. He was "seized with a strange distemper," and on the 7th January 1701 started for Old England, where, we are told, he "arrived well, after a troubled stormy voyage, to his fair mistress to whom he was more welcome than to the company, who at first hotly resented his disappointing them of his service, but it soon cooled to kindness, having

little to say to him. Soon after which he married, and much transported in the sweet embraces of his mistress." [1]

Meanwhile Littleton's position at Hugli was becoming extremely
embarrassed. His authority was scouted by the majority of the
English in Bengal. Two of his council as well as a number of young
men in the New Company's service had fallen victims to the climate.
The greater portion of his military guard had died or deserted. He
had no pilots acquainted with the soundings of the Ganges. It was not
till the 20th January 1700, after paying a considerable sum of money
to the Indian Government, that he was permitted to trade, and even
then the grant was only for a time and had to be renewed at a ruinous
cost. In vain did he write to Norris, urging him to conclude his negotiations with the Mogul and procure an Imperial rescript without delay.
The Embassy, as has been seen, was abortive, and no rescript ever
came. [2]

The English Company had had its day. The fortunes of the elder
Company had been all this while steadily improving at home and abroad.
It had been continued as a corporation by act of parliament [3] in 1700;
and two years later the differences between it and the new creation
were settled by an amicable agreement which led to the eventual union
of the two. [4]

---

[1] *Hedges' Diary*, II, 134 to 136. Also Bruce's *Annals*, III, 300 to 303.
[2] Bruce's *Annals*, III, 349, 399, 415 to 418.
[3] *Ib.*, III, 294, 422 to 426.
[4] 11th April 1702.

CHAPTER III.

1701 TO 1703.

THE man who played the chief part in the history of Calcutta
during the first three or four years of the eighteenth century was
" our good and faithful servant" John Beard. Nominated writer on
the 5th October 1681, he accompanied his father to India on board the
Defence with Governor Hedges.[1] He shared the perils of the struggle
between the English and the Mogul, and was one of the Bengal Council
at the time of their expulsion[2] and sojourn at Madras. After the
foundation of Calcutta he sat as second on the Council, of which
Charles Eyre was the Chief. It seems to have been about this time

---

[1] He arrived in India, 17th July 1682.
[2] On the 26th November, 1688, he volunteered to serve under Heath in
the attack on Balasor (Long's *Notice*, p. 14).

he married his wife Mary,[1] by whom he had two children, Charles and Elizabeth. When Eyre went home for the first time in 1699, Beard succeeded to the Agency in Bengal; but he had not held office for fourteen months, when, as has been already said, he was superseded by Eyre. Many men would have refused to descend to the second place after having filled the highest; but Beard on this occasion showed his common-sense and self-control by resolving to serve on under Eyre. Accordingly, when seven months later that home-sick lover hurried off to England on the plea of ill-health, Beard again ruled in Calcutta, this time with the enlarged powers of an independent President.

During his first government Beard had had to deal with troubles caused by Sir Edward Littleton and his lofty pretensions, which he had resisted with spirit and propriety; he now had to meet a series of attacks on the English by the native powers.[2] For many years past Aurangzēb had been greatly annoyed by the depredations of pirates who harassed the trade of the eastern seas and the pilgrims on their way from Surat to Mecca. He had often suspected that the English were really responsible for these outrages; and when he found the old and the new Companies accusing each other of piracy, his suspicions seemed to be confirmed. At any rate, he determined to teach them a lesson. At the end of the year 1701, a proclamation was issued ordering the arrest of all Europeans in India. "Inasmuch as the English and other Europeans," it ran, "notwithstanding that they have entered into a contract to defend our subjects from piracies, have seized and plundered Musalman ships, therefore we have written to all governors and *dīwāns* that all manner of trade be interdicted with those nations throughout our dominions, and that you seize on all their effects, wherever they can be found, and take them carefully in your possession, sending an inventory thereof to us. And it is likewise further ordered that you confine their persons, but not to close imprisonment."[3] In consequence of these orders, Dāūd Khān blockaded

---

[1] The maiden name of Mrs. Beard is uncertain. Beard is called the brother of John Pitt, Consul at Masulipatam. It appears from the register of marriages and burials at Madras that John Pitt married twice—on the 5th August 1686 Elizabeth Northey, who was buried on the 7th February 1689; and on August 15th Sarah Wavell. A copy of the will of Sarah Pitt is in the British Museum (Egerton MSS., 1971), from which it seems clear that she was not in any way connected with John Beard. But perhaps Elizabeth Northey was. The Madras register records the burial of Mrs. Elizabeth Ivory on the 2nd December 1702. The Pitt correspondence shows that this Elizabeth Ivory was probably Beard's mother-in-law. She may have married more than once.

[2] *Hedges' Diary*, II, 104, 105.

[3] Wheeler's *Madras in the Olden Time*. Edition of 1882, p. 210.

Madras from February to May 1702. In Bengal, the servants of the old Company at Patna, Rajmahal, and Cassimbazar were, in February 1702, seized with all their effects. On the 30th March the execution of the order was extended to all European factories. To the new Company the blow was severe. They had neither anticipated it nor prepared to meet it. At one stroke they lost no less than Rs. 62,000, and instant ruin stared them in the face. But the injury done to the old Company was not great. The bulk of their wealth was safe in Calcutta, and the native government soon grew tired of keeping in confinement a few English merchants from whom nothing could be extorted.[1]

Beard displayed firmness and good sense all through these troubles. He knew how to conciliate and also how to resist. In 1700, when the governor of Hugli had threatened to send a judge to Calcutta to administer justice amongst the natives living under the protection of the English flag, Beard by a bribe had induced 'Azīmu-sh-Shān to forbid it.[2] In 1702 the Mogul officer ordered the Company's goods at Calcutta to be seized. But Beard had now made additions to Fort William strong enough to ward off any attack made by a Bengali power, and he determined that if he was to spend money he would rather spend it in powder and shot than "to be always giving to every little rascal" who thought he could do some injury to the English. He mounted additional guns, drafted men from the ships to work them, and so raised the number of the garrison to a hundred and twenty men.[3] This show of resistance daunted the governor, and in June the Prince again interfered in favour of the English. Beard had, however, to repeat his lesson later on in the same year. A present of five thousand rupees given to the governor to allow the transit of the Company's goods incited him to make further exorbitant demands. Beard stopped all the Mogul's ships going to Surat and Persia for nine days, and the governor, fearing to offend the Emperor, gave way. The treasurer was treated with the same spirit. This official offered to sell his favours for twenty thousand rupees, an offer which Beard peremptorily rejected.[4]

This was the last opportunity given to Beard to show his mettle. The year 1703 was mainly occupied in making arrangements for duly carrying out the union of the two Companies. A member of

---

[1] *Hedges' Diary*, II, 105. Bruce's *Annals*, III, 506.
[2] Stewart's *Bengal*, 218.
[3] *Hedges' Diary*, II, 106, 107.
[4] Bruce's *Annals*, III, 444, 445, 506, 507.

M

Counoil and two factors of each Company made inventories of their respective dead stocks, and balanced up the accounts. To prevent any dispute occurring at the commencement of the united trade, the office of President was to be temporarily abolished. Beard and Littleton were to be placed on a dignified shelf, and directed to wind up their masters' separate affairs, while the business of the united trade was to be carried on by a Council of the four senior servants of each Company.[1]

In the year 1704 these arrangements were completed. The servants of the English Company, with their effects, were all placed in security within the walls of Fort William, and Calcutta rejoiced in the government of no less than three Councils. In the first place there was the Council for the management of the separate affairs of the old London Company, at the head of which was John Beard. Then there was the Council for the separate affairs of the new English Company, which left Hugli for Calcuttta in May, and at the head of which was Sir Edward Littleton. And lastly there was the Establishment Council for the management of all the United Company's affairs in Bengal. This last body was constituted as follows :—Mr. Robert Hedges and Mr. Ralph Sheldon, cash keepers; Mr. Winder, store keeper, Mr. Russel, export warehouse keeper ; Mr. Nightingale, import warehouse keeper, Mr. Redshaw, charges general keeper, or bakhshī; Mr. Bowcher, zamīndār, to collect the rents and keep the three native towns in order; and Mr. Pattle, secretary. It was presided over in alternate weeks by Hedges and Sheldon, and on account of its incessant quarrels and disputes soon became the laughing-stock of all India.[2] The "rotation government," as it was called, came into power on the 1st of February. "At ten o'clock in the morning," says the consultation book of the new Council, "being the time appointed by President Beard to deliver possession of the garrison and dead stock, etc., to us, we waited on him accordingly, and being met in the old Company's consultation room, all the Company's servants and the free inhabitants of Calcutta being present, President Beard wished us joy of our new trust. But his long indisposition having weakened and disabled him from speaking, he desired Mr. Sheldon to make a public declaration that in pursuance of the order from the Court of Committee, and in conformity to the Deed of Union and Quinquepartite Indenture, he does now resign the fort and

---

[1] *Hedges' Diary*, II, 105, 106, 208, 209.
[2] *Summaries*, §§ 13, 46.

all the dead stocks, together with all the lands and privileges, to us, the established Council for the management of all the United Company's affairs in Bengal." President Beard then received the keys of the fort from the Ensign, the chief of the guard, and gave them to the new Council, by whom they were given back again to the Ensign to keep. After the ceremony all the English in Calcutta were entertained at the expense of the Council. Then all the members of the Council except two proceeded to Hugli to take possession of the dead stock there.[1]

The old Company's President and servants were forced to remove from the fort and establish themselves in hired houses in the town.[2] Their Council day was altered to Tuesday so as not to clash with the meetings of the United Trade Council, which was now the head Council in Calcutta.[3] Poor old President Beard did not long survive the indignity of being thus a second time superseded in the government of the town for which he had done so much. His bodily infirmities steadily increased. At the end of the year he determined to go on a voyage to Madras for the benefit of his health.[4] Here he stayed during the first six months of 1705 without finding any alleviation. He was also troubled about money matters. "He has been telling me," writes Pitt, "of the unkindness of the old Company in refusing their bills-of-exchange, and has requested my writing in his behalf." [5] Death, however, soon came to end his troubles. On the 7th July, as the Madras records tell us, "John Beard, Esq., President for the old Company's affairs at Bengal, from whence he came sick, and has ever since continued so, did this afternoon depart this life at St. Thomas' Mount." On the evening of the 15th his body was buried at Fort St. George by the Chaplain, James Wendey. "Governor Pitt and the Council, with all the inhabitants and a company of soldiers, accompanied the corpse to the burying place, when the soldiers fired three volleys, and afterwards forty great guns were discharged." [6]

It is sad to think that one who had long served his masters with so much ability and loyalty should have been thus cast aside by them when no longer of any use, and left to die amidst pecuniary embarrassments. But the end of his rival was far more sad, because dishonourable. From the very first Littleton seems to have neglected the

---

[1] *Summaries*, § 47.
[2] *Ib.*, §§ 19, 35.
[3] *Ib.*, § 14.
[4] *Ib.*, §§ 41, 133.
[5] *Hedges' Diary*, II, 106.
[6] See Madras Consultation Books and the Burial Register at Madras.

Company's business, and before long he stooped to dishonesty. He kept
back the accounts of his transactions in order to conceal their nature,
and invested a considerable amount of the Company's capital in specu-
lations of his own by means of advances made nominally to natives
who were really his own creatures and agents. His unfaithful management aroused the suspicions of his colleagues, amongst whom was
Robert Hedges, formerly in the employ of the old Company in the
time of his uncle, Sir William, but now serving the new Company as
second in the council at Hugli. In April 1702, Hedges, with the
help of Winder, the third in the Council, made efforts to restore order
and put an end to the growing defalcations.[1] But in the end Littleton
wore out the patience both of his Council and of his employers, from
whom his proceedings could not be kept secret. At the beginning of
the year 1704, the Court wrote secretly to Hedges and the rest of the
Council, directing them to "use all fair means imaginable to induce
Sir Edward Littleton to come to a just accommodation of their affairs
transacted by him." They were not for putting any real hardship on
him or having any public difference with him, but they aimed at a just
and true account of their own. If, however, Sir Edward should kick at
these measures and obstruct their proceedings, they were to produce the
enclosed letter marked "A," by which Littleton's commission was
revoked and annulled, and his authority taken from him.[2] These
instructions reached Hedges and his colleagues in the middle of 1704
when they had removed to Calcutta, and as members of the Council
of eight were engaged in the business of the united trade. Their
interest in the affairs of the defunct English Company was on the
wane, and Hedges in particular was unwilling to deprive its chief of
the empty name of President, for he knew if he did so he would be
pushed into Littleton's place and would lose his seat in the United
Council over which he now presided on alternate weeks. They therefore
gladly caught at the repeated cautions given in the letter to act gently
and avoid a scandal, and at the fact that Sir Edward had no visible
effects to discharge his liabilities, and resolved on these grounds to
suspend action and await further orders.[3] Next year all pretext of
delay was taken from them. Peremptory orders were given to
produce letter "A," Littleton was stripped of his powers, and the
consequence was that Hedges lost his seat on the United Council and

---

[1] *Hedges' Diary*, II, 217.
[2] *Ib.*, II, 213.
[3] *Ib.*, II, 216.

had to content himself with the *otium cum dignitate* of President of
the Council for the separate affairs of the English Company.[1] The
disgraced man, soured in his mind, isolated and hopelessly involved in
his circumstances, was left to drag out a miserable existence in Calcutta,
writing scurrilous letters, and heaping up ribald abuse upon those whom
he regarded as the authors of his ruin. He died suddenly on 24th
October 1707, after five days illness, of fever, without having done anything to arrange his affairs. In the famous award of Lord Godolphin
the name of the unhappy Sir Edward Littleton " was dishonourably
enshrined, as his debt of Rs. 80,437-8 due to the Company he served
was adjudged to remain to the English Company on their Additional
Stock, and not to be added to their United Stock as a debt in the East
Indies."[2]

---

[1] *Hedges' Diary*, II, 215.
[2] *Ib.*, II, 218 to 222; and *Summaries*, §§ 219, 222, 279.

CHAPTER IV.

THE EARLY DAYS OF THE ROTATION GOVERNMENT AND ITS EFFORTS TO COME
TO TERMS WITH THE LOCAL RULERS.

1704 TO 1707.

*The clearest account of situation and prospects of the Rotation
Government on assuming office is to be found in the letters despatched
by Beard to his masters in the year 1702. In these a strong contrast
is drawn between the position of the old Company and that of the new.
The one had received Imperial patents exempting it from all imports,
and allowing it to issue passes for the free transport of its goods. The
other had no such privileges, but was under a security bond to pay
customs, and already owed three years' payment. In which position
would the United Company stand? No doubt it would claim all the
privileges and immunities of the London merchants; but would these
privileges be conceded? Might not the Mogul choose to regard it as
the successor of the recent establishment and hold it responsible for the
English Company's debts? Or, at any rate, might he not very well
demand that it should take out fresh patents at the cost of further
donations to the Imperial exchequer and the local officers? The position
of the English had been seriously imperilled by the rivalry of the
two Companies, and Beard was sure that the opportunity now afforded

to the Mogul Government to squeeze more money out of them was far too good to be missed. He foresaw years of tedious negotiation, and he advised his masters to put little faith in Eastern diplomacy. If they wished to gain any substantial advantages, they must have recourse to stronger measures. Bitter experience had stamped this lesson on his mind; that in dealing with an Indian government "force and a strong fortification were better than an ambassador." [1]

In February 1703 Governor Pitt wrote from Madras to the Court at home in much the same strain about the Mogul officials :—" You will see they have a great mind to quarrel with us again, and it is most certain that the Moors will never let your trade run on quietly, as formerly, till they are well beaten. Besides, your having suffered your servants to be treated after that most ignominious manner at Surat for many years past has encouraged them to attempt the like in all your settlements, and I hear in Bengal that they *chawbuck* Englishmen in their public *darbars*, which formerly they never presumed to do, and the *junkaneers* all over the country are very insolent; only those within our reach I keep in pretty good order by now and then giving them a pretty good banging." [2]

These views were to a great extent justified by the events of the next few years. During the whole of its term of office the Rotation Government were harassed with arbitrary attempts to impede their trade. Sometimes their petre boats were stopped by a petty landholder or an impudent customs officer. At another time their goods and servants were seized by an extortionate governor. Constant efforts were made to come to terms with the Mogul, efforts which were as constantly frustrated, owing to the mistakes of the English agents, the rivalry of other European nations, and the changes which were constantly taking place in the opinions and *personnel* of the native rulers.

The government of Bengal at this period recalls the methods of the Roman emperors. Just as Augustus took care to assign to each province a procurator of the imperial revenue to be a check on the legate who was entrusted with the administration, so in the rich provinces of Bengal, Bihar, and Orissa, the jealousy of Aurangzēb had placed side by side with the imperial governor an imperial treasurer, Murshid Quli Khān. While the indolent Prince 'Azīmu-sh-Shān was turning his attention more and more away from his government to the future of the

[1] Bruce's *Annals*, III, 507 to 509.
[2] *Hedges' Diary*, III, 80.

Mogul succession, his more active colleague, who was originally entrusted with nothing but the collection of the revenue, was gradually gathering into his own hands all the powers of the state.

It was to Murshid Quli Khān that the Rotation Government addressed themselves with a view to securing letters patent, or at least an order extending to them the immunity from imposts previously enjoyed by the old Company. Such an order, though not at this time absolutely indispensable to the English in Bengal, was certainly very desirable. Fort William was, as a military work, useless, and its garrison of one or two hundred men was chiefly employed in protecting the Company's boats on their way down from Patna, and in forcing a passage for them when their progress was stopped. It is true that, as long as they held command of the sea, the position of Calcutta was secure, that they could always threaten a refractory Indian government with the seizure of its ships, and that both the Mogul and its officers were well aware of the advantages which the empire derived from foreign trade. Still in the disputes which constantly occurred with obstructors, it was as well to be able to appeal not merely to force or to interest, but also to law.

In 1703 the English merchants had, as usual, been much annoyed by the interruption and disturbance which they experienced at the hands of petty officers and local land-holders. They had also failed to convince Murshid Quli Khān that the London Company by any other name might enjoy the same privileges as before. The Bengali agents whom they employed to represent them at the local courts had only spent money to no purpose, and in the end had all been withdrawn. Their employers had been compelled to make to the imperial treasury two separate contributions of three thousand rupees. Without payment of a large sum of money the Indian Government refused to recognise the fusion of the two companies or to admit the lawfulness of the succession. When the Rotation Government assumed office on the 1st February 1704, it was still unrecognised and unrepresented—the bastard offspring of an illegitimate union. The Council were therefore not unnaturally "apprehensive of troubles with the government," and for more than a month did not venture to issue passes for the free transit of merchandise in their own name.[1]

On the 13th March, however, they agreed to use their own seal, a very practical assertion of the rights they claimed to have inherited

---

[1] *Summaries,* § 48, 59.

from their predecessors.[1] At the same time, in consequence of orders received from the prince at Rājmahal, they determined to renew their negotiations.[2] On the 27th March an agent named Rām Chandra was sent to the governor of Hugli,[3] and on the 14th June, Rājāram, an old diplomatic hand, was appointed their representative to go southwards through Midnapore to Balasor and meet the treasurer on his way back from Orissa. In their instructions to Rājāram the Council were careful to define their position. " Tell Murshid Quli," they said, "that the Companies have amalgamated, and that we expect that a new head will shortly be appointed. We are now one Company with one factory, and we shall therefore, according to agreement, make but a single annual payment of Rs. 3,000. As for the Rs. 15,000 which he demands for the release of our trade, we refuse to pay it at all. Our trade should never have been hindered." [4]

Then followed the higgling and hukstering which regularly characterises Indian negotiations, both great and small. The governor of Hugli requested that an Englishman might be deputed to visit him, and that presents should be made to himself and the officers of his Court. The Calcutta Council complied with his requests, and was in consequence asked to give more.[5] On the other hand, the treasurer who had received no less than Rs. 30,000 from the Dutch, scorned to take a paltry present of goods from the English, demanded hard cash, and was not to be satisfied with Rs. 15,000 or even Rs. 20,000.[6] At the beginning of 1707 he consented for the sum of Rs. 25,000 to give an order to the English for free trade. By the end of January, Bugden and Feake, under an escort of Mogul troops, left Calcutta for Cassimbazar, taking with them everything necessary to renew the trade there, and also money enough to pay for the order.[7] But before the necessary arrangements could be completed, when the party had been only a few weeks in Cassimbazar, tidings reached Bengal which completely altered the situation, and they were ordered to come down at once to Calcutta, bringing all the Company's effects with them, including the rupees provided for Mushid Quli Khān.[8]

---

[1] *Summaries,* § 62.
[2] *Ib.,* § 65.
[3] *Ib.,* § 70.
[4] *Ib.,* § 95.
[5] *Ib.,* § 93, 117, 119, 126.
[6] *Ib,,* § 125.
[7] *Ib.,* §§ 189, 192.
[8] *Ib.* § 197, 199.

In his camp, beneath the walls of the city of Ahmadnagar, from whence in 1684 he had gone forth at the head of a mighty host, bent on the conquest of the South, Aurangzēb had, for some time past, lain dying. For many days he continued to give public audience and administered justice, but death was clearly stamped upon his face. The aged Emperor had fought his last battle, and yet the mountain rats were at large and the South was unsubdued. He had failed. He was dying. He knew it, and knew that he must die alone. His eldest living son, Shāh 'Ālam, was far away in Cabul. He now resolutely ordered the two remaining sons to depart. Kām Bakhsh, the younger and best beloved, was sent to Bījāpūr; A'zam was dismissed to Malva.[1] Then all the horror of remorse and despair settled upon that lonely soul. It might have seemed that the integrity of his fifty years of rule had atoned, and more than atoned, for the means by which he had gained his throne. But Aurangzēb was a puritan whose stern sense of justice could allow no such plea. Even his best acts now seemed to him of no value; what then was he to think of his worst? His gloomy creed left him no hope. At times utter despair broke down the barrier of his stoic self-control, and he poured forth in letters to his sons the whole anguish of his heart. "Many were around me when I was born, but now I am going alone. What am I, or why came I into the world? I cannot tell. I bewail the moments which I have spent forgetful of God's worship. I have not done well by the country or its people. My years have gone by profitless. God has been in my heart, yet my darkened eyes have not seen His glorious light. The army is confounded and without heart or help, even as I am, apart from God, with no rest for the heart. Nothing brought I into this world, but I carry away with me the burthen of my sins. Though my trust is in the mercy and goodness of God, yet I fear to think of what I have done. Without hope in myself, how can I hope in others? Come what may, I have launched my barque upon the waters.......Farewell! Farewell! Farewell!"[2]

On the 4th March 1707, after saying the morning prayer and repeating the creed, Aurangzēb was suddenly called to his rest. "Oh! that my death may be on a Friday," he had often exclaimed; and his wish was granted.[3] His simple burial was also in accordance with his

---

[1] Khāfī Khān in Elliot's *History of India*, edition of 1877, Vol. VII, pp. 384 to 386.

[2] Scott's *Dekkan*, Vol. II, Pt. IV, p. 8, edition of 1794.

[3] Irādat Khān in Scott's *Dekkan*, Vol. II, Pt. IV, p. 10.

express command: "Carry this creature of dust to the nearest spot. There commit him to the earth with no useless coffin." [1]

Prince A'zam was only forty miles distant from the court when he received the news of his father's death, and hastened back without a moment's delay. He at once laid claim to the empire. Most men had thought him "fit to rule, had he not ruled." But like Galba he forfeited all esteem and all sympathy before he was fairly seated on the throne. He slighted the nobles, he harassed the soldiers with foolish orders, he disgusted all alike by his parsimony. With overweening confidence in himself, he put no trust in any other human being, not even in his own son, Prince Bēdār Bakht. " In short," says the historian, "I cannot enumerate all the ill omens to the fortune of A'zam Shāh which proved that the will of Providence had decreed that the kingdom should be given to his brother. He who prideth himself is lost. When the will of God hath decreed an event, all things work together to bring it to pass." [2]

Very different was the conduct of Shāh 'Ālam at this trying juncture. Relying on the help of his two sons, Mu'izu-d-Dīn and 'Azīmu-sh-Shān, and above all on the help of his able lieutenant Mun'im Khān, he made a bold push for the throne. On the 10th March, two days after he had received the news of his father's death, he set out for Peshaur, and by April he was at Lahore. Here he paused for a short while to organise his party, and then pressing onwards in time to secure Delhi and Agra, joined 'Azīmu-sh-Shān, who had come up with twenty thousand horse from Bengal. [3]

The contest for the empire of India was now practically decided. The race had been won by the elder brother. Shāh 'Ālam had shown himself superior to A'zam in prudence, in ability, and in resources; he was now to show himself superior in generosity. He offered to divide the empire with the defeated competitor, but A'zam disdained a compromise. His answer was a line from Sa'dī: " Though ten dervishes can sleep under the same blanket, one country cannot hold two kings." He had already passed Gualior, where he had left Asad Khān in charge of the ladies of his court. He crossed the Chambal, and marched upon Agra. The direction of the main body of his army was retained in his own hands, but Prince Bēdār Bakht was allowed to command the right of the advanced guard, while Zū-l-fikār Khān led the left. [4]

1 See also Stanley Lane-Poole's *Aurangzib*, p. 204.
2 Iradat Khān in Scott's *Dekkan*, pp. 11, 12.
3 Khāfī Khān in Elliot's *History*, VII, 392, 393.
4 *Ib.*, 396, 397.

On the morning of the 10th June 1707, the two armies were only
a few miles distant from each other. Ignorant of the nearness of his
brother, Shāh 'Ālam had ordered an advance of his whole army southwards, and had sent on his own tents under a small escort commanded
by Rustam 'Alī Khān. With still greater negligence the ill-paid, ill-
disciplined troops of A'zam were toiling over the hot plains toward
Agra. The van, under Prince Bēdār Bakht, was some miles in advance
of the main body, and Zū-l-fikār Khān, inclining far to the left, was
almost out of sight, when he suddenly came upon Rustam 'Alī Khān.
The escort was routed and fled, leaving their commander with the tents
and the artillery in the hands of Zū-l-fikār. Both sides were now
aware of their proximity, and prepared for the battle of Jājū.[1]

It was close upon the summer solstice. The Indian sun put forth
the full measure of his strength. Sky and earth were burning hot.[2]
Whirling sands enveloped the combatants, who could keep themselves
from fainting only by opening their armour and pouring skins of
water over their naked bodies.[3] On hearing of the approach of the
enemy A'zam started, as if stung by a scorpion. His eyes rolled, his
face was distorted with passion as he pulled up the sleeves of his dress,
and called frantically for his war elephant. It was brought to him.
Standing erect upon his moving throne, and twirling a short, crooked
staff round his head, the madman hurried forward at the head of his
troops and thrust himself into the gap between the two wings of the
advanced guard.[4] Before him was nothing but vast clouds of dust;
but soon the clouds opened, and under cover of a heavy cannonade
two columns of attack were pushed forward till they were about three
hundred yards off. At this short distance they poured a most
destructive fire into the tightly compressed masses of A'zam's troops,
who found themselves unable to deploy or make any effective resistance.
The winds in their courses fought against the southern army, blowing
strongly in their faces, so that while their arrows and rockets fell short,
every shot fired by Shāh 'Ālam's troops took effect.[5] The Rajput
chieftains fell; their followers began to disperse; and Zū-l-fikār
Khān, who cared very little about the success of A'zam, declared that
it was time to retire from the contest. This advice only made his

---

[1] Irādat Khān in Scott's *Dekkan*, II, Pt. IV, p. 31.
[2] *Ib.*, 30.
[3] *Ib.*, 35.
[4] *Ib.*, 34, 35.
[5] *Ib.*, 36, 37. Also Khāfī Khān in Elliot's *History*, VII, p. 398.

master more furious: "Go with your bravery," he shrieked; "save your life wherever you can. I cannot leave this field. For princes it is either throne or tomb." [1]

Zū-l-fikār accordingly withdrew towards Gualior, and left the ill-fated prince with two or three hundred men to fight to the last. One by one they were shot or cut down, the gallant young Bēdār Bakht and his brother, the Ṣufawī Khān, and all the great officers of the household. A whirl of sand blew in the face of A'zam, and from it issued Mun'im Khān with a picked band of men. "It is God," cried the wretched prince, "not men that are against me." His elephant, pierced with wounds and deserted by its drivers, became unmanageable; he stood up to direct it, when an arrow struck him in the forehead, and he fell back dead. Seeing this, the prisoner Rustam 'Alī climbed up the elephant, cut off the dead man's head, and hastened to lay it at the feet of the conqueror. Shāh 'Ālam turned with horror from the ruffian and burst into tears. [2]

But the fight for the empire of India was not quite over. Kām Bakhsh still remained to be dealt with. Though at Calcutta people seem to have thought seriously of this young man, it was not supposed at Delhi that he would be able to offer any real opposition. [3] He had already been weighed in the balances and found wanting. Sent by Aurangzeb to govern Bījapūr, he had in a short time made himself infamous by his treacherous and bloodthirsty proceedings. The chief men of the south left him and returned to their lands, while his army dwindled away. [4]

In 1708 Shāh 'Ālam arrived at Aurangabad. He was unwilling to proceed to extremities, and before advancing to Haidarabad, where Kām Bakhsh was encamped, he wrote offering terms: "Our father assigned you the government of Bījapūr: we give you in addition Haidarabad, and will esteem you dearer than our children. Spare the blood of the true believers, and let there be peace." [5] Kindness, however, only provoked the foolish fellow to greater insolence and extravagance. As Shāh 'Ālam drew near to Haidarabad, all Kām Baksh's troops deserted except a few thousand of the sorriest troops and a small corps of artillery. Yet he must needs sally forth from the city to give

---

[1] Khāfī Khān in Elliot's *History*, VII, 398, 399.
[2] Irādat Khān in Scott's *Dekkan*, pp. 38, 39.
[3] *Ib.*, 53.
[4] *Ib.*, 50, 51.
[5] *Ib.*, 54.

battle. The lying prophets who surrounded him had said, "Go up and prosper!" and he preferred their smooth sayings to the warnings of those who could already see his forces scattered upon the hills as sheep without a shepherd.[1] In spite of the reluctance of Shāh 'Ālam, another fractricidal battle was fought. Kām Bakhsh with his two sons was seized and carried to the oratory close to the imperial tent. He was desperately wounded. In the evening his brother came and sat beside him, covered him with his own mantle, and offered to feed him with his own hands. "It was never my wish," he said, "to see you thus." "Neither was it mine," replied the other, "that one of the race of Timur should be a cowardly captive." He died refusing to be comforted, refusing even to allow the European surgeons in attendance to dress his wounds.[2]

---

[1] Irādat Khān in Scott's *Dekkan*, p. 55.
[2] *Ib.*, 56, 57. Also Khāfi Khān in Elliot's *History*, VII, 406, 407.

CHAPTER V.

HOW THE ROTATION GOVERNMENT COMPLETED THE BUILDING OF FORT WILLIAM,
BUT FAILED TO COME TO TERMS WITH THE LOCAL RULERS.

1707 TO 1710.

A CONTEMPORARY view of these important events is given in the Calcutta consultation books, which chronicle the various steps in struggle as information was received about them, and which show very clearly their effect on the fortunes of the English in Bengal. When on the 3rd April 1707 news was first received that the Mogul was dead, great was the consternation of the Council. They had but too good reason to fear that their growing trade would be swept away by the coming flood of civil war and anarchy. Immediate steps were taken to secure a store of provisions at Fort William. Orders were sent to the English agents in the district near Calcutta to return to head-quarters, bringing the Company's effects there, if possible. Sixty additional black soldiers were taken into the Company's service and posted round the settlement.[1] From the agent at Patna tidings soon came of the movements of A'zam Shāh and of the counter-efforts of 'Azīmu-sh Shān to support the cause of his father, Shāh 'Ālam. The Sultan,

---

[1] *Summaries*, § 197.

they said, had seized on the Imperial treasures, had threatened to
levy a tax on all the merchants, and had demanded a lac of rupees
as a contribution towards raising forces to fight against A'zam.[1]

With this demand the English neither could nor would comply.
On the contrary, after their first panic was over, they began to see that
the death of Aurangzēb might turn out very much to their advantage.
While the attention of the Indian rulers was concentrated on the fight
for the succession, Fort William might be considerably strengthened,
and two new bastions were accordingly built by the riverside without
delay.[2] It happened, therefore, that at the time when the Council
heard of 'Azīmu-sh Shān's requisition they had laid aside their fears
and were rather in a confident mood. A threatening message was
despatched to Patna. "If any of our people there are plundered," said
the Council, "we will take satisfaction at Hugli, or anywhere we find
it convenient so to do."[3]

On the 11th July a letter arrived from Patna with the news that
Shāh 'Ālam had obtained an entire victory, and that A'zam and his
two sons had fallen in battle. The Council, however, seem always to
have been unwilling to believe in the new emperor's prospects. The
story of the great victory at Jājū was dismissed as "being only
merchants' advices from Agra," and little credit was given to it.[4]

In November they learnt from a native agent that Murshid Quli
Khān was not only to continue Treasurer, but was also to be 'Azīmu-sh-
Shān's deputy in the government of Bengal, and that he had expressed
a desire to see the English merchants settled at Cassimbazar and to
come to terms with them about the granting of an order for free trade.[5]
The Council, however, were not at all anxious to renew their former
negotiations. The country was still in a very unsettled state.[6] In the
south, Kām Bakhsh was in possession of many strongholds and said to
be making all the preparations he could for war. It was considered very
doubtful whether he or Shāh 'Ālam would eventually secure the Imperial
throne.[7] In Bengal, too, disorder was rife. The safeguarding of the
Company's saltpetre boats, always an anxiety to the Council, had now
become so difficult that they were on the point of giving up the Patna

---

[1] Summaries, § 198.
[2] Ib., § 202.
[3] Ib., § 203.
[4] Ib.. § 210.
[5] Ib.. § 221.
[6] Ib., § 226.
[7] Ib., § 235.

factory altogether.[1]   But towards the middle of 1708 the conduct of a
newly-appointed governor of Hugli brought matters to a crisis.
This officer, who had at first seemed friendly, suddenly changed his
attitude. He wished, no doubt, to secure his share in the money which
the English were expected to present to the new emperor and the new
government, and he therefore tried to force them to carry on their
negotiations through him. The Council were sufficiently alive to the
importance of keeping on good terms with the Hugli governor, and
did all they could to gratify him by sending him presents and polite
messages, but they wished to keep the negotiations with the Supreme
Government in their own hands.[2] In July the "hotheaded phousdar"
began to resort to violence. He prohibited the local merchants from
dealing with the English, abused the English representative, imprisoned
the English servants. An attack on Fort William seemed imminent.
Only two private ships were then lying in the Hugli, and the garrison
amounted to about a hundred and eighty men. But the Council were
wanting in courage. They ordered ships and men, such as there were,
to be in readiness, and on the 10th July " summoned all the European
and Christian inhabitants and the masters of ships, acquainting them we
expect some trouble from the governor of Hugli. We ordered that
they forbear to go to Hugli for some time, and that they should be in
readiness under arms on summons to prevent any insolence he may
design us, or in case there should be occasion to act anything against
him, that they be ready thereto. They all showed a readiness and
declared they would be ready on all summons." The Council also
ordered the Portuguese Christians to be trained for arms by the factory
ensign and to appear under arms once a week to exercise.[3] In the end
the courage of the defenders of Calcutta was not put to the test. Two
days after these warlike preparations had been made the Council received
a letter from the Prince's Qāṣidār Mīr Muḥammad Dafar. " I have
been," he said, "to the governor of Hugli, and I told him that it was
not well to interfere with the English and stop their trade, and that
if he persisted in it, he would repent. The governor answered me
that the English trade had been stopped by order of the Treasurer, and
that as for imprisoning their servants and agents it was not done by
his orders nor with his knowledge." Mīr Muḥammad therefore
advised his English friends to wait a few days, by which time

---

[1] *Summaries*, § 226.
[2] *Ib.*, §§ 225, 231, 239, 240.
[3] *Ib.*, § 246.

he hoped to make everything right, and the Council gladly accepted his mediation.[1]

The defiant attitude of the governor of Hugli had the effect of making the English Council a little more anxious to come to terms with the new government of Bengal. A fort no doubt is better than an ambassador, but an ambassador is not altogether to be despised. A good deal of trouble, it was clear, would be saved if they could procure a grant from the emperor Shāh 'Ālam, or even an order from Murshid Quli Khān. At the end of April 1708 they sent an agent to Rajmahal to renew the negotiations for securing free trade to the English in Bengal. The Government of Fort St. George had already requested the new emperor to confirm the privilege granted to the English by his father Aurangzēb, but no grant had yet been issued by him for the whole of the Company's factories, and there was consequently some fear that the Prince and the Treasurer would withhold their orders. Nevertheless the Council put a bold face on the matter, and stoutly declared that they were daily expecting the imperial letters-patent which they would send for the Prince and the Treasurer to see just as they had sent with their agent copies of former grants to the Company.[2]

The usual higgling and blustering followed.

"Fifteen thousand rupees," said the Council, " for your order; otherwise we retaliate." [3]

"Impossible," said the Prince and the Treasurer.

"We have sent up another fifteen thousand rupees and three looking-glasses, one for His Highness and two for your Excellency." [4]

"The Dutch have given us thirty-five thousand rupees for their privileges, and we think that you should do the same." [5]

"Thirty-five thousand rupees will ruin us," cried the Council; "indeed, we cannot possibly give more than twenty thousand." [6]

A month later they received a letter from their agent at Rajmahal, Çivacharan, stating that he had paid the Treasurer and the Prince thirty-six thousand rupees for their order, and had drawn a bill-of-exchange on the Company for that amount. The Council were not unnaturally indignant at these unauthorised proceedings, and even thought of

---

[1] *Summaries*, § 247.
[2] *Ib.*, §§ 239, 240.
[3] *Ib.*, § 244.
[4] *Ib.*, § 249.
[5] *Ib.*, § 254.
[6] *Ib.*, § 285.

refusing to honour the bill. After a long consultation they decided on sending one of their most trustworthy native servants, Fāzil Muhammad, to Rajmahal with orders to send Çivacharan under a guard to Calcutta to answer for his conduct.[1] On the 22nd, October Fāzil Muhammad returned from Rajmahal bringing still more unpalatable news. The Prince and the Treasurer, he said, although they had promised to give the new order for freedom of trade for thirty-six thousand rupees, now absolutely refused to do so for less than fifty thousand rupees as a present to themselves and a hundred thousand rupees to be paid into the emperor's treasury at Surat.[2]

In this extremity the Council could only turn to the governor of Hugli for help. He had lately given up his hostile attitude, and for the sum of three thousand rupees had promised to formally satisfy all the privileges hitherto enjoyed by the English at Hugli.[3] The Council therefore agreed to write to him and tell him that they would accept his offer to act as negotiator between them and the Government of Bengal.[4] At first the governor of Hugli represented that it would be impossible to obtain any grant at the rate offered, but on the Council's threatening to seize all the Mogul shipping in the Hugli and order all English subjects to withdraw from Bengal, he changed his tone, and professed that for thirty-five thousand rupees he would procure the English letters patent from the Prince and an order from the Treasurer.[5] This promise was, however, purely of a diplomatic character. As the sequel showed, the Hugli governor did nothing and could do nothing for the English. In December 1708 Mr. Cawthorpe, the English agent at Rajmahal, was ruthlessly seized by the Prince, who refused to set free his prisoner or to let the Company's boats pass, till he had received a bill-of-exchange for fourteen thousand rupees.[6]

Once, again, the shadow of the greater struggle for empire falls across the scene giving pause to local wranglers and for the time hushing the rising bickerment. On the 24th December 1708 the Council received a letter from Madras, saying "that Shāh 'Ālam was advanced near Golconda and like to get the better."[7] On Wednesday, the 16th February 1709, they learned from several sources that there had been

---

[1] *Summaries*, § 258.
[2] *Ib.*, § 263.
[3] *Ib.*, § 260.
[4] *Ib.*, § 263.
[5] *Ib.*, § 272.
[6] *Ib.*, §§ 280, 287.
[7] *Ib.*, § 284.

" an engagement between the King Shāh 'Ālam and his brother Kām
Bakhsh near Golconda, wherein the King had an entire victory and
slew his brother and one or more of his sons, and vanquished his party,
so that now 'tis believed the kingdom will soon be at quiet and the
Government more orderly." From Madras, too, came a letter confirming
the death of Kām Bakhsh, and informing them that negotiations were
in progress to secure an Imperial grant.[1]   On the 31st March 1709 the
Council, considering that the victory of Shāh 'Ālam opened up a fair
prospect of peaceable times, agreed that the garrison should be reduced
to one hundred and thirty-seven men.[2]   At the end of April they took
vigorous steps to chastise the watchmen at Kidderpur, who had " of late
been very troublesome in stopping the Company's boats with goods."
Thirty soldiers and twenty black gun-men were got to fetch them up for
punishment, and the six men who actually offered a resistance with
swords were tied to a post, given twenty-one stripes with a split rattan,
and then remanded for further punishment.[3]

The confidence felt by the Council in the coming peaceable times
and their summary treatment of the impudent watchmen are to be
attributed not merely to the victory of Shāh 'Ālam, but also to the fact
that in consequence of that victory 'Aẓimu-sh-Shān and Murshid Quli
Khān had at the beginning of the year left Bengal and gone to the
Imperial Court. In their stead Sher Bulland Khān was sent to be chief
manager of the provinces of Bengal, Bihar, and Orissa. In June
Mr. John Eyre and Mr. Pattle were deputed to meet the new ruler,
who at first seemed particularly well disposed to the English and gave
them permission to go on with their business as usual till they could
produce a formal order.[4]   In a very short time, however, they heard
from Mr. Pattle that Sher Bulland Khān had stopped all the boats at
Rajmahal.[5]   A present of goods worth two thousand rupees was rewarded with more fair speeches, but notwithstanding all his promises Sher
Bulland refused to make the smallest real concession. " He positively
demands forty-five thousand rupees, on the receipt of which he will
give us his order for free trade, and when the present diwān is confirmed or a new one sent he will procure a writ from him, without
which he is resolved to admit of no more delays from us, but will stop

---

[1] *Summaries*, § 294.
[2] *Ib.*, § 304.
[3] *Ib.*, § 309.
[4] *Ib.*, §§ 322, 326.
[5] *Ib.*, § 330.

all our business, having called all the merchants at Muqsūdābād to give in an account of what goods they have provided for us in order to their paying custom. The governor further adds that the Prince last year forced from our Patna boats seventeen thousand rupees, and if we comply not that we shall see what he can do. On these advices we meet early this morning to consult what to do in these unsettled times, and cannot find any remedy ; for since the new King is come to the throne we have had no order from him to trade as usual, which is the advantage the government takes hold of. Therefore it is resolved we write immediately to Mr. Pattle, ordering him to make an end of it the best way he can, for it is certain if we comply not the governor will again stop our Patna fleet, which, as the year before, will not be let loose till a large sum is extorted as also custom to be paid on our goods which we have bespoke of the Cassimbazar merchants, which will be of very ill consequence." [1] So Mr. Pattle paid Sher Bulland Khān the forty-five thousand rupees and obtained in return the governor's order of the freedom of the English trade in Bengal, Bihar, and Orissa, as also the governor's particular orders to Hugli, Rajmahal, Dacca, and Muqsūdābād, acquainting them that he had given the English a general order.[2] And Walī Beg, the superintendent of the King's treasury, who had been most useful to Mr. Pattle in helping to get the order, was graciously pleased to visit Calcutta at the end of September, where he was "received very civilly," and had a present of one thousand rupees value made him.[3]

Meanwile Governor Pitt at Madras had entered into important negotiations with the Mogul court, which were destined to occupy the attention of the English in India for the next eight years, and of which the first steps taken are significant in many ways. They show among other things how hard it is to tolerate a neighbour and how easy it is to love any one sufficiently remote. The Calcutta Council, as has been pointed out, felt no enthusiasm whatever for the cause of Shāh 'Ālam ; the English in the far south were anxious to support him. It is also interesting to note the value of personal influence, Thomas Pitt, Esq., President of the Company's affairs on the coast of Coromandel, being able to form lasting friendship with many of the Indian officials such as were quite impossible to the headless government of Fort William in Bengal. Of the well-wishers thus secured, the most important was the

---

[1] *Summaries*, § 335.
[2] *Ib.*, § 337.
[3] *Ib.*, § 338.

Lord High Steward of the King's household, Zainu-d-Dīn Khān, whose
name is persistently corrupted by the records into Zoodee Khān. It
was in July 1708, when Shāh 'Ālam was anticipating a conflict with
Kām Bakhsh, and was therefore anxious to conciliate as many supporters
as possible, that Zainu-d-Dīn Khān despatched a letter to the Governor
of Fort St. George, "professing great kindness and tendering his
service in any affair." The letter was received with due solemnity,
presents were made to "Zoodee Khān's Lady," who happened to be
residing at St. Thomé, and letters were sent in answer to the Mogul's
Court, requesting the confirmation of the privileges granted by
Aurangzēb. More correspondence followed, and the feelings between
the English and the High Steward grew very friendly.[1] During the
first half of the year 1709, Pitt was busy preparing a sumptuous
present for the King, which he intended to send to him at Golconda,
and a part of which was actually despatched by sea to Masulipatam.
But after the defeat of Kām Bakhsh, the King withdrew to Aurangabad,
and thence to Delhi, and in September Pitt was deprived of his office.
Consequently the whole scheme dropped for the time.[2]

Pitt had urged upon the Calcutta Council the expediency of
joining in embassy, but in vain.[3] Their attention was entirely
taken up with their affairs at Rajmahal and Muqsūdābād, and they
had no leisure to think of sending to such distant places as Aurangabad
and Delhi. In November Sher Bulland Khān, for whose order they
had recently paid so much, was removed from the government of
Bengal, and in the absence of any higher authority the official who was
acting in Murshid Quli's place as treasurer took upon himself to stop all
the Company's goods and boats, requiring the sum of twenty thousand
rupees before he would let them pass. The Council refused to comply
with this "unreasonable demand," and resolved on strong measures. The
treasurer to gain time abandoned his aggressive attitude and promised
everything.[4] The dispute would have no doubt run the usual course
had not the treasurer been fortunately killed in dispute with some
regiments of horse about arrears of pay.[5] After this the English seem to
have been left in peace for the rest of the year 1710. Murshid Quli Khān

---

[1] Wheeler's *Madras*, pp. 272, 274, 275, 277.
[2] Wheeler's *Madras*, pp. 284, 285.
[3] *Summaries*, § 336.
[4] *Ib.*, §§ 352, 359.
[5] *Ib.*, § 362.

returned to Bengal, but he did nothing to molest them.[1] On the other hand, Zainu-d-Dīn Khān was in April appointed by the emperor himself to be governor of Hugli and admiral of all the seaports on the coast of Coromandel. His letter on this occasion to the Governor of Madras shows very clearly his kindly relations towards Pitt and the English. "As there is a great friendship between us," he said, "and you have often informed me that it was your opinion that if all the seaports under the King's dominions were under the admiral as a company, he might settle the sea affairs, destroy the pirates, enrich the seaports, and encourage the sea merchants to come and depart, which will increase their profit; and you desired me to use my utmost endeavours to obtain this, which I have done; and on account of our friendship have undertaken this great business myself, and if it happens otherwise, the discredit will be the same to us both. For I have no other hopes than the safety of all subjects, the security of merchants going or coming by sea, extirpation of pirates, and the enrichment of the King's sea-ports. So your Honour must use your endeavours in this matter likewise, and advise all of our native agents and merchants everywhere to trade freely without suspicion of any danger, and augment their trade. I want your advice, if you think it proper to send some of the King's ships to bring elephants from the other coast. The King has ordered me to build a fort at Balasor and enrich your factory. After I arrive at Hugli I will observe how affairs are managed and advise your Honour. And now I must desire you to think of means how things may best be carried on for the King's advantage and your company's, that so all persons may live happy and serve their Maker. For I have neglected other business and undertaken this on your account, in hopes to get a great name by it; and within five, six, or twelve months' time, if it is your request that I should take in the other seaports, as also Surat, I can procure it, and we must endeavour to promote both our fames. For if we agree we can conquer the whole world, and clear the seas of all dangers for the merchants. As to the present, I have wrote you lately to send it to Bengal, according to the King's orders, which be sure you do. For it is very necessary that you send a present, and when I come to Hugli I will advise you of all other matters ; and you should send an agent with me, or write your people at Calcutta to send one. For I shall want him on several occasions. I heartily wish you all health and prosperity."[2] Zainu-d-Dīn Khān reached Hugli in May.[3] Janarddana Set, the

---

[1] *Summaries*, § 375.
[2] Wheeler's *Madras*, 289.
[3] *Summaries*, § 381.

Company's broker who had gone up to meet him, returned and told the Council that he had been received with marked kindness and that the admiral would like to come on a visit to Calcutta, but understood that it was customary for them to pay the first visit. The Council accordingly sent Mr. Chitty and Mr. Blount to Hugli to "visit and discourse" with the new governor.[1]

The days of the Rotation Government were now rapidly drawing to a close. On the 18th July a letter was received from the Hon'ble Antony Weltden, Esq., announcing that he had been sent out by the Company to be Governor and President of the Council, and had just arrived at Balasor. Samuel Blount of the Council was at once sent down the river with a letter of congratulation and various conveniences for the President and his family, and many other besides hastened, of their own accord, to meet their new Chief. On the evening of the 20th July Weltden reached Calcutta. He was "met at his landing by most of the Europeans in the town and the natives in such crowds that it was difficult to pass to the fort where he was conducted by the worshipful John Russell and Abraham Adams, Esquires, and the Council. The packet was opened and the commission read, after which the usual ceremony given on such occasions by firing guns and the keys of the fort delivered." [2] In September Zainu-d-Dīn Khān came to Calcutta to return the visits paid to him, and was received "with all the respect and civility due to him on this occasion" and with a suitable present.[3] At the end of October he was able to inform the Council that he had received a favourable letter from Farrukhsiyar, who represented his father 'Aẓīmu-sh-Shān at Rajmahal, together with a dress of honour for the President to be delivered at Hugli. On Wednesday the 1st November 1710 the President, accompanied by Hedges, Chitty, Blount, and several others, went up to Hugli. There the President received the dress of honour and a letter, with a fine horse, and returned to Calcutta on Friday. The following Monday the Prince's letter was read in Council, and it was agreed to send him a present in return, as he was the son of the favourite son of the emperor, and might, therefore, help them to procure an imperial grant.[4]

Of the external relations of the Rotation Government little more remains to be said. England was during the whole of this period at

[1] *Summaries*, § 383.
[2] *Ib.*, § 391.
[3] *Ib.*, § 405.
[4] *Ib.*, § 411.

war with France and in alliance with Holland, but of this the only indications are one or two acts of civility to the Dutch Governor of Chinsurah, and occasional fears as to the movements of French ships recorded in the consultation books.

On the other hand, far too much space seems to be given up to disputes about the constitution of the Council itself. Long and heated discussions took place about the rules of succession. The managers at home had ordered that the Old Company's servants were to have the first, third, fifth, and seventh places, and that the New Company's servants should have the second, fourth, sixth, and eighth. If this rule were rigidly carried out when the first place fell vacant, it would be filled not by the second in the Council, but by the third; and this method of promotion being followed all along the line, the new member of Council would at once take seventh place, and not the eighth. Yet the managers appear to have ordered that the next who succeeded was to be the eighth of the Council. These contradictory rules furnished a long succession of hard cases and bitter disputes, which were only terminated by once again reading the letters on the subject from London and resolving, in spite of the protests of the New Company's servants, that the Old Company's places are the first, third, fifth and seventh in the Council.[1]

Another fruitful root of bitterness was the question whether either Hedges or Sheldon, on becoming President of the Council for the separate affairs of his own company, could retain his seat on the United Council. At the end of 1704, two whole months were spent in disputing upon the point, and numerous letters were sent home from both parties, each accusing the other of disloyalty and disobedience. It was in the end decided that neither Hedges nor Sheldon need resign, but this decision was not observed. When on the death of Beard at Madras in 1705, Ralph Sheldon was appointed President of the Council for the Old Company, he was compelled to give up his place in the United Trade Council, and the same fate befel Robert Hedges, who much against his will superseded Littleton on the 1st November 1705. In September the whole question was re-opened by the receipt of a letter from England. The Governors of the Old Company stated that they did not wish a separate President for their affairs now that Mr. Beard was dead. Consequently, Ralph Sheldon was displaced, and being no longer President of the Old Company's affairs wished to take his seat again as a Chairman of the United Trade Council. On the 24th September he sent

---

[1] *Summaries*, §§ 177, 212.

a letter to the Council asking to be reinstated. On this a stormy discussion ensued, half the Council being for it and half against. In the end, finding they could come to no decision, they determined "to cast lots as our masters have bidden us in times of disagreement." The lots fell for Sheldon, who was accordingly re-elected. But the matter did not end here. Having taken back one of their former Chairmen, the Council felt that they could not do less than offer to take back the other, and sent a letter to Hedges to that effect. Hedges, however, wrote back arguing that Sheldon should not have been re-elected, and refusing to be re-elected himself unless the Council would admit that they had no right in the first place to force him to resign. Many letters passed on both sides. In his last, Hedges declared that he was justly turned out on becoming President of the New Company, and that he could not see how the recent orders from home justified the action of the Council. He, therefore, refused to be re-elected, and added that he was returning home to England and would lay an account of the whole affair before the Managers in London.[1] Sheldon, however, continued to sit as a Chairman of the Council till the beginning of 1709, when illness compelled him to ask permission to take a voyage on the *Mary* smack, in the hopes that the sea air might restore his failing health.[2] But the voyage was never taken, or, if taken, proved of no avail. Ralph Sheldon died in Hugli at the end of April,[3] and was buried in the old Calcutta graveyard, where his tombstone with the following inscription is still to be seen :—

> RUDOLPHUS SHELDON
> Armiger et
> Illustris Sheldoni-
> ani stematis haud in-
> digna Proles,
> Mortalitatis suæ
> exuvias in spe bea-
> tæ resurrectionis
> sub hoc tumulo de-
> posuit Aprilis 26,
> 1709,
> Aetat. 37.

---

[1] *Summaries*, § 178.
[2] *Ib.*, § 295.
[3] *Ib.*, § 310.

CHAPTER VI.

WHEN the English first came to Calcutta their position was precarious and ill-defined. The land in the neighbourhood being to a large
extent wild and uncultivated, there was little or nothing to prevent any
body of men that chose from seizing a piece of unoccupied ground and
squatting on it. In this way the Setts and Bysacks had, more than a
hundred years before, founded Govindpur, and the English, coming
to Calcutta with the good-will and, probably, at the suggestion of these
very Setts and Bysacks, had nothing more to do than to take as
much waste land as they needed, clear it, and build houses and offices.
They trusted that the natural strength of the position would protect
them, and that the acquiescence of the government would leave them
undisturbed in their new home.

The first settlement at Sūtānuṭī seems to have consisted of mud and
straw hovels with a few masonry buildings. Its chief defence was
the flotilla of boats lying in the river. The renewed settlement
established by Charnock in 1690 was of the same nature; but as time

went on the number of masonry buildings increased, and in 1696 the beginning of a fort was made. The English also attempted to raise some sort of revenue from the land upon which they had squatted. In 1694 such partial duties as the agent at Calcutta could then raise are reckoned as amounting to only one hundred and sixty rupees a month,[1] and from the records which remain it would appear to have been even less. For instance, in the account of the revenue for August 1695, the total receipts from shop-rents, fines, fees, and duties are set down as Rs. 75-0-6. The expenses are equally trifling. Besides Rs. 69-12 for servants' wages, the items of expenditure are one rupee for paper, ten annas for a whip, four annas for "rice for ye thieves," and one anna for "making a jamp."[2]

The letters patent granted by Prince 'Aẓīmu-sh-Shān in 1698 changed all this. The English Company gained a definite status in the eyes of the Indian Governors. It became the Collector[3] of the three towns, Sūtānuṭī, Calcutta, and Govindpur. As such it was empowered to levy internal duties and customs on articles of trade passing through its districts and impose petty taxes and cesses on the cultivators; as such it managed the lands and exercised jurisdiction over the inhabitants. The exact relations of a Collector to the supreme government are a matter of dispute. Ordinarily, we are told, the Collector realized the public revenue arising from the land under him, and, after deducting a commission of ten per cent. and various other small charges, transmitted the sum to the Imperial treasury. In the case of the Company this sum was fixed. In short, the Council at Calcutta paid the Mogul an annual rent of twelve hundred rupees, more or less, and was free to tax and govern the place almost as it pleased.[4]

In consequence of this change in the position of the Company, a new member was added to the Council to represent it in its new capacity. Henceforth a special officer, known as the Collector, was appointed to gather in the revenue of the three towns and to keep them in order. In 1700 Ralph Sheldon became the first Collector of Calcutta,[5] and from him through many an inheritor whose name is now part of the history of British India, the line of the Calcutta Collectors

---

[1] Bruce's *Annals*, III, 172.

[2] See the *Chutanuttee Diary* for the year. India Office Records.

[3] *Zamīndār*.

[4] The exact legal position of the Company is very perplexing. See Stephen's *Nuncomar and Impey*, II, p. 26. Also Hamilton's *East Indies*, edition of 1727, II, p. 13.

[5] See above, p. 157.

runs in unbroken succession down to the present day. On the 1st February 1704, Benjamin Bowcher, the second of the Calcutta Collectors, took over charge of the office,[1] which he filled till his death on the 24th September 1705. On the 8th October John Cole succeeded him;[2] but in April 1706 Arthur King was ordered to act in his stead.[3] On the 3rd October 1706, after a good deal of discussion about the proper constitution of the Council, it was settled that John Maisters should be Collector.[4] In February 1707 the post was filled by Abraham Adams,[5] but in August of that year Adams was made Secretary and was succeeded by William Bugden.[6] He remained in the office till April 1709, when he was promoted to be Import Warehouse keeper. His place in the Council was given to William Lloyd, but as Lloyd was away from Calcutta, the duties of Collector were discharged by Samuel Blount during the rest of the year 1709,[7] and by Spencer for the first half of 1710.[8] In July, on the arrival of President Weltden, the Calcutta Collectorate was entrusted to John Calvert.[9]

Although the Company seem to have claimed all the land between the river and the Salt Lake, from Govindpur to Sūtānuṭī, as within their sphere of influence, the land which they actually rented at this time amounted to about 5,077 bighas, or 1,861 acres, that is, about one-third of the present area of the town. The primary duty of the Collector was to gather in the revenues accruing from this area. The principal receipts were from the ground rents, which the Company was empowered to levy up to a maximum of three rupees a bigha, but besides these the Company drew considerable sums from various aids and benevolences, from tolls levied on the markets and ferries, and from other miscellaneous town duties.[10]

The Collector rendered an account of the revenue to the Council month by month. The "balances paid into cash" are regularly recorded in the consultation books, and sometimes the details as well. From these entries it is comparatively easy to trace the growth of

---

[1] *Summaries*, § 46.
[2] *Ib.*, § 148.
[3] *Ib.*, § 162.
[4] *Ib.*, § 179.
[5] *Ib.*, § 191.
[6] *Ib.*, § 212.
[7] *Ib.*, § 310.
[8] *Ib.*, § 360.
[9] *Ib.*, § 392.
[10] See for instance 16, §§ 4, 8.

the Calcutta revenues.   In 1704 the average monthly cash balance shown by the Collectorate accounts is four hundred and eighty rupees: during the next few years this balance increases at the rate of one hundred rupees a year, till in 1707, it amounts to eight hundred and eighty-five rupees.   In 1708 it is a thousand and ten rupees; in 1709 it is thirteen hundred and seventy rupees; in 1710 it is stationary.[1]   In the time of Holwell the average net monthly balance varies from two thousand five hundred to three thousand eight hundred rupees.   It may be set down as three thousand five hundred.[2]

These figures are interesting not only in themselves, but also for the evidence they furnish as to the early development of Calcutta in size and population.   The growth of the revenues was the direct consequence of the growth of the settlement, and, if we could be certain that the revenues were regularly collected, would give us a measure of it. Regarded in this light the Collectorate accounts would show, that in the six years, from 1703 to 1708 inclusive, Calcutta doubled itself, and that between then and 1710 it increased more than thirty-five per cent. In the whole of the forty years which followed, Calcutta only increased threefold.

Unfortunately we have every reason to believe that the collection of the revenue was most irregular, and we cannot tell whether the increase in any particular year may not be due to some improvement in the collecting agency.   When, therefore, we further try to arrive at some definite account of the population in those early days, we lose all firm foot-hold, and become involved in perplexities.   The whole subject "suffers from a plethora of probabilities."   Nevertheless, though well aware that my results can only be rough and tentative, I shall yet not shrink from giving figures, this being the only way in which we can hope to gain clear ideas.   To help us in our task we have a survey of the Company's lands made in the year 1706,[3] and two contemporary estimates of the population, one by Alexander Hamilton who spent some years in Calcutta under the Rotation Government,[4] and the other by John Zephaniah Holwell just before the taking of the city by Siráju-d-Daula.[5]   Hamilton, who was a private merchant and therefore prejudiced against the Company and all connected with it, sets down the

---

[1] The monthly net balances are given in the *Summaries passim*.
[2] Holwell's *Tracts*, 3rd edition, 1774, p. 241.
[3] *Summaries*, § 207.
[4] Hamilton's *East Indies*, II, 18.
[5] Holwell's *Tracts*, 209.

population as from ten to twelve thousand. He does not say of what year he is speaking; but it is reasonable to suppose that his estimate is based on the survey in 1706. Holwell, one of the greatest of the Calcutta Collectors, on the basis of a survey of his own, argues that in 1752 the total population from which the city revenues were drawn, must have amounted to 409,000. There can be no doubt that this number is far too large. In order to reach it, Holwell has included a considerable area of land, which, though now a part of Calcutta, did not then belong to the Company at all, and has reckoned forty-eight inhabitants to each bigha,[1] a density of population hardly yet reached in the most crowded quarters of the city. We shall probably be making a very liberal allowance if we fix it at twenty to a bigha in 1752, and we shall strictly confine our attention to the Company's lands from which alone it drew rent.

It appears, then, from Holwell's account, that the total area of the land owned by the Company, exclusive of Jannagur, which lies outside the Maharatta ditch, was about 5,243 bighas, and thus the population of the settlement, reckoned at the rate of twenty inhabitants to a bigha, was about one hundred and five thousand. Taking this as our starting-point, and assuming that the increase of the population was proportional to the increase in the average monthy net balances, we should reach the following conclusions. At the beginning of the Rotation Government, the population of the Company's lands would be fifteen thousand; in 1706, when the survey was made, it would be over twenty-two thousand, that is double Hamilton's estimate; in 1708 it would be thirty-one thousand. From this it would rapidly rise to forty-one thousand in the years 1709, 1710. These calculations would only apply to the lands under the management of the Company, that is, to about a third of the whole area included within the Maharatta ditch. If we were to guess at the total population within these limits, we should have to increase the figures by fifty or sixty per cent., or perhaps even to double them.

For administrative purposes the Company's land was split up into four divisions. The smallest but most populous of these was the Great Bazar, where the houses occupied more than 400 bighas out of 488. Beyond lay the large division of Town Calcutta, an area of 1,717½ bighas. In 1706 only 248 bighas were occupied with dwellings, the rest of the division being under cultivation or left waste; but the surveyor notes that 364 bighas are shortly to be used for houses.

---

[1] A bigha is about one-third of an acre.

The northern division, Sūtānuṭī, is estimated to contain 1,692 bighas, of which only 134 were inhabited. In the southern division, Govindpur, only 57 bighas out of 1,178 were inhabited. Thus the total amount of inhabited land in 1706 was only 841½ bighas; and if we were to suppose as before that there were as many as twenty persons living on each bigha, the total population of the settlement in 1706 would be 16,830. It might be argued that the population was not so dense at that time, and that a lower proportion should be taken, which would bring the estimate into agreement with Hamilton. But the calculations which have been based on the growth of the revenues indicate a much large number, and this seems to be nearer the truth. Of the rest of the land, 1,525 bighas were rice fields and 486 bighas gardens. Plantains were grown on some 250 bighas, tobacco on 187, vegetables on 150; 307 bighas were granted rent free for the use of Brahmans; 167 bighas were manor[1] land; 116 were taken up with roads and ditches, wells and ponds; 1,144 bighas were waste.[2]

The position of the English with regard to these lands is clear. The Company had not the absolute possession of the land, but only the rights of a Collector. It could sell, grant, or lease the manor and unoccupied lands, and from the occupiers of the tenanted lands it could demand a rent not exceeding three rupees a bigha; but it had no powers of sale or resumption on failure to pay the ground-rent. Arrears of rent could only be recovered by distraint and by the sale of the moveable property of the occupier. When the Company made a grant of land, it gave with it a deed which conveyed to the grantee his title to the property, and specified the conditions under which it was held.[3] The form of these deeds was extremely simple. Written in Bengali and in English, and signed by the zamindar, they merely gave the date, the name of the grantee, the amount of the land, its situation, and its rent.[4] In the same way, whenever land already occupied changed hands, a new deed had to be taken out. By a resolution passed on the 12th June 1707, it was ordered that all deeds should be registered, should be renewed once a year, and should be shown every month at the time of paying rent. We may, however, suspect that this resolution, like many others made by the Council, was by no means rigidly enforced.

---

[1] *Khamar.*
[2] *Summaries,* § 207.
[3] *Ib.,* § 83.
[4] The deed books from 1758 onwards are preserved in the Calcutta Collectorate.

Each of the four divisions of the settlement was administered through a separate office. As a revenue officer, the Collector had under him a staff of clerks and rent gatherers,[1] which gradually grew with the growth of the revenue. The pay of these servants seems to have been miserably small.[2] One of the results of the survey of 1706, was the discovery that the rent gatherers had been making false returns and farming out lands for their own advantage. The corrupt officers were discharged, and it was decided that the pay of the clerks in charge of the land records should be raised to four rupees a month;[3] but as a matter of fact, the order was not carried out.

Still more difficult was it to discover a reliable "black collector." During the first ten years of the Calcutta collectorate several men were tried in the post and found wanting. As long as Ralph Sheldon was collector, the "general supervisor" was a certain Nandarāma; but soon after Bowcher had succeeded Sheldon, Nandarāma fell under suspicion, and in August 1705, Jagatdās was made " black collector."[4] He does not seem to have given satisfaction. In 1707 the post remained vacant for several months, during which Nandarāma again acted as the assistant to the Collector.[5] No sooner was he displaced then all sorts of complaints were preferred against him, and it appeared that he had been guilty of extensive peculation.[6] On being given up by the Governor of Hugli, whither he had fled for refuge, the Council ordered him to be imprisoned while the Collector looked over the accounts. The drum was beaten all about the town, and notice was given to all the native inhabitants that whosoever had any money or effects of Nandarāma in his possession should not deliver them up to him or any of his family till his case had been decided.[7] During Weltden's government, Jagatdās was again "black collector," and was accused of being concerned with the president in extensive frauds on the Company.

These incidents seem typical. The dishonest "black collector" is a recurring feature in the internal administration of Calcutta, and it is a feature which need not excite surprise. In all probability the pay of

---

[1] *Summaries*, § 205.
[2] *Ib.*, §§ 4, 8.
[3] *Ib.*, § 206.
[4] See *Ib.*, Addenda, § 420.
[5] *Ib.*, § 306.
[6] *Ib.*, § 316.
[7] *Ib.*, § 320.
[8] He had from 30 to 50 rupees a month. See Holwell's *Tracts*, 187.

the " black collector " was absurdly small.[8] It was the vicious policy of the Company to under-pay its servants, and it was notorious that these servants, both high and low, derived the greater part of their income from their perquisites and from private trade. If the English Collector was not content with his pay but had recourse to indirect means to augment it, why should not his Bengali personal assistant follow so good an example? When in 1752 Holwell accused Govinda-rāma Mitra of dishonesty, the celebrated "black collector" defended himself by pointing out that every deputy of this description was allowed similar privileges, and that he could not from his wages keep up the equipage and attendance necessary for an officer of his station.[1]

But the Collector was not merely the gatherer of the Calcutta revenues, he was also the magistrate in charge of the native inhabitants. As magistrate he had under him a small police force, of which the numbers must be inferred from the scanty notices found in the Consult-ation Books. On the 16th February 1704 it is ordered that a native superintendent of police, 45 constables, two beadles, and 20 watch-men shall be taken into pay,[2] and on the 27th December 1706, in consequence of various outrages committed in the town, the Collector was ordered for the present to entertain 31 watchmen.[3] The accounts of the four offices in Calcutta show a total of only 30 constables and some 40 watchmen, but it is quite possible that some were told off to do duty in the fort. In Holwell's time the head-quarters of the Collector were in Town Calcutta,[4] but in the days of the Rotation Government they would seem to have been in the Great Bazar, in which were sta-tioned the native superintendent and the greater part of the police force, and which, in addition to the usual drummer employed in every quarter of the town to assist in the publication of important notices, was in 1712 able to boast of two trumpeters.

In Holwell's time the Collector presided over two separate branches of administration, the Collector's office, which dealt with land and revenue questions, and the Magistrate's court, which dealt with both civil causes and criminal offences where natives only were concerned. This was practically his position under the Rotation Government. But at that time the Council made many attempts to take away the sole jurisdiction from the Collector, and deputed three of their

---

[1] Holwell's *Tracts*, pp. 196, 197.
[2] *Summaries*, § 52.
[3] *Ib.*, § 188.
[4] Holwell's *Tracts*, 207.

number to form a court of justice. When first constituted in August
1704,[1] it was ordered to sit every Saturday from nine to twelve
in the morning, but it does not seem to have met very regularly.
In September 1705,[2] in May 1709,[3] and in July 1710,[4] we find notes
in the consultations to the effect that the sittings of the court of
justice had been suspended for the time. On 29th April 1706 a
registrar was appointed for the court.[5] The duty of the court was to
hear and determine small controversies: the hearing of important cases
was reserved for the full Council. We have an example of their
administration of criminal justice in 1706. In August of that year
they ordered that a number of thieves and murderers who had been
recently caught should be branded on the cheek and turned on the
other side of the water.

Although in great emergencies the Council might extemporise a
volunteer force out of the European and Christian inhabitants,[6] the
regular garrison of the fort consisted only of some hundred and fifty
men, divided into two companies, each having a captain, or lieutenant,
and an ensign. There were besides four armourers, and a master-at-
arms.[7] These two weak companies, besides defending the Fort, had to
undertake the safeguarding of the Company's boats up and down the
river as far as Patna, and had sometimes to help to maintain order in the
town. They were, no doubt, trained after the model of Marlborough's
armies. Their uniform seems to have been red trimmed with blue.[8]
The soldiers were partly Portuguese, hired in the country, and partly
English, recruited from home, perhaps by some young gentleman who
wished to hold a commission under the Company.[9] Their lot does not
seem to have been enviable. Without any of the excitement or glory
of war, they had to discharge the harassing duties of river police.
Till the year 1710, they had no proper barracks to live in, but had to
find lodgings for themselves, as best they could, anywhere in the town.[10]
Till the autumn of 1707, there was no hospital for the numbers among

---

[1] *Summaries*, § 105.
[2] *Ib.*, § 147.
[3] *Ib.*, § 315.
[4] *Ib.*, § 394
[5] *Ib.*, § 168.
[6] *Ib.*, § 246.
[7] *Ib.*, § 304.
[8] *Ib.*, § 395.
[9] *Ib.*, Addenda, § 442.
[10] *Ib.*, § 366.

them who were sick and dying.[1] Very few of these poor lads ever saw their native land again, and half of them never even reached India.[2] Yet it was upon them that the merchants depended for the safety of the river and the defence of Calcutta.

More important even than the fort and the garrison were the Company's ships and sailors, for the English power was founded on the command of the sea. The Company's business in Bengal required two fleets. Besides the great sea-going ships, there were a large number of small sloops and boats which carried on the trade of the river, and brought down the saltpetre from Patna. The great ships did not come up the river farther than Calcutta, for the navigation of the river was then as now very difficult. It would have been impossible had it not been for the splendid service of pilots which the Company had established in 1668. At the beginning of the Rotation Government this service, it would seem, included three pilots, three masters, three boatswains, and three or four apprentices.[3] A large number of English pilots must also have been employed on Indian and other foreign ships. In 1708 we find the Council threatening to stop all the Mogul shipping and paralyse the trade at Hugli and Rajmahal by ordering all the English captains in the employ of the Indian government to repair to Calcutta.[4] Altogether nothing can be more striking than the hold upon the river which the English had acquired even at this early date.

---

[1] *Summaries*, § 218.
[2] *Ib.*, § 308.
[3] *Ib.*, Addenda, § 416.
[4] *Ib.*, § 272.

CHAPTER VII.

Such was the somewhat rough machinery of Government by which Calcutta was at this time administered and its trade protected. When we search the records for information as to the life of the place, we find very little said about those who constituted the great majority of the inhabitants. Of the Bengali families only one stands out with any distinctness, the great family which sprang from Mukundarāma Sett, who with the assistance of the four Bysacks colonized Govindpur in the sixteenth century.[1] Eighth in descent from the founder was Kenarāma, the father of Janārdana, Vārānasi, and Nandarāma Sett. Of these Janārdana, the eldest brother, a fair, stout and good-looking man, was the Company's broker in the days of the Rotation Government. Liberal and high-minded, like his better-known son Vaiṣṇava Charan, he commanded the respect and confidence of all who came into contact with him. His wife, Ṭunumani, was noted for her good works, for the charities which she endowed at Bindrabun, and for the twelve temples of Çiva which she built at Katrunga.[2] Janārdana was

---

[1] G. D. Bysack's *Kalighat and Calcutta*, in the Calcutta Review, XCII, p. 319.

[2] I am indebted to Babu G. D. Bysack for this information.

appointed the Company's broker on the 18th October, 1707.[1]   He is
mentioned more than once in the records, and was evidently the most
important of the Company's native servants.[2]   On the 9th February
1712 he died, and was succeeded as broker by his brother Vārānasi
Sett.

   The records notice more than once the celebrated Armenian merchant, Khojah Israel Sarhad, the nephew of the great Khojah Phanoos
Khalanthar.   In the preceding period Sarhad had done good service in
helping to secure the grant of the three towns from Prince 'Aẕīmu-sh-
Shan.   In the days to come he was to still further distinguish himself
as a diplomatist when sent with the embassy to Farrukhsiyar; but
at the present time he does not seem to have been on the best terms
with the Council, who, on the 2nd May 1707, actually went to the
length of seizing his goods to recover the money which he then owed
the Company.[3]

   As regards the life of the English in Calcutta, our information is
sufficiently abundant.   Besides the numerous hints and touches supplied
by the records, we have two contemporary accounts, one by Captain
Alexander Hamilton and the other by Parson Benjamin Adams.   Both
are interesting and important; but before accepting either we must in
each case examine the circumstances under which our witness gives his
evidence.

   Benjamin Adams, "a sober, virtuous, and learned man," had been
appointed by the Court to the Bay on the 22nd November 1699, at the
recommendation of Hewer, the friend of Pepys, and of Eyre, the late
Agent at Calcutta.   Four days later he had been ordained priest, and
at Christmas-tide, when Eyre, newly knighted, set out for India in the
Fame to resume service under the Company as President and Governor
of Fort William in Bengal, Adams sailed in his patron's train.   He
brought with him a collection of modern books which Hewer had presented to the Company's library at Calcutta, a very acceptable addition
to a place so far removed from the civilizing influences of literature.

   Adams seems also to have brought with him a rather poor opinion
of the spiritual state of his intended flock, and the belief that it was
his mission to effect a thorough reform.   The natural results followed.
When a young priest comes to a strange land, and with little knowledge
of life, and no knowledge of the society he is addressing, begins to

---

[1] *Summaries*, § 183.
[2] *Ib.*, §§ 215, 311, 319, 381, 383.
[3] *Ib.*, §§ 312, 327.

criticise, admonish, rebuke and condemn, he must not be surprised if he finds himself laughed at and neglected. This was what befell Adams. Calcutta thought well and spoke well of its new Chaplain, but it did not pay much attention to his views on social reform. To Adams the experience was a bitter disappointment, and he wrote home painting the condition of Calcutta in the most sombre colours.[1]

"The missionary clergy abroad," he says, "live under great discouragement and disadvantage with regard to the easy and successful discharge of their important office. For, to say nothing of the ill-treatment they meet with on all hands, resulting sometimes from the opposition of their chiefs, who have no other notion of chaplains but that they are the Company's servants sent abroad to act for, under, and by them, upon all occasions, and sometimes from the perverseness and refractoriness of others, it is observable that it is not in the power to act but by legal process upon any emergent occasion, when instances of notorious wickedness present themselves. And because that cannot conveniently be had at so great distance [since all important cases have to be referred to Madras,] hence it comes to pass that they must suffer silently, being incapacitated to right themselves upon any injury or indignity offered, or, which is much worse, to vindicate the honour of our holy religion from the encroachments of libertinism and profaneness.

"This everybody knows, and that knowledge is constant ground for licentiousness and ill-manners, to those especially whose dissoluteness prompts them to level both persons and things when that may serve to the gratifying of their own extravagant and wild humour and interest.

"Were the injuries and indignities small and trivial, and such as in time by a competent care and prudence might either be avoided or redressed, a man might choose to bear them with patience rather than give himself the trouble of representing them to superiors. But notorious crimes had need be notoriously represented, or the infection would grow too strong and epidemical.

"For what, for instance, can any man say to that incestuous as well as adulterous marriage of Sir Nicholas Waite, President of Affairs for the New Company at Surat, with his niece, at a time when he expected his own lady by the next shipping? Or to that other adulterous marriage of William Warren, Surgeon to the Factory at Calcutta, with Elizabeth Binns, a widow there, though admonished, advised, and cautioned to the contrary, when she, and everybody that knew Mr. Warren,

---

[1] Hyde's *Bengal Chaplaincy in the reigns of William and Mary and Anne: Indian Church Quarterly*, Vol. V, 1892. Also *Hedges' Diary*, II, 318, 319.

knew also that he was married to another woman, who would have come out to him, if he had had a mind to it? But it seems that the obligations of marriage, or anything else, are of little consideration with Mr. Warren, being a man of most pernicious principles and debauched manners.

"I might instance in several things of this nature which occur daily, to the great scandal of our Christian profession among other Europeans, not to mention how easily the more strict and reserved among the heathens may reproach us in that particular enormity, which I have been speaking of." [1]

I think it would be most unfair to construe Adams's words into an indictment against the whole of the English colony in Calcutta. That offences against good morals were then far more common and far more serious than they are now, we cannot doubt. We do not expect to find purity in the lower waters of a stream which is tainted at its source, and the beginning of the eighteenth century was the nadir of our morality. We do not expect the wall to stand firm when its buttresses have been removed, and Calcutta was then so far away from London that all the common moral restraints and supports were to a great extent inoperative. We know that many of the exiles in that distant land formed unions, sometimes lawful, sometimes unlawful, with Portuguese and Indian women. We know that many of them were largely denationalized. The records make mention far too frequently of their quarrels and their punch-houses. They testify painfully to the prevalence of slavery. But for all that, there is no reason to believe that the majority of the Anglo-Indians of that time were not, as they always have been, sober, earnest, generous, and faithful. The charges made by Adams are sweeping enough, but only two definite cases are quoted, of which one occurred not at Calcutta but at Surat, which was supposed to be the godliest of the Company's factories. Against the solitary instance of Dr. Warren's misconduct, we can set the lives of men like Beard, Hedges, and Adams himself, whose excellence we know from the letters and documents which remain; and we need not doubt that could we read the recorded lives of all who lived at this period, the numbers of those who fell far short of the recognized standard of right conduct would be comparatively few.

If we turn from Adams to Hamilton we get a rather different picture. The captain, who from 1688 to 1723 was engaged in voyaging,

---

[1] *Hedges' Diary*, II, 319, 320.

by land and by sea, between the Cape of Good Hope and Japan, has given us the results of his eastern experiences in two gossiping volumes published in 1727. As a private trader he had to suffer many things at the hands of the Company's covenanted servants, and he consequently writes with a certain animus against them and their doings. He makes no mention of Dr. Warren; but he retails with evident relish the various scandalous stories which were current about Job Charnock and his Indian wife:[1] he also takes care to inform us of the corrupt practices of President Weltden, whose "term of governing was very short," but who "took as short a way to be enriched by it, by harassing the people to fill his coffers." "Yet he was very shy," continues Hamilton, "in taking bribes, referring those honest folks who trafficked that way to the discretion of his wife and daughter, to make the best bargain they could about the sum to be paid and to pay the money into their hands. I could give many instances of the force of bribing both here and elsewhere in India, but am loth to ruffle the skin of old sores." [2] It is unfortunate, perhaps, that Hamilton did not give other instances. As it is, these are the only serious charges which he has to make. One of them concerns an earlier period of our story and has already been disposed of; the second relates to a man who was sent out by the Court to Bengal, and, therefore, tells very little against the character of the English in Calcutta.

Hamilton's account of the religious state of the place is quaint. "In Calcutta all religions are freely tolerated but the Presbyterian, and that they brow-beat. The pagans carry their idols in procession through the town; the Roman Catholics have their church to lodge their idols in, and the Muhammadan is not discountenanced; but there are no polemics, except what are between our high Churchmen and our low, or between the Governor's party and other private merchants on points of trade." [3]

This brings us to the great sin of the English in Calcutta, their quarrelsomeness and violence. In one of his most amusing books, Jules Verne has described the strange results produced in the citizens of Quiquendone by the experiment of Dr. Ox. The waggish man of science contrived to fill the sleepy Flemish town with oxygen gas, and the worthy Quiquendonians, who used to be no more animated than sponges or corals, became straightway changed, morally and physically.

---

[1] Hamilton's *East Indies*, edition of 1727, vol. II, p. 8.
[2] *Ib.*, II,10.
[3] *Ib.*, II, 13, 14.

The very babies became insupportable; the High School boys rebelled; the burgomaster, Van Tricasse, hitherto incapable of deciding anything, now made twenty different decisions a day, scolding his officials and insulting his oldest friend, the Counseller Niklausse. They quarrelled in the streets; they fought with pistols; the police lost all control. At length, not satisfied with attacking each other, they determined to declare war on their neighbours at Virgamen, in consequence of an insult more than seven hundred years old.

It might well be supposed from all that is recorded about the days of the Rotation Government that a similar experiment was in progress in Calcutta. The wranglings and janglings of the double-headed government were notorious throughout India.[1] Page after page of the Consultation Book is filled with miserable disputes as to who should succeed to the Council and what should be his position. From the Council Chamber the disease spread far and wide. Captain South was ready to fight with Hedges about his salutes:[2] Littleton spent the last years of his life in abusing his colleagues:[3] even parson Adams was admonished to be more peaceable.[4] The ladies quarrelled about their places in church;[5] the sailors quarrelled with the landsmen;[6] the Company's servants with the private traders. For, although, as Hamilton puts it, "the conscript fathers of the colony disagree in many points among themselves, yet they all agree in oppressing strangers who are consigned to them, not suffering them to buy or sell their goods at the most advantageous market, but of the Governor and his Council who fix their own prices, high or low as seemeth best to their wisdom or discretion, and it is a crime hardly pardonable for a private merchant to go to Hooghly to inform himself of the current-prices of goods, although the liberty of buying and selling is entirely taken from him before."[7] "The colony has very little manufactory of its own, for the government being pretty arbitrary, discourages ingenuity and industry in the populace; for by the weight of the Company's authority if a native chances to disoblige one of the upper house, he is liable to arbitrary punishment either by fine, imprisonment, or corporal sufferings."[8]

---

[1] *Hedges' Diary*, II, 106.
[2] *Summaries*, § 87.
[3] See above, pp. 164, 165.
[4] *Summaries*, § 167.
[5] *Ib.*, § 158.
[6] *Ib.*, 154; and *Addenda*, § 417.
[7] Hamilton's *East Indies*, 12, 13.
[8] *Ib.*, 14.

From the hints given us in the records and from the little that
Hamilton tells us about the social life of Calcutta, it would seem to
have been much the same as it was twenty or thirty years before.
Its main features were preserved, but it was larger and freer. The
English sailed up and down the river as they pleased, and on land
from the south mark at Govindpur to that in the north near Bara-
nagar, from the river to the salt lake, they were supreme.[1] The mode
of life was still to a great extent moulded on the pattern of an Oxford
college. The established discipline still required residence inside the
factory walls, and daily attendance in church for prayers,[2] and at the
Company's table for dinner.[3] But these regulations were yielding to
the force of circumstances. The garrison, which consisted of some
one hundred and fifty soldiers, had to be quartered in the town.[4] On
various pretexts the Company's servants were given a diet apart, and
allowed to rent lands and build separate houses for themselves, till at
last, in May 1713, the general table was abolished on the score of
economy. In 1708 it was agreed that as the town was rapidly growing
and provisions were accordingly becoming dearer, the diet money must
be increased. In future the two chairmen were allowed sixty rupees
each a month, and the other married members of the Council thirty
rupees.[5] Their salaries, however, remained unaltered. The two chairmen and the chaplain received each £100 a year, and the members of
the Council £40, "to be paid in the country as the Court and the
managers direct at 2s. 6d. per rupee."[6]

As in Hugli, so here the Company had its garden to furnish the
Governor's table with herbage and fruits, and some fish ponds to serve
his kitchen with good carp, calcops, and mullet. "Most of the inhabitants of Calcutta," says Hamilton, "that make any tolerable figure
have the same advantages; and all sorts of provisions, both wild and
tame, being plentiful, good and cheap, as well as clothing, make the
country very agreeable.

"On the other side of the river are docks made for fitting and
repairing their ships' bottoms, and a pretty good garden belonging to
the Armenians, that had been a better place to have built their fort
and town in for many reasons. One is, that where it now stands,

---

[1] See above p. 191.
[2] *Summaries*, § 120.
[3] *Ib.*, § 139.
[4] *Ib.*, § 366.
[5] *Ib.*, § 266.
[6] *Ib.*, § 118.

the afternoon's sun is full in the fronts of the houses, and shines hot on the streets that are both above and below the fort; the sun would have sent its hot rays on the back of the houses, and the fronts had been a good shade for the streets. [1]

"Most gentlemen and ladies in Bengal live both splendidly and pleasantly, the forenoons being dedicated to business, and after dinner to rest, and in the evening to recreate themselves in chaises or palankins in the fields, or to gardens, or by water in the budgerows, which is a convenient boat that goes swiftly with the force of oars. On the river sometimes there is the diversion of fishing and fowling, or both; and before night they make friendly visits to one another, when pride or contention do not spoil society, which too often they do among the ladies, as discord and faction do among the men." [2]

I may add that they sometimes went hunting, and that occasionally the whole Council took a holiday trip up the river.

Being a man, Captain Hamilton has not condescended to tell us about the costume of the period. No doubt, though always a little behind the time, they did their best to keep up with the prevailing fashions, and the beauty and fashion of Calcutta, when they took their promenade on the green before the fort, arrayed themselves in dresses which recalled those worn by Bellinda and Sir Plume at Hampton Court five years previously.

In private life, however, the dwellers by the steamy banks of the Hugli adopted attire much less formal and exquisite. Even at the meetings of the Council the members thought of comfort rather than dignity, and we must picture them dressed in muslin shirts, long drawers, and starched white caps, sitting in the consultation room, with a case bottle of good old arrack and a goglet of water on the table, which the Secretary, with skilful hand, converted into punch as occasion arose. [3]

For all this the life led in Calcutta in these earliest days would not, according to modern ideas, appear either so splendid or so pleasant as it did to Hamilton. Books were scarce; outdoor games rare. We hear nothing of card playing [4] or dancing. There was no race-course, no spacious esplanade, no hotels, no theatres, no assembly rooms. Their

---

[1] Hamilton's *East Indies*, II, 11, 12.

[2] *Ib.*, 12.

[3] Letter from *An Old Country Captain* in the *India Gazette*, February 24th, 1781.

[4] I find mention of a card table in a list of goods sold in 1719.

wildest excitement must have been to sit in Mistress Domingo Ash's parlour, sipping arrack punch and listening to the story of the most recent quarrel amongst the dignities or the news brought by the latest ship ; how a Dutch vessel had been chased by a French cruiser from the gulf of Mocha towards the Malabar Coast ; and how the chaplain had refused to surrender one of his servants to justice, and had so come into conflict with Mr. Russell; how the English had failed to re-establish the factory at Banjar; and how Mr. Hedges had refused to resume his seat on the Council.

If Dame Fortune's wishing shoes, about which Hans Andersen has so much to tell us, were in existence and could be procured in Calcutta, I do not think the most discontented inhabitant of the modern city would be well advised to wish himself back into the days of the Rotation Government. If he did, he would probably find much more cause for complaint and regret than even the Councillor Knap when transported by the magic of the shoes to the times of King Hans. Imagine such a one with the fateful coverings on his feet leaving the General Post Office late at night on his way home. He has been employed till past nine o'clock in making up and sealing bags of letters and parcels, and wishes with all his heart that he had lived centuries ago when communications were less numerous and less rapid. The shoes work at his wish. He steps out of the great portico into the Calcutta of age of Good Queen Anne. The lofty buildings, the pavement, the lamps, the metalled street, the carriages, the tram-lines, all disappear. By the faint glimmer of the moon he can see a rough roadway. Beyond lies the only thing in the old town with which the modern citizen is familiar, the great " tank " with the grassy green surrounding it. To the south are bushy trees, thatched hovels, and pools of stinking water, which render the path leading to the burial-ground and the fields anything but inviting. The Post Office has vanished, and behind him in its place stand the red walls of the fort. He turns and walks northwards, following them, till he reaches the gate. It is shut. Leaving on his right the great avenue to the eastward, and the new church, he passes up the broad street to where the lights show that people are still up and stirring. He stumbles into a large garden and finds himself in the porch of a low single-storeyed dwelling, where, let us hope, despite his strange Victorian garb, he is welcomed and allowed to rest his bewildered head. In the morning, if the spell should still last, fresh surprises would await him. The majority of the English inhabitants are living in bungalows in the quarter of Calcutta which extends to the north of the great tank, their main reservoir of sweet water. Along the avenue to the eastward, which leads from the fort to the Salt Lake, there are but a few newly-built houses. To the south of the green, before the fort, there are plenty of eligible sites for building. Some plots have been taken up already by the Company for its stables, hospital, barracks, and powder magazine. There are as yet no Court House and no Court-house Street. The green extends right up to the Rope Walk, which modern Calcutta calls Mission Row. At the back of the town is the immemorial pilgrim path from Chitpur to Kālighāṭ, which is intersected by the Eastern Avenue at the "cross roads," where criminal justice is publicly meted out to offenders. On every side there are large wastes of unreclaimed land. The place reeks with malaria. A very hasty glance at his surroundings fills our translated citizen with a hearty desire to return to modern times, and with that the charm is at an end.

But is it fair thus to view the old settlement from the stand-point of modern progress? Perhaps not; yet tried even by the low standard of its own day it was extraordinarily unhealthy. Death overshadowed every living soul. Hamilton says that in one year, out of twelve hundred English in Calcutta, no less than four hundred and sixty died between August and the January following.[1] No direct confirmation of this terrible mortality bill is to be found in the records; but both in August 1705, when a second surgeon was appointed to assist Dr. Warren, and in October 1707, when it was resolved to build a hospital, we are informed that the sick and dying were superabundant.[2]

---

[1] Hamilton's *East Indies*, II, 7, 8.
[2] *Summaries*, §§ 145, 218.

CHAPTER VIII.

WHEN we remember that the town had at this time no proper drains, no good water-supply, and very few solid buildings or open roads, the unhealthiness of Calcutta is not much to be wondered at. No doubt during the whole period of the Rotation Government great efforts were made towards supplying these deficiencies. Private houses sprang up in all directions,—by the riverside, along the roads, out in the fields. On the 27th March 1704, the Council ordered a book to be prepared in which "leases, bills of sale, and agreements made by the freemen inhabitants of Calcutta" should be entered, "the Secretary's fee to be two rupees for registering the same,"[1] and in the Consultation Book itself we have noted from time to time a good many transactions relating to lands and houses. There was, however, no proper agency to supervise these private enterprises, or to carry out public works and improvements. Consequently, as Hamilton observes, "the town was built without order, as the builders thought most convenient for their own affairs; every one taking in what ground best pleased them for gardening, so that in most houses you must

---

[1] *Summaries*, § 68.

P

pass through a garden into the house; the English building near
the river's side, and the natives within land."[1]

The arsenal of Calcutta, and seat of the Company's Government in
Bengal, took from 15 to 20 years to build, and was even then not
completed.[2] As it stood by the riverside in 1710, Fort William was
in shape "an irregular tetragon of brick and mortar." Its north
side was 340 feet long, its south side 485 feet; its east and west sides
710 feet.[3] At the four corners were four small bastions which were
connected by curtain walls about 4 feet thick and 18 feet high. They
were built of small thin bricks strongly cemented together with a com-
position of brick-dust, lime, molasses, and cut hemp.[4] Each of the four
bastions mounted ten guns, and the east gate, which projected, carried
five. The bank of the river was armed with heavy cannon mounted
in embrasures on a wall of solid masonry, and the space between this
river wall and the west curtain was closed at each end by small cross
walls with palisaded gates. There were, however, no proper ditches or
military outworks of any kind to protect the other three sides of the
fort. Within, a block of low buildings running east and west cut the
fort into two sections, which were connected by a narrow passage.
The northern section of the Fort had one small water gate, and in its
centre an oblong building with a row of columns down the middle. The
southern and larger section had two gates, one leading to the river and
the landing stage, the other opening out to the eastward and giving
access to the town. In the middle of this section was the Governor's
house, which Hamilton describes as "the best and most regular piece
of architecture that I ever saw in India."[5] This building formed
three sides of a quadrangle. The west and principal face was
245 feet long. In the centre of this face was the main door of
the Governor's house, and from it a colonnade ran down to the water-
gate and the landing stage. Entering the doorway and turning to
your left you ascended the great flight of stairs which led to the hall

---

[1] Hamilton's *East Indies*, II, 9.

[2] For the topography of the fort see my article on the subject in the
Journal of the Asiatic Society of Bengal, Pt. I, 1893, pp. 104 to 127; also Mr.
Roskell Bayne's *Note on the remains of portions of Old Fort William*, in the
same *Journal*, Pt. I, 1883, pp. 105 to 119.

[3] I get these lengths by actual measurement. They are the extreme dimensions. Orme gives other measurements, which were probably taken from centre
to centre of the bastions.

[4] Hamilton's *East Indies*, II, 13.

[5] *Ib.*, II, 11.

and the principal rooms. The south-east wing contained the apartments of the Governor. A raised cloister ran round the three sides of the court enclosed within the building. All round the fort, chambers and arcades were built against the curtain walls, their roofs serving as ramparts. To those lying south of the east gate a melancholy interest attaches. They were the scene of the Black Hole tragedy.

Something but not all of the history of these buildings can be collected from the records. As early as 1693, Sir John Goldsborough had marked out the site of the fort with a mud wall, but the English did not venture to begin to build till the rebellion of Çubha Singha in 1696. It appears from the Sūtānuṭī diary that on the 1st January 1697 they were "employed in fortifying themselves ;and wanted proper guns for the points." For the present they only asked for ten, from which it may be inferred that only one bastion was then in existence. The so-called fort, in fact, consisted merely of three or four walls with a square brick tower at the north-east angle, built to look like a warehouse for fear of exciting the jealousy of the Mogul. In the year 1700 and 1701 the question of strengthening the fortifications was forced upon the Council at Calcutta by the return of Sir Charles Eyre, who had been sent out from home for this very purpose.[1] Upon his hasty departure the work was taken up by Beard, who, at the beginning of 1702, was able to report that he had made such substantial additions to Fort William that it was strong enough to ward off any attack by the Country Powers.[2] The additions probably included the building of a new bastion at the south-east angle, and the encasing of the old square bastion at the north-east angle with flanks and salients to give it a more proper military shape. The remains of all these works, now buried beneath a mass of modern erections, have from time to time been brought to light by excavations made in the course of laying down new foundations. In 1883 Mr. Roskell Bayne examined the site of the north-east angle of the fort, and measured all the old walls. The masonry work was found to be of good material and very hard to break into. The walls of the old square bastion were more than six feet thick. Those of the new outer bastion were still thicker. They "were battered," says the engineer, " with a fall in of about one in ten, and the outer faces were finished with a thin coat of lime plaster of a rich crimson tint and

---

[1] For these statements, see ante, pp. 143, 149, 157.
[2] Bruce's Annals, II, 444, 445.

reticulated in imitation of stone work, the stones being about 1 foot 6 inches long by about 9 to 10 inches deep."[1]

When on the 1st February 1704 President Beard handed over to the Rotation Government the garrison and factory, the fortifications consisted of nothing but three or four walls, with two bastions at the north-east and south-east corners of the enclosure. It was not till the death of Aurangzēb in 1707 that anything further was done to strengthen the fort. During the confusion of the interregnum two regular bastions were built on the water-side to correspond with those on the land side. The military paymaster was ordered " to see it well performed out of hand, and to that end to take all the materials in the town that are necessary thereto, that it may be quickly erected, for we may not meet with such an opportunity again."[2] The signs of haste were still visible in the north-west bastion, when its remains were dug up in 1883. Its courses of bricks were irregular; its outlines confused; its dimensions contracted.[3] In February 1709 the English took a further step of the greatest importance to the health and safety of their settlement. On the east side of the fort lay a small pond of water. By deepening and lengthening it, additional security was given to the south-east angle of the fortification, and a large reservoir was provided of water, far sweeter and healthier than the brackish Hugli which had hitherto been the drink of the garrison. The earth taken out of the excavation was used to fill up the space between the two new bastions and the bank was faced with rubble and ballast.[4] In February 1710 they began to build a wharf before the fort, facing it with brick and raising a breastwork on which to plant cannon.[5] Lastly, to complete these improvements in the external surroundings of the place, a clearance was made to the south where the ground was choked up and close set with trees, small thatched hovels, and standing pools of stinking water. In August the paymaster was ordered to clear the ground and open the way directly before the factory, " continuing the present walk already made further into the open field, filling up all the holes, and cutting small trenches on each side to carry the water clear from the adjacent places into the large drains."[6]

---

[1] Roskell Bayne in *Journal of the Asiatic Society of Bengal*, Pt. I, 1883, p. 109.

[2] *Summaries*, § 202.

[3] Roskell Bayne in *Journal of the Asiatic Society of Bengal*, Pt. I, 1883, p. 110.

[4] *Summaries*, § 296.

[5] *Ib.*, § 365.

[6] *Ib.*, § 398.

While such was the progress of the external defences of the factory, the growth of the internal buildings was no less slow. It would seem that originally the principal buildings occupied the northern end of the enclosed space. At first they were of the meanest description. The Company's store places, outhouses, and stables consisted of nothing but mud walls and thatched roofs. Brick and mud were probably the materials used for the armoury and factory, of which the former occupied the centre of the north ward, while the latter seems to have stood on the site of the dividing block of buildings afterwards assigned "to the young gentlemen in the Company's service."[1] In 1706 the old factory house was hardly fit for habitation. It had long been falling into decay, and had been so much injured by recent storms that it had given way in places. It was accordingly ordered to be pulled down, and other lodgings were prepared for the gentlemen that lay in it.[2] Meanwhile, in the south ward, the new Governor's house was being built, which so much excited the admiration of Captain Hamilton. This fine piece of architecture was put together with considerable deliberation. It seems to have been commenced in 1702[3] and not to have been finished till the middle of 1706. At the beginning of 1704, when Littleton enquired what accommodation could be given to him in Calcutta, he found that there were but few good rooms finished in the new house,[4] and, in fact, the first floor was not completely roofed in till just before the rainy season of that year.[5]

Every year, as the Company's trade developed and the number of the Company's servants, civil and military, increased, the difficulty of finding room for them all became more pressing. On all sides warehouses were erected against the walls, under the pleasing belief that they strengthened the fortification.[6] In other cases accommodation had to be sought outside the fort altogether. In 1707 for example, the authorities

---

[1] This is conjecture. It is certain that the old buildings were at the north end ; and when I dug up the foundations of the dividing block of buildings in 1892, I found the foundations of older " brick-in-mud " buildings beneath.

[2] *Summaries*, § 164. I suppose that the old factory house was condemned as soon as the new house was completed.

[3] *Ib.*, § 24.

[4] *Ib.*, § 45.

[5] *Ib.*, § 50.

[6] Thus in May 1708 the Council strengthened the fortification by continuing the sorting warehouse, which was built inside the south curtain till it reached the new south-west bastion (*Summaries*, § 248); and in the next year they rebuilt the whole of it in a more solid manner (*Summaries*, § 300).

in Calcutta were at last induced to attend to the needs of the soldiers and sailors, who every year fell sick and died in large numbers, owing to the cruel manner in which they were neglected. After frequent representations had been made by the doctors, the Council agreed on the 16th October that a convenient spot, close to the burial ground, should be pitched on as the site of a hospital, and contributed two thousand rupees towards the building expenses. The rest of the money was raised by public subscription.[1] Of this institution Hamilton has expressed a somewhat modified approbation. "The Company," he says, "has a pretty good hospital at Calcutta, where many go in to undergo the penance of physic, but few come out again to give account of its operation."[2] In 1710, in order to put a stop to the unwholesome practice of allowing the soldiers to lodge in the town, the hospital was walled round and barracks erected for them to live in under the supervision of their officers.[3]

But of all the buildings erected at this time without the fort, the most important was the Church of St. Anne. The first proposals for a separate place of worship in Calcutta were made in September 1704, in a joint letter to the Council by Benjamin Adams and by William Anderson, the former Chaplain of the "English Company" at Hugli. At that time, owing to the union of the two Companies, the English inhabitants had become so numerous that there was "no place able to contain the congregation that would meet at divine service if there were rooms sufficient to contain them," and the Council lent a willing ear to the suggestions of the two clergymen. To the building fund, to which the commanders of ships, the Company's servants, and the free inhabitants had liberally contributed, they added Rs. 1,000,[4] and when towards the end of October Adams was obliged to make a sea-voyage to Madras for his health, they furnished him with a letter to the authorities of Fort St. George to enable him to raise money there too.[5] The site first assigned to the Church was a plot of ground in the "Broad street,"[6] but in deference to a chorus of objections on the part of the inhabitants, who threatened to withdraw their subscriptions, it was changed for another immediately opposite the east curtain of the

---

[1] *Summaries*, § 218.
[2] Hamilton's *East Indies*, II, 11.
[3] *Summaries*, § 366.
[4] *Ib.*, § 113.
[5] *Ib.*, § 127.
[6] *Ib.*, § 128.

Fort.[1] The work of building now began in right earnest. Adams, however, continued to collect subscriptions till September 1706, when he called a conference and arranged that the raising of funds, as well as the supervision of the building, should be left to lay agency. In a somewhat mysterious letter to the Council, dated the 19th of the month, he gives as his reason for this step, that "Brother Anderson had not reputation enough among the gentlemen to obtain their subscriptions" and that he himself is about to resign his Chaplaincy at Michaelmas. Therefore "at this juncture it were more advisable that the collection should proceed upon indifferent trustees." "And I wish," he adds, "with all my heart, they may collect more money than I did last year, which will enable them to do what is useful if not ornamental to the Church; and that in any corner of the world would be acceptable news to your friend and servant, Benjamin Adams."[2] In spite of the wishes of the worthy clergyman the trustees do not seem to have done much for the Church. In February 1707 it was found that the work was at a standstill owing to the want of proper or regular proceedings, and Edward Pattle and John Maisters were ordered to take the matter in hand at once. They were to receive subscriptions, supervise the building, and see that it went on regularly, and to make a monthly report to the Council.[3] The work now proceeded rapidly. Early in the following year it had advanced so far that Anderson was able to write to the Bishop of London and ask him to arrange for the consecration. By the beginning of 1709 the Church was complete. On the 9th May, Anderson, as Bishop's Commissary, laid before the Council the commission to consecrate, and received permission to execute it.[4] On the 5th June, being the Sunday after Ascension Day, the Church was duly dedicated to the service of God in the name of St. Anne.[5]

The structure of St. Anne's has recently been studied with loving care by Mr. H. B. Hyde,[6] and by a comparison of various views and plans, its most important dimensions and features have been ascertained. The length of the Church was eighty feet. The interior consisted of a nave about twenty feet broad, with a high-pitched roof divided by rows

---

[1] *Summaries*, § 134.
[2] *Ib.*, § 176.
[3] *Ib.*, § 190.
[4] *Ib.*, § 318.
[5] *Ib.*, § 328.
[6] See his article on *the Bengal Chaplaincy in the reigns of William and Mary and Anne* in the *Indian Church Quarterly*, Vol. V, 1892.

of pillars from the north and south aisles. At the east end was a circular apse for the sanctuary. The west end was a massive section containing the vestibule, the vestry, and the tower staircase. The tower itself, which was twenty feet square, was divided into three storeys and surmounted by a balustrade. In 1712 a bell, sent out by the Court, was ordered to be hung in a convenient handsome place over the porch, and an octagonal spire was in consequence added to the tower. For nearly fifty years the sacred edifice continued to be the chief ornament of the English settlement in Bengal, and in the earliest view of Calcutta you may see its lofty steeple rising into the sky, above all the buildings of the fort.

In the foregoing pages I have tried to trace the main outlines of the early history of the English in Bengal, up to and including the story of the Rotation Government, in the years 1704 to 1710, and I hope that, in the light of what I have written, the extracts from and summaries of the Bengal Records, given in this and subsequent volumes, will be intelligible and interesting to the reader. I have tried to bear in mind that history is the exposition of a coherent series of social changes. I have tried to show the necessity for the English settlement at Calcutta, and I have begun to sketch the consequences of this settlement. The story of the first twenty years suggests three points of view from which to follow the subsequent course of events, the external relations of the English Government, the effect of the settlement on the character of the English settlers, and lastly its effect on the character of the natives of the country.

The external policy of the English was determined by the nature of the Mogul Government, a Government which exacted constant supplies of tribute from the Lower Provinces, and yet was unable in return to secure peace and good order. The great object of the Viceroy of Bengal and of his subordinates was to extract from the country enough gold and silver to satisfy the demands of Delhi and their own cupidity. The European trading companies were their great mines of wealth, which they worked vigorously. So anxious were they to get every golden egg they could from their foreign geese, that they often came near to killing the geese themselves. The English, to defend themselves against these exactions, took refuge in Calcutta, where the strength of their position enabled them to make more advantageous terms with the nabob of Bengal. During the twenty years of which this volume treats, these advantages were seen to be very real. The English settlement advanced by leaps and bounds, and its progress would have been still greater, had it not been for the disputes between the rival companies, and the uncertainty of the nature of the English legal position, an uncertainty which was remedied, as will be seen in the next volume, by the English embassy to Farrukhsiyar.

The second point of interest is the effect of the settlement in Bengal on the English themselves. The first settlers became very largely Indianised in their manners and customs; but as time went on, and the English became more numerous, they were better able to resist the influences by which they were surrounded, and preserve their own national characteristics. Towards this safeguarding of the English character the settlement at Calcutta must have greatly contributed.

The effect of the English settlement on the natives of the country is not very noticeable in the story as far as I have brought it, yet this perhaps is the most important point of all. In Calcutta the English made many of their first experiments in ruling India. Ralph Sheldon is the first English Collector and Magistrate in Bengal.[1] Poor and unworthy as the administration of the early settlement may seem to modern eyes, we can have no doubt that it presented a very favourable contrast to the government of the surrounding districts, a contrast which was not forgotten in 1757. The development of the administration of Calcutta and the introduction of British order and justice should be among the most interesting points upon which the volumes of records which I have yet to summarise may be expected to throw light.

---

[1] The principal regulations introduced, or intended to be introduced, by the Permanent Settlement are found in force in Calcutta under the Rotation Government. The English Council, as the permanently-settled collector, makes a survey of its lands. The rent is paid at the customary rate of not more than three rupees a bigha. Every tenant has to take out a deed declaring the area of his land and the rent due on it. The native officers in charge of the land records are converted into "rent-gatherers" in the pay of the Collectorate. See *Summaries*, sections 205, 206, 207; and compare Sir W. W. Hunter's *Bengal M. S. Records*, edition of 1894, Volume I, Historical Dissertation on Land Rights, especially pages 55, 61, 67, 120.)

SUMMARIES

OF THE

BENGAL PUBLIC CONSULTATION BOOKS

FOR THE YEARS 1704 TO 1710.

DIARY[1] AND CONSULTATION BOOK

OF THE

LONDON COMPANY'S COUNCIL AT FORT WILLIAM IN BENGAL.

From December 1703 to the end of November 1704.

1.—SALE OF THE COMPANY'S COPPER.

BEING in great need of money they agree to dispose of the Company's copper at the present low rate, namely 100 maunds, at 24 rupees per maund.

December 2nd.

2.—MONEY FOR THE STEWARD.

The charges general keeper, wanting money for the steward and other expenses, is paid four hundred rupees.[2]

December 6th.

3.—EXPENSES FOR OCTOBER 1703.

The general expenses for the month of October 1703 were brought in, read, and passed.

December 6th.

October accounts of the Governor's Company.

				Rs.	A.	P.
Charges general	...	...	...	103	13	6
Diet	...	...	...	677	4	6
Merchandise	...	...	...	91	14	3
Servants' wages	...	...	...	296	6	6
Cattle	...	...	...	38	0	0
Weaving shop	...	...	...	40	15	6
General stores	...	...	...	13	14	0
Durbar [*Darbār*]	...	...	...	2	8	0
Factors' provisions	...	...	...	61	0	0
By Lotmond Vacquelle [*Lakshman, Vakīl*]	...	...	1	0	0
By profit and loss by 94 ch. 2 pun cowries[3] not passable at 32 pun per rupee	...	...	47	1	0
		Total	...	1,373	13	3

---

[1] This diary, and the diaries which follow, except where a note occurs to the contrary, are contained in the bound volumes of Bengal Public Consultations in the India Office, Range 1, Nos. 1 and 2.

[2] About once a month he seems to have had the same sum more or less given him.

[3] That is 94 *kāhans* and 2 *pans* of *kawris* : 16 *pans* made 1 *kāhan* ; and 2 *kāhans* 1 rupee.

Accounts of the English Company.

				Rs.	A.	P.
Charges general	...	...	...	47	3	3
Cattle	...	...	...	23	1	6
Repairs	...	...	...	26	3	3
Mary Smack	...	...	...	133	5	6
Servants' wages	...	...	...	124	8	6
New house	...	...	...	60	11	0
Butler's room	...	...	...	28	12	6
Summer house	...	...	...	57	11	3
Garrison	...	...	...	813	1	9
Cash sent to Parransow [?*Prān Çāhā*] at Jessore to provide timbers		...	...	300	0	0
				1,594	10	6
Expenses added ; both Companies together		...		2,968	7	9

4.—REVENUE FOR OCTOBER 1703.

December 6th.

The account of the revenues collected out of the three towns and bazar for the month of October by Ralph Sheldon was perused and passed, the particulars being as follows :—

Accounts of the Revenue of the three Towns, month of October 1703.

Paid by Bassar [Bāzār].					*Credit.*			
	Rs.	A.	P.			Rs.	A.	P.
For servants' wages, etc.—Catwall [*Kotwāl*]	4	0	0		By rent of houses ...	327	10	6
					Batta [*Baṭṭā*]—			
Four writers, Rs. 18-8; fifteen peons, Rs. 31; ten paikes [*pāiks*], Rs. 15-8...	65	0	0		297-10½ sicca 10 p.c. ...	29	12	3
					1 ditto ...	0	1	6
					22 ,, ...	1	14	0
					(7 currt.)			
Four rent-gatherers, Rs. 6-4; drummer and piper, Rs. 1-12 ...	8	0	0			359	6	3
Hollocore [*halāl-khor*] ...	0	12	0		By sundry petty incomes—			
					Recovery of debts ...	7	1	0
Paper, 6a; ink, 2a ...	0	8	0		Fines ...	4	0	0
					Peons' pay on business ...	0	6	0
	78	4	0		Marriage fees ...	1	12	0
					Sallamie [*Salāmī*] ...	1	8	0
					Duties on firewood ...	3	8	0
					Customs on grain, etc., taken in specie and sold for ...	14	15	6
Balance paid into cash ...	314	4	9					
	392	8	9			392	8	9

Calcutta.

Paid.	Rs.	A.	P.
For servants' wages, etc.—			
Sheekdar [*shiqdār*], Rs. 4;			
three mundels [*manḍal*],			
Rs. 2	6	0	0
One Putwarie [*paṭwāri*],			
Rs. 2; five peons, Rs. 10	12	0	0
Mending the cutcherrie and			
mats	1	9	3
Cloth to tie up the papers	0	4	0
Mending the highways ...	1	11	0
A seerpau [*sar-o-pā*] to two			
mundells [*manḍals*] ...	2	1	0
	26	2	3

Credit.	Rs.	A.	P.
By rent of houses and land...	203	15	3
Batta [*Baṭṭā*] on houses			
at 10 p. c.	20	6	3
	224	5	6
By sundry petty incomes;—			
marriage fees, 7 rupees;			
recovering debts, Rs. 2-7;			
sallamie [*salāmī*], Rs. 22;			
fines, Rs. 2; batta, 7 annas;			
fruit sold, 4 annas 3 pie;—			
Equals altogether	34	2	3
New bazar—			
Mart rent, Rs. 2; duties on			
goods, Rs. 1-7¾; weighers'			
duties, Rs. 1; batta, 5½			
annas	4	13	3
Pole money received, sicca...	20	8	6
Batta	2	0	9
	285	14	3

Soota Loota.

Servants' wages, etc.—		Rs.	A.	P.
Shikdar [*shiqdār*] •	...	3	0	0
Putwarrie [*paṭwāri*]	...	2	0	0
Five peons	...	10	0	0
Ink and paper ...	...	2	1	0
		17	1	0

	Rs.	A.	P.
By rent of land and houses	134	3	0
Batta at 10 p. c.	13	6	9
Petty incomes, nine marts of			
this month...	54	15	0
Batta at 10 p. c.	5	8	0
Weighers' duties, Rs. 5; batta			
8 annas	5	8	0
Cuttie Mangun [? *Kuṭṭi*			
mangan], Rs. 14-8½; batta			
Re. 1-7	15	15	6
Duties on fruits out of gardens	5	9	3
Fines, Re. 1; recovering debt,			
3 annas	1	3	0
Sallamie, 8 annas; pole mo-			
ney, 32 sicca, annas 7 ...	32	15	0
Batta, Rs. 3-4	3	4	0
Assaurie [? *āshāṛi*] by the			
fishers, Rs. 6-5	6	5	0
Batta, 10 annas	0	10	0
	279	6	6

Govingpore.

	Rs.	A.	P.			Rs.	A.	P.
To servants' wages, etc.—				By rent of houses and land	160	0	0
Sheekdar, Rs. 4; patwarrie,				Advance on cowries received	1	0	0
Re. 1-8; spreading, Re. 1	6	8	0	Batta at 10 p. c.	16	0	0
Charges on the three towns—				Sundry petty incomes, goods			
Vacquell [*Vakīl*], Rs. 5.				received in specie and sold			
2 writers, Rs. 6, 8 cahars				for	2	13	0
[*kāhārs*], Rs. 8	19	8	0	Sallammie	2	0	0
Ink and paper Re. 1-3, oil				Pole money sicca ...	47	4	0
annas 12	1	15.	0	Batta	4	11	9
To the Government peon ...	1	4	3	Assurie by fishermen ...	8	0	0
	29	3	3	Batta	0	10	9
	72	6	6		242	7	3
To balance into cash ...	735	5	6		565	4	9
	807	12	0		807	12	0

JOHN CALVERT, *Sect.*　　　　JOHN BEARD.
　　　　　　　　　　　　　　　　JONA. WHITE.[1]
　　　　　　　　　　　　　　　　RALPH SHELDON.
　　　　　　　　　　　　　　　　JOHN RUSSELL.

5.—PETRE BOATS STOPPED.

The Company's petre boats arrive at Rajmahal and are there
December 30th. stopped because they had neither the Prince's
nor the Dīwān's *sanad.* Mr. Redshaw has
gone there to see after them. They send him a thousand rupees, and
order him to clear the boats at any price; otherwise the saltpetre will
not be at Fort William in time for shipping.

6.—BUILDING EXPENSES.

The charges general keeper receives four hundred rupees to pay the
December 30th. workmen on the building and to procure some
fine chunam [*chūnām.*]

7.—TAKING FROM THE MOORS.

John Matroon, chief mate of the President's ship *Monsoon,* coming
December 30th. into the river, took out of a Moor's ship some
cowries, stores, etc. The President hearing of
this ordered that the goods should be given up to the Council and

<hr>

[1] White died on the 3rd January, 1704, in the 34th year of his age. His tombstone is in St. John's Churchyard, Calcutta, in the Charnock mausoleum.

reserved, in case any demand should be made, as it might prove disadvantageous for the Company, if the Moors complained. Finally, the goods were sold at public auction, and the money they fetched paid back.

8.—REVENUE FOR NOVEMBER 1703.

December 30th.

The account of the revenues collected out of the three towns and bazars for the month of November 1703, and was perused and passed, the particulars being as follows:—

Bazar.

Debts.		Rs.	A.	P.	Credit.				Rs.	A.	P.
To servants' wages—					By rent of land and houses.				112	5	0
Catwall ...	...	4	0	0	Sicca at 10 per cent.						
Four writers	...	18	8	0	100 0 0	10 0 0					
Fifteen peons	...	31	0	0	2 0 0	0 3 0					
Ten paikes ...	...	15	8	0	1 9 0	0 2 0					
Four rent gatherers	...	6	4	0	1 0 0	0 1 0					
Hollocore ...	...	0	12	0					10	6	0
Drummer and piper	...	1	12	0	(Current 17 12).						
Paper and ink	...	0	8	0	By sundry petty						
		78	4	0	incomes, *i.e.*, for the amount of one year and rent of ground for leases granted to the English, *i e.*, Sir Charles Eyre's compound—						
					Large ...10 1 0						
					Ditto, smaller ... 5 13 6						
					Gunner Price, 1 ditto 3 4 9						
					19 3 3						
					Batta at 10 per cent. ... 1 14 9						
									21	2	0
					Sallammie ... 4 8 0						
					Peon's pay ... 1 1 0						
									5	9	0
					Fines ... 6 4 9						
					Marriage duties .. 2 0 0						
									8	4	9
					Recovering debts ¼ part				3	5	0
					Duties on firewood ...				3	8	0
					Customs on grain, etc., taken in specie and sold						
To balance paid into cash		112	8	9	for				26	5	0
		190	12	9					190	12	9

Calcutta.

Debts.	Rs.	A.	P.	Credit.	Rs.	A.	P.	Rs.	A.	P.
To servants' wages, etc.—				By rent of land						
One putwarie [*patwārī*]	2	0	0	and houses ...	99	1	3			
Two mundells [*maṇḍals*]	1	8	0	Batta at 10 per cent.	9	14	3			
One peon	1	8	0					108	15	6
Sheekdar [*shiqdār*] ...	4	0	0	By sundry petty						
	9	0	0	incomes—						
				Salammie ...	3	0	0			
				Recovering debts	7	4	0			
				Fines ...	4	0	0			
								14	4	0
				New buzzar, *i.e.*—						
				Mart rents ...	2	0	0			
				Duties on goods						
				sold for ...	1	7	0			
				Weigher's duties	1	0	0			
				Batta ...	0	5	0			
								4	12	0
								127	15	6
Debts	9	0	0	Credit ...127	15	6				

Soota Loota.

	Rs.	A.	P.		Rs.	A.	P.
To servants' wages—				By rent of houses,			
Sheekdar ...	3	0	0	etc.	67	12	0
Putwarie ...	2	0	0	Batta	6	12	3
	5	0	0	Incomes of eight			
Five peons ...10	0	0		marts 121 ca. 10 pa.	52	3	9
Charges on the new				Batta	5	3	6
settled houses, *i.e.*				Weigher's duties	5	8	0
Two paikes ...	2	8	0	Cuttie Mangun	6	0	0
One drummer ...	0	8	0	Batta	0	9	6
	13	0	0	Sallamie	2	0	0
Charges on making a				Incomes of 105 new			
new buzzar in set-				settled houses, this			
tling 105 houses,				being the 1st			
being for 7 months,				month rent was			
charges allowed	40	0	0	taken	10	11	0
(Calcutta debts Rs. 9							
added on)	67	0	0		284	12	0

Govingpore.

	Rs. A. P.	Rs. A. P.		Rs. A. P.	Rs. A. P.
Servant's wages—			By rent of houses,		
Sheekdar ...	4 0 0		etc.	54 12 0	
Putwarie ...	1 8 0		Batta ...	5 7 6	
		5 8 0			60 3 6
			Fines ...	5 0 0	
			Sallammie ...	1 0 0	
					6 0 0
New buzzar—1 peon ...	1 8 0				350 15 6
Drummer	0 12 0				126 5 0
		7 12 0			224 10 6

Expenses on the three towns.

				Rs. A. P.	Rs. A. P.
Vacqueel	...	...	...	5 0 0	
Paper	...	...	...	1 0 0	
Ink	...	...	...	0 3 0	
					6 3 0
Two writers	...	...	...	6 8 0	
Cahars	...	...	...	8 0 0	
					14 8 0
Given to the putwaries of the towns and the head tenants for encouraging and paying the full year's rent as customary			...		30 14 0
					51 9 0
Rs. 67+7-12+51-9=126-5	...	...		126 5 0	
To balance paid into cash	...	...		224 10 0	
					350 15 6

9.—GETTING THE PETRE BOATS PASSED.

The Council received notice that the Company's saltpetre was cleared and had come up the river to Calcapore, [Kālkāpur.] Knowing that there was so little water at Calcapore that the large boats could not pass, the Council sent up two of its own members with six soldiers, and with money and presents for the Governor and officers of Muxadevad in case they should hinder the boats. They order them to load the petre on to smaller boats, and bring it along as quickly as possible.

January 10th, 1704.

Q

10.—PRESENTS FOR MAQSŪDĀBĀD.

January 10th.   List of presents sent to Muxadevad—

Looking glasses	...	...	...	1 of 10 inches.
Ditto	...	...	...	2 „ 12 „
Sword blades	...	...	...	2 „ 14 „
				5

Flintware 38, viz.—

Cups 3. Carpet glass 4.

Beetle box 5 lbs., a plate and cover	...	1
Candlesticks	...	...	...	2
Pigdannye (*Pikdāni*)	...	...	...	2
Hubbubles	...	...	...	3
Knife hafts	...	...	...	2
Rose-water bottles	...	...	...	7
Plates	...	...	...	2

Velvet blue 4 yards, broad cloth (fine).
Red cloth 1 piece   22½ yards.
Green cloth 1 piece   24   „

Broad cloth, coarse—
     Red, 2 pieces   44   „
     Do., 1 piece   10   „

11.—EXPENSES, NOVEMBER, 1703.

The accounts for the month of November are brought in and January 10th.   passed.

NOVEMBER 1703.

Accounts of the Old Company.

				Rs.	A.	P.
Charges general	...	...	...	95	1	6
Weaving shop ...	...	...	...	35	2	6
Merchandise ...	...	...	...	77	0	3
Cattle ...	...	...	...	38	0	0
Diet ...	...	...	...	683	5	3
Servants' wages	...	...	...	294	14	0
Madras Presidency	...	...	...	34	0	0
Durbar ...	...	...	...	51	7	6
General stores ...	...	...	...	72	11	3
Factors' provisions	...	...	...	223	2	0
By what paid into cash being the amount of Captain Perrin's accounts of stores brought	...			2,507	15	9
				4,112	12	0

Accounts of English Company.

				Rs.	A.	P.
Charges general	...	...	...	70	3	6
Repairs	...	...	...	17	0	0
Servants' wages	...	...	...	127	8	0
Cattle	...	...	...	25	2	3
Repairing the small budgrow	...	...	...	57	14	9
Ditto three tow-boats...	...	...	...	53	12	9
Charles and Betty sloop	...	...	...	309	15	6
Building a butler's room...	...	...	...	8	9	9
Building a summer-house...	...	...	...	113	14	9
New house	...	...	...	61	3	0
Timbers	...	...	...	209	14	3
Household necessaries	...	...	...	21	0	0
				1,169	2	6
				4,112	12	0
				5,281	14	6

12.—APPOINTING THE ROTATION GOVERNMENT.

Letters arrive from England appointing Messrs. Hedges, Sheldon,

Sunday, January 30th, 1704. Winder, Russell, and Bowcher, and three others to be the Council for the United Trade. The Councils of the Old and of the New Company are to go on as usual for their Separate Trade; and each Council is to have a President of its own. But for the United Trade, the Council is to consist of four members of the Old and four members of the New Company's Service; and the two senior members of this Council are to take it in turns to be Chairman of the Council, week by week.

The following were appointed to the United Trade Council in 1704:—

Mr. Ralph Sheldon, Charge of books.

Mr. John Russell, Warehouse-keeper.

Mr. George Redshaw, Charges general.

Mr. Bowcher, Jemidar [*Zamīndār*].

Mr. Hedges and Mr. Sheldon were to be Chairmen in alternate weeks.

The Managers' letter also ordered the Old Company to give up the charge of the garrison and all dead stock into the hands of the United Trade Council; and the New Company likewise to give up all their dead stock.

13.—MAKING OVER CHARGE.[1]

The Council for the United Company formally took charge of
garrison, dead stock, and the like in Calcutta;
and some of the Council went to Hugli to take
possession of dead stock of the New Company.

Monday, January 31st.

14.—DAYS OF MEETING.

The United Trade Council was to hold its meetings on Mondays,
and so, to avoid clashing, the Old Company
altered their day to Tuesday.
The United Trade Council was to be the head Council in Calcutta.

February 8th.

15.—PAYING OFF THE NATIVE SERVANTS.

"Ordered that all the black servants that look after the Company's
factories and dead stock in the country be
dismissed and paid off till the 1st of February,
and the houses, etc., be delivered to the Council for the Managers of
the United Trade."

Tuesday, February 22nd.

16.—DR. WARREN'S ALLOWANCE.

Doctor Warren, the surgeon of the garrison, was taken by the
United Trade Council into their service. He
begs that the Old Company will not on that
account stop his allowance. He will still have twenty-three of the Old
Company's servants to look after. The Old Company's Council agree
that his stated salary may be allowed him, but no other benefits
from the old Company.

February 22nd.

17.—DECEMBER EXPENSES.

The accounts for the month of December are brought in and passed.[2]
It is agreed that they shall be entered under the
headings of "Account of the Company of Merchants of London" and "Account of the English Company."

February 22nd.

---

[1] See below, Addenda § 414.
[2] In the Bazār accounts for January we have, " Making a new Goola at Govingpore Mart-
place, Rs. 11-5-6."

DECEMBER 1703.

Account of the Company of Merchants of London.

				Rs.	A.	P.
Charges general	...	...	...	146	6	0
Merchandise	...	...	...	179	7	0
Servants' wages	...	...	...	296	8	3
General stores	...	...	...	101	3	3
Madras Presidency	...	...	...	2,145	0	0
Cattle	...	...	...	38	0	0
Diet	...	...	...	770	9	6
Weaving shop	...	..	...	5	15	3
Patana Residency	...	...	...	2	2	0
				3,685	3	3

Account of the English Company.

Charges general	...	...	...	64	13	9
Repairs	...	...	...	19	7	3
Cattle	...	...	..	25	5	9
New house	...	...	...	116	2	9
Servants' wages	...	...	...	127	12	0
General stores	...	...	...	45	12	0
Summer-house in garden	...	...	34	15	0
Mary Smack	...	...	...	82	4	6
William Do.	...	...	...	101	15	0
Charles and Betty Sloop	...	...	68	13	3
				737	5	3
				= 4,422	8	6

18.—RALPH SHELDON MARRIED.

"This morning Mr. Ralph Sheldon was married to Mrs. Elizabeth Halsey by Mr. Benj. Adams."

February 29th.

19.—HOUSE FOR THE OLD COMPANY.

"Wanting a house for lodging for the Company's servants which must be out of the factory; Mr. Bowridge's two houses are ordered to be taken at 50 rupees per month for a twelve month together."

March 2nd.

20.—DIET MONEY.

"Having left it to the choice of fifteen of the Company's servants (who are to be put to diet money) whether they would have 15 rupees per month each person, and servants and cookroom, necessary firewood, candles, etc., or 20

March 7th.

rupees per month as the New Company's servants have, and they having pitched upon the 20 rupees, agreed that they be allowed it from the 1st of March."

21.—OUTSTANDING DEBTS.

"Several merchants being in the Right Hon'ble Company's debt, and having houses and grounds in the town, agreed that they be sold, and the money brought to the Company's credit; also that the bad debts standing out of the several factories, and what bad debts of this place which were contracted and occasioned by the fire in President Eyre's time be wrote off in order to adjust our master's affairs and bring them to a quicker conclusion."

March 14th.

22.—TIMBER.

The old Company sent to buy timber in July 1702; but the timber arrives now, when they have no need of it. It is ordered that it be offered for sale to the United Trade.

March 22nd.

Upon further enquiry about the timber they found that the Charges General Keeper had provided the timber that had just arrived, and other timber too, for the use of the garrison, *since July* 1702. Hence, though the timber was paid for out of the old Company's cash, and "the hazard of the timbers were on their account," the United Company ought to be charged with the money. "It is therefore agreed that the said timbers be delivered the Council for the Managers and that the United Company be charged therewith accordingly."

March 28th.

23.—SALARIES.

"The salary due to the Right Hon'ble Company's servants unto the 25th of March, being 2,015 rupees, six annas, 10 pies, agreed that the same be paid them. Those that entered into the Manager's Service (United Trade Council), their account salaries are to be made up to the 25th of February, at which time they had their discharge from the old Company."

March 28th.

24.—EXPENSES IN JANUARY 1704.

The accounts for the month of January were brought in and passed.

April 12th.

ACCOUNTS FOR JANUARY 1704.

Accounts of the Company of Merchants of London.

				Rs.	A.	P.
Charges general	...	...	...	163	15	3
Servants' wages	...	...	...	357	15	9
Merchandise	...	...	...	170	15	6
Cattle	...	...	...	38	0	0
Pilots' wages	...	...	...	502	8	0
Madras Presidency	...	...	...	565	0	0
General stores	...	...	...	87	14	3
Factors do.	...	...	...	153	0	0
Diet	...	...	...	691	5	6
Weaving shop	...	...	...	25	8	9
				2,756	3	0

Accounts of the English Company.

				Rs.	A.	P.
Charges general	...	...	...	105	12	6
Repairs	...	...	...	52	6	0
Building the new houses	...	...	316	5	9
Building a summer house	...	...	105	11	9
The *Mary* smack	..	...	...	469	6	9
William do.	...	...	...	489	12	6
Charles and Betty sloop	...	...	318	7	3
Repairing two budgerows	...	...	15	1	3
Servants' wages	...	...	...	129	4	0
Cattle	...	...	...	26	11	6
General stores	...	...	...	45	14	0
Timber	...	...	...	365	5	0
Garrison	...	...	...	2,159	0	6
				4,599	2	9

25.—PUBLIC-HOUSE LICENSE.[1]

April 12th.

Charles King paid a hundred and fifty rupees for a license to keep a public house and place of entertainment.

26.—BORROWING.

April 12th.

About this time we find the Company borrowing various sums of money, and paying interest at the rate of one per cent. per mensem.

---

[1] See below, Addenda, § 415.

27.—REDSHAW ARRIVES FROM PATNA.

"Mr. George Redshaw being arrived from Patna and received into
April 19th.   the United Trade Council, agreed that he take
charge of the general stores, and that Mr. John
Russell have the charge of the godowns delivered him from Mr. Ralph
Sheldon, who has charge of the Right Hon'ble Company's books."

28.—SELLING GUNS.

"There being an oppertunity (*sic.*) to dispose of some Gunns its
April 25th.   agreed that the Charges General Keeper Mr. John
Russell dispose of as many as he can, not under
nine Rupees per hundred."

29.—THE PRESIDENT'S TABLE.

"The President (Old Company) brought in his account of stores
May 9th.   provided for his table for the month of April,
agreed that the Charges General Keeper pay the
same, being 115 rupees 10 annas."

30.—SELLING GOLD.

"Being apprehensive that gold will fall upon the arrival of the
May 16th.   Madras shipping, agreed that what pagodas are
in chest be sent to Hugly by the podar and be
disposed thereof for rupees."

31.—EXPENSES FOR APRIL 1704.

20th June.   *Charges General for April.*

				Rs.	A.	P.
Charges, merchandise	...	...	...	1,084	15	3
Servants' wages	...	...	...	206	8	0
Repairing and making a cook-room	...	...	9	7	6
Cattle	...	...	...	40	8	0
Diet	...	...	...	415	10	9
Cojah Surhaud to be charged to his account	...	159	1	3
By what paid into cash account	...	...	1,000	0	0

32.—TRADE IN PATNA.

The English trade is stopped in Patna owing to the necessity of
12th July.   paying custom dues. The Mogul had granted a
free trade, and sent notice of the same to the

Prince in Patna, under the seal of his Grand Vizier, but the Prince still refused free trade unless the Company made him a large present. The old Company do not wish for any such pass now, as they are not responsible for the trade. They therefore send a letter to the United Trade Council telling them the result of the negotiations. The United Trade Council agree to stop the trade in Patna till they see what the Dutch will do. The old Company therefore send to recall their agent at Patna.

The United Trade Council resolves after all to continue the settle-
August 15th. ment at Patna. Consequently Mr. William Lloyd and William Cawthorp, the Old Company's Servants, who have not yet returned, are ordered to stay where they are and to enter into the United Trade Service.

33.—FOR FEAR OF THE FRENCH.

A ship is detained from taking stores from Calcutta to Madras,
August 15th. owing to the danger apprehended from the French ships, which are hovering round coast.

34.—OLD SERVANTS MAY BE TAKEN BACK.

The Old Company and the New Company both agree that if at
August 22nd, 1704. any future time any of their servants who have had their discharge in order to serve the United Trade should leave the United Company's service and wish to return to their old service, they may be taken back.

35.—BEARD'S HOUSE-RENT.

The President having moved out of the Factory in March to make
September 5th. more room for the 'Manager's servants' requires house-rent. He is to be allowed fifty rupees a month, payable from March 1704.

36.—SALE BY OUTCRY.

Many parcels of goods about this time are sold by auction or "public
September 5th. outcry at ten per cent. more than invoice price." The custom was to post a notice of the sale on the gates of the Fort two or three days before the auction.

37.—THREE MONTHS' EXPENSES.

The general expenses for the months of May, June, and July,
September 12th. having been perused, are ordered to be passed.

May.

				Rs.	A.	P.
Charges, general	...	...	...	80	6	9
Charges, merchandise	...	...	...	11	15	0
Servants' wages	...	...	...	219	13	0
Charges, Darbar	...	...	...	120	0	0
Cattle	...	...	...	54	12	0
Diet	...	...	...	362	9	9
		Total	...	849	8	6

June.

Charges, general	...	...	...	145	12	3
Charges, merchandise	...	...	...	18	12	9
Servants' wages	...	...	...	194	0	0
Cattle	...	...	...	43	12	0
Diet	...	...	...	751	5	9
Factors' provisions	...	...	...	55	0	0
General stores	...	...	...	910	12	0
				2,119	6	9

July.

Charges, general	...	...	...	160	13	6
Merchandise	...	...	...	11	12	0
Diet	...	...	...	415	15	6
Servants' wages	...	...	...	202	10	6
Cattle	...	...	...	41	4	3
Factors' provisions	...	...	...	25	0	0
				857	7	9

38.—SALE OF GOODS FROM PATNA.

The Right Hon'ble Company had some goods returned from Patna
to sell at " Public Outcry." They hoped to get
September 19th. ten per cent. on the invoice prices, but failed to
do so, "goods being fallen considerably here, there not being those
demands for them as in former years."

39.—EXPENSES FOR AUGUST 1704.

The account of the expenses in August is brought in and passed.

October 24th. It contains the same items as the July account, and almost invariably the same amounts, with this one item added:—

By provisions for Madras   ...   ... Rs. 1,588-7-6

40.—THE OLD COMPANY'S SERVANTS.

List of Right Hon'ble Company's Servants in the Bay of Bengal, according to their precedency and station in Calcutta.

NAMES.	Dignity,	Arrival in India.	Salary	Present salary.	
1	2	3	4	5	6
			Rs.	Rs.	
The Hon'ble John Beard President.	Writer ...	17th July 1682 ...	10	300	
The Worshipful Ralph Sheldon.	Do. ...	9th June 1688 ...	5	40	Elected by the Managers 31st Jan. 1704.
Mr. John Russell ...	Factor ...	3rd Dec. 1694 ...	15	40	
Mr. George Redshaw ...	Writer ...	3rd Feb. 1694 ...	5	40	
Mr. Edward Pattle ...	Do. ...	31st Oct. 1692 ...	5	40	
Sen. Merch. James Ravenhill ...	Do. ...	17th July 1692 ...	10	40	
John Calvert ...	Factor ...	12th Aug. 1700 ...	15	...	
William Mercer ...	Do. ...	„ „ ...	...	...	
Jacob Loveday ...	Do. ...	„ „ ...	...	...	
John Mountenay ...	Do. ...	„ „ ...	...	...	
Peter Vansittart ...	Do. ...	„ „ ...	...	...	
Samuel Feake (accompt.) ...	Writer ...	26th May 1700 ...	5	40	
Philip Middleton ...	Factor ...	25th Aug. 1702 ...	15	...	
1 Doctor William Warren ...	Doctor ...	....	...	36	
Richard Smith ...	Writer ...	12th Aug. 1700 ...	5	...	
Francis Silvestre ...	Do. ...	25th May 1701 ...	5	...	
John Deane ...	Do. ...	25th Aug. 1702 ...	5	...	
Samuel Wittewronge ...	Do. ...	„ „ ...	...	...	
18 Servants in all of Company.					

Account of the Right Hon'ble Company's servants taken into the Hon'ble Manager's service since the 25th of January 1704.

Benjamin Adams, Chaplain.

William Bugden, Senior Merchant.

William Lloyd, Junior Merchant, at Patna.

Thomas Curgenven, Junior Merchant, by the Manager's Consultation, elected 16th February 1703-4.

William Cawthorp, Factor, by the Manager's Consultation, elected 16th February 1703-4.

Henry Waldo, Factor, by the Manager's Consultation, elected 16th February 1703-4.

Benj. Walker, Factor, discharged the service according to his own request, by the Manager's Consultation, elected 16th February 1703-4.

William Walker, Factor, by the Manager's Consultation, elected 16th February 1703-4.

James Williamson, Factor, by the Manager's Consultation, elected 16th February 1703-4.

Doctor William Warren, by the Manager's Consultation, elected 16th February 1703-4.

Edward Halsy, Writer, by the Manager's Consultation, elected 16th February 1703-4.

Thomas Long, Writer, gone for England in the Dutches, by the Manager's Consultation, elected 16th February 1703-4.

Charles Boone, Writer, by the Manager's Consultation, elected 16th February 1703-4.

Dead of the old Company's Servants, never taken into the Manager's service.

3 { Mr. Jonathan White, 23rd January 1703-4.
James Tisser, Factor, 25th April 1704.
Thomas Ashby, Factor, 23rd July 1704.

DIARY AND CONSULTATION BOOK

OF THE

LONDON COMPANY'S COUNCIL AT FORT WILLIAM IN BENGAL.[1]

From December 1704 *to November* 1705.

41.—BEARD'S DEPARTURE.

"The President [Beard] going for Fort St. George, thinks it needful to retrench the Company's expenses, and therefore there is allowed no more servants than is hereafter mentioned, *i.e.*—

December 12th, 1704.

1 Poddar [*Padar*] to assist the Buxie [*Bakhshī*].
1 Chubdar [*Chob-dār*] Barrahmull.
1 Chief peon Lottlow and six more.
6 Guallis [*Gowalās*], 1 Budgrow manjee [*mānjhī*].
2 Horse-keepers and horse meat."

42.—LEASES IN 1703.

Thirty leases were given to the inhabitants in Calcutta in the year 1703.

April, 1705.

43.—OLD DIARIES IN CALCUTTA.

We find in April 1705 a list of all the books and diaries then in Calcutta. Apparently these diaries dated back from 1684, for we have "A diary of the Patna Factory, 1684." The first for Calcutta was in 1688—"Chuttanuttee diary, 1688." At the end of the list of diaries is written, "A large chest full of old books and papers, so much defaced that nothing can be made of them."

April, 1705.

---

[1] Calcutta Diary, No. 7. Received per ship *Northumberland* on the 23rd August 1706. Birdwood Records, RRa 7.

DIARY AND CONSULTATION BOOK

OF THE

UNITED TRADE COUNCIL AT FORT WILLIAM IN BENGAL.

From January to November 1704.

44.—LETTERS BY THE "DUTCHESS."

Letters are brought to Fort William by the ship *Dutchess*. After a hasty consultation, the members of the committee agree to open them at once, without waiting for the arrival of Mr. Nightingale from Dacca, and to send a letter to Mr. Benjamin Bowcher, telling him of the arrival of the letters, and asking him to join them soon. They agree to allow the purser of the ship to deliver all private letters. They also agree to send a letter to Sir Edward Littleton at Coxe's[1] to tell him that they have a letter sealed with the English Company's seal, and directed to him as President of the English Company in India, and that it states that he is to continue in his office.

Saturday, January
29th, 1704.

45.—QUARTERS FOR LITTLETON.

Sir E. Littleton, " coming up the river, called here, and being seated among us, and at the head of our table, was desired to choose whether he would have an apartment provided for him within the Fort, or elsewhere in the town. He thinks that a house in the town will be most convenient

January 30th.

---

[1] Coxe's Island at Saugor. In the old charts in the place of the modern Saugor Island we have three detached islands, Saugor, Coxe's Island, and the Isle of Dogs, Saugor being the most southerly. The name Coxe's Island, or more properly Cock's Island, or Cock Island, is found as late as 1807.

for him, there being but few good rooms finished in the new house within the Fort."

46.—CONSTITUTION OF THE UNITED COUNCIL.

On seriously considering the orders received from the Hon'ble Court of Managers in London, they conclude
January 31st.
that the meaning of the letters is that they should elect two Chairmen, one for the New and one for the Old Company, to take the chair alternately each week. They send a letter to President Beard telling him to give up to Joint Council, the Garrison and all the Dead Stock, also the Grants, Privileges and Phirmaunds of the Three Towns. They agree that the United Council is to choose servants both from the New and Old Company's servants, and that neither party is to grumble at the other. An equal number of servants are to be appointed from the New and from the Old Company. Mr. Ravenhill is to be passed over and Mr. Pattle appointed in his stead.

"Agreed that the charge each of us takes in
February 2nd.
the management of the Hon'ble Manager's affairs be as follows:—

Mr. Robert Hedges and Mr. Ralph Sheldon—Cash-keepers.

Mr. Winder—Accompt General.

Mr. Russell—Warehouse-keeper of Goods Exported.

Mr. Nightingale—   ,,   ,,   Imported.

Mr. Redshaw—Charges General Keeper.

Mr. Bowcher—Jemidar [*Zamindār*], to collect the rents, and to keep the three Black Towns in order, and that he officiate as Buxie [*Bakhshi*] until Mr. Redshaw arrives.

Mr. Pattle—Secretary.

47.—BEARD MAKES OVER CHARGE.

" Yesterday at 10 o'clock in the morning, being the time appointed by President Beard to deliver possession of the
February 2nd.
garrison and dead-stock, etc., to us, we waited on him accordingly, and being met in the Old Company's consultation room, all the Company's servants and the freemen inhabitants of Calcutta being present, President Beard wished us joy of our new trust. But his long indisposition having much weakened and disabled him from speaking, he desired Mr. Sheldon to make a public declaration that in pursuance of the order from the Court of Committees and

in conformity to the deed of Union and Quinquepartite Indenture, he does now resign the Fort and all the dead-stock, together with all the lands and privileges to us the Established Council for the management of all the United Company's affairs in Bengal."

President Beard then received the keys of the Fort from the Ensign who was chief of the guard, and gave them to the Council, by whom they were given back to the Ensign. After the ceremony all English in Town, both the Company's servants and freemen, were entertained at the expense of the Council. All the members of Council, except Mr. Bowcher and Mr. Pattle, then proceeded to Hugli to take possession of the dead-stock at Hugli, and also if necessary to visit the Governor of Hugli, and make a declaration to him about the Company's affairs.

48.—TAKING OVER CHARGE.

They agree to write to Sir E. Littleton, the President of the New Company, to order him to give up all the dead stock and privileges of New Company into hand of Council; also to tell Sir E. Littleton that the management of all public affairs for the English nation is vested in them.

February 3rd.

An order is sent to Josia Townsend to bring the *Anna* Ketch up the river Hugli to convey the goods of the New Company down to Fort William.

They agree to borrow 8,000 Sicca Rupees of the New Company to be repaid when they receive their treasure. The money is to be sent to Fort William on a boat guarded by two soldiers.

Enquiries are made of Sir Edward Littleton whether any prisoners are under confinement by order of the New Company. If there are any they are to be sent to Fort William. Two prisoners under charge of murder are sent to Fort William and kept in guard there.

February 4th.

In order to avoid disturbance, they determine not to acquaint the local Indian Government with the change of administration till all their goods are safe in Calcutta. It is agreed that Sir Edward Littleton's seal in Hugli, and Beard's seal in Calcutta, shall be used for *dastaks* till affairs be settled.

February 5th.

It is agreed that both Presidents be allowed a house, palanquin and budgerow, out of the dead-stock of their respective Companies.

February 16th.

49.—THE UNITED COUNCIL'S SERVICE.

They take into the service of the United Council eight of the Old
February 16th.   and eight of the New Company's servants—

New Company's Servants.	Old Company's Servants.
William Champion.	Thomas Curgenven.
Abraham Addams.	Henry Waldo.
Edward Darell.	Benjamin Walker.
Josia Chitty.	William Walker.
John Brightwell.	James Williamson.
John Eyre.	Edward Halsey.
George Hussey.	Thomas Long.
Ralph Emes.	Charles Boone.

50.—NEW BUILDINGS.

Timbers and materials being already provided sufficient to cover
and finish the first floor of the New House, it
February 16th.   is agreed that that part of the building be
perfected, if possible, before the rains set in, the rooms being very
much wanted for the accommodation of the Company's servants.

It is also agreed that the stables and other necessary outhouses
be enlarged as much as present necessity requires.

51.—RENT.

They order ninety rupees be paid to "the Prince's¹ Jaggeerdar
[Jāgïr-dār]," being part of the rent due at this
February 16th.   time for the three towns, viz., "Calcutta, Goving-
pore, and Chuttanuttee [Govindpur and Sūtānuṭī]."

52.—POLICE.

It is ordered that one chief peon, and forty-
February 16th.   five peons, two chubdas [chob-dārs], and twenty
guallis [gowalās] be taken into pay.

53.—TIME OF MEETING.

They agree to meet on Mondays and Thurs-
February 19th.   days at 9 o'clock in the morning.

---

¹ Prince 'Aẕīmu-sh-Shān.

54.—A LIST OF GOVERNMENT PAPERS.

"A list of some of the Government papers relating to priviledges
of trade, granted formerly to the English nation,
also of what have been procured by the Hon'ble
the English Company trading to the East Indies, for their affairs in
Bengale—

February 19th.

Date.

1. Copie of Cha Chehanas Phirmaund [Shāh Jahān's
   farmān] from Agra to Bengall in the 11th year of
   his reign.   1638

2. Copie of Aurenzeeb's Phirmaund [Aurangzēb's *farmān*]
   from Agra to Bengall, in the 11th year of his
   reign.   1667

3. Copie of Cha Sujahs Nishaan [Shāh Shujā's *nishān*]
   for a free trade in Bengall in the 28th year of Cha
   Jehan's [Shāh Jahān's] reign.   1652

4. Copie of Sultan Azzum Tarras Nishaan [Ā'zạm Tārā's
   nishān] for a free trade in Bengall, procured by
   Sir Matthias Vincent.   1678

5. Copie of a Phirwanna [*parwānah*] from Agra Mahmuud
   Jemma [Āghā Muḥammad Zamān] for a free trade
   in Orixa, granted to Mr. Cartwright in the 6th year
   of Cha Jehans reign.

6. Copie of Hedges Sophy Cawn [Ḥājī Sūfī Khān],
   Duan [Dīwān] of Bengall, his Phirwanna [*parwānah*] for a free trade, in the 21st year of Auren-
   zeeb's reign, procured by Sir Matthias Vincent.   1678

7. Copie of Assid Cawn [Asad Khān], Chancellor to the
   King, his Phirwanna for a free trade in the 23rd
   year of Aurenzeeb.   1680

8. Copie of Shastah Cawn Meerul Omrah [Shāyista Khān
   Amīru-l-Umarā], his Phirwanna for a free trade in
   the 23rd year of Aurenzeeb.   1680

9. Two copies of Aurenzeeb's Phirmaund for freeing the
   English from *Tridgia* (*sic*) or Toll Tax (*sic*) in
   Bengall.[1]   1680

---

1 Perhaps this is a mistake of the copyist for " *Jizyah* or Poll Tax."

R

10. One Husboll Omer[1] of Alla Rezze ['Alī Raẓā] the Prince's Duan [*Dīwān*], for a free trade and five copies of the same.

11. An order from the Prince for the draining (*sic*)[2] of the Nishaan.

12. Copie of a Hookum Oomer from the Prince.

13. Two copies of the Prince's Nishaan.

14. Copie of Siaid Issard Cawn [? Sayyad 'Izzat Khān] his Phirwanna, upon Alla Rezze ['Alī Raẓā], the governour of Hugly.

15. Siaid Issard Cawn's his Phirwanna for a free trade in Hugly, and another of the same for Hugly.

16. Siaid Issard Cawn's order for ground in Hugly and copie of the same.

17. Four copies of Issard Cawn's Phirwanna.

18. Issard Cawn's Phirwanna for a free trade in Mauld and Rajam[LL.]

19. Issard Cawn's order for ground at Ballasore and copie of the same.

20. Meer Jerulla's (*sic*) [Mīr Jār-ullah] order to the Choukee's [*chaukīs*] and copie of the same.

21. Copie of the Prince's order for the mint.

22. Meer Abbas Cooly [Mīr 'Abbās Qulī] (the Princes Berderbux his Gomasta) [Prince Bēdār Bakht's *gumāshtāh*] his order to the Chowkies [*chaukīs*].

23. Copies of the King's Husbool Hookum [*ḥasbu-l-ḥukm*] for securing the persons and effects of all Europeans.

24. Cart Lullab Cawn [*Kārṭalab Khān, i.e.*, Murshid Quli Khān] (the King's Duan) his order for the clearing of the effects of the Europeans in Hugly—another of the same for Ballasore.

25. The Prince's order and copie thereof for clearing the English from the King's Hussboolkookum.

---

1 That is "ḥasbu-l-amr," according to command, the initial formula of the document used as the title of the document in the same way as "ḥasbu-l-ḥukm."

2 Surely this a mistake for "drawing."

26. Enaut Elles ['Ināyat ullah's] Original Sunnud [*sanad*] and two copies of the same on the back of which the Morchelcha[1] is inserted.

27. An Husbool Omer from Cartullub Cawn [*Kārṭalab Khān*] (the King's Duan) and two copies of the same."

"And these are all the papers we received from them relating to the Government or Durbarr [*Darbār*] affairs.

ROBERT HEDGES.
RALPH SHELDON.
JONATHAN WINDER.
JOHN RUSSELL.
BENJAMIN BOWCHER.
EDWARD PATTLE."

55.—SALTPETRE.

"The *Dutchess* being to be dispatched forthwith for Fort St. George, ordered that Ralph Seldon and Jonathan Winder do go to visit the saltpetre bought of the Old Company and compare it with the musters we agreed on, that it be weighed off and sent on board."

February 21st.

56.—FURTHER AMALGAMATION OF THE COMPANIES.

All the Old Company's servants at Patna, etc., are to come to Calcutta before they are received into the United Company's service. This is done to avoid paying custom to the Mogul for past trade, as it would be "an ill precedent at the beginning to make the United Trade stand security for past transactions."

•February 21st.

57.—SHIPS DESPATCHED.

They despatch ships to Madras, "the season not being so late, but several European and country ships have been despatched after this time." The latest time for despatch was the 15th of March.

February 21st.

58.—A MEETING OF COUNCIL.

February 24th.   *At a Consultation, present :*

| Ralph Sheldon. | Jonathan Winder. |
| Robert Hedges. | John Russell. |

Benjamin Bowcher.

---

1 Probably *Muchalkā*, bond.

1st.—Paid on account of the revenues of the three towns, in Hughly, being Colsa [*Khālisah*] as customary—

		Rs.
New sicca	... ...	100
Batta	... ...	11
Do. current money	...	3
	...	114

2nd.—Agreed that the general books of this Presidency for the United trade begin the primo February, and to be balanced to the last of April as customary, and that the books that were kept apart by the Old and New Company's servants for the United trade be delivered to Mr. Jonathan Winder to be entered as they are now stated.

3rd.—Mr. Benjamin Bowcher having been on board ship *Dutchess* to muster the ship's company, he brought in his report that there were sixty-one men which are twenty-three less than Charty Party; part of them were taken out in the Downs, and the rest died on the passage as the Captain reports.

4th.—Wanted a master to navigate the *Hugly Anna* Ketch to Fort St. George and Charles Hopkins offering his services, being an able man, ordered that we accept of him at the wages of fifty-six rupees per month, and that he get the Ketch forthwith ready.

5th.—Having desired the Presidents and Councils for the Old and New Company to defer paying the three thousand rupees which is due from each of them to the Government lest there might follow some ill-conveniency, we now agree and approve that it be forthwith paid by each Company's vacqueel [*vakil*] in their name and that they take discharge for the same, and that they declare they are discharged their employments, and the vacqueels for the United Company which will be appointed by us will answer for the English nation.

6th.—The Muster Roles of the soldiers that came from Hughly and of Fort William were brought and referr'd till Monday in the election who shall continue.

7th.—Ordered that there be fifty tunns of petre laden on board the *Hugly Anna* Ketch for Fort St. George and filled up with rice, &c., for that port, and that the vessel be recommended to the Governor and Council there for their use, if they have occasion, by which means the expense of the Company's small craft may be raised, and that the *William* Smack and *Rising Sun* Smack be laid up till a proper time for their saile, or to be sent to the Fort, if they may have occasion for them there.

8th.—The President and Council for the Old Company having acquainted us that they have ordered the black servants in all the subordinations that look after the factories be discharged from the salaries they pay them to the 31st January, wherefore it is ordered that the same servants be continued in the manager's pay till we shall see reason to order it otherwise.

9th.—The eight thousand sicca borrowed of the New Company ordered it be paid them, also that a pylot be sent them for ship *Union* which they desire.

10th.—The President and Council for the New Company advising that they are withdrawing their English servants from Balasore, 'tis agreed we continue the English in any subordination at present, but what dead-stock cannot be brought away immediately thence be continued in the charge of the black servants of their factory till further orders, and that they may expect their pay from us.

RALPH SHELDON.

ROBERT HEDGES.

JONATHAN WINDER.

JOHN RUSSELL.

BENJAMIN BOWCHER.

MR. PATTLE *indisposed.*

59.—THE GARRISON.

"Being apprehensive of troubles with the Government and not having lately heard from Surrat, Agreed that the souldiers be continued as they are entered in the Muster Roles but as Any die or are hereafter discharged the Vacancies not to be filled up till the Number be reduced below One hundred men."

March 3rd.

60.—FACTORY WEIGHTS.

"Agreed that the factory weights be adjusted and that the factory maund be just $74\frac{2}{3}$, that is $\frac{2}{3}$ of weight averdupoise."

Saturday, March 4th.

61.—NIGHTINGALE JOINS THE COUNCIL.

March 6th.

Mr. Robert Nightingale having arrived from Dacca yesterday, is ordered to take his charge of the warehouse of goods imported.

62.—THE UNITED COMPANY'S SEAL.

March 13th.

"Agreed that our own Seal be henceforth used for the *Dusticks*."

63.—SALTPETRE.

March 13th.

Some trouble had lately arisen about getting saltpetre, the most profitable export at this time. The Hugli merchants refused to deliver it at Calcutta without an advance of price. At last the Council agree to give them an anna, or a little more, per maund extra. This is agreed on hastily at the last because of the arrival in Balasor road of seven Dutch ships and one French ship in search of saltpetre.

64.—SALE OF TREASURE.

March 18th.

"Being in present want of money, ordered that a chest of Treasure be sent to Hugly to be sold for ready money."

65.—A VAKIL FOR HUGLY.

March 20th.

"We having promised on the 15th instant to send a Vacqueel [*vakīl*] to the Government of Hugly within a few days, the Prince his Muttsudies [*mutaṣaddī's*] order being come to the Governor of Hugly to send all the European Vacqueels to Rajahmaul [Rajmahal]; and it being necessary that we have somebody there to answer and stop all complaints; resolved that we nominate a person to attend at Hugly."

66.—CURRENT EXPENSES.

March 21st.

Mr. Benjamin Bowcher, the Paymaster, wants money to defray the expenses of the garrison, to pay for stores for Madras, and to buy timber to finish the first floor of the house. It is ordered that he be paid 4,974 siccas and thirteen annas at the rate of 205 siccas per 240 sicca weight.

67.—RĀMACHANDRA TO BE VAKĪL.

They select Rāmachandra as *vakīl* for Hugli. His salary is to be
March 23rd. 20 rupees per month. He is to have five rupees
for his horse, and two peons are allowed to attend
him as is the custom with *vakīls.*

68.—HOUSES AND LEASES.

"James Johnson having let his newly-erected house outside the Fort
March 27th. to Benj". Whitley, the Indenture was brought
before us, and it is agreed that a book be prepared
in which are to be entered this and all other leases, bills of sale
and agreements made by the freemen inhabitants of Calcutta. The
Secretary's fee to be two rupees for registering the same.

Mr. Benjamin Bowcher, desiring a piece of ground to build a
house on, agreed that he have leave to build on the parcel of ground
lying between the row of trees which stand from Mr. Meverell's house
to the waterside, and Mr. Bowridge his ground. The ground granted
to Mr. Benj. Bowcher to build on is on consideration that he is to
build two godowns of brick which he is to let out for the convenience
of European shipping."

69.—THE ZAMĪNDĀR'S ACCOUNTS.

Mr. Bowcher having given in his account of the bazar and three
March 27th. towns, the balance, being Rs. 449-9-3, was paid
into the Company's Cash.

70.—RĀMACHANDRA'S INSTRUCTIONS.

It is ordered that Rāmachandra, the *vakīl*, be sent at once to
Hugly. He is to write down in his own language the following
directions :—

"He is to declare to the Governor, the *Buxie* [*Bakhshī*], and *Wacca*
March 27th. *Nevis* [*Wāqāyānavīs*], that we have appointed
him Vacqueel in Hugly for the affairs of the
English. If the Governor expect a visit from us, he is to give us notice,
and to tell the Governor we did design it, and desired to know when it
would be a fit time for him to receive us. If the Governor requires
reasons of our withdrawing Vacqeels from the Duan's [*Dīwān's*]
company and from Dacca, he is to answer we kept them there a long
time in vain and at great expense, which is a discouragement, and

makes us unwilling to be at such fruitless expenses; he also is to desire the Governor befriend us in writing to] Prince's and the the King's Duan. If questions be asked concerning the Union of the two companies, he is to say both Presidents are displaced, and that there is but one English Company, who have appointed a Council to manage their affairs. He is to give us constant advices, and to expect directions from us, what answer he is to give in case any material questions asked."

71.—TIMBER FOR BUILDINGS.

They send an order for wood to build Mr. Bowcher's house. The
March 28th.
boatswains and masters of the Company's vessels are to bring up what timber, etc., is necessary, for which 'Mr. Bowcher is to pay the freight, as is customary.'

"Two large boats belonging to Company lately come from Jessore
March 30th.
with timbers for the new buildings, being very old, ordered that they be sold."

72.—DARBĀR CHARGES.

It is ordered that a *hundred* sicca rupees be put into the hands of
March 30th.
Rāmachandra to defray petty *darbār* charges in Hugli.

73.—A LEASE GRANTED TO BEARD.

"Delivered His Honor, Mr. Beard, a lease, dated the 1st April, for
April 1st.
1 bigah 16 cottahs squares of ground for 5 rupees 6 annas 6 pies per annum." [1]

74.—GARRISON EXPENSES.

April 3rd.
" *Two thousand* rupees are paid for the expenses of the garrison.

75.—A LEASE GRANTED TO JOHN WATTS.

"Gave a lease to Mr. John Watts for a parcel of ground lying
April 6th.
between the Portuguese Church and the lane to the buzzar, containing 1 bigah and 10 cottahs squares, the rent of which is 4 rupees eight annas per annum."

---

[1] This is the customary rent, *viz.*, 3 Rs. a bigah.

76.—DIET MONEY.

Mr. Ralph Sheldon is allowed for his diet and house rent *forty*
rupees per month, on account of his living out of
April 6th.
the factory. The rest of the married men of the
Council are only to have *thirty* rupees per month.

77.—A LOCAL SURVEY.

Mr. Benjamin Bowcher having no employment just then as bakhshī
is ordered to survey and inspect into the revenues
April 16th.
of the three towns. He is to measure everyone's
compound, to see that they have not more than they pay for, to measure
all waste ground, and to send into the Council a particular account of
what each man pays. Mr. Ralph Ems is ordered to assist him in this.

78.—RĀMACHANDRA REPRIMANDED.

The *vakīl* Rāmachandra at Hugli misrepresents the Company's
affairs by saying that they have no Agent. They
April 18th.
send for him to reprimand him and to give him
a message for each *darbār.*

79.—THE COUNCIL'S LETTERS.

They agree that all letters coming for the Council are to be taken
to the Chairman for the week, and if they are
• April 18th.
important he is to call a special Council. He is
also to call a special Council on the receipt of letters from England,
Fort St. George, &c.

80.—WEIGHING SALTPETRE.

As there has been some dispute with the pursers of the ships about
saltpetre, the pursers requiring 1℔ in draught
April 24th.
extra allowed to them overweight if they weigh
the petre, they order the warehouse-keeper to weight it before sending
it on board.

81.—FACTORY EXPENSES.

One thousand rupees is paid to Mr. George Redshaw to defray the
April 24th.   general expenses of the Factory.

82.—LOOMS IN THE FACTORY.

Eighteen looms are ordered to be fitted in the factory in order to
make canvas, in the rainy season, for the use of
April 24th.
the Company's sloops.

83.—NEW PAṬĀS.

Mr. Bowcher, the zamīndār, is ordered to call on all the black
inhabitants, who have no writing for their tene-
ments, and to give them writings, they paying
the Company *Salāmī*, and he causing their ground to be measured.
Also those who have writings from former zamīndārs are to surrender
their old writings and have new writings given them gratis.

April 27th.

84.—RENT.

They order 485 siccas to be paid to the Government for the rent
of the three towns.

May 1st.

85.—AN EXPLOSION.

" The powder workhouse through carelessness of the workmen blew
up, and in it perished Bickerstaff, a soldier who
came on the *Dutchess*, also eleven Gentues and
one Mahometan."

May 9th.

86.—THE COMPANY'S BROKER.

They choose a broker, Deepchund Bella [Dvīpchand Bella], to deal
with the Native Merchants at a salary of one-
eighth of an anna per rupee on the net amount
of goods brought, and that he receive the same from the merchants."

May 9th.

87.—QUARREL BETWEEN HEDGES AND CAPTAIN SOUTH.

Mr. Hedges proposing several questions, they are entered as
follows :—

May 17th.

1. " Is either of the Chairmen obliged to
answer the challenge of every bully that pretends to be affronted and
challenges him to fight ?

2. " Are any other of the Council obliged to fight on a like
challenge ?

3. " If one of the Chairmen be challenged, without offering abuse
for the Council, is the party challenged only affronted, or the whole
Council?

" In answer to the former questions 'tis our opinions as follows:—

1. " The trust reposed in us by the Hon. United Comp. obliges
us to the contrary, and not to engage in such quarrels.

2. " The Council are under the same obligations, and are not to
answer challenges.

3. " If a Chairman or any of the Council be challenged without giving occasion, more particularly on the public affairs, the whole Council are affronted; but if any one gives abuse, each person is to answer for himself; but all ways and means are to be used to prevent such quarrels."

These questions came up in the Council because a certain Captain South had challenged Mr. Hedges to combat, alleging that Mr. Hedges had insulted him by not having the Fort guns fired when the Captain's ship arrived. The Governor and Council at Fort St. George took up the matter. Ralph Sheldon in a letter to Fort St. George declares that it is not customary to salute captains with guns, and that he and the other married men who live out of the Fort could not so salute them if they would.

88.—SALE OF LAND.

A compound belonging to Herrene a Dhringie was sold to
May 17th.   Mr. Sheldon at public auction for rupees 160.

89.—THE " CASSIMBUZZAR."

"The *Cassimbuzzar* Sloop returned to us, having sprung her mast
May 19th.   at Tana reach, about 4 miles below the Factory."

90.—DUTCH DESERTERS.

Some Dutch sailors who had deserted were found and sent back to
May 22nd.   their Captain, who promised to forgive them and
take them back. Otherwise it would have been necessary to send them to the Dutch Council in Hugli, who were bound to prosecute all fugitives of their nation and to execute all found guilty.

91.—THE "NEW COMPANY" LEAVE HUGLI.

The 'New Company are rose from their house at Goolgaul[1] and
May 22nd.   gone to Calcutta.'

92.—CAPTAIN RAYMOND.

They refuse again to have anything to do with Captain Raymond's
May 22nd.   cargo; he must manage it himself, taking all
risks.

---

[1] Ghōlghāṭ at Hugli. This is a " copy of the Vacca."

93.—DIPLOMATIC RELATIONS.

Finding out from Rāmachandra, the *vakīl* at Hugli, that Mīr
Ibrāhīm, the *Faujdār* or Governor of Hugli, is
preparing to meet Murshid Quli Khān, the
King's Dīwān, and that at present we have no *vakīl* at the Dīwān's
Camp, we agree to send a *vakīl* to follow him. Also hearing that
the Governor of Hugli is vexed that we have not sent him a present
or an Englishman to visit him, we order Rāmachandra to tell him
that we will visit him whenever he appoints time and place, and
that he is welcome to anything out of the warehouse. In return, we
want him to intercede with the King's Dīwān to give us a *sanad* to
free us from the present interruptions and disturbance from petty
officers in our trade.

June 6th.

94.—MENDING THE ROADS.

"Agreed that all petty fines from the black inhabitants be put to
the use of mending the highways and filling up
the holes to make the town more wholesome and
convenient, and that Mr. Bowcher take care of the same."

June 12th.

95.—INSTRUCTIONS TO RĀJĀRĀMA.

The King's Dīwān[1] of Bengal being on his return from Ořissa,
they send a *vakīl* to meet him as he has entire
power over the trade, and the King's customs
and dues, and should he be hostile, might interfere or even stop
their trade. They give the *vakīl*, named Rājārāma,[2] orders to tell
the King's Dīwān that the companies have amalgamated, that at
present there is no head, but that one will be shortly appointed, that
the Company will only pay Rs. 3,000 for grants and privileges, as
it is but one Company with one factory, and the agreement is Rs. 3,000
for one Company, although Rs. 6,000 have been paid by the two Companies. They refuse to pay the sum of Rs. 1,500 rupees demanded by
Government for the release of their trade, because that trade should never
have been hindered, and because the petty officers had impeded them in
their trade, and lessened the trade so much that they could not pay
such a sum.

June 14th.

---

[1] Murshid Quli Khān.
[2] Rājārāma had "great knowledge in the affairs of Bengal." See Bruce's *Annals*, III, p. 461.

Here follows a " list of things given to the Vacqueel to be given by him as presents to the Duan's under-officers " :—

"Broad cloth, 10 yds. (fine).

Aurora do. 10 do.

Ordinary do. 10 do.

One pair of pistols.

One Japan shield.

Four black spirit cases.

Looking glasses: four of several sorts.

Six pairs of penknives and scissors.

Four hundred rupees to be given to the Vacqueel for expenses and charges."

96.—A LEASE GRANTED TO JAMES JOHNSON.

They give James Johnson a lease for his house and grounds, dated
June 21st.   14th June 1704, containing two bighas and four cottahs of ground. Rent Rs. 7-6.

97.—RAYMOND'S CHARTER PARTY.

Captain Raymond demands the rest of his Charter Party money.
June 26th.   They order it to be paid him.

98.—A LEASE GRANTED TO DR. WARREN.

A lease is granted to Dr. Warren for two bighas and eighteen
• June 26th.   cottahs of ground out in the fields. Rent
• Rs. 8-11-3 per annum.

99.—FACTORY EXPENSES.

July 3rd.   They pay to Mr. G. Redshaw Rs. 500 for factory expenses.

100.—A MURDER.[1]

A squabble arises between the natives and the sailors, in which
July 20th.   the sailors are attacked, and one killed. Some of the natives are arrested, but, as at this time there was no Court of Judicature in Calcutta, nothing was done to the natives.

101.—BORROWING MONEY.

The Company are short of money, and borrow from a Mrs.
August 14th.   Margaret Wallis and her daughter at 1 per cent. per month.

---

[1] See below Addenda § 417.

102.—A PRISONER SENT TO MADRAS.

They decide to send Captain Alexander Delgardno to Madras.
Captain Delgardno was put in confinement by
Sir Edward Littleton when he was Consul. He
is accused of the murder of Jos. Handy. At this time Madras was the
only station that possessed a Court of Judicature.

August 14th.

103.—RĀJĀRĀM SENT TO MEET MURSHID QULI KHĀN.

It is agreed that Rājārām be ordered to proceed from Midnapore
to the Diwān's Camp at Balasor, in order to
intercede with the Diwān to grant us his *sanad*
for our freedom of trade for want of which we suffer many inconveniences, and are likely to have a fresh stop put to all our trade.
If unreasonable sums are asked by the Diwān or his officers, the
vakil is to acquaint us before he concludes with the Diwān.

August 14th.

104.—A WILL.

Mr. Joseph Morsse, mate of the *Dutchess*, lately deceased, having
appointed Mrs. Mary Morsse his sole executrix
by his last will and testament dated 30th May
1704; it is ordered that the Secretary copy the same in the book for
registering wills.

August 18th.

105.—A SMALL CAUSE COURT.

It is ordered that Mr. Robert Nightingale, Mr. George Redshaw,
and Mr. Benjamin Bowcher do meet in some
convenient place between the hours of nine and
twelve in the morning, every Saturday, to hear and determine small
controversies, but if anything difficult and of moment happens it is to
be heard in full Council.

August 18th.

106.—SALTPETRE.

One of the chief exports at this time was saltpetre. The English
Directors in all their letters demand quantities
of saltpetre. This year the difficulty seems to
have been to get it fine enough. They receive a letter from the
Council and President of Madras urging them to make haste and buy
what saltpetre they can, either coarse or fine, or there will be none to

August 18th.

send to the English Directors, as four French ships are on their way to buy saltpetre.

107.—A SHIP'S CARGO.

List of cargo [1] provided for Ship Scipio, Fort William, August 24th, 1704.

			Tons.					
Saltpetre	...	...	200					27,000
Baftaes	...	...	6	3,600	at	1	8	5,400
Lack Cowries	...	...	10	6,000		1	8	9,000
Cossaes	...	...	5½	2,000		5	8	11,000
Tanjeebs	...	...	5	2,000		6		12,000
Mulmulls	...	...	6	2,400		8		19,200
Dooreas, Fine	...	...	5	2,000		8		16,000
Soosies, Fine...	...	...	2½	1,000		8		8,000
Neckcloths	...	...	3	1,200		8		9,600
Dimothy	...	...	1	400		6		2,400
Taftaes	...	...	2½	1,000		5	8	5,500
Allebannies	...	...	2	800		3	8	2,800
Photaes	...	...	3	1,200		2		2,400
Tanjeebs, Flowered	...	...	2	800		10		8,000
Raw Silk	...	... }	37		500	4	8	90,000
Muctah	...	... }			144	2	8	14,400
Ginger, &c. gruss goods	...	...	49½			,,	,,	14,700
Cotten yarne	...	...	10			,,	,,	5,200
	Total	...	350	..	...	...		262,600

108.—MEMORANDUM ON THE CURRENCY.

September 1st.

The Council is alive to the fact that it would be much better for the Company to coin their own treasure, instead of selling it in chests, but the freedom of the mint is not allowed them, without the payment of heavy custom dues, which they refuse to do.

109.—PACKING CARGO.

September 4th.

Two thousand rupees are provided for packing stuff for the *Scipio's* cargo.

110.—BRIBING THE PRINCE'S JÁGÍRDÁR.

September 4th.

"Jeetmull Carrowrie [Jitmal Karoṛī], the Prince's Jaggerdar [Jāgīrdār], often troubling us about advance rent, that he pretends to be due to his master,

---

[1] The names of the goods should read thus : " Saltpetre, *baftas*, lac-cowries, *khāṣas*, *tanjíbs*, *malmals*, *doriyas*, *sūsís*, neck-cloths, dimity, taffetas, ? *alvānis*, ? *patkas*, *tanjíbs* flowered, raw silk, *mogta*, ginger goods, and cotton yarn."

and there being no other way to put it off, without making application to his superior, or giving him a small present, agree to give him a small present to value of Rs. 30."

111.—THE RIVER TARIFF.

Agreed that the Company's sloops have due credit in their books for what they carry down, or bring up from European ships, or to or from Balasor, that they may not stand at more than they are worth, and that the two Warehouse-keepers take care to give an account to the Accountant of what private goods are sent down on freight, and what quantity of bales, &c., are sent down for the Company's Association, and that the freight be charged as follows, *viz.* :—

September 11th.

To and from Balasore road—

Every Chest or Bale, Butt or Cask, two rupees each;

Saltpetre, Red Cowries, Lead, Iron, and all weighty goods, Rs. 15 per one hundred maunds;

Cordage, Coyer, and the like, Rs. 16 per one hundred maunds;

And from below in the river in proportion.

The river tariff to be charged, in charging the merchant, so that the vessels may not be a charge to the Company.

112.—A LICENSE RENEWED.

"Deningo Ash, her licenses for distilling Arrach, and selling Punch being expired on the 1st of August last— Ordered that they be renewed from that day on the same terms. She paid last year that is Rs. 800 for distilling, and Rs. 200 for selling punch for one year."

September 11th.

113.—PROPOSALS FOR A CHURCH.

A liberal contribution having been made by both the freemen of the place and the Company's servants towards building a Church for the public worship of God, and the Rev. Mr. Anderson and the Rev. Mr. Adams having asked help of the Company, because "the town is increasing, and there is no place in it able to contain the congregation that would meet at divine service, if there were rooms sufficient to contain them," it is agreed that one thousand rupees be given by the Company for this purpose.

September 11th.

*Copy of the Paper read by the Rev. Mr. Anderson and Mr. Adams before
the Council.*

"To the Hon'ble the Council for all affairs of the Right Hon'ble
United Company in Bengal.

Gentlemen,

How much the Christian religion suffers in the esteem of these
infidels and in the real effects of it even among ourselves for want of a
place set apart for the public worship of God, we can none of us be
ignorant; and if we have any concern at all for the honour of God
or any zeal for the advancement of the Christian religion in the world,
we cannot but lament the great disadvantage which we do at present
labour under from thence.

It was a deep sense of these things that induced us to set on foot a
subscription towards the building a church, which though it might at
first look like a design too big for us, yet, we have already succeeded
in beyond our hopes. Gentlemen, the very good encouragement you
have been pleased to give us in it has laid us under an obligation of
returning you our hearty thanks for it, and we now do it as becomes
us in the station we are now in. The commanders of ships have been
very generous upon this occasion; and all other gentlemen, whether
servants to the Right Hon'ble Company, or other inhabitants of the
place, have contributed freely and cheerfully to the work.

Gentlemen, the design is apparently noble and worthy of all the
encouragement that can be given it. 'Tis for the service and credit
of the English Company trading to these parts; 'tis for the honour
of the English nation; and above all 'tis for the honour of that Religion,
which we are all bound to maintain, and which, especially considering
where we are, we can never be too zealously concerned for.

But because the work we are going about ought to bear some
proportion to the end for which it is designed and consequently cannot
be accomplished with a small charge, therefore we hope, gentlemen, you
will think it reasonable to make some considerable addition to what
we have hitherto collected from private hands on account of the
Hon'ble Company, who, as they are likely to reap the most lasting
benefit from the undertaking, so they cannot be but abundantly
satisfied with what you shall think fit to do in it. The work we are
undertaking has been neglected too long already; we intend therefore
to put it off no longer, but set about it as soon as possible; in order to
which we desire, gentlemen, you will assign us a spot of ground, which

s

may be proper to our purpose, and that we suppose will be agreed on all hands to be as near the Factory as it conveniently may.

We are,

GENTLEMEN,

Your most affectionate Friends and humble Servants,

WILLIAM ANDERSON.

BENJAMIN ADAMS."

114.—SEIZURE OF A DEBTOR.

Rāmachandra, the *vakil*, sends the Company notice that one of the debtors of the King is in Calcutta, and that unless he is seized and given over to the King, the Company will be held responsible for his debts. He is seized, and sent under a guard of peons to the Governor of Hugli.

September 14th.

115.—A MARKET FOR GOVINDPUR.

Mr. Bowcher proposing to have a market ordered at the town of Govindpur, by which the Company will receive a considerable benefit in time, it is resolved that the same be ordered forthwith.

September 18th.

116.—THE ZAMINDĀR'S ACCOUNTS.

Mr. Bowcher brought in the account of the Revenues of the three Towns and of the Buzzar. The Balance amounts to 587 rupees 15 annas and 6 pies, which was paid into the cash account as usual.

September 19th.

117.—PRESENTS TO THE LOCAL OFFICERS.

They receive a letter from Rājārāma, the *vakil*, telling of his arrival at the Dīwān's and that the Dutch had already got their perwanna to clear their business, having satisfied the Prince with presents, and that if the English Company did the same, they could get their perwanna forthwith. They write an answer to Rājārāma telling him to find out how much the present to the Prince himself and all other charges will be, and if it is not unreasonable they will send it. He is to take care that the perwanna is in as full terms as formerly, and also that it is to clear their business in Patna. The *vakil* is also to try and put off the European goods for the present to the Prince.

October 2nd.

A report comes in from Rāmachandra *vakil* from Hugli stating that the native princes there require large presents before they will clear the business of the Company, they having been used to such large sums from both Companies. It is agreed to give them 3,000 rupees in European goods to be given to the several officers according to the following list:—

"Account of the presents made to the several officers belonging to the Government of Hugli.

To					Rs. A. P.			Rs. A. P.		
	To the Governour.									
1	Piece of broadcloth, violet,	16	yds.	...	114	0	0			
1	,, ,, green,	24	,,	...	80	0	0			
1	,, ,, scarlet,	23½	,,	...	120	0	0			
1	,, ,, ordinary,	,,	,,	...	80	0	0			
2	Sword blades	...	...	...	5	0	0			
1	Pair pistols	...	...	...	22	0	0			
1	Birding gun	...	...	...	22	0	0			
1	Large looking glass, 30 inches	...	...	...	33	0	0			
1	Flintware at 1-6	...	...	...	60	0	0			
								541	9	0
	To									
	Mahomet Rara, Ecbarnavees and Cossowda.[1]									
3	Pieces of broadcloth, Aurora, £7-7-6			...	117	0	0			
2	,, ,, ordinary	..	...	...	80	0	0			
1	Piece ,, scarlet	...	...	...	120	0	0			
1	Pair of pistols	...	...	...	22	0	0			
2	Sword blades	...	...	...	5	3	0			
1	Gun	...	...	...	22	0	0			
1	Looking glass, 30 inches	...	...	...	33	8	0			
	Flintware ...	...	...	...	60	0	0			
								524	9	0
	To									
	Ooja Mahomet, Buxie.[2]									
1	Piece fine broadcloth, green,	24	yds.	...	80	0	0			
1	,, ,, scarlet,	22	,,	...	120	0	0			
1	Pair pistols	...	...	...	11	0	0			
1	Gun	...	...	...	22	0	0			
1	Looking glass, 18 inches	...	...	...	7	10	0			
1	Flintware ...	...	...	...	60	0	0			
								300	10	0
	To									
	The Droga of the Buxbunder Vizt.[3]									
1	Piece of fine broadcloth, scarlet,	22	yds.	...	120	0	0			
1	,, ,, ,, Aurora	...	...	59	0	0			
1	,, ,, ,, ordinary	...	...	40	0	0			
1	Looking glass, 18 inches	...	...	...	7	10	0			
1	Pair pistols	...	...	...	22	0	0			
1	Flintware	...	...	...	36	0	0			
								284	10	0
			Carried over	...	...			1,651	6	0

[1] Muḥammad Dārā, *Akhbārnavīs and qāṣid-dār.*

[2] *Khwājah* Muḥammad, *Bakhshī.*

[3] *Dāroghah* of the *bakhshbandar.*

s 2

		Rs. A. P.	Rs. A. P.
	Brought forward ...	...	1,651 6 0
	To		
	The Cozzee¹ Vizt.		
2	Pieces broadcloth, Aurora	118 0 0	
1	Looking glass, 18 inches ...	7 10 0	
2	Sword blades	5 3 0	
1	Piece ordinary broadcloth	40 0 0	
	Flintware ...	30 0 0	
			200 13 0
	To		
	Ramkisna Mutsiedie² Vizt.		
2	Pieces ordinary broadcloth	80 0 0	
1	Looking glass, 18 inches	7 10 0	
1	Sword blade	2 9 6	
			90 3 6
	To		
	Coja Mahomets Naibe³ Vizt.		
2	Pieces ordinary broadcloth	80 0 0	
1	Looking glass, 18 inches	7 10 4	
1	Sword blade	2 9 6	
			90 3 6
	To		
	The Droga of the Mennerah⁴ Vizt.		
2	Pieces ordinary broadcloth	80 0 0	
1	Sword blade	2 9 6	
1	Looking glass, 18 inches ...	7 10 0	
1	Pistol	22 0 0	
			112 3 6
	To		
	The Cossianavis⁵ Vizt.		
1	Piece broadcloth, Aurora ...	59 0 0	
1	Sword blade	2 9 6	•
1	Looking glass, 18 inches ...	7 10 0	
	Flintware ...	12 0 0	
			81 3 6
	To		
	The Governor Naibe⁶ Vizt.		
1	Piece of broadcloth, Aurora	59 0 0	
1	Gun	22 0 0	
1	Pistol	11 0 0	
1	Looking glass, 18 inches...	7 10 0	
			99 10 0
	To		
	The Governor Muttsuddie⁷ Vizt.		
1	Piece of broadcloth, Aurora, at 7-6	15 0 0	
1	Sword blade	2 9 6	
1	Flintware ...	15 0 0	
1	Looking glass, 18 inches ...	7 10 0	
			40 3 6
	Carried over ...	...	2,365 14 6

¹ *Qāsi.*
² Rāmakrishṇa, *mutaṣaddī.*
³ Khwājah Muḥammad's *nāib.*
⁴ *Dāroghah* of the *menṛ.*
⁵ *Khāṣ-navīs.*
⁶ Governor's *nāib.*
⁷ Governor's *mutaṣaddī.*

				Rs.	A.	P.	Rs.	A.	P.
	Brought forward		..		...		2,365	14	6
	To								
	The Munchee[1] Vizt.								
4	Yds. of Aurora at 7-6 per yard ...	...		12	0	0			
1	Sword blade (ordinary) ...	...		0	9	6			
	Flintware ...	...		6	0	0			
							18	9	6
	To								
	The Buxies Naibe[2] Vizt.								
1	Piece of Aurora cloth ...	...		59	0	0			
1	Gun	...		22	0	0			
1	Pistol	...		11	0	0			
1	Looking glass, 18 inches ...	...		7	10	0			
							99	10	0
	To								
	Cojah Mahomets Muttsuddies.[3]								
5	Yds. of Aurora cloth at 7-6 ...	...		15	0	0			
1	Looking glass, 18 inches ...	...		7	10	0			
1	Sword blade, ordinary ...	...		9	6	0			
	Flintware	...		6	0	0			
							29	3	6
	To								
	Droga of the Buxbunder, his Mutsuddie.[4]								
5	Yds. of Aurora cloth at 7-6 ...	...		15	0	0			
1	Looking glass, 18 inches ...	...		7	10	0			
1	Sword blade, ordinary	...		9	6	0			
	Flintware	...		6	0	0			
							29	3	6
	To								
	Meerbars Drogah.[5]								
1	Piece of ordinary cloth ...	...		40	0	0			
1 *	Looking glass	...		7	10	0			
1	Sword blade •	...		2	9	6			
							50	3	6
					...		2,592	12	6
	Cash given to the Government servants ...				...		200	0	0
					...		2,792	12	6

118.—SALARIES.

"The Company's Servants, Factors, and Writers desiring their
Salaries, the usual day being past, the Secretary
October 2nd.   is ordered to draw a list of all the servants, their
stations and time of entering into the United Service, and that they
have the Salaries advanced them, as the Company directed in the

---

[1] *Munshi.*

[2] *Bakshi's nāib.*

[3] Khwājah Muḥammad s *mutaṣaddī.*

[4] *Dāroghah* of the *bakhshbandar's mutaṣaddī.*

[5] *Mīr-baḥr's dāroghah.*

General Letter to Fort St. George, which paragraph the Governor and Council remitted us according to our desire, the Court of Managers having not acquainted us what salary they have allowed each person."

"Having determined the Salaries of the Factors, and Writers,

October 8th.
ordering them what the Managers direct in their letter to Fort St. George, 'tis unanimously agreed by all the Council, being voted from the lowest to the highest, that the Chairmen have £100 each, and the others of the Council £40 each, to be paid in the country, as the Court and Managers direct at 2-6 per rupee, the two Chaplains £100 each per year."

119.—TAKING THE PRESENT TO HUGLI.

Messrs. Russell and Nightingale are ordered to take the present to

October 7th.
Hugli, and visit the Faujdār. They are to give him his present in person, and see that two of the Company's Factors, who go with them, give the presents to the other officers.

120.—MORNING PRAYER AT 8 A.M.

"A letter read from the Chaplain, Mr. Adams, complaining that

October 9th.
Mr. Hedges took too much on himself in altering the hour of morning prayer in the factory. Answer him that it was not Mr. Hedges' doing, but that the Council wished that the morning prayer in the Factory might be at eight in the morning, and not at ten, as the latter hour interfered with business."

121.—PAYING THE SALARIES.

The account of the amount of the salaries was given by Mr. Winder,

October 12th.
the Accountant. It amounted to sicca rupees 4,949-2-3. He is ordered to place the same to the salary account, in the name of and to the amount for each servant of the Company. The cashier is ordered to pay each man in siccas.

122.—AN INTESTATE'S ESTATE.

"Ordered that Mr. Bowcher do together with Mr. Redshaw take

October 12th.
an account of the estate of Mr. John Johnson, a free merchant lately deceased intestate—as we apprehend, and if no will is found, Mr. Redshaw is to put the deceased's goods to public outcry."

123.—THOMAS CURGENVEN.[1]

An application is made by Mr. Thos. Curgenven, who asks that he may have the salary of £40 per annum.

October 16th.

He is only allowed a salary of £30 per annum as a junior merchant until advice has been taken of the Company at home as to what they wish their men to receive.

124.—THE COTTA WAREHOUSE.

October 27th.

The cotta or pricing warehouse is opened. The goods are to be sorted and priced as soon as possible.

125.—MURSHID QULI KHÂN DEMANDS MONEY.

They receive a notice from the *vakil* Rājārāma at Balasor to the effect that the Dīwān will not take a present of goods, but that he will have money. The Dīwān

October 27th.

also refuses to receive money as though the two companies were one. He wants 30,000 rupees, as large a sum as he used to receive when they were two. Rājarāma proposes that, if the Company are willing, he will offer the Dīwān 15,000 rupees, and try and persuade him to accept it, and give them his *sanad* for trade accordingly. They agree to allow the *vakil* to do this, but to tell him to get Patna also included in the *sanad* if possible.

126.—THE HUGLI OFFICERS DEMAND LARGER PRESENTS.

Some trouble is caused by the native officers at Hugli, who demand larger presents than those sent. Rāma-

October 30th.

chandra, the *vakil* at Hugli, reports that three of the *bakhshis*, or-officers, of the Dīwān will not accept their presents unless they be augmented by Sicca Rupees 1,100. If this be not done, they will obstruct the trade as much as they can. They agree to delay complying as long as possible, and then to send the money by Mr. Winder and Mr. Redshaw. They are to pay it privately, concealing it from all the other *darbār* officers, for fear that they too may demand more. They also agree to send with Mr. Winder and Mr. Redshaw 30 soldiers, to overawe, if possible, the native officers, but the soldiers are on no account to commence hostilities.

127.—ADAMS GOES TO MADRAS.

Mr. Adams, the Chaplain, goes to Madras for his health, bearing a letter to help him to raise money there for the

November 2nd.

Church in Calcutta.

---

[1] Thomas Curgenven had influence. He was the nephew of the Rev. T. Curgenven, Rector foFolke, who married Dorothy, sister of Thomas Pitt, Governor of Fort St, George,

128.—A SITE FOR THE CHURCH.

"The contribution money to build a Church, being mostly collected by the two Chaplains, ordered that a sufficient piece of ground to build it on be appointed in the Broad Street, next or pretty near to Captain Wallis his house, between that and Mr. Soames's, and that a broadway be left on the side next the river fully sixty feet broad clear from the Church."

November 6th.

129.—GOODS OF INTESTATES SOLD BY AUCTION.

William Champion, factor, dies leaving a will. Nicolas Audney, of the *Rising Sun*, Smack, and George Moore, one of the gunner's crew, die intestate. Their goods were sold by public auction and the money paid into the Company's cash account.

November 27th.

130.—DISPUTES IN THE UNITED COUNCIL.[1]

Quarrels arose between servants of old and New Companies now joined in Council on the following question. Although the affairs of the United Company were now managed by the United Council, there still existed two other Councils in Calcutta. There was a separate Council for winding up the separate affairs of the Old London Company, of which Mr. Beard was President, and there was another separate Council for winding up the affairs of the New English Company, of which Sir Edward Littleton was President. Neither of the Presidents had a seat in the United Council. If Beard were to go away for a short time from Calcutta, Mr. Ralph Sheldon, who was next in succession to him among the Old Company's servants, would officiate for him as President of the separate Council for the Old Company's affairs. Would he then for the time cease to be a Member of the United Council? Similarly, in the temporary absence of Sir Edward Littleton, Mr. Robert Hedges would become President of the separate Council for the New Company's affairs. Would he then temporarily cease to be a Member of the United Council? After much discussion it is settled that neither Hedges nor Sheldon need resign his seat in the United Council. Many letters are sent to the Court of Managers at home from both parties, each accusing the other of not wishing to obey the orders of the Court of Managers at home.

November and December.

---

[1] Of this Governor Pitt writes: "In Bengal all things are pretty quiet, only jangling in the Rotation Government, all talkers and no hearers." (Brit. Mus. Add. MSS. 22, 848, No. 70.) And two months later to the Secretary at the East India House: "For the Rotation Government in Bengal 'tis become the ridicule of all India, both Europeans and Native." (To John Styleman, Dec. 1704.) See *Hedges' Diary*, II, .106.

DIARY AND CONSULTATION BOOK

OF THE

UNITED TRADE COUNCIL AT FORT WILLIAM IN BENGAL.

From December 1704 *to the end of November* 1705.

181.—BAD LANGUAGE FINED.

Benjamin Walker was fined twenty rupees for abusing Mr. Hedges
December 3rd, 1704.   by using bad language to him.

132.—FRIENDLY RELATIONS BETWEEN DUTCH AND ENGLISH.

" Passed by the Dutch Commissary to repair on board his own ship
December 11th.   when was fired 21 guns as usual."

" Passed by the Dutch Director who came ashore to take leave of
President Beard before the President departed for Madras."

133.—BEARD GOING TO MADRAS.

" President Beard departed down the river in order to go board the
December 17th.   *Chambers* frigate for Madras."

134.—FRESH SITE FOR THE CHURCH.

" The ground pitched on for building the church on being objected
December 22nd.   against by many inhabitants of the town, who
are so dissatisfied about it, that they who have
not already paid their contributions refuse, and resolve not to pay it,
except the ground be changed; it is therefore agreed that it be built
opposite to the west[1] curtain at a convenient distance from the wall of
the Fort."

135.—SENT TO ENGLAND TO BE TRIED.

Captain Delgardno, who was imprisoned for murder in 1702, was now
December 25th.   sent to England to be tried. He was first sent on
board ship *Tavistock* as prisoner, but refusing to
go that way, was allowed to go as passenger.[2]

---

[1] This should be *east*. Had the church been built opposite the *west* curtain, it would have
been in the river.

[2] On August 14th, 1704, Captain Delgardno was ordered to be sent to Fort St. George,
Madras, to be tried.

136.—HARD TERMS.

Rājārāma arrives from the Dīwān's camp. He states that the
22nd January 1705.   Dīwan positively insists on twenty thousand
                         rupees. The United Company think it abso-
lutely necessary to procure the Dīwān's *sanad*, as without it they cannot
have the benefit of the mint, nor yet work the Cassimbazar factory.
They therefore resolve to agree to demand, and order Rājārāma to
return to the Dīwān's camp at Burdwan to acquaint the Dīwān of
their decision.

137.—FRENCH CRUISERS AT FORT ST. DAVID.

They hear news that five French ships have arrived at Fort St.
12th February.   David's roads probably designed to cruise for
                        English shipping.

138.—ROBBERIES IN CALCUTTA.

"There having been several robberies committed in the Black Town,
23rd February.   ordered that a corporal and six soldiers be sent
                        to lodge in the Catwall's [*Kotwāl's*] house, to
be upon call to prevent the like in future."

139.—ALLOWANCES.

The Company's servants complain of the bad table kept, and ask
27th February.   for diet money. It is agreed that they shall be
                        allowed twenty rupees each per month. They
are also to be allowed oil for lamps, but not candles.

140.—THE ABUSE OF DASTAKS.

"Ordered that a paper be fixed to the factory gate prohibiting any
26th March.   man procuring dusticks [*i.e. dastaks*] for goods
                        not for his own account or for account of some
Englishman under the Company's protection."

141.—PUNCH-HOUSE LICENSES.

"Ordered that the licensed punch houses do pay their license money
7th May.   out of hand, they being most of them behind
                        hand more than 12 months."

142.—A FRESH SURVEY.

"Ordered that Mr. Bowcher, jemidar, [*zamīndar*,] take a fresh
16th July.   account of every house under the Company's
                        government, and survey all the ground that is
occupied either in tillage, gardens, or any other plantation."

143.—BEARD DIES; SHELDON TAKES HIS PLACE.

"Mr. Ralph Sheldon, one of the Chairmen in the Council of United
Trade and second in Council of Old Company, is
August 14th. promoted to be President of Old Company,
President Beard[1] having died away from Calcutta." In consequence
of this promotion, Sheldon has to give up his place in the United Trade
Council, as neither the President of the Old Company nor the President
of the New Company can sit in United Trade Council. The Directors
in England had sent orders that if either President died, the second in
the Council was to succeed him, until orders arrived from England
either ratifying or annulling his appointment.

144.—A PUNCH-HOUSE LICENSE.

One hundred rupees are paid for a punch-house
August 14th. license.

145.—NEW DOCTOR.

"The place and season being very sickly renders it impossible for
one Doctor to attend all the sick, and that none
August 20th. may perish for want of due attendance in sickness,
there being no mates or assistants to Dr. Warren, and he very sick, 'tis
unanimously agreed that Mr. Gray, who was Surgeon to Metchlepatan
Factory for the New Company, be taken into the United Trade Service
at the same salary that Dr. Warren has, but Dr. Warren to have precedence, having served the longest time in India."

146.—A DUTCH SHIP PASSES.

"A large Dutch ship passed by in order to proceed to a town
below near the mouth of the river, where gene-
September 3rd. rally their large ships lades."

147.—THE SATURDAY COURT OF JUSTICE.

It is ordered that Mr. Winder and Mr. Pattle do sit in Court every
Saturday after this week to do justice there.
September 6th. This Saturday Court had been discontinued
owing to illness.

---

[1] Further details about Beard are given in the introduction to these summaries.

148.—NEW ZAMĪNDĀR.

Mr. Benjamin Bowcher, the *Zamīndār*, died of fever at 10 o'clock last night. Mr. Jonathan Winder is to officiate as *Zamīndār*, till a new one can be appointed.

September 24th.

They must wait for full Council for that, some of them being away.

October 8th.   Mr. John Cole is appointed *Zamīndār*.

149.—FOR THE BETTER DESPATCH OF SHIPPING.

In consideration to provide for the despatch of shipping, 'tis resolved that we meet in consultation on Mondays and Thursdays at 7 o'clock and finish consultation

October 9th.

at 9 o'clock, and go to the warehouse to price goods. A summons to be sent out by the Secretary the evening of the day before the Counsel to put men in mind. This rule is to be in force till after the autumn shipping is despatched.

150.—SHALL WE PAY THE DĪWĀN ?

Another long discussion takes place as to whether Rājārāma shall be authorized to pay thirty thousand rupees to the Dīwān at Hugli for his *sanad*. The question is

October 18th.

still left open till they hear further news. If they decide that the money is to be paid, Rājārāma is to pay it at once, and so prevent the saltpetre boats being stopped on their way down the river.

151.—SALTPETRE BOATS.

They had news from Mr. Chitty and the others who had gone with him to procure saltpetre that they had already started for Calcutta, so that they might

October 21st.

any day arrive at Hugli.

News arrives from Mr. Chitty of the grounding and sinking of four of the saltpetre boats on the sands at Barr; the other boats were " saved with much pain."

October 21st.

152.—MILITARY APPOINTMENTS.

November 2nd.   Woodville is appointed Lieutenant of the soldier in the garrison.

November 5th.   Dalibar is appointed Ensign.

153.—DESPATCHING SHIPS.

They order all captains to bring their ships up the river and anchor near the Fort for the quicker despatch of business. The great month for despatching the winter European shipping seems to have been November.

November 5th.

DIARY AND CONSULTATION BOOK

OF THE

UNITED TRADE COUNCIL AT FORT WILLIAM IN BENGAL.

———◆———

From December 1705 to December 1706.

———◆———

154.—BUYING SILENCE.

A couple of sailors belonging to the ship *Herne*, then lying in the
harbour, attacked some natives and killed one
peon, who was in the Company's service. The
Council directly they heard of the affair sent for the relatives of the
murdered man, and bought their silence about it for 50 rupees;
being afraid that if it came to the native Governor's ears, he would
make it an excuse, not only for forcing the Company to pay a heavy
fine, but also for stopping their trade.

January 14th, 1706.

155.—THE PATNA FACTORY.

Two members of the Council, Maisters and Chitty, are to be sent
to the Patna Residency with money and presents.
They are to superintend the factory and trade at
Patna. The Council at Calcutta seem most anxious to keep the Patna
factory going.

January 14th.

156.—NEW DUTCH CHIEF.

"Passed by the New Dutch Chief[1] with
several servants for Hugli."

January 27th.

157.—ZAMĪNDĀRĪ ACCOUNTS.

'Mr. John Cole brought in the account
and revenue of the three towns balance being
Rs. 614-10-0.

March 4th.

158.—PRECEDENCE.

The Council received a letter, dated February 18th, from Mr. Arthur
King, a factor in the Company's service, who
considers himself insulted because the Surgeon's

March 4th.

---

[1] Willem de Roy.

wife has taken her place in church above his wife. He asks the Council to order that his wife shall be placed above the Surgeon's wife in future. This letter was opened by the Chairman, Mr. Russell, who persuaded King to withdraw it, that the matter might be settled privately. King now writes again to say that the Surgeon's wife continues to "squat herself down" in his wife's place, and that, if they would not see to it, he would let them know that they as well as he "had masters in England," and that they must hold themselves responsible for any disturbance or unseemly conduct that may arise in church in consequence.

159.—DOUBTS ABOUT THE SANAD.

The Council still hesitates to take out the *sanad* at Hugli, because
March 11th.
they are waiting to be advised from Surat how the affairs of the Dutch are settled. The Dutch are there with a fleet, and are threatening to burn the town, which "if they should do, would be of ill consequence to all Europeans."

160.—PROVISIONS.

"Being a cheap season for grain," it is ordered that the charges
April 2nd.
general keeper do provide a thousand rupees worth of wheat and "100 maunds of oil, and that it lie by for garrison stores, which, if no occasion for use here, may serve for provisions for the coasts."

*161.—IRON FOR CHURCH BUILDING.

The overseers of the church send five hundred rupees worth of
April 4th.
copper to Balasor to provide iron for building the church.

162.—KING MADE ZAMĪNDĀR.

Mr. Arthur King is ordered to act as Zamīndār instead of Mr. Cole.
April 8th.
Mr. Cole had been ordered to take charge of the Import Warehouse, but the execution of the order was delayed till April, as the books were all adjusted each year in that month, and it was easier to move officers then.

163.—ENCOURAGING POOR TENANTS.

"It formerly being a custom for all people who sold small houses or
April 15th.
compounds to pay one-fourth part of the money they sell them for to the Company: and that the merchants or others that sold large houses or compounds paid but 2 per

cent. Considering this is very hard upon the poor people, ordered that all people pay for the future 5 per cent., which we think to be reasonable and an encouragement to the poor tenants who paid in proportion a great deal more than the richer sort."

164.—THE OLD FACTORY.

" The old factory house having for several years been decaying, and

April 18th.   more especially of late with the great storms, has given way in several places insomuch that those gentlemen that lie in it declaring it dangerous to stay any longer there. We have had the chief carpenter and bricklayer with several others to survey it, whose opinions are that if it not soon taken down it will fall of itself, ordered therefore that lodgings be prepared for the gentlemen that lay in it, and that the house be pulled down to prevent any mischief that may happen."

165.—PESHKASH.

They send the Government of Hugli three thousand siccas as

April 22nd.   *peshkash* for the past year.

166.—RETURN TO CASSIMBAZAR.

"Send a letter to King's Duan at Muxodabad to the effect that

April 22nd.   upon the encouragement he has given we design to settle Cassimbazar on the arrival of our shipping, and in the meantime we shall send up our people to repair our factory."

167.—MR. ADAMS ADVISED TO BE MORE PEACEABLE.

A quarrel arose between Mr. Benjamin Adams and Mr. Russell.

April 25th.   Mr. Adams's native servant attacked one of the native servants of the Company and beat him. For this Mr. Russell orders him to be imprisoned; but Mr. Adams shuts him up in his own house, and refuses to give him up. Both Mr. Adams and Mr. Russell appeal to the Council, who decide that the " said servant was justly punished for beating one of the Company's officers who was merely doing his duty." The Council then send for Mr. Adams, and advise him to be of a " more peaceable temper, and to be civil and respectful to the Government for the future."

168.—JOHN CALVERT.

Mr. John Calvert is ordered to be assistant to the cashier and regis-

April 26th.   trar of the Court of Justice.

169.—REPAIRS AT HUGLI AND CASSIMBAZAR.

"The house at Hugly, formerly the new Company's Factory,

May 2nd.

beginning to decay, and considering the use made of it by the United Company's servants when ordered up thither about the Company's affairs, agreed that it be kept in repairs, as the United Company have the use of it till the right owners lay claim to it."

May 20th.

"Send a man to repair Cassimbazar Factory, also timber for same."

170.—OUR OWN WEAVERS.

Last year they employed several weavers in their own towns, but

May 20th.

the men proved to be so poor that they could not carry out their contracts in time. This year they agree to still employ their own weavers as they wish to encourage weavers to settle in the town, but they decide that the weavers must be overlooked. Accordingly they appoint a native who is to give out the orders, and see that he has security that the men can carry out what they undertake. For this he is to have three per cent. on the said orders.

171.—TWO LICENSES.

Two native merchants are given licenses; the one, "Gossa," to sell

•May 20th.

ganja for which he pays the Company Rs. 180 per year, and the other, "Sufferally, Serong," to provide the ships with lascars for which he pays Rs. 65.

172.—THREATENING THE GOVERNOR OF HUGLI.

The Governor of Hugli will not give a full receipt for the peshkash

June 4th.

given him, but stops the trade, hoping to get a larger present. They agree that it would be a very bad precedent to give him more. They therefore send Mr. Nightingale with thirty soldiers to Hugli who will, if possible, compel the Governor to let trade go on through fear of hostilities with English.

Mr. Nightingale returns from Hugli having extorted a promise

June 17th.

from the Governor not to obstruct English trade in future.

173.—VISIT FROM THE GOVERNOR OF HUGLI.

"This day the Governor of Hugli came to visit us and was received

July 7th.

with great civility." They had a lodging prepared for him in town, and each Chairman visited

T

him in turn. He stayed till the 14th and had presents of cloth and flintware given him before he left. Both on his arrival and on his departure the Fort guns and the guns on the ships in the harbour saluted him.

174.—MORE PRESENTS.

"We have received advice from Mannick Chund that the King's Diwān has ordered his *naib* at Patna to permit our business to pass as formerly, also that he will give his *sanad* for our free trade in Bengal upon paying him piscash [*peshkash*] of Rs. 3,000 (*sic.*)[1] The King's Commissioner of the Customs of Bengal having visited us, and considering it lies in his power to obstruct our affairs, it is agreed we present him and his servants in European goods to the amount of Rs. 200.

July 18th.

175.—BRANDING THE THIEVES.

"A few days ago there were taken several robbers and thieves; the former have taken and murdered several people; it is therefore agreed what persons we have in custody and what more may be taken, that the gentlemen belonging to the Court do burn such persons on the cheek, and turn them on the other side the water."

August 29th.

176.—LETTER FROM MR. ADAMS.

A letter from Mr. Adams announces that he intends to resign his Chaplaincy at Michaelmas.

September 19th.

" To the Hon'ble Council of Managers—

"Sirs,—This is to acquaint you that I intend to officiate among you no longer than Michaelmas, so in the interim shall give Mr. Anderson warning which yet I bind myself hitherto not to divulge that I might gather what money I could for the Church before I left you, for I found Brother Anderson had not reputation enough among gent. here to obtain their subscriptions. But now since matters are otherwise determined I am lett loose from restraint, being free from those obligations I was under before to raise money, and I am glad for your sakes and the Church that the result of yesterday's Conference was so fortunate, for absolutely speaking though it were by far more proper in itself and withall more profitable for the Church that the Ministers should gather the contributions, yett at this juncture it were more advisable for

---

[1] This is obviously a mistake for Rs. 30,000.

the above reason that the election should proceed upon indifferent Trustees, and I wish with all my heart they may collect more money then I did last year, which will enable them to do what is useful if not ornamental to the church; and that in any corner of the world would be acceptable news to Yr. friend and servant.—B. ADAMS.

"Fort Wm., 7 bre 19, 1706."

177.—DISPUTES ABOUT PLACES IN COUNCIL.

They receive another letter from the managers in England, confirm-ing the Council of the United Trade, and stating that the Council was to adhere to the orders already given about the place of every one in the Council. A long and stormy debate follows. At last they pass a resolution to do as their masters order; and it is agreed "that the four of Council for Old Com-pany do take their station as 1st, 3rd, 5th, and 7th in the United Council, and the two 1st do take the chair alternately every week as formerly established, and in case of mortality on either side, the next who shall succeed must be the 8th person of this Council."

September 21st.

Mr. John Cole is excluded from the Council. According to the list sent by the Hon'ble Directors, Mr. Arthur King is to take his place.

"Agreed that the undermentioned persons take the charge and management of the following affairs of the Hon'ble Company:—

September 23rd.

Mr. Edward Pattle ...	...	Accomptant.
Mr. Robert Nightingale	...	Export Warehouse-keeper.
Mr. William Bugden	...	Import ditto.
Mr. John Maisters ...	...	Buxie [Bakhshi].
Mr. William Lloyd ...	...	Jemindar [Zamindar].
Mr. Arthur King ...	...	Secretary.

Maisters and Lloyd were away settling the factory at Patna. Till their return Mr. Arthur King was to act as *Bakhshi*, and Mr. Waldo as *Zamindar*, and Mr. Abraham Adams as Secretary.

178.—MORE DISPUTES. THEY CAST LOTS.

They receive another letter from England, in which the Governors of the Old Company state that they do not wish for a separate President for Old Company affairs now that Mr. Beard is dead. Consequently Mr. Ralph Sheldon is displaced.

September 24th.

T 2

Now begins another quarrel in Council. Mr. Ralph Sheldon, not being any longer President of the Old Company's affairs, wishes to take his place again as one of the Chairmen of the United Trade Council. He sends a letter to the Council asking to be reinstated. Half the Council are for allowing it, half against it. In spite of much stormy discussion, they cannot come to any decision. They therefore "agree to cast lots as our masters have bidden us in times of disagreement." The lots fell for Mr. Sheldon, who was accordingly re-elected.

The Council then send a letter offering to re-elect as the other Chairman Mr. Hedges, the President of New Company, who had been obliged to resign for the same reason as Mr. Sheldon. Mr. Hedges writes back arguing that Mr. Sheldon should not have been re-elected, and refusing himself to be re-elected, unless the Council own that they had no right in the first place to force him to resign. Many letters pass between Mr. Hedges and the Council. At last, in his final letter, he says that he believes he was justly turned out on becoming President of the New Company, and that he cannot see that the recent orders from home justify the action of the Council. He therefore refuses to be re-elected and adds that he is returning home to England directly to lay an account of the whole affair before the Managers in London.

"Agreed that Mr. Winder is therefore to continue to act as New Company Chairman on United Trade Council."

179.—THEY AGAIN ARRANGE THE COUNCIL.

October 3rd.

In October they seem again to alter the position of the Council—

Mr. Ralph Sheldon	...	} Chairmen and Cashiers.
Mr. Jona. Winder	...	
Mr. John Russell	...	Book-keeper.
Mr. Robert Nightingale	...	Export Warehouse-keeper.
Mr. Edward Pattle	...	Import ditto.
Mr. William Bugden	...	Buxie [Bakhshī].
Mr. John Maisters	...	Jemindar [Zamīndār].
Mr Arthur King	...	Secretary.

"Mr. Waldo to be Jemidar till Mr. Maister's arrivall."

180.—LICENSES.

"Granted licenses to Mingo Ash and Govind Sondee [Govinda-sundar] to distil arrack and keep houses of entertainment."

October 3rd.

181.—PROSPECTS AT CASSIMBAZAR.

They agree to send people to work the Cassimbazar factory if the
October 18th.   King's Dīwān will give them a good *sanad*.
From this factory they seem to have expected to
get "much profit for our masters, though present expenses be heavy."

182.—NO GRATUITY FOR ADAMS.

Mr. Adams[1] applies for his salary and gratuity money. He is to
October 18th.   be paid his salary, but no gratuity, on account
of his " behaviour to the Council."

183.—JANARDDAN SETT, BROKER.

On this day Janarddana Sett was appointed Broker in place of
October 18th.   Dvipchand Bella, deceased.

184.—WORRIED ABOUT PETRE BOATS.

They are as usual much worried about the saltpetre boats which are
October 31st.   stopped over and over again on their way down
the river by the various officials. They send
orders to pass them at any price; they give presents everywhere.

They privately receive news that Mr. Calvert and Mr. Spencer,
two of the Company's servants who had been sent up to clear the
saltpetre boats, and had arrived at the Rajmahal river's mouth, were
attacked by 'chowkies' in their passage up the river. The Council
determine to send Mr. Edward Pattle with an ensign and twenty
soldiers to help Mr. Calvert and Mr. Spencer bring the boats down.

Mr. Pattle and his escort were attacked by *chaukidārs*; and several
November 25th.   men wounded. As they had the Dīwān's orders
to let them pass, the Council determined to send
to the King's Dīwān, and demand satisfaction, and also to send a
complaint to the Prince at Patna.

185.—A FRENCH SHIP ON THE WEST COAST.

They received a letter from the Dutch Governor of Negapatam,
November 25th.   stating that one of his vessels had been chased
by a French ship from the gulf of Moca towards
the Malabar Coast.

186.—SANAD FOR CASSIMBAZAR.

The Dīwān of Maqṣūdābād gives his *sanad* for trade, in Cassimbazar,
November 25th.   and for clearing the Company's petre boats. The
Dīwān will send his passport with ten horsemen
and footmen to attend the Englishmen appointed to go to Cassimbazar.

---

[1] Further details about Mr. Adams will be found in the introduction to these summaries.

DIARY AND CONSULTATION BOOK

OF THE

UNITED TRADE COUNCIL AT FORT WILLIAM IN BENGAL.

From December 1706 to December 1707.

187.—BUGDEN AND FEAKE TO CASSIMBAZAR.

They agreed to send Mr. W. Bugden and Mr. Samuel Feake to

December 4th.

Cassimbazar on the arrival of the purwanna and horsemen from the Dīwān.

188.—POLICE.

Several robberies having been committed in the town by 'country

December 27th.

robbers,' who killed and wounded several of the Company's native servants and others, it is "thought necessary to keep greater guard on the towns for the Company's tenants' safety, wherefore the jemindar [*zamīndār*] is ordered to entertain 31 pikes, or black peons, for the time present, to prevent like mischief in the future."

189.—ESCORT TO CASSIMBAZAR.

The King's Dīwān's people arrive in Calcutta to escort Mr. Bugden

January 17th, 1707.

and his company to Cassimbazar. They are lodged in the town for a few days. Then, Mr. Bugden and his people being ready, they all set out for Cassimbazar. Mr. Bugden took with him everything necessary to start the factory well at Cassimbazar, also money to pay the Dīwān for his *sanad*.

190.—CHURCH BUILDING.

The new Church which was building had apparently been more

February 10th.

or less at a standstill for some time owing, says the consultation book, to want of proper or regular proceedings. By order of the Council, Messrs. Edward Pattle and John Maisters are now to take the matter in hand. They are to receive subscriptions for the building fund, to see that the work of building goes on regularly, and to give a monthly account to the Council of what they do.

191.—ABRAHAM ADAMS.

Mr. Abraham Adams is appointed to be jemindar [*zamīndār*] and to
February 14th. look after the three towns and bazar. He is also
to sit in the Court of Justice in the room of
Mr. William Bugden.

192.—NEWS FROM MR. BUGDEN.

News is received from Mr. Bugden and his company. It appears
February 19th. that when they arrived at Cassimbazar they
found that the Dīwān would not give them a
sanad unless the 25,000 sicca rupees, which he declared the Company
had promised him, were first paid. Mr. Bugden therefore sends to
enquire of the Council what answer he shall give. They send back
a message to the effect that Mr. Bugden is to answer that as soon
as the Dīwān's *sanad* is in his (Mr. Bugden's) hands, the Dīwān
shall receive the money, but not before. If the Dīwān will not
agree to this, Mr. Bugden and his company are to return to Calcutta.

193.—THE SUB-ACCOUNTANT'S SALARY.

The sub-accountant is to receive £40 per annum above his salary
February 19th. to encourage him to keep the books well, this
being the custom at Fort St. George and
other leading factories.

194.—BIG GUNS.

Some big guns had been sent out from England for Fort St. George,
February 27th. but it was found a very difficult matter to convey
them there. They were therefore in the factory
at Calcutta. After a good deal of correspondence between the two
forts, it was agreed that Fort William should buy the guns, but should
undertake to sell them again to Fort St. George, if at any time the
means of conveying them there could be found.

195.—SLAVES.

"There being slaves often ordered for sale, and they desiring a
February 28th. supply on the West Coast at York Fort, and just
on the ships going they are not to be had, there-
fore we think it necessary that the Buxie [*Bakhshī*], Mr. Arthur King,

buy up what slaves he can get from time to time, and keep them in a compound with a guard for that purpose, giving them victuals from the Company, and make them work at the house or otherwise as there may be occasion, so as to keep them in health; he must take care that they are most men and boys, and few women or girls, and see they are sound, wholesome, and well shaped when bought."

196.—IRREGULAR BUILDINGS FORBIDDEN.

Finding that several of the inhabitants had built walls and digged tanks in their several compounds without leave from the Government at Fort William, the Council ordered that an "order be wrote up and put at the gate to forbid all such irregular proceedings for the future."

March 10th.

197.—DEATH OF AURANGZĒB.

The whole town and factory are thrown into confusion by the news that the Mogul is dead. As these tidings were received from several sources people were found to credit the story, and great was the consternation at the Fort.

April 3rd.

A hasty Council was summoned and determined,

To stop as much as possible all paying out of money, and as a revolution is expected, order all the men that are near enough, such as Messrs. Darrell and Spencer, to come back with what money and charters they have belonging to the Company;

To send out a sergeant and 20 soldiers to meet Messrs. Darrell and Spencer, and bring them home safely;

To write to Messrs. Bugden and Feake at Cassimbazar to hold themselves in readiness to come to Calcutta and bring all the Company's effects with them.

On April 7th, at another Council meeting, the following resolution is passed:—" Considering the Emperor's death and the scarcity there may be of provisions, and the want they may have at Madras, agree to order that 5,000 maunds of rice and 1,000 maunds of wheat be provided by Mr. Arthur King for the use of the garrison, and to supply Fort St. George if they should be in want of the same."

April 7th.

A second order is despatched to Messrs. Bugden and Feake to come down at once, and bring all the Company's treasure they have, also the rupees provided for payment of the *sanad*. What broadcloth and other cloth they have they are to try and dispose of, but if they cannot it is to be left with Herry Kissen [*Harikrishṇa*], their banyan.

Fearing that the neighbouring zamīndārs in case of trouble in the country may prove troublesome and rob and plunder the Company's towns, unless the Company have a force equal to theirs, they "order that sixty black soldiers be taken into the company's service and posted round the towns."

198.—NEWS FROM PATNA.

Letters are received from Messrs. William Lloyd and Cawthorp at Patna, confirming the news of the Emperor's death, which was on the 23rd February, 1706, and that the Sultan had seized on Assud Khawn's [Asad Khān's] and the ? Vinrahs treasure as well as on that of the Emperor, and that he designed to raise a contribution on the merchants to levy forces in order to defend the country. The Council sent Messrs. Lloyd and Cawthorp an answer immediately telling them to get all the petre in as fast as they can, that they may "come away with the same." If it is necessary, they are to bribe to get the petre through. If they are forced to leave either goods or money behind them, they are to leave it in charge of what native servants they can trust.

April 14th.

The following week they receive another letter from Messrs. Lloyd and Cawthorp, to the effect that they cannot come down as there is little or no water in the river, and that should they make the attempt, they expect the Dīwān's people will stop them. The Council send them back an answer that they must do all in their power to come down, and bring the petre, and that they are to endeavour to sell what treasure they have to the Shroffs if the Shroffs will have it.

April 21st.

199.—WITHDRAWING.

The Council at the same time write a letter to Mr. Bugden[1] at Cassimbazar ordering him to dispose of the treasure he has in the same way. They also register an order that only merchants round Calcutta are to be dealt with, as owing to the unsettled state of the country they cannot trust any money out in the far provinces such as Dacca, Suntoos, Hundiall,

April 14th.

---

[1] As far as can be gathered from the consultations, Messrs. Bugden and Feake did not come back to Calcutta from Cassimbazar until May 22nd, or perhaps later. Mr. Bugden took his place in Council in June.

Malda, etc.; no place, says the order, that is more than "two or at the most three days' journey off."

200.—PUNCH-HOUSE LICENSE.

April 21st.

"Two hundred rupees received from Mr. Wheatley for two years' license money for his punch-house."

201.—NEGLECTING TO REGISTER.

April 21st.

"Josiah Jounsen was fined Rs. 25 for neglecting to register a house he had bought in the town."

202.—NEW WATERSIDE BASTIONS.

April 28th.

In both the last consultations there had been some talk as to the advisability of strengthening the Fort, and on the 28th of April the following resolution was passed:—"The Emperor being dead, and now being the properest time to strengthen our Fort, whilst there is an interregnum and no one likely to take notice of what we are doing, it is therefore agreed that we make two regular bastions to the water side to answer those to the land, and the Buxie is ordered to see it well performed out of hand, and to that end to take all the materials in the town that are necessary thereto, that it may be quickly erected, for we may not meet with such an opportunity again."

203.—FORCED CONTRIBUTIONS.

May 12th.

Bad news was received from Patna on May 12th to the effect that the factory there was being watched. The Sultan, and his son, the Prince, had demanded one lac of rupees as a contribution towards raising forces. Messrs. Lloyd and Cowthorp refused the money, so the Prince had the English *Vakil* seized and also the other native servants who belonged to the Company.

June 3rd.

Decided to write a letter to the Dīwān, desiring him to write to the Sultan at Patna, asking him "to give favour to the English there and to stop the people from interfering with trade." At the same time a letter was sent to the Company's *Vakil* at Patna, telling him that if the Company's people there "are plundered, we will take satisfaction at Hugli, or anywhere we find it convenient so to do."

204.—THE NORTH-WEST BASTION.

In building the north-west bastion, it was found necessary to

June 3rd.

build on land that beyond to the trustees of Governor Beard's estate. "Having occasion for one-third of President Beard's '(deceased) compound to build the north-west bastion upon, and to keep the fort clear from any building, and since it will not be very much prejudice to the dwelling-house and warehouse for which, as well as the whole compound, he has a lease for 31 years, paying a quit-rent for the same, agreed that the trustees for the deceased's house and compound be allowed 300 rupees to repair the damages, rebuild the wall, etc., and what ground is taken away, so much quitt-rent as is in proportion to the whole to be deducted out of the yearly payment."

205.—REGULATION OF THE THREE TOWNS.

In July 1705, the Company had ordered a survey and measurement

June 12th.

of the three towns; this was now completed and submitted to the Council. On examining it they found that the Company was being cheated, many persons not paying for half the ground they possessed. They agreed, therefore, to pass the following resolutions—

That the rent-gatherers or the jemindar [zamīndār] do give the inhabitant a puta. [paṭā] or ticket with a note affixed to it for the amount of rent he shall pay annually.

The tickets are to be brought in monthly when the rent is paid and to be renewed once a year. The rent-gatherers are to keep a book and duly enter each ticket.

The tax-gatherers are also to give in a yearly account of the increase or decrease of the inhabitants.

206.—NEW PAṬWĀRĪS.

The Council also discovered that the black rent-collectors had been

June 12th.

making false returns and farming out lands for their own advantage, so they issued an order that "all such land be given up and the black putwarries [paṭwārīs] be turned out of office as soon as possible, and new ones elected in their places, and to encourage the new putwarries. Each one shall have his wages increased to four rupees per month."

June 12th. # FORT WILLIAM.

JUNE 1707.

Account of Ground in Buzzar, and three Towns, as it was last measured.

BUZZAR.

			B.	c.	
Houses	...	...	401	10¾	
Wells	...	...	15	3½	
Plantins	...	...	7	4¾	
Sunaporea [? *Ġūnya-poṛa*]	...	...	9	3	
Ditches	...	...	3	12	
Gardens	...	...	19	3	
Flowers	...	...	0	6	
Cotton	...	...	0	3	
Green trade	...	...	0	10	
Tobacco	...	...	0	11	
Sursah [*Sarshyā*]	...	...	0	17	= 458-4
			458	4	

			B.	c.		B. c.	B.	c.
Bammons [*Brahmans*], etc.	...		26	8¾				
Wells	...		0	13				
Sunahpurah [? *Ġūnya-poṛa*]	...		1	0		458-4 +	30	5¾
Ditches	...		1	7		= 488		9¾
Gardens	...		0	17				

$$30 \;\; 5\tfrac{3}{4} = 488 \; \bullet 9\tfrac{3}{4}$$

B. c.

GOVENPORE.

			B.	c.
Houses	...	...	57	9
Paddee [*Padi*]	...	...	510	11
Green trade	...	...	35	14
Beatle	...	...	0	2
Tobacco	...	...	139	16
Gardens	...	...	59	2
Plantins	...	...	12	3
Bamboo	...	...	4	10
Grass	...	...	18	0
Wells	...	...	10	3
Tancks	...	...	0	9
Ditches	...	...	1	6
Commer	...	...	17	9
			866 14 = 866 14	

GOVENPORE—*concluded.*

			B.	c.
Bommons [*Brahmans*]	...	...	57	16
Jungall	...	...	83	14
Wast ground	...	...	169	12

		B.	c.
		311	13 = 1,178 7

TOWN CALCUTTA.

			B.	c.		Rs.	A.
Houses	...	...	248	6	3 Rs. &	2	0
Paddie	...	...	484	17	&	1	12
Plantins	...	...	169	18	&	2	8
Green trade	...	...	77	18	&	2	4
Tobacco	...	...	38	7	&	2	12
Cotton	...	...	19	15	&	1	12
Gardens	...	...	70	1	&	2	0
Grass	...	...	15	9	&	0	4
Bamboos	...	...	1	16	&	3	12
Flowers	...	...	6	2	&	1	4
Ditches	...	...	0	9	to pay into the ground		
Assah [?*Áu¢*]	...	...	11	9	measure.		
Commer	...	...	72	10			

		B.	c.
		1,216	17

			B.	c.	
Bommons [*Brahmans*], &c.	...	...	109	15	
Jungall	...	...	363	15	to be bought to act as
Waste ground	...	...	27	3	inhabited.

		B.	c.
		500	13 = 1,717 10

SOOTA LOOTA.

			B.	c.	
Houses	...	...	134	4	
Assah [?*Áu¢*]	...	...	2	6	
Paddee	...	...	515	6	
Green trade	...	...	32	19	
Plantins	...	...	60	7	
Gardens	...	...	147	7	
Tobacco	...	...	8	6	
Sugarcanes	...	...	0	11	at Rs. 3
Bamboos	...	...	1	1	
Grass	...	...	11	16	
Null [?*Nala*]	...	...	0	18	,, ,, 3-14
Cotton	...	...	14	7	
Flowers	...	...	2	17	
Sunapurah [F*¢ünya-pora*]	...	2	0		
Reeds for matts	...	...	0	4	
Ditches	...	...	10	19	
Commer [*Khamar*]	...	...	76	14	

		B.	c.
		1,022	2 = 1,022 2

SOOTA LOOTA—*concluded.*

			B.	c.		
Tancks and ways	...	...	72	6		
Jungall	...	...	487	1		
Bommons [*Brahmans*]	...	...	111	3		
					B.	c.
Total—			670	10	= 1,692	12
Buzzar	...	...	488	9¾		
Govenpore	...	...	1,178	7		
Town Calcutta	...	...	1,717	10		
Soota Loota	...	...	1,692	12		
			5,076	18¾		

208.—PESHKASH.

The Governor of Hugli had been paid his peshkash for the year, and on June 21st his receipt for three thousand rupees for peshkash for the year was produced in Council and ordered to be put " in the chest amongst other papers of like nature."

Saturday, June 21st.

209.—CAPTAIN PERRIN AND THE "SCEPTRE.

At this same Council Captain Blair, the Commander of the ship *Sceptre*, lodged a complaint about the treatment he had received, as he was proceeding up the river in his ship, towards Hugli. A boat full of soldiers and officers from the Fort had been sent after him with orders to bring him back ; and the reason alleged was that several persons in the factory were owed money by Captain Charles Perrin who was said to be the owner of the ship *Sceptre*. In his complaint, which is read before the Council, Captain Blair protests that Captain Charles Perrin sold the ship at Madras, and is not now her owner. Even if Captain Perrin were the owner, the Council of the Fort would have no right to detain his ship and cargo at the suit of private persons. The Court dismiss the complaint. They say they fully believe the ship belongs to Captain Perrin. No evidence has been brought to prove that he was not still the owner. They must therefore detain the ship, and moreover send officers and men to unload her and bring the goods into the Company's warehouses, there to be sold for as much as they will fetch, and the debts paid. When that has been done Captain Blair may carry out his owner's orders by going to Hugli and there shipping a return cargo. The Council has a right to seize

Friday, July 4th.

and stop any cargo the owner of which is a debtor in their Courts.
The unloading of the ship, however, seems to have been put off for a
few weeks to allow of witnesses being brought to prove that it is
no longer Captain Perrin's ship. The ship is to be kept under a
guard until further orders from the Council.

210.—NEWS OF SHĀH 'ALAM'S VICTORY.

The Council receive a letter from Messrs. Lloyd and Cowthorp,
July 14th. dated the 28th of June, from Patna, stating that
the native merchants had received advices from
Agra to the effect that Shaw Allum's [Shāh 'Ālam's] and Azzemshaw's
[Ā'zam Shāh's] forces had met and fought about 20 days before the
date on which Mr. Lloyd wrote, that "Shaw Allum [Shāh 'Ālam]
had obtained an entire victory, and that Azzem Tarrah [Ā'zam] and
his two sons were slain in the battle. This being only merchants'
advices from Agra, therefore can give but little credit to it."

211.—THE "SCEPTRE" RELEASED.

The Council find that they were mistaken about ship *Sceptre*.

July 24th. "Ship *Sceptre*, David Blair, Captain, was
arrested and detained in the Port of Calcutta by
Ralph Sheldon, in behalf of Thomas Pitt, Esq., and the owners of
ship *Unity*, and by Robert Nightingale, in behalf of the orphans of
Benjamin Bowcher, deceased, and William Walker, deceased, his estate,
the fourth day of June, on which the Council for the United Trade in
this place gave an order for said ship being detained here under a
guard till further satisfaction, whether or no Captain Charles Perrin
(whose ship this was formerly and was supposed to be concerned
therein, and on whose account the arrest was lain) was directly or indirectly concerned therein: if so, that his creditors might have satisfaction, and now there appearing before us Mr. James Peachy, one of the
owners of said ship, who came lately from Madras, producing his certificate from the Court of Madras, and Mr. William Wear's hand,
register of said Court, that the demands of said Thomas Pitt, Esq., etc.,
owners of the *Unity*, were invalid and of no effect as per copy of said
certificate here annexed appears, and the demands of Mr. Robert
Nightingale, on his own and several accounts, being the same foundation as the owners of the *Unity*, it is therefore agreed that said ship
Sceptre with her cargo and tackling be delivered to Mr. James Peachy,
part-owner of said ship, there appearing at present nothing appertain-
ing to Captain Charles Perrin, he the aforesaid Mr. James Peachy

giving us a full discharge that there has been no detriment to ship or cargo by her detention."

212.—DEGREES AND OFFICES.

Another dispute about the places in the Council arises between the Old and New Companies' servants. This time Messrs. John Maisters and Arthur King brought the affair before the Council, complaining that the old Company's men took the best places. Again they read the letters on the subject from the Directors in London, and again they decide that the Directors wished the places to be as follows:—

August 7th.

Old Company's servants ...	...	1	3	5	7
New ,, ,, ...	...	2	4	6	8

The Council is to stand thus:—

1. RALPH SHELDON.	5. EDWARD PATTLE.
2. ROBERT NIGHTINGALE.	6. ARTHUR KING.
3. JOHN RUSSELL.	7. WILLIAM BUGDEN.
4. JOHN MAISTERS.	8. ABRAHAM ADAMS.

Their several offices are to be:—

RALPH SHELDON	} Cashiers.
ROBERT NIGHTINGALE	
JOHN RUSSELL	Book-keeper.
JOHN MAISTERS	Export wareshouse-man.
EDWARD PATTLE	Import ,,
ARTHUR KING	Buxie [*Bakhshi*].
WILLIAM BUGDEN	Jemindar [*Zamindār*].
ABRAHAM ADAMS	Secretary.

In spite of the discussion and apparent settlement, the New Company's men still feel themselves aggrieved. Mr. A. Adams enters a protest in the consultation book, objecting that "should there now be a vacancy on the old Company's side, he that fills it comes in over my head, and will be 7th, and I shall continue 8th, which is directly contrary to the Hon'ble Company's order."

213.—A SUB-BAKHSHI.

On account of Mr. King's ill-health, it was found necessary to appoint a *Sub-Bakhshi.* Mr. A. Adams was therefore ordered to act in that capacity, and Mr. Waldo, one of the factors, was to take his place as Secretary.

August 14th.

214.—THE COURT OF JUSTICE.

The Council decided that Messrs. Pattle and Bugden should sit in
the Court of Justice instead of Messrs. Maisters
and King.

August 25th.

215.—THE SETT'S GARDEN.

September 11th.   The following resolution was entered—

"In consideration that Jonundun Seat, Gopaul Seat, Jadoo Seat Bon-
narsyseat, and Jaykissen[1] will keep in repair the highway between the
Fort's land mark to the norward on the back side of the town, we have
thought fit to abate them 8 annas in a bighā of their garden rent, which
is about Rs. 55 in the whole less than it is ordered in consultation the
12th of June last, and they being possessed of this ground which they
made into gardens before we had possession of the towns, and being
the Company's merchauts and inhabitants of the place."

216.—MONEY WANTED TO CLEAR SALTPETRE.

Messrs. Lloyd and Cawthorp sent to Calcutta for money to clear the
saltpetre, which they hope to despatch at the end
of the month.

September 22nd.

217.—DEATH OF KING.

Mr. Arthur King, Member of the Council for the New Company,
died on the 27th. At the Council, held the next
day, Mr. Edward Darell of the New Company
was appointed eighth in the Council. He is to act as Secretary
instead of Mr. Waldo. Mr. Adams of course takes King's place as
Bakhshī, he having really filled that office since August 14th.

September 29th.

218.—BUILDING THE HOSPITAL.

The Council had been asked two or three times to put up a hospital
of some kind for the soldiers. They now pass the
following resolution :—"Having abundance of
our soldiers and seamen yearly sick (this year more particularly our
soldiers), and the doctors representing to us that for want of a
hospital or convenient lodging for them, is mostly the occasion of their
sickness, and such a place will be highly necessary as well for the
garrison and sloops as the Company's Chaiter Party shipping to keep
the men in health, it is therefore agreed that a convenient spot of

October 16th.

---

[1] *i.e.,* Janarddana Sett, Gopāla Sett, Jādu Sett, Vārānasi Sett, and Jaikrishṇa.

U

ground near the Fort be pitched upon to build a hospital on, and that the cashiers pay out of the Company's cash for the said occasion towards perfecting it the sum of 2,000 rupees, and what more may be gathered in by subscription from the Commanders of European and Country shipping and the inhabitants, which is to be forwarded and gathered in by Mr. Ab. Adams, who is to look after the building of the same under the direction of the Council."

219.—DEATH OF LITTLETON.

"Sir Edward Littleton,[1] late President of the New Company, departed this life on the 24th instant at night, and was decently buried on the 25th at night. Mr. Adams, Bakhshí, with his assistants, Mr. Hussy and Mr. Cook, sent the next morning (the doors, &c., being sealed up with the Company's seal, and a guard set on the house overnight), to overlook his papers to see whether there was any will, which does not yet appear. Ordered that a further strict search be made by them, and if none appears, that they take an inventory of all his goods and necessaries and bring it to the Council for their perusal and further orders."

October 27th.

220.—ENSIGN DALIBAR.

Dalibar, an ensign in the Company's service, was tried by the Council and sentenced to be kept as a prisoner on the guard for one month, and to lose two months' wages for entering the house of one Mr. Harris, Master-at-arms, and abusing and ill-treating Mr. Harris's wife.

October 27th.

221.—MURSHID QULI TO BE DEPUTY GOVERNOR.

The *Vakíl* at the Dīwān's camp wrote that the Dīwān, Murshid Quli Khān, "is ordered by the present King, Allum Shaw ['Álam Shāh], to be the Subah's Naib [Sūbadār's nāib] of this province." He has sent to tell the *Vakíl* that he would like the English to settle the Cassimbazar Factory. He also talks of sending the *Vakíl* to Calcutta with his *parwāna* to bring up the English merchants. The *Vakíl* says he is trying to avoid being sent, if possible, for he knows the Council would not wish it, and he asks the Council to send him orders. They agree to tell him in answer that they will write him an excuse to delay time till the year's shipping is gone, and they have further assurance of the settlement of the Government.

November 1st.

---

[1] More details about Sir E. Littleton will be found in the introduction to the summaries.

222.—LITTLETON'S GOODS SOLD.

Proof having been brought in that Sir E. Littleton had died
without a will, orders are given that his goods be
sold at public outcry, and the money paid into
the Company's cash.

November 1st.

223.—GETTING ANXIOUS ABOUT SALTPETRE.

The Council was getting anxious about the saltpetre boats for
which they were waiting. The winter shipping
could not be despatched till they came. "We
not having of late advices from Patna, believe our cossits [qáṣids] are
miscarried, and we are advised by the merchants that our boats have
left Patna. Ordered that the ensign and 40 men be sent up to clear
the boats, and bring them down to Calcutta and that Mr. Waldo be
sent with them."

November 6th.

DIARY AND CONSULTATION BOOK

OF THE

UNITED TRADE COUNCIL AT FORT WILLIAM IN BENGAL.

———◆———

From December 1707 to December 1708.

———◆———

COURT OF MANAGERS.

At beginning of this year.

1. MR. R. SHELDON.	5. MR. EDWARD PATTLE.
2. ,, ROBERT NIGHTINGALE.	6 ,, ABRAHAM ADAMS.
3. ,, J. RUSSELL.	7. ,, W. BUGDEN.
4. ,, MAISTERS.	8. ,, EDWARD DARELL.

Zamíndár.—MR. W. BUGDEN.

224.—THE PETRE BOATS ARRIVE.

On the 2nd of December, Mr. Cawthorp reached Calcutta from

December 2nd.

Patna. The petre boats had not yet arrived, and some anxiety was felt about them as they had been sent off before Mr. Cawthorp started from Patna. On the 11th, much

December 11th.

to the relief of the factory, the boats arrived, escorted by Mr. Waldo, and the soldiers who had gone to meet them. They had been hindered by the shallowness of the river which was almost dry. Mr. William Cawthorp had come to Calcutta to see after the presents that he had promised, in the name of the Company, to the Governors of Rajmahal and Dustuck-maul for letting the saltpetre boats pass. The Governors had sent *chobdárs* to receive the presents. Mr. Edward Pattle was therefore

December 18th.

ordered to deliver twenty yards of broadcloth, six sword-blades, and six hookahs for the Governor's present to each *chobdár* and five rupees each for themselves.

225.—GREETING THE NEW GOVERNOR OF HUGLI.

On January 5th they hear that a new Governor has arrived at

January 5th, 1708.

Hugli, and they agree to send Mr. John Russell and Mr. Darell to visit him, and desire his friendship. The usual ceremonies, *salāms*, and the like are to be gone through by them in order to gain his favour.

226.—WHAT TO DO ABOUT PATNA.

They are much exercised in their minds as to what they shall do

January 19th.

about the Patna Factory. In the present state of country it is not safe to spend much money in keeping it up, and yet it is not wise to abandon it too suddenly.

On 19th January they came to the following resolution :—"Having considered about the Patna residence, of a further investment for this year, finding we cannot possibly gather all the Company's effects there, for the servants to come away this season. We therefore deem it best for the Company's interest to continue it and to make a small investment (not venturing too much money at a time up) so as to get all things together to come away the first of next season, if the affairs of the Government do not appear better than at present."

227.—ZAMĪNDĀRĪ ACCOUNTS FOR NOVEMBER 1707.

The accounts of the three towns and buzzar for November last were

•
February 2nd.

brought in by Mr. Bugden, zemindar, at this Council ; they amounted to Rs. 976-13-3,

228.—MORE PETRE BOATS TO BE CLEARED.

Some more saltpetre boats had been despatched from Patna at the

February 9th.

beginning of the year, and had not been heard of. Hence the following order in the Consultation Book :—" The Company's saltpetre boats having left Patna some time, and we suppose by this time may be arrived at Rajmahal, ordered that Mr. Calvert, with a sergeant and 35 soldiers, proceed to Cassimbazar, or futher, if occasion be, to clear them of the troublesome chowkies and bring them down to us."

229.—CAWTHORP AGAIN SENT TO PATNA.

At this same Council they decide to send Mr. Cawthorp again to

February 9th.

Patna to help Mr. Lloyd. Cawthorp is to send a letter to tell Lloyd to be in readiness to come away by the 1st of August.

230.—ZAMĪNDĀRI ACCOUNTS FOR DECEMBER 1707.

The zamindār's accounts for the three towns and buzzar for December were brought in and passed, the amount being Rs. 792-10.

February 23rd.

231.—PRESENT FOR THE NEW HUGLI GOVERNOR.

They receive news at the factory that the Dutch and French have both sent presents to the new Governor of Hugli, and that he was pressing for his present from the English. They therefore agreed to send him the usual present of European goods by Mr. Darrell.

February 23rd.

232.—PILOTING OUTSIDE SHIPS.

Antonio de Rota, a head pilot, was brought up before them and charged with using their sloop to attend a ship that belonged to outside merchants. They resolve this time only to fine him, but to caution him that for the next offence he will be turned out of the " Company's service, towns, and protection."

March 1st.

233.—ABATEMENT OF RENT IN GOVINDPUR.

The following resolution was passed relating to the rents of Govindpur:—" We having had several complaints from the inhabitants of Govenpore that they are not able to pay the rent, we last ordered in consultation and desire some abatement, agreed that there be a small allowance made them according to the list that was brought in by Mr. William Bugden, Jemindar [*Zamīndār*], and that the list be annexed next to this consultation."

March 25th.

Account of what the Govenpore tenants are willing to pay.

B.	c.	Rs.	Rs.	A.	
57	9	Houses, 2, and some	2	8	per bigah.
510	11	Paddy, 1.			„ „
35	14	Green trade	1	8	„ „
	2	Beetle	3	0	„ „
139	16	Tobacco	2	0	„ „
59	2	Gardens	1	8	„ „
12	3	Plantains	2	0	„ „
4	10	Bamboos	3	0	„ „
18	0	Grass	1	0	„ „

234.—ZAMĪNDĀRI ACCOUNTS FOR JANUARY 1708.

The account of the revenue for January of the buzzar and the three towns amounted to Rs. 966-10-6.

March 25th.

235.—KĀM BAKHSH AND SHĀH 'ĀLAM.

The Council received a letter from Madras, telling them of the

April 15th.   unsettled state of the country. "No one can be sure who will reign—whether Shaw Allum [Shāh 'Ālam] or Cawn Bux [Kām Bakhsh.''] The latter, they said, "is making all the preparation he can for war, and taking several strongholds."

236.—PASSAGE AND LICENSE MONEY.

Messrs. Darrell and Waldo bring in an account of the passage and

April 15th.   license money paid to the Company for the year 1707. It amounted altogether to 1,898 rupees. Of this sum the license money amounted to Rs. 1,300. The sums paid by the three punch-house-holders were at follows :—

					Rs.
Domingo Ash,	2 licenses	...	...		500
Goviusunder [Govindasundar],	2	,,	...	...	500
Charles King,	2	,,	at Rs. 150 each		300
					1,300

237.—TROUBLE AGAIN IN HUGLI.

The Governor of Hugli had sent for their merchants and "tried

April 19th.   to get them to give him an obligation that they will not trade with us." On hearing what had occurred, the Council wrote to their *vakīl* at Hugli telling him to go and ask the Governor why he wishes to stop the trade, and also to find out on what terms the Dīwān's *sanad* may be obtained.

238.—ZAMINDĀRI ACCOUNTS FOR FEBRUARY 1708.

The zamīndār's accounts for the month of February last, brought in

April 26th.   and passed, amounting to Rs. 1,340-9-9.

239.—LETTER TO THE GOVERNOR OF HUGLI.

They write a letter to the Governor of Hugli acquainting him that

April 26th.   "according to the Prince's Husbulumers [*ḥashu-l-amrs*] and King's Duan's [Dīwān's] orders to our black servants at Rajamahal, we are now despatching a Vacqueel [*Vakīl*] there to tend the Prince and King's Duan's orders, and that we desire his (the Governor's) recommendation to the Duan as he promised us." As they are sending a *vakīl*, Çivacharan, to Rajamahal, they will not need the Governor's services as negotiant.

240.—HOSTILITY OF THE GOVERNOR OF HUGLI.

They receive another letter from their *vakil* at Hugli, from which they gather that the Governor has greatly changed to them, and is anything but friendly. On this they agree to send the *vakil* to Rajamahal without delay lest in case the Governor should manage to prejudice the Prince and Dīwān against them. The *vakil* is to start at once, taking with him copies of the former grants to the East India Company for the Prince to see. There is some fear that the Prince and Dīwān will withhold their *parwānas*, because the new King, as far as they know, has not yet given his *parwāna* for the whole of the factories of the East India Company. The *vakil*, if he questioned on this subject, is to say that they daily expect it, and will send the imperial order for the Prince and Dīwān to see, and that if it does not come before a certain date, they will pay customs.

April 26th.

241.—ADDITION TO THE FACTORY.

" We being in great want of a warehouse to sort the silk in, agreed that the sorting warehouse to the south be carried out to the point: there being one wall already, the charge will be but small, and it will be a strengthening of the fortification."

May 3rd.

242.—BENJAMIN WHEATLEY'S LICENSE.

"There being more due, Rs. 150 from Benj. Wheatley, account revenues, for his license for keeping a punch-house, was this day paid into cash."

May 10th.

243.- ZAMĪNDĀRI ACCOUNTS FOR MARCH 1708.

The Zamīndār's accounts for March were brought in and passed; they amounted to Rs. 968-13-9.

May 31st.

244.—THREATS OF RETALIATION.

They receive a letter from their *vakil*, telling them that he must have more money to give amongst the young Prince's and the Dīwān's officers. They send the *vakil* a bill of exchange for fifteen thousand rupees and tell him that he must try and take out the sanad at once, and that they send him such a large sum in order that he may do so. He is also to complain to the

June 30th.

Prince that the "delay about the sanad is stopping our trade and that his mutsuddis also stop our trade and do us injury." If the Prince and Dīwān do not redress the wrong that has been done at once, the Company will take measures to get redress in some other way. They wrote at the same time to the Governor of Hugli, who is doing all he can stop to their trade, and tell him that they will retaliate when and where they find an opportunity.

245.—ZAMĪNDĀRI ACCOUNTS FOR APRIL 1708.

July 5th. The zamīndār's accounts for the month of April were brought in and passed. They amounted to Rs. 1,948-3-3.

246.—ALARMING ATTITUDE OF THE GOVERNOR OF HUGLI.

July 5th. The Governor of Hugli refuses to redress our wrongs, and insults our *vakīl* and servants, and is keeping some of our black servants and one Englishman in prison, and still threatens greater severity. This letter causes great uneasiness at Calcutta. The Council immediately proceed to put themselves in an attitude of defence, fearing the Fort may be attacked. "Therefore it is agreed that we order all our guards with ships *Dolbon* and *Success* (having none of the Company's ships here) to be in readiness, lest this hot-headed Pousdar [*Faujdār*] should endeavour to commit any outrage on our towns-people or settlement." They also agree "that forthwith we give an account of this matter to the Prince and King's Duan by the hands of our Vacqueel at Rajmahal by two expresses on purpose, ordering him out of hand to make complaint to them that we may have relief and justice in this affair."

July 10th. Things look serious for the Fort. They, therefore, decide that they will acquaint all the European and Christian inhabitants in their towns with what has happened.

"Having summoned all the European and Christian inhabitants and the masters of ships acquainting them, we expect some trouble from the Governor of Hugli, he having imprisoned our people and stopped our goods. We ordered that they forbear to go to Hugli for some time, and that they are in readiness under arms on summons to prevent any insolence he may design us, or in case there should be occasion to act anything against him, that they are ready thereto." "They all," adds the Consultation Book, "showed a readiness and declared they would be ready on all summons." The Council also order the black Christians to be trained for arms by the factory ensign. "The ensign having got all the black Christians together, we ordered that they appear under arms once a week to exercise. That they may be in readiness till further orders."

247.—MEDIATION OF THE PRINCE'S QĀSIDĀR.

Two days after these preparations for war had been made they

July 12th.

receive a letter from Mīr Muḥammad Dafar, the Prince's Qāṣidār. "I have been," he said, "to the Governor at Hugli and I told him that it was not well to interfere with the English and stop their trade, and that if he persisted in it he would repent." The Governor answered that the English trade had been stopped by order of the Diwān, and that as for imprisoning their servants and gumāshtāhs it was not done by his orders nor with his knowledge. Mīr Muḥammad Dafar advises the English to stop sending up ships to Hugli for a day or two, by which time he hopes to make things smooth. The Council in reply write: "We will gladly take your advice. Will you ask the Governor of Hugli to dismiss from his service the officers who imprisoned our men?"

248.—ZAMINDĀRI ACCOUNTS FOR 1707.

An account is brought in showing that the revenue to the Company

July 12th.

from the rents of the buzzar and three towns for the year 1707 amounted to Rs. 792-11-4 (sic).

249.—MORE RUPEES FOR RAJMAHAL.

They receive another letter from the vakīl at Rajmahal, telling them

July 15th.

that he must have still more money before he can get the sanad. They agree to send him another fifteen thousand rupees. The vakīl also asks for three looking-glasses to be sent him, one for the Prince and two for the Diwān.

250.—INCREASE IN THE REVENUES.

The Company's revenues for the year past being collected and

July 15th.

adjusted, it was found that the year dating from May 1707 to the end of April 1708, the increase in income amounted to Rs. 5,756-5-6.

251.—FARMĀN FOR MADRAS.

They receive a letter from Madras, telling them that the "Pher-

July 26th.

maund that the Emperor had sent them for Fort St. George by the hands of one Mulla Abdull Phasill [Mulla 'Abdu-l-Faẓl] would come by way of Bengal." The

letter asked the Council to make inquiries after the messenger and to
assist him by sending him on by ship to Madras.

252.—MUḤAMMAD RAẒĀ.

Some of their business at Hugli is cleared by means of a friendly
July 31st.   merchant named Muḥammad Raẓā.

253.—ZAMĪNDĀRI ACCOUNTS FOR MAY 1708.

The Zamīndār's accounts for May last brought in and passed,
August 9th.   amounting to Rs. 816-9-5.

254.—INCREASING DEMANDS.

They receive notice from their *vakīl* at Rajmahal that the Prince
        and Dīwān have now increased their demands to
August 9th.
        thirty-five thousand rupees for their sanad.   The
Dutch had already given this sum, and so the Prince and Dīwān wish
to force the English to do the same.   The Council decide that they
cannot give such a sum.   They write to their *vakīl* telling him to offer
twenty thousand rupees.   If the Prince and Dīwān refuse to accept
it, the *vakīl* is to come away, and when he comes to Calcutta the
Council will again consider the matter.

255.—COPY OF THE NEW MADRAS ḤASBU-L-AMR.

They receive a long letter from Madras, sending them on a copy of
August 24th.   the New King's *Hasbu-l-amr* for Madras.

256.—ZAMĪNDĀRI ACCOUNTS FOR JUNE 1708.

The Zamīndār's accounts for the month of June were brought in
August 30th.   and passed, amounting to Rs. 806-13-9.

257.—NEW BRICK STABLES.

The Company's stables falling down, "being only mud," the Council
        give an order to Mr. Adams, Bakhshi, to have one
September 1st.
        built of brick "that may be durable;" he is to
build it in a convenient place."

258.—ÇIVACHARAN'S NEGOTIATIONS.

They receive a letter from Çivacharan, the *vakīl* at Rajmahal
        stating that he had paid the Dīwān and the Prince
September 6th.
        thirty-six thousand rupees for the *sanad*, and had
drawn a bill of exchange on the Company for that amount.   The Council

is very angry about this as they had ordered him on no account to give more than twenty-five thousand rupees. At first they thought of refusing to honour the bill; but, after a long consultation, considering that the time of year for despatching the winter shipping was at hand, and that it would injure their trade not to have the *sanad*, and to be on bad terms with the Prince and the Dīwān, they agreed to pay it. In his letter the *vakīl* assures them the *sanad* of the Prince and the Dīwān is such that now they will not need the Emperor's *Farmān*. Though the Council had decided to honour the bill when it came to hand, they resolved to send some trusty person up to Rajmahal to look into the *vakīl's* affairs, as they felt sure he was not dealing fairly with them.

At this Council they resolve to send up their *ākhūnd*, by name
September 15th. Faẓl Muḥammad, to Rajmahal. He is to take with him a new *vakīl* and to send Çivacharan to Calcutta under a guard to answer to the Council for his conduct. The *ākhūnd* is to make enquiries as to how the money sent up to Çivacharan has been spent.

259.—OUT OF LIQUOR.

"The Company's European ships having not yet arrived and their
September 16th. covenanted servants being out of liquor, ordered that the wine and fruit arrived from Persia be divided amongst them as customary."

260.—OVERTURES FROM THE GOVERNOR OF HUGLI.

The Governor of Hugli sends them word that if they will again
September 28th. offer him for his grant the sum of three thousand sicca rupees, he will accept it, and their trade can be free in his domains. The Council send for the *vakīl* who was at Hugli before, and tell him to start for Hugli, taking the money with him. He is not to pay the money to the Governor before he has received a receipt entitling the Company to all their former privilege at Hugli.

261.—ZAMĪNDĀRI ACCOUNTS FOR JULY 1708.

The Zamīndār's accounts for the bazar and the three towns for
September 28th. the month of July were brought in and passed. They amounted to Rs. 911-13-9.

262.—LICENSES.

"Mr. Edward Darrell paid into cash 1,000 rupees for two licenses granted to Domingo Ash and Black Jack for leave to keep a Punch-house and distil arrack, due 29th of September."

October 4th.

263.—SERIOUS NEWS FROM RAJMAHAL.

The *ákhúnd* returned from the Dīwān's camp and told the Council that, after having promised their *sanad*, the Prince and Dīwān now refuse to give it for less than fifty thousand rupees as a present for the Dīwān and Prince and a hundred thousand rupees to be paid into the Emperor's treasure at Surat. The *ákhúnd* had tried every means he could to lessen their exorbitant demands, but had not succeeded. The Dīwān and the Prince, he said, were determined to have a large sum from the English. After much consultation the Council agree to write to the Governor of Hugli and tell him that they will now accept his former offer of acting as negotiant between them and the Prince and the Dīwān. They ask him on what terms he will agree to try and procure their sanad for them. "This," says the consultation book, "is a very unaccountable method of doing our business at the Prince and Duan's camp by the Governor of Hughli: but the Dutch have introduced this unaccountable method, which we are obliged to follow, but we doubt not they will find a great inconvenience to attend their master's affairs by it, the Government having already obliged them to give a bill of exchange to Surat for 100,000 rupees."

October 22nd.

264.—ZAMĪNDĀRI ACCOUNTS FOR AUGUST 1708.

The Zamīndār's accounts for the month of August were brought in and passed, amounting to Rs. 950-15-7.

October 25th.

265.—DEATH OF JOHN MAISTER.

Mr. John Maister, the second in the Council on the New Company's side, having died on the 18th instant, Mr. Josiah Chitty was appointed to the Council to fill up the vacancy. He was to take his place as eighth of the Council.

October 25th.

"Mr. Maisters being export warehouse-keeper, and now the place being vacant, Mr. Abraham Adams is ordered to take the charge upon him, and Mr. Edward Darrell the Buxie's charge and Mr. John Chitty to be Secretary."

266.—DIET MONEY INCREASED TO MEET THE GROWING EXPENSES OF CALCUTTA LIFE.

The diet money allowed to the Council was found not to be sufficient now, so the Council agree to increase it. They enter both their reason for so doing and the amount to which it is to be increased in a letter sent to London. "The inhabitants of the town increasing, by which provisions grow dearer, and the allowance of diet to the Chairmen and Council not near defraying their expenses, it is therefore judged equitable that a larger allowance be given, so that it may at least defray the charges of their table for eating, and considering that the Chairmen are at a far greater expense than the others by entertaining strangers, it is thought fit for each Chairman sixty rupees per month, and the other six of Council 30 rupees per month, which the Buxie is ordered to pay monthly."

October 25th.

267.—PROVING MAISTERS' WILL.

"Mr. Robert Nightingale and Mr. Edward Darrell being appointed Mr. John Maisters' executors and having accepted the same, produced his last will and testament, and the witnesses, Mr. John Calvert and Dr. Lewis Demenny, appearing and taking their oaths on the Holy Evangelist that they were present when Mr. John Maisters signed his last will and testament, ordered that the same be registered."

November 1st.

268.—AN ORPHAN.

"Mrs. Susanne Child being dead some time and left no will; and there being only one child and no one to take care thereof, agreed that Mr. Adams looks after what effects she has left behind, and take care that the rents of the houses be paid towards maintaining the child to Mrs. Rose."

November 1st.

269.—CAPTAIN HAMILTON MORTGAGES HIS HOUSE.

"Captain Alex. Hamilton having made over or mortgaged his dwelling-house in this town for the sum of Rs. 2,902 appearing before us and agreeing thereto, ordered that the said overture be registered in the book for that purpose."

November 8th.

270.—DARRELL DIES.

November 8th.   Mr. Darrell, sixth in Council, died.

271.—PETRE BOATS TO BE CLEARED BY FORCE.

As the boats were being stopped on their way down the river owing
to the hostile attitude of the Prince and Dīwān,
the Council resolved to send and tell Captain
Woodville and Mr. Spencer to take a good force of about twenty
soldiers and ten gunners and bring down with them all the boats
carrying goods that have the Company's *dastak*.

November 15th.

272.—THREATENING THE MOGUL GOVERNMENT.

They hear from the Governor of Hugli that he cannot get the *sanad*
for them at the rate they offer. The Prince and
Dīwān are still determined to have an enormous
sum. Rather than comply with these exorbitant demands the Council
resolves to retaliate on the Prince and Dīwān, in two ways. They will
stop all the shipping subject to the Mogul Government as it passes their
port; and they will command all English subjects to repair at once to
Calcutta. This last step would affect the entire shipping of Hugli and
Rajmahal, as nearly all the best Captains in the employ of the Dīwān
and the Prince were Englishmen.

November 22nd.

Through the native merchants the Governor of
Hugli made them the following overtures :—

November 27th.

"That if we would give Rs. 35,000 sicca, he will procure us the
Prince's Nishaun [*Nishān*] and Kings Duan's grant the same as we
formerly had in every respect, and that we shall be at no further charge
for any expenses to the mutsuddies [*mutaṣaddīs*] or others and no
demands for the bill of exchange to Surat, and that we shall have a
seerpaw [*sar-o-pā*] and horse as usual with all the other customary
signs of friendship."

They agree to what he proposes, attributing his coming to terms so
soon to "our former resolution of sending a good force to clear our
boats in the country and our declaration of stopping Moorish ships."

273.—ZAMĪNDĀRI ACCOUNTS FOR SEPTEMBER 1708.

The Zamīndār's accounts from the bazar and the three towns for
September were brought in and passed, amount-
ing to Rs. 850-14-1.

November 27th.

DIARY AND CONSULTATION BOOK

FOR THE

AFFAIRS OF THE Rt. Hon. COMPANY IN BENGAL KEPT BY RALPH SHELDON, Esq., AND THE COUNCIL.[1]

------◆------

Commencing January 1708.

------◆------

274.—SALARIES.

"Account salary due to the Company's covenant servants amounting
September 1708. to rupees 400 sicca, as per account brought in, being due the 26th instant. Agreed that the cashier pay the same."

275.—OLD COMPANY'S DEBTS.

"Having received a general letter from the Hon'ble Old Company
October 6th. the 4th instant per ship *Dispatch* of the 16th April 1708, wherein they acquaint us that they have directed the Governor and Councill of Madrass to clear all our debts and send us money to invest what shall remain of these stock there, which we account will be considerable, since the Governor and Councill of Madrass writes us that they have more than double the amount of the Company's debt in Bengall due from the United Company, which by the United Generall letter to Madrass we observe is ordered to be paid out of the stock that is coming out for that place this year. So we judge it highly necessary that we agree for what fine goods we can get ready to be sent home this season, on the best terms we can, since it is so late in the year that we cannot expect to have them cheap."

---

[1] Fort William Diary and Consultation and Charges General. Commencing January 1707-8. Ending December 1708. Received per *Howland*, 31st August 1709. Birdwood Records, RR*a* 8.

276.—NO MORE SALARIES ON THE SEPARATE ACCOUNT.

"The Hon'ble Company in their general letter seeming to disapprove of the charge we are at for salary, &c., on their separate account, and we are willing to give them satisfaction (notwithstanding we have now and shall have their business to negotiate) in all things, we therefore do agree and resolve that no further charge of salary or anything else be charged or paid on their separate account form this day forward, except Mr. Deane's allowance, who has no benefit of the United Service, and what usual reward is given to the accountant."

October 6th.

K

DIARY AND CONSULTATION BOOK

OF THE

UNITED TRADE COUNCIL AT FORT WILLIAM IN BENGAL.[1]

December 1708 to December 1709.

THE UNITED COUNCIL, DECEMBER 1708.

MR. RALPH SHELDON.	MR. ROBERT NIGHTINGALE.
,, JOHN RUSSELL.	,, ABRAHIM ADAMS.
,, EDWARD PATTLE.	,, JOSIAH CHITTY.
,, WILLIAM BUGDEN.	,, JAMES LOVE.

  ,, RALPH SHELDON and MR. ROBERT NIGHTINGALE, *Chairmen and Cashiers.*

  ,, JOHN RUSSELL, *Book-keeper.*

  ,, A. ADAMS, *Export Warehouse-keeper.*

  ,, EDWARD PATTLE, *Import Warehouse-keeper.*

  ,, JOSIAH CHITTY, *Secretary.*

  ,, WILLIAM BUGDEN, *Zamīndār.*

  ,, JOHN LOVE, *Bakhshi.*

277.—LOVE SUCCEEDS DARELL.

Mr. Love is appointed to the Committee to succeed to eighth place, Mr. Darell, the fourth man for the New Company, having died last month.

December 2nd.

278.—RENT.

The rent for the three towns being due, the Council ordered 485 rupees to be paid to the Hugli Government.

December 2nd.

---

[1] Received in England by Ship *Stretham*, September 1st, 1710.

279.—LITTLETON'S ESTATE.

Mr. Adams brought in the account of estate left by Sir Edward
Littleton, the balance of his estate being 14,455
rupees 8 annas.

December 7th.

280.—FOURTEEN THOUSAND RUPEES TO CLEAR THE BOATS.

A letter was received from Mr. Cawthorp, who was at Rajmahal,
stating that he had drawn a bill on the Company
for fourteen thousand sicca rupees in order to
clear the boats. He had been forced to pay this sum to the Prince, who
had stopped the Company's boats and imprisoned him until the money
was paid. On the receipt of this letter, the Council was very angry.
They had already paid a large sum for the *sanad* of the Dīwān and the
Prince; they therefore refused to honour the bill, and wrote as follows
to Mr. Cawthorp:—" We having agreed with the Governor of Hughli
for the Prince's Neshawn [*nishān*] and the Duan's sunnud and for clearing our goods from all parts of Bengall, ... we think we shall
sufficiently pay for the Prince's favour without this great imposition."

December 13th.

281.—MORE TROUBLES WITH THE NATIVE GOVERNMENT.

The native Government was so very troublesome "at Patna and
all the way up" that they agree to write to
Mr. Lloyd to come away with all the Company's
effects as soon as possible. They also agree to write to the *Faujdār*
of Hugli, and to send up the *ākhūnd* to tell him that the boats are
stopped at Rajmahal and that the Prince and Dīwān want twelve
thousand rupees to clear them, which makes the Council "suspect
that the phousdar [*i.e. faujdār*] has not acquainted the Prince with the
agreement between the Company and himself. Therefore we request
the favour of him forthwith to give us a letter to the Prince or Duan
that he has agreed the business with us here and that our boats may be
cleared immediately."

December 13th.

282.—LITTLETON'S MONEY PAID TO THE NEW COMPANY.

It is ordered that all the money that Sir Edward Littleton had left
be paid to the New Company, who claimed it
under a bill of debt for 23,808 rupees 3 annas,
signed by Sir Edward Littleton, and dated April 1704.

December 20th.

x 2

283.—NEWS FROM BANJAR AND BENCOOLEN.

Mr. Cunningham, late President of Banjar, and Mr. Edwards, second [1]

December 21st.

arrived in the Company's ship *Anna*. They had been trying to settle the Banjar [2] factory, but had failed. A Council was called immediately on their arrival to hear what news they brought and to give them a welcome. They told of their failure to re-establish the factory at Banjar, and that now even their endeavours to get a cargo for their ship had been frustrated by the hostile Government. They said that the Managers in England were expecting their vessel home with the rest of the winter shipping, and they begged of the Council to find her a cargo and despatch her at once. They also brought a message from the factory at Bencoolen, to the effect that that factory was greatly in need of stores, and not able to buy rice, because of the disturbed state of the country. The Council order the *bakhshī* to provide suitable lodgings for Mr. Cunningham and Mr. Edwards and also to see after getting a cargo for the ship, so that she may be despatched with the other winter shipping. They order rice and grain to be got ready to send to Bencoolen at once.

284.—SHĀH 'ĀLAM NEAR GOLKONDA.

They receive a letter from Madras, containing letters from Mr. Hastings at Vizagapatam. The letter "advises

December 24th.

us that Shaw Allum is advanced near Golcondah

---

[1] Mr. Cunningham and Mr. Edwards appear to have wished to take service in Calcutta, but this the Council would not allow till they had their master's orders on the subject. The matter could not be decided quickly. It would take at least a year to write to their Hon'ble Masters in England and have an answer back. So Mr. Edwards and Mr. Cunningham seem to have settled down in Calcutta, calmly waiting for an answer.

[2] Banjar, or Banjarmasin, in the south-east of Borneo, was long regarded by the English as a desirable place for an intermediate station to facilitate the exchange of European and Chinese produce. In 1614, 1615, the old Company kept agents there for a short time ; and in the years 1699 to 1702 the new Company made various efforts to get a footing there. At last, in 1704, events seemed to take a favourable turn. The King granted the English permission to erect a fortification for the protection of their establishment. Accordingly on the union of the two Companies the Court decided to concentrate their trade at Banjarmasin, where a strong fortification was to be erected. Soon, however, in consequence of disputes with the natives a war broke out, in which the English took five Banjarese villages. Of these four were restored in consideration of three thousand dollars ; the fifth, Banjarmasin, was retained for the residence of the English. Here they built a factory, and soon began to carry matters with a high hand. But the Chinese, being jealous of the proportion of trade in pepper which the English had acquired, and foreseeing that their fortifications would enable them to overawe the inhabitants, stirred up the Banjarese to make a sudden attack on the English on the 27th June 1707. After a severe struggle they were driven off, but the loss of the English was so great that the survivors escaped with difficulty on board the ships, carrying with them the Company's treasure, but leaving some fifty thousand dollars on shore. The death of Agent Barré left them without a head, and it was resolved to abandon the place.

and like to get the better." They also "ask us for sundry things for present, for Shaw Allum if our ships be come."

285.—CAWTHORP STILL DETAINED AT RAJMAHAL.

They receive another letter from Mr. Cawthorp saying that he cannot come down till they send the money for the Prince. They decide to delay answering him till they hear again from the Governor of Hugli.

December 27th.

286.—FOUR BAD CHARACTERS SENT TO ENGLAND.

"Hans Ffoert, Peter Harnalston, Simon Jansen, and John Van Eck be sent to England on board the ship *Harland*, they working for their passage home. They having committed several robberies at this place, and that they have protected several other thieves, and have received goods from them; as has been plainly made appear to us; therefore we think it very convenient to rid the town of such troublesome persons; agreed we advise the Company thereof."

December 27th.

287.—THE FOURTEEN THOUSAND RUPEES MUST BE PAID.

They again receive a letter from Mr. Cawthorp, and also one from Captain Woodville, who had gone up to help to bring down the boats, saying that the saltpetre boats are all detained at Rajmahal because the Prince has not received the fourteen thousand sicca rupees he demands. As far as Mr. Cawthorp and Captain Woodville can gather, the *Faujdar* of Hugli has not done anything in their favour, nor has he the power so to do. The Council agree to write to Mr. Cawthorp and to the shroffs to say that they will pay the money. The shroffs are to supply it and draw a bill on the Company.

January 3rd, 1709.

288.—NIGHTINGALE RESIGNS THE SERVICE.

Mr. Nightingale, the Chairman on the New Company's side, finding his health failing him, and wishing to go to England, applies for and receives his discharge from the Company's service. He is allowed to go to England in one of the Company's ships on the payment ninety-six rupees, the equivalent of £12, which seems to have been the usual amount of passage money from India to England at that time. He has the entire use of the great cabin.

January 6th.

289.—REARRANGEMENT OF THE COUNCIL.

Mr. Adams is to become Chairman for the New Company in Mr.
Nightingale's place ; Mr. Josiah Chitty is to be
Export Warehouse-keeper ; Mr. James Love,
Buxie ; and Mr. Samuel Blount is to be elected to fill the vacant
place left in the Council, that is the fourth place, in the New
Company, or eighth in the Council. He is also to be Secretary.

January 6th.

290.—JOSIA TOWNSEND FINED FOR DISOBEDIENCE.

" Josiah Townsend having brought up the Company's vessel (*Mary*
Smack) contrary to his orders received from us,
and now having present occasion for him, think it
not convenient to give him any bodily punishment ;[1] agreed that for
the present we fine him three months' pay and return him with all
expedition with the vessel into Ballasore road, for fear the Company's
shipping should be there and want one to bring them into the river."

January 10th.

291.—UNSETTLED STATE OF THE DECCAN.

They received a letter from Madras, telling them that the country
is as unsettled as ever, and that the competitors
for the throne have not yet met, but that a
battle is daily expected.

January 17th.

292.—ZAMĪNDĀRI ACCOUNTS FOR NOVEMBER.

The zamīndār brought in the accounts of the bazar and the three
towns for the month of November, the balance
being Rs. 837-9-2.

February 4th.

293.—MRS. HILL SELLS HER HOUSE.

" Mrs. Hill being desirous to sell her dwelling-house, and there
having been public notice given by bills on the
gates, and no demands appear, agreed that Captain
Herbert have liberty to buy the same and that the sale be registered."

February 7th.

---

[1] Was this Townsend connected with Joseph Townshend who died the 26th June, 1738, and
whose tombstone is still to be seen in St. John's Churchyard, Calcutta.—
" Here lies the body of Joseph Townshend, Pilot of the Ganges. Skilful and industrious,
a kind father and useful friend, who departed this life the 26th June, 1738, aged 85 years."
This Townsend also figures in a local ballad which connects him with Job Charnock.

294.—DEATH OF KĀM BAKHSH.

On Wednesday, the 16th, they received advices from several shroffs of note and from the Hugli Government of an
February 18th. "engagement between the King Shaw Allum [Shāh 'Ālam] and his brother, Cawn Bux [Kām Bakhsh], near Golgondah [Golconda], about 40 days since, wherein the King had an entire victory and slew his brother and one or two of his sons, and vanquished his party; so that 'tis now believed the kingdom will soon be at quiet and the government more orderly."

They receive from Madras confirmation of the death of Kām Bakhsh. The Madras Council also tell them that
February 19th. they are sending up a present to the King in order to procure the necessary *farmāns.*

295.—ILLNESS OF SHELDON.

"Mr. Sheldon being very much indisposed, and has been for these last two months without relief, and the Doctor
February 28th. advising him to take the sea air for which end he desires the *Mary* Smack with Mr. Adams, the gunner (who is a navigator), with the Doctor to send him out to sea for ten or fifteen days.—Agreed that the Master of the Smack be ordered to get her ready and to take care that all necessaries and stores are on board to send Mr. Sheldon out and in as he may direct."

296.—DIGGING THE GREAT TANK.

"The Company having given us liberty and directions to make drains and necessaries for the Fort, and we having
February 28th. a small tank to the eastward which in some measure defends our bastion and yields good water, when in the months of March and April the river water is brackish, which being necessary to be enlarged and deepened to keep the water good and constantly in it.—Agreed that we lengthen the same what may be thought convenient and deepen what is made, so that the next season at least we may reap the benefit, and the Buxie is ordered to pay the charge and enter it under the head of drains; also that he fill up the earth between the two waterside bastions even with the earth of the said bastions, and throw rubbish, ballast, etc., to face it which holds very well and answers the end."

297.—INCREASING THE REVENUE.

They come to the conclusion at this time that the towns did not
yield the profits they ought, so they ordered
that—

February 28th.

"The Zamīndār or Rent-gatherer is to consider of the best means
and easiest ways possible to raise the revenues and see that all our
former orders of consultations for the benefit thereof be put in execution and that he bring his report in."

298.—THEY CONTINUE THE PATNA FACTORY.

After much consultation they agree to continue the Patna factory,
"now the Government is more settled, and now
that the Government and Council of Madras are
hoping to get a phirmaund for the whole of the Company's factories
from the King." A letter had been received from England a few
days before this, ordering them to keep on the Patna factory if they
possibly can. They therefore send a letter to Mr. Lloyd telling him
still to continue the factory, and to see about buying in goods for the
coming season.

February 28th.

299.—ZAMĪNDĀRI ACCOUNTS FOR DECEMBER.

The accounts of the revenues from the bazar and the three towns
for December were brought in and passed, the
balance being Rs. 1,010-7-10.

March 5th.

300.—REBUILDING THE PRICING WAREHOUSE.

The import warehouse-keeper gave notice that the warehouse used
for pricing the goods was in a very bad state.
On the following resolution was passed :—

March 8th.

"The warehouse we price goods in being very much out of repair,
the timber rotten, and the water in the rains falling down and damag-
ing the goods, and the outward wall of both godowns being cutcha,
agreed that we build that pucka and repair the whole out of hand, that
it may be fit for sorting goods the ensuing season."

301.—HUNTING.

March 12th.   "Mr. Chitty gone a hunting."

302.—PIRATES.

The Council receive a letter from Madras, telling them that the
King is not willing to grant the Company a
March 23rd.   *farmān* unless they will undertake to secure their
ships from pirates at sea.

303.—ZAMĪNDĀRI ACCOUNTS FOR JANUARY.

The January accounts of the bazar and the three towns were passed,
March 28th.   the balance being Rs. 1,699-3-1.

304.—REDUCTION OF THE GARRISON.

March 31st.   It is agreed to reduce the garrison.

"Shaw Allum [Shāh 'Ālam] being now entire victor and sole
King, and we having a prospect of peaceable times, 'tis agreed that
we reduce the soldiery to less number, *i.e.*—

                    1 Captain.
                    1 Ensign.
                   60 Soldiers.
                   ──
                   66 Drummers and Corporals included.
                   66 The second Company.
                    1 Master of Arms.
                    2 Portuguese Armourers.
                    2 Bengal Armourers.
                   ──
                  137 Men in all."

"Ordered that they are reduced to the above number, and the
Buxie is ordered to see he pays no more from this time forward, and
will save the pay of 30 men per month."

305.—TWO ASSISTANTS SENT TO PATNA.

Mr. Lloyd wanting help at Patna, it is agreed that "Mr. Cawthorp
and Mr. Gibbon do proceed to Patna so soon as
March 31st.   they can by land to assist in the investment
there, and that Mr. Frankland be sent afterwards with the boats⌡with
what goods we send."

306.—THE BLACK ZAMĪNDĀR.

Apparently the Company had some difficulty in finding a man
to fill the post of Black Zamīndār, who was likely
April 4th.   to prove honest, as some time back in last year

they were looking for one, and according to the following notice had only just found such a man:—

"The Black Zamīndār's place in taking care of the bazar and the three towns being void for several months, during which time Nunderam has acted, we having now found a fit person to fill it up, one Rambudder having given under his hand, and Santose Mullick being bound for his well and honest performance, agreed that forthwith he enter upon that business and have wages as the former man had in. his place."

307.—TONNAGE, PASS-MONEY, FINES AND LICENSES.

The account of the last year's tonnage, pass-money, English fines and punch license money was brought in by
April 11th. Mr. Blount, the Secretary; it was passed and paid into cash, the amount being 1,665 rupees.

308.—SOLDIERS FOR CALCUTTA.

The ship *Recovery* arrived from England having on board soldiers for Calcutta sent out by the London Directors.
April 14th. Only nine private soldiers out of thirty arrived in Calcutta, the rest having died on the voyage. With the soldiers came Captain Child and one Sergeant.

309.—PUNISHING THE KIDDERPORE CHAUKĪS.

Mr. Josiah Chitty and other servants of the Company made complaint against the *chaukīs*. They said that they had
April 25th. been "affronted and abused very much by Kidderpore *chaukī* in their going down aboard the ships." The *chaukīs* had also "of late been very troublesome in stopping the Company's boats with goods." Accordingly the Council agreed to "send down thirty soldiers and twenty black gun-men to fetch some of them up to punish them, so as they may not be so impudent for the future."

"Yesterday the soldiers and black gun-men as was ordered in that consultation went to Kidrepore *chaukī*: when
April 26th. landed, one of them with cutlass cut one of our sergeants, almost half through his body, but before he fell he shot the man, that wounded him, dead, upon which our men took several of their people prisoners, and have now brought them before us. We have found six of them that actually opposed our men with drawn swords. We have considered it and believe it will be for the Company's

interest to have them severely punished to deter the other troublesome *chaukīs* from committing the like. Agreed that each of them be tied to the post and have 21 strokes with a split rattan, and be kept for a further punishment."

310.—DEATH OF SHELDON.

They receive news of the death of Mr. Ralph Sheldon[1] at Hugli. His body is brought down to Calcutta to be buried there. Mr. John Russell is appointed Chairman in Mr. Ralph Sheldon's place; Mr. Edwin Pattle is to be Accountant; Mr. Bugden is to be in charge of the Import Warehouse; and Mr. Lloyd is to be the new Member and Zamīndār; but as he is at present in Patna, Mr. Blount is to take charge of the Zamīndār's place and the Secretary's office until Mr. Lloyd comes home.

April 26th.

311.—DEPUTATION TO MĪR MUḤAMMAD RAZĀ.

They receive notice that "Mīr Muḥammad Razā, Commissioner of the Prince's treasury, is in a few days expected to pass through Hugli in his way to meet Sher Buland Khān, who is coming into Bengal as chief manager of the provinces of Bengal, Bihar, and Orissa . . . . . . Now this Muḥammad Razā being the treasurer's friend as well as chief officer under him for his private affairs, and having been always very ready to serve the Company, agreed that we send Janarddana Sett, our broker, and the *Ākhūnd* to Hugli to wait on him, and present him with a present to the value of Rs. 500 which present we promised him last year for accommodating affairs between us and the Hugli Government. If so be that Muḥammad Razā stay at Hugli two or three days, then they are to advise us of it, on which it is agreed that Mr. Chitty do proceed to Hugli to wait on him from the Council . . . . . . Now the favours we are to desire of them are these:—On the arrival of our people at camp to visit Sher Buland Khān in order to procure a *sanad*, that he assist us all he can."

April 28th.

312.—COJAH SARHAD IN DEBT.

"Cojah Sarhad being indebted to the Company, and he having considerable value of goods in his house, agreed that we get two peons there, that there be nothing carried away."

May 2nd.

---

[1] Further details about Sheldon will be found in the introduction to these summaries.

313.—TROUBLE BREWING FOR SHĀH 'ĀLAM.

A letter is received from Madras with the following news :—

"They say the Rashpoots [Rājpūts] are in arms and design to oppose the march of King Shaw Allum: that the Governor [of Madras] daily expects an answer to his letter; wrote to the Lord High Steward about getting a phirmaund ; that they believe there will be greater trouble than here has been yet between the father and his four sons."

May 2nd.

314.—ZAMĪNDĀRI ACCOUNTS FOR FEBRUARY.

The account of the revenue of the bazar and three towns for February was brought in and passed; the balance amounted to Rs. 1,028-15-4.

May 2nd.

315.—THE COURT OF JUSTICE.

The Council ordered that "Messrs. Bugden, Love, and Blount sit in Court, there having been none of late."

May 2nd.

316.—DISHONEST TAX-GATHERER.

They agreed to write to the Governor of Hugli to give up a rent-gatherer of theirs who had been caught cheating at Calcutta and had fled to him for protection. "Several complaints having been made against Nandarāma, that was employed in gathering in the Company's rents. He going with Mr. Sheldon to Hugli, and hearing thereof, fled from justice; but since we hear that he is at Hugli and he has given money to the Government upon their promise of protecting him.—Agreed we write to the Governor and demand him, he being our servant, that we may have satisfaction for the abuse to the Company."

May 4th.

317.—MISBEHAVIOUR OF CAPTAIN CHILD.

Captain Child is ordered to be "confined upon the guard until further consideration," because "we think him not a fit person to be trusted." "On the second night being on duty he committed a great disorder and disturbance in the town," and also "several complaints have been made against him," and "two women claim him as husband."

May 4th.

318.—COMMISSION TO CONSECRATE St. ANN'S.

"Mr. William Anderson, the Company's Chaplain at this place, came

May 9th.

before us and produced a commission from the Lord Bishop of London to consecrate the church newly built in this place. Agreed he be permitted to execute said commission as usual on such occasions "

319.—KINDNESS FROM MUḤAMMAD RAZĀ.

Janarddana Sett and the *ākhūnd* returned from Hugli, where

May 12th.

Mīr Muḥammad Razā had received them very kindly, and promised to do all he could for the Company. Mīr Muḥammad also writes the Council a letter, wherein he says "he will make the Company's business his own."

320.—NANDARĀMA GIVEN UP.

They receive an answer from the Governor of Hugli. He gives up

May 12th.

Nandarāma to them, and is sorry he protected him against justice. Nandarāma is ordered to be imprisoned, whilst Mr. Bugden looks over his accounts, and the bazar drum is to "be beat about the town to give notice to all the black inhabitants that whosoever has any money or effects of Nandarāma in their possession, that they do not deliver them to him, or to any of his family till such a time that we have inspected into the town accounts, and find out what he has wronged the Company of."

321.—NEW BUDGEROWS.

"Some of the Company's budgerows being very old and hardly

May 12th.

worth repairing any more, ordered that Mr. Love do build a new one, and when that is finished that he dispose of one of the old ones."

322.—DEPUTATION TO THE NEW GOVERNOR.

They send a *vakīl* to meet Sher Buland Khān, the new Governor.

May 20th.

They give him orders to act entirely on the advice of Muḥammad Razā. As soon as the Patna *vakīl* can be got down to Calcutta, they are going to send him as he is acquainted with Sher Buland Khān, and with him they will send Mr. Chitty, one of the Council.

323.—ZAMÍNDÁRI ACCOUNTS FOR MARCH.

The account of the revenues of the bazar and the three towns for

May 20th.

March last was brought in and passed, the balance being Rs. 890-3-7.

324.—CHITTY REFUSES TO WAIT ON THE NEW GOVERNOR.

Mr. Chitty refuses to go to wait on Sher Buland Khān, so Mr.

May 26th.

Pattle is to go instead. No reason is given for Chitty's refusal to obey the Council's orders. In the Consultation book it is recorded that " Mr. Chitty's reasons for not wishing to go to wait on Sher Buland Khān, which seem to us just and right, are annexed next after this Consultation." But they are not.

325.—BAPTISM AT CASSIMBAZAR.

" The Dutch Chief of Cassimbazar having several times desired our

May 30th.

Chaplain to go up there and baptise his child, and he has now renewed his request, as Mr. Anderson has now advised us in his letter to us of this day's date, and desires we would give him liberty to comply with the same.—Agreed that he go after the consecration of our church is over."

326.—NEGOTIATIONS WITH THE NEW GOVERNOR.

They agree to send Mr. John Eyre with Mr. Pattle to meet Sher Buland Khān.

June 1st.

" Yesterday arrived a messenger from Sher Buland Khān, and brought us a *parwāna* for our business to go on as usual, till we can conveniently send one to him to procure a *sanad* which we design as soon as we hear he is arrived at Maqṣūdābād. Agreed we make the messenger a present to the value of 120 rupees being necessary for the Company's affairs, and what is customary. "

327.—COJAH SARHAD WILLING TO PAY.

Cojah Sarhad, who owed them money, petitions to have the peons,

June 1st.

who are watching his house, taken away, as he is willing to pay the money he owes. The Council gives an order accordingly.

328.—CONSECRATION OF ST. ANN'S.

" The church lately built in this place was consecrated and called

Monday, June 6th, 1709.   St. Ann's. "

329 —ZAMÍNDÁRI ACCOUNTS FOR APRIL AND MAY.

The accounts for the month of April of the bazar and the three
towns were brought in and passed, the balance
June 16th.   being Rs. 2,014-3-6.

The accounts for the month of May of the bazar and the three
July 11th.   towns were brought in and passed, Rs. 2,014-3-6.

330.—BOATS STOPPED AT RAJMAHAL.

They receive a letter from Mr. Pattle, telling them that the boats
are stopped at Rajmahal by order of Sher Buland
July 15th.   Khán because the Company were hesitating about
the price of a *sanad*. Sher Buland Khán asked more for his *sanad*
than the Company wished to give. They agree to write to Mr. Lloyd
telling him to get the *sanad* on any terms he can, " as the stopping
of boats up the river will prevent our sending off ships in time."

331.—STORES FOR BENCOOLEN.

They receive a couple of letters from Bencoolen, asking them to
send stores and provisions to the factory there as
July 25th.   soon as possible.

332.—A PRESENT FOR THE ṢUBAHDÁR.

Mr. Pattle writes asking for English goods to give as a present
to Sher Buland Khán. In answer to his letter
August 10th.   they send him goods worth 2,000 rupees.

333.—ZAMÍNDÁRI ACCOUNTS FOR JUNE.

The accounts of the revenues of the bazar and the three towns for
June are brought in and passed, the balance being
August 22nd.   Rs. 1,129-12-3.

334.—IRON FOR THE CHURCH WINDOWS.

" The Hon'ble Court of Managers ordering us to give iron for the
church windows, and there being now due on that
August 22nd.   account Rs. 1,310-9-3, agreed that the cashiers
pay the same."

335.—DISAPPOINTING NEGOTIATIONS.

They receive another letter from Mr. Pattle at Cassimbazar telling
them that the Ṣubadár had received him kindly,
September 3rd.   and promised him his utmost assistance in the
Company's affairs, and that " he, the Subah [Ṣūbadár], had wrote to
the Governor of Hugli not any ways to molest our business." " We

were all very glad at this, and hoped for the sunnud soon," says the Consultation Book. But their joy did not last long, for on the very same evening they received bad news.

"Last night late received from Mr. Pattle a letter dated the 30th of August, acquainting us that the Subah, notwithstanding all his promises, positively demands 45,000 rupees on receipt of which he will give us his perwanna, and when the present Duan is confirmed or a new one sent, that he will procure us his sunnud, without which he is resolved to admit of no more delays from us but will stop all our business having called all the merchants at Muxodabad to give in an account of what goods they have provided for us in order to their paying custom. The Subah further adds that the Prince last year forced from our Patna boats 17,000 rupees, and, if we comply not, that we shall see what he can do." . . . . "On these advices we meet early this morning to consult what to do in these unsettled times, and cannot find any remedy ; for since the new King is come to the throne, we have had no order from him to trade as usual which is the advantage the Government takes hold of. Therefore it is resolved we write immediately to Mr. Pattle, ordering him to make an end of it the best way he can, for it is certain if we comply not, the Subah will again stop our Patna fleet, which (as the year before) will not be let loose till a large sum is extorted, as also custom to be paid on our goods, which we have bespoke of the Cassimbazar merchants, which will be of very ill consequence."

336—NEWS FROM MADRAS.

September 6th.

They receive a letter from Madras telling them that the Council there was sending presents to the great Mogul and also black Ambassadors to negotiate at his Court for a King's phirmaund, and advising them to do the same. "They also tell us that a French ship had arrived at Pondicherry and is cruising about and has taken a Dutch ship, and they wish us to keep a vessel cruising about off Point Palmiras from the 1st of November to the 10th of January to advise all ships to avoid them."

337.—SHER BULAND KHÂN'S ORDER.

September 29th.

"Received a letter from Mr. Pattle at Cassimbazar, enclosing Subah Seer Bullund Cawn's perwanna [the Ṣūbadār Sher Buland Khân's parwânah] for our free trade in Bengal, Bihar, and Orissa, and the Subah's particular orders to Hugly and Rajamahal, Dacca and Muxodabad, acquainting them that he had given us a general perwanna."

338.—WALĪ BEG.

The letter also goes on to say that Walī Beg, the *dārōgha* of the King's treasury, who had been most useful in helping Mr. Pattle to get the *sanad*, was coming to Hugli and would like to come on to Calcutta and visit the English. Mr. Pattle advises them to offer the *dārōgha* a present when he arrives at Calcutta.

September 29th.

Walī Beg visits Calcutta, is "received very civilly," and has a present of 1,000 rupees value made to him in broadcloth, and the like. He promises to do all he can to keep the peace between the Hugli Government and the Company.

October 1st.

339.—ZAMĪNDĀRI ACCOUNTS FOR JULY.

The accounts of the revenues of the bazar and the three towns for the month of July are brought in and passed, the balance being Rs. 1,352-3.

October 1st.

340.—A NEW GUNNER.

"Mr. William Adams, gunner of the Fort, having been indisposed in his health, has leave to go to England; and here being one Captain Henry Harnett, who was sent for from Madras, and is a very ingeneous man, understanding fortifications, etc., very well, agreed that he be gunner and have the same allowance as the former had, and he take charge of the gunner's stores. He is also to assist the Buxie as master of attendance in taking care of the sloops in fitting them. He also undertakes to make the drains about the town as our masters have ordered. In consideration of these services, agreed he have further allowance of 30 rupees per mensem."

October 3rd.

341.—PETRE BOATS ON THEIR WAY.

Mr. Surman and some soldiers are to go up the river to meet the saltpetre boats that are coming down from Patna. The boats have been released, now that the Company have the Ṣūbadār's *sanad*.

October 3rd.

Y

342.—SALARY BILLS.

October 3rd.

The account of the half-yearly salaries due to the Company's servants was brought into Council and passed the sum total of the salaries being Rs. 4,345-3-7.[1] The cashiers are ordered to pay the same forthwith.

343.—MORE NEWS FROM MADRAS.

October 9th.

They receive another letter from Madras about the present for the great Mogul. The Madras Council inform them that they have heard rumours that the King is going to Delhi. If this be true, the Council at Calcutta had better not send the present to Surat, but by way of Patna to Delhi. The letter also again speaks of the trouble caused by the French cruiser off the coast of Pondicherry. A meeting of the Council was called to know what should be done about the Frenchman, with the result that they "ordered Captain Dan Wilkinson to take the *London* sloop and cruiser between Point Palmiras and the sea reefs, the place where our pilots commonly leave ships when they carry them out."

344.—BLOUNT MARRIES WIDOW WALDO.

October 12th.

Mr. Samuel Blount was married to Mrs. Waldo, widow of Mr. Henry Waldo.•

345.—MADRAS RUPEES.

October 17th.

The Company was losing money on the Madras rupees.

"The Government having often refused to take Madras rupees into the King's treasury, has caused their batta to fall from 9 to 7 per cent. Agreed we write to Madras advising them thereof, and that if any of our master's ships should arrive with them belonging to Bengal, they send us down the silver uncoined, which will turn to a much better account than Madras rupees; and now we have got the Subah's perwanna. We design to coin the Company's treasure at Muxodabad, which will be much more advantageous than Madras rupees should they ever rise again to 9 per cent."

---

[1] The sum total only is given.

346.—HOW TO ESCAPE THE FRENCH SHIP.

On account of the French ship cruising about, they determined to
send out the ships two together, "so that it will
not matter if they don't meet the Dutch fleet till
the Cape of Good Hope be reached."

October 17th.

347.—ZAMÍNDÁRI ACCOUNTS FOR AUGUST.

The accounts of the bazar and the three towns for August were
brought in and passed, the balance being
Rs. 1,198-1-10.

October 27th.

348.—LLOYD TAKES HIS SEAT.

"Mr. William Lloyd arrived here the 29th ultimo with the Hon'ble
Company's boats of goods from Patna. He
being eighth person in this Council is ordered
to take his place accordingly."

November 3rd.

349.—WALDO'S DOCTOR'S BILL.

"Mr. Blount brought in a Doctor's bill paid by Mrs. Waldo for
attendance and physic to her husband in his
sickness, our Doctor being sick at that time."
Ordered that the Buxie pay the same.

November 3rd.

350.—ZAMÍNDÁRI ACCOUNTS FOR SEPTEMBER.

The accounts of the bazar and the three towns for September were
brought in and passed, the balance amounting to
Rs. 1,111-3-1.

November 10th.

351.—PROTECTION AGAINST THE FRENCH.

The Council agreed to send two soldiers and an officer with each
ship "that goes out" in case they are attacked
by the French before they get to Madras. The
soldiers are to be put on land again at Madras and to return to
Calcutta by the next ship.

November 10th.

DIARY AND CONSULTATION BOOK

OF THE

UNITED TRADE COUNCIL AT FORT WILLAM IN BENGAL.

From December 1709.

Council.

JOHN RUSSELL.	ABRAHAM ADAMS.
EDWARD PATTLE.	JOSIAH CHITTY.
WILLIAM BUGDEN.	JAMES LOVE.
WILLIAM LLOYD.	SAMUEL BLOUNT.

Chairmen and Cashiers	...	John Russell and Abraham Adams.
Accountant	...	Edward Pattle (away at Cassimbazar).
Export Warehouse-keeper	...	Josiah Chitty.
Import ditto	...	William Bugden.
Buxie [*Bakhshī*]	...	James Love.
Jemindar [*Zamīndār*]	...	William Lloyd.
Secretary	...	Samuel Blount.

352.—EXACTIONS AND THREATS.

December 1st.

On the 29th of September last they had after much difficulty obtained the Ṣūbadār's *parwānah*. Some time in November the Ṣūbadār was turned out of his Governorship, and the Dīwān was now trying to stop all the Company's boats and goods, requiring the sum of Rs. 20,000 more before he let them pass, which "unreasonable demand cannot be complied to."

Therefore they resolve to write to the Governor of Hugli and "acquaint him that if the boats of goods that are stopped are not cleared, we will not let any of the Moor's ships pass." They also agree that they will send up forty soldiers and thirty black gunners to clear the "boats that are stopped higher up the country," and that Mr. Spencer and Ensign Dalibar go to command them.

353.—CAPTAIN CHILD ORDERED HOME.

"Captain Francis Child having very much misbehaved himself

December 12th. insomuch that we can't think it safe to trust him, we have therefore ordered him to England on the ship *Herne* with one of his wives, the other we have ordered home on board the *Stretham*."

354.—CHITTY TO OFFICIATE AS ACCOUNTANT.

"Mr. Edward Pattle being still at Cassimbazar, and there therefore

December 19th. being no one to fill the accountant's place, it is agreed that Mr. Chitty fill that post till Mr. Pattle returns."

355.—CAPTAIN HAMILTON'S DEBTS.

They order that Captain Alexander Hamilton's house "be sold at

Monday, December 26th. public outcry" in order to defray his debts. The house was sold for Rs. 2,500.

356—DEATH OF THE NEW MADRAS GOVERNOR.

They received news from Madras of the death of the newly-appointed

January 6th, 1710. Governor of that place, Gulston Addison.[1]

357.—ZAMĪNDĀRI ACCOUNTS FOR OCTOBER AND NOVEMBER.

The accounts of the bazar and the three towns for the two months

January 8th. of October and November last were brought in and passed; the balance being for October Rs. 1,910-13-11, for November Rs. 1,025-1.

---

[1] Gulston Addison, born in 1673, was the son of the Very Rev. Launcelot Addison, Dean of Lichfield, and of Jane, the sister of the Right Rev. William Gulston, Bishop of Bristol, and was a brother of the celebrated Essayist. Dean Addison had, in fact, four children by his first wife, "each of whom for excellent talents and singular perfection was as much above the ordinary world as their brother Joseph was above them." Joseph was the eldest, and Gulston the Dean's second son. Launcelot, the third son, born in 1680, was a demy and afterwards a Fellow of Magdalen College, Oxford. About the time of Gulston's death, he visited Fort St. George, and died there in 1711.

Thomas Pitt was superseded in September 1709, after being Governor of Madras for more than eleven years. On the 17th September the *Heathcote* arrived with a packet from England. The next day the packet was opened and found to contain a letter dismissing Pitt from the service and "constituting Gulston Addison, Esq., in his room." "He immediately read the cash and tendered the balance thereof, ... but the new Governor desired the payment for that time might be deferred for that he was very much indisposed." Addison died the 17th October 1709, while Pitt was still in Madras. At the time of his supersession Pitt says:— "They have made a very good choice in him for Governor, but God deliver us from such a scandalous Council."

358.—APPOINTING EVERY ONE IN THEIR PROPER STATIONS.

"Agreed, the shipping being now gone, that we appoint every-
one of the Council in their proper stations, viz.,
January 17th.   Mr. Pattle being at Cassimbazar, ordered that
Mr. Chitty do take the charge of the accountant's office, and Mr. Bugden
of the export warehouse and Mr. Love of the import warehouse, and
Mr. Blount, Buxie."

359.—PATTLE'S PROCEEDINGS.

They received a long letter, dated 14th January, from Mr. Pattle,
telling them that he had visited the Dīwān and
January 17th.   was promised a *sanad* "which is written out."

They determined to send three of the Company's factors to assist
Mr. Pattle. Mr. Pattle also wrote that the Dīwān had sent to clear their
boats at Bidiepore, so there is "no need now to send Mr. Surman
and Ensign Dalibar to clear them."

360.—NEW SECRETARY AND NEW ZAMĪNDĀR.

For some reason not given, an order is issued that for the present
Mr. Calvert is to act as Secretary and Mr.
January 17th.   Spencer as Zamīndār.

361.—NEW ARRIVALS FROM ENGLAND.

A ship from home arrived bringing nine covenant servants and
thirty soldiers for Calcutta, also a certain
January 23rd, and 26th.   Mr. Gerard Cook, who brought papers stating
that he was to be gunner to the Fort. The Council at Calcutta had
already made Captain Henry Harnett gunner. Consequently they
determined upon keeping two gunners "as there is so much to be
done in looking after the Fort drains, etc.," and by way of giving the
gunner something to do they agree "to begin upon the drains at once"
so as to do what they can "before the rainy season."

The work allotted to the other nine covenant servants who came
out was as follows:—

Accompt. Office	⎰ Michael Cotsworth. ⎱ John Lloyd.
Export Warehouse	⎰ Waterworth Collett. ⎱ John Pratt.
Import Warehouse	Edward Crisp.
Buxie's assistant	John Cole.
Secretary's Office	⎰ Thomas Falconer. ⎰ John Farmer. ⎱ John Cateral.

362.—SET ON BY NAQDĪS.[1]

"This morning we received advice from Mr. Pattle that the Duan was dead of the wounds he had received from the Nuggadees [Naqdīs] when they set on him to endeavour to procure their pay and having not yet had any satisfaction continue ten thousand of them in arms near that place."

January 26th.

363.—SURMAN SENT TO PATNA.

They order Mr. Surman to go to Patna with money and goods for the factory. He was to remain up there until further orders.

January 30th.

364.—SOLDIERS TO MEET THE BOATS.

They send soldiers to meet the Patna boats and to bring them down.

February 9th.

365.—A WARF BEFORE THE FORT.

"We have duly considered the Company's orders in relation to building a warf before the Fort, and find it will be a great security to the banks and a strengthening thereto; it is therefore agreed we instantly set about it, and make it with brick and raise a breastwork and plant cannon there."

February 9th.

366.—BARRACKS IN THE HOSPITAL.

"There being a great many English soldiers in the garrison who, if they lodge about the town as usually, will create sickness and other inconveniences to themselves and others, therefore 'tis agreed the hospital be walled round and that barracks be made in it for the soldiers to lodge in, and that some of the officers do likewise lodge there, and see a good decorum kept amongst them."

February 13th.

---

[1] The Naqdī regiments of horse were so named from being paid in money. It is said that, on a previous occasion, 'Abdu-l-Wāḥid, the commander of one of these regiments, tried to waylay and assassinate Murshid Quli Khān. With this intent he and his troops accosted the treasurer in the street while on his way to pay a visit of ceremony to Prince 'Aẓīmu-sh-Shān. They demanded their arrears of pay in an insolent manner, and attempted to prevent him from proceeding. But Murshid Quli, perceiving their object, put himself at the head of his armed retinue, and forced his way to the palace. He accused 'Aẓīmu-sh-Shān of being party to the conspiracy, complained of the insult he had received to the Emperor Aurangzéb, and, considering it no longer safe to remain in the same place with the Prince, removed to Murshidabad.

367.—ZAMĪNDĀRI ACCOUNTS FOR DECEMBER.

Mr. Blount, acting as Zamīndār, brought in the accounts of the

February 16th.

revenue for the bazar and the three towns for December, the balance being Rs. 1,084-14-11.

368.—PATTLE TO BE RECALLED.

The Council resolve to recall Mr. Pattle until a new Dīwān be

February 16th.

appointed, as nothing can be done about the *sanad* before that. They also order all the native merchants to deliver their goods straight to the Company's warehouses in Calcutta, so as to allow trade to go on as well as it can under the circumstances.

369.—ROSE'S WILL.

"Mrs. Rose, widow of Captain Rose, who died some time ago, has

February 16th.

produced her husband's will, witnessed by Elizabeth Browne and Thomas Clausade and Charles Pittman; the two former witnesses are dead and the third at sea, but Mr. Browne, who was husband to the first witness, does declare that to the best of his knowledge it was her signing, ordered this will be entered next this Consultation."

WILL.

In the name of God, Amen. I, Richard Rose, of Calcutta, in the Bay of Bengal, Mariner, being very sick and weak in body but of perfect mind and memory, praised be God for the same, therefore knowing 'tis appointed for all men once to die, do make and ordain this my last will and testament, that is to say, first, I recommend my soul into the hands of God that gave it, and my body I recommend to the earth to be buried in a Christian-like and decent manner, and touching such worldly estate wherewith it has pleased God to bless me with, I give, devise and dispose of in manner and form following.

Imprimis—I give and bequeath to my loving wife, Sarah Rose, all my estate, goods, and chattels, after my debts and funeral charges being paid and satisfied, wherewith at the time of my decease I shall be possessed or invested, and I do revoke all other former wills or deeds of gift by me at any time made, and ordain this to be my only last will and testament, and I do make and ordain my said loving wife, Sarah Rose, my sole executor of these presents.

In witness whereof I have hereunto set my hand and seal this eleventh day of October A.D. 1706.

Memorandum.

I give to my Cozen William Mercer my seal ring.

RICHARD ROSE.

Sealed and delivered, published and declared in the presence of—

ELIZABETH BROWNE.

THOMAS CLAUSADE.

CHARLES PITTMAN.

370.—ZAMĪNDĀRI ACCOUNTS FOR JANUARY.

February 27th.

The accounts for the bazar and the three towns for January last were brought in and passed, the balance being Rs. 1,386-2.

371.—ZAINU-D-DIN KHĀN.

February 27th.

The Council receive a letter from Madras telling them "that Zoody Cawne [Zainu-d-Dīn Khān], the great man at the King's Court with whom Governor Pitt was treating withall for a Phirmaund [*farmān*], had wrote them a kind letter, and that he was coming to Bengal to be Subah [Ṣūbadār] of Hugli and Admiral of all the sea ports on the coast of Coromandel, and that they would have us on his arrival here. keep in good friendship with him."

372.—TAKING A HOLIDAY.

March 13th.

"The shipping being now all despatched and contracts being made with the merchants for goods against next shipping, agreed that we go to Rewhigh for a few days to take the air and to recreate ourselves with hunting; ordered that the Buxie [*Bakhshī*] get boats and necessaries for our going."

373.—THE PRINCE AT RAJMAHAL.

March 29th.

"The Prince who is Subah [Ṣūbadār] of Bengal is now at Rajamahal, at which place the Company's boats bound to Patna are stopped; agreed to send Mahmud Assum [Muḥammad A'zam], our Vacqueel thither, to attend on that durbar."

374.—REPAIRS AT CASSIMBAZAR.

March 29th.

They agree to repair the Cassimbazar factory, as they hope to settle there next season, and the factory was very much out of repair.

They therefore order Mr. Acton to go up to Cassimbazar and remain there to see the work well done.

375.—NEWS FROM LLOYD.

They receive a letter from Mr. Lloyd, who is at Rajmahal, telling

March 31st. them that "the Patna boats were stopped there by reason that all the officers of the Government were gone from that place to meet the Prince, who was coming hither, and that there was none to give passes. Afterwards when they arrived they demanded large sums to clear the boats ; these he would not pay, but he must pay something. He told them too that Murshid Quli Khān was made Dīwān of Bihar and Bengal, and that he would come through Patna on his way to Bengal. The Council write at once directing Mr. Lloyd to try to procure *sanads* for both Patna and Calcutta from Murshid Quli when he is in Patna.

376.—NATHANIEL JONES'S WILL.

The will of Nathaniel Jones was sworn to by the witnesses, and

March 31st. the Council ordered that it be " entered next this Consultation."

WILL.

Will of Nathaniel Jones, dated 18th January 1709-10, Calcutta.

" In the name of God, Amen. I, Nathaniel Jones, of Calcutta, being very sick of body, but of perfect mind and memory, thanks be given to God therefore, and calling to mind my mortality, that it is appointed for all men once to die, do make and ordain this my last will and testament in manner and form following :—

First of all I give and recommend my soul into the hands of Almighty God that gave it, and for my body I recommend it to the earth, to be buried in a Christian-like and decent manner at the direction of my executor, nothing doubting of a blessed resurrection on the last day ; and as touching such worldly goods and estate wherewith it hath pleased God to bless me in this life, I give, devise and dispose of the same in the following manner and form :—

Imprimis—As a legacy I give and bequeath unto my dear mother, Sarah Rose, out of my estate, the whole garden adjoining the house where I now live in *Amen Corner* to her and her heirs for ever. I also as a token of my filial respect do leave her two hundred rupees and a free possession of the house in which we live without any charge or molestation till such time as she shall think fit to remove, and to my young brother, William Rose, I give all my wearing apparel, buckles, buttons, cane and guns, as a token of my love, and to my friend, Thomas Hubbard, my best buckanering[1] piece, to keep for my sake, and to my dear wife, Sarah Jones, I give and bequeath the whole remainder of my estate, to be possessed and enjoyed by her, but if she should prove with child by me, my will is she possess one-half of the remainder of my estate, and the lawful heir of my body, the other half, to him or her, for ever; and in case my dear wife should die a widow without an heir, then it is my desire my remaining estate be given to my young brother, William Rose, aforesaid; and I do hereby make and ordain my kind friend, Mr. James Love, my only and sole executor of this my last will and testament. In witness whereof I have hereunto set my hand and seal in Calcutta, this eighteenth day of January, Anno Domini, one thousand seven hundred nine and ten.

NATHANIEL JONES. (Seal.)

Signed, sealed, and delivered in the presence of us. (The above interlinement was done before signing.)

Sealed, and witness hereof—

JOHN WATTS.
CHARLES MIDDLETON.
THOMAS HUBBARD.

377.—ZAMÍNDÁRI ACCOUNTS FOR FEBRUARY.

Mr. Spencer •brought in the accounts of the bazar and the
April 13th. three towns for February, the balance being Rs. 1,314-2-8.

378.—COOKE'S PAY.

Mr. Gerrard Cooke makes an application concerning his pay; he is
May 1st. ordered to receive the same pay as former gunners, Rs. 50 per month.

379.—PATTLE ARRIVED FROM RAJMAHAL.

Mr. Pattle, who has evidently arrived from Rajamahal, is ordered
May 8th. to "sit on Saturday in the Court of Justice with Mr. Love and Mr. Blount." He is also ordered to take charge of the general books for 1710.

380.—ZAMÍNDÁRI ACCOUNTS FOR MARCH.

The accounts of the bazar and three towns for March were brought
May 22nd. in and passed, the balance being Rs. 1,003-15-2.

---

[1] Buccaneering piece (F. *fusil boucanier*): a long musket used in hunting wild oxen (Murray).

381.—THE NEW GOVERNOR OF HUGLI.

"The new Governor of Hugli being near at hand at Hugli agreed that the Broaker do go up to meet him to compliment him on his arrival in his new government. He has wrote a very civil letter promising his kind assistance in our Masters affairs; he is a greater man than has ever been Governor of Hugli; he is also made Governor of Ballasore and of all sea ports here and on the coast of Coromandell; he was put into these places by the King himself, and is independent of any Duan or Subah." "By Governor Pitt's advises last year," we learn "that he has been always very civil to our nation and is the Prince whom Governor Pitt, &c., were treating with about procuring a Phirmaund."

May 25th.

382.—OLD HORSES.

"Three of the Company's horses being old and worne out ordered the Buxie put them up at outcry."

May 30th.

383.—ZAINU-D-DĪN KHĀN.

The broker they had sent to visit Zainu-d-Dīn Khān returned and told them that he had been received with marked kindness by the faujdār, and that the faujdār would like to come to Calcutta to visit the Company; only he had been told that it was customary for them to visit him first. So the Council agree to send Messrs. Chitty and Blount to Hugli to "visit and discourse with him."

June 5th.

384.—WILLIAM WHITE'S WILL.

The witnesses swore before the Council to the authenticity of the last will and testament of William White, dated 26th May 1710.

June 13th.

WILL.

In the name of God, Amen. I, William White, merchant, now residing in Calcutta, in Bengal, at the writing hereof am of sound and perfect memory (though not of health of body), considering the uncertainty of this mortal life, do make this my last will and testament in the manner following, revoking all other wills by me heretofore made, and first and principally I commend my soul unto the hands of Almighty God, my Heavenly Father and Jesus Christ, his only son, my blessed Saviour and Redeemer, trusting by and through his merit, death and passion to obtain everlasting life. My body I commit to the earth to be decently buried at the discretion of my executors hereafter named, and for the worldly estate it has pleased God to bless me with, I give and bequeath the same as follows :—

First my will and mind is I do hereby give and bequeath unto my sister, Elizabeth King, one hundred rupees, current of Bengal, for mourning, as also a mourning ring, now by me with a cypher on it.

Item.—I give and bequeath unto Dr. Philip Richardson the sum of forty rupees, current of Bengal, for his care of me in my sickness.

Item.—I give and bequeath unto Mr. Thomas Smyth and Mr. John Cole each of them twenty rupees, current of Bengal, to buy them rings.

Item.—I give and bequeath unto my niece, Elizabeth King, all my personal estate that shall be found remaining and to appertain to me after the discharge of my just debts and legacies aforementioned.

Item.—My humble request is to the Hou'ble Chairmen and Council of this place that my body may be entered in the same tomb my deceased brother, Mr. Jonathan White, lies.[1]

Item.—I appoint and desire Mr. Thomas Smyth and Mr. John Cole to be executors of this my last Will and Testament.

Item.—I desire and request that the abovenamed executors do take care of what shall be found remaining of my estate to be sent to England to my sister, Elizabeth King, for the use of her daughter, Elizabeth King.

CALCUTTA,
The 26th May 1710.   WILLIAM WHITE.   (Seal.)

Witnesses.

Signed and delivered where no stamped paper is to be had in the presence of us—

WATT. COLLETT.

THOMAS WRIGHT.

"A true copy from the orginall examd."

JOHN CALVERT, *Secretary.*

385.—SCARCITY OF RICE.

Rice was very scarce this year, not only in Calcutta but in Madras and Bombay too. Two or three ships had put into Calcutta, asking for supplies of rice. The

June 15th.

---

[1] The tombstone of Jonathan White is still to be seen in St. John's Churchyard: see *ante*, p. 4.

Company therefore regulate the price at which it is to be sold to the poor people.

"There being now a very great scarcity of rice to that degree that the poor are ready to starve, agreed we order to be sold in the bazar, the fine at one maund for a rupee, and the coarse at maunds 10 for a rupee and to encourage the same: it is ordered that the Buxie sell five hundred maunds of the Company's at that price; by reason a great many of the country people hoard it up in hopes of getting a great price for it."

386.—PRESENT TO THE GOVERNOR OF DACCA.

They agree to send a present to Khwājah Muḥammad Maḥmud Razā, Governor of Dacca, "where a great part of the Company's goods come from" as "'tis in his power to do the Company's affairs a great deal of prejudice."

June 15th.

387.—ROBERT OWEN'S WILL.

June 15th.　　　　The will of Robert Owen, sworn to before the Council by the witnesses.

WILL.

"In the name of God, Amen. I, Robert Owen, in Madras, born in the Parish of St. Benedict, London, Mariner, son of Thomas Owen Vintner and Citizen of London, being in perfect health and memory, thanks be to Almighty God, and calling to remembrance the uncertain estate of this transitory life, and that all flesh must yield unto death when it shall please God to call, do make, constitute, and declare this my last will and testament in manner and form following, revoking and annulling by these presents all and every testament and testaments, will and wills, heretofore, by me made and declared either by word or writing, and this is to be taken only for my last will and testament and none other, and first being pennitent and sorry from the bottom of my heart for my sins past, most humbly desiring forgiveness for the same, I give [my soul] unto Almighty God, my Saviour and Redeemer, in whom and by the merits of Jesus Christ, I trust and believe assuredly to be saved and to have full remission and forgiveness of my sins, and that my soul with my body at the general day of Resurrection shall rise again with joy, and through the merits of Christ's death and passion possess and inherit the Kingdom of Heaven, prepared for His elect and chosen, and my body to be buried in such place as shall be most proper, and now for settling my temporal estate and such goods, debts, and chattels, as it hath pleased God far above my deserts to bestow upon me, I do order, give, and dispose of the same in manner and form following. That is to say, first, I will that all those debts and duties as I owe in right and conscience to any manner of person or persons whatsoever, shall be well and truly contented and paid or ordained to be paid within convenient time after my decease by my executrix hereafter named. In witness hereby I have hereunto set my hand and seal this fourteenth day of July A.D. 1709.

Imprimis—I give unto my well-beloved friend, Mr. Robert Glessde, merchant, in Madras, the sum of 20 pagodas, current of Madras, for to make mourning and ten pagodas for a ring.

Item.—To my dear and well-beloved friend, Elizabeth Browne, of Madras, whom I likewise constitute and make and ordain my only and sole executrix of this my last will and testament, all and singular goods, money, and whatever else it has pleased God to endow me with either in England or any other place after my debts and charges of my funeral is paid, leaving my interment to the discretion of my said executrix, and I do hereby utterly disallow, revoke, and disannul all and every other former testament, wills, legacies, bequests and executors by me in any way before this time named, willed and bequeathed, ratifying and confirming this and no other, to be my last will and testament. In witness whereof I have hereunto set my hand and seal this fourteenth day of July A.D. 1709.

[ROBERT OWEN.]

Signed, sealed, and delivered, where no stamped paper is to be procured, in the presence of us—

HENRY HARNET.

JOS. BERNERS.

EDWARD ROGERS.

A true copy from the original examined per

JOHN CALVERT, *Secretary.*

388—LAND FOR A DRY DOCK.

"Mr. Samuel Blount desires of the Council to give him the small
June 23rd.   piece of ground that lies between Mr. Russell's warehouse and the house built by Dr. Warren which for the benefit of shipping he is to make a dry dock of. Agreed he has it, paying ground-rent for the same."

July 3rd.   The will of Mrs. Sinclare sworn to by the witnesses before the Council.

WILL.

In the name of God, Amen. This tenth day of June 1710, I, Sarah Sinclare, inhabitant of Calcutta, being very sick and weak in body, but of sound and perfect mind and memory (praise be given to God for the same) and knowing the uncertainty of this transitory life on earth, do make this my last will and testament in manner and form following, (viz.) :—First and principally I recommend my soul to Almighty God, my Creator, and my body to the earth from whence it was taken, to be buried in such decent and Christian-like manner as to my executors hereafter named shall think meet and convenient, as touching my worldly estate, my will and meaning is the same shall be employed and bestowed as hereafter by this will is expressed, and I do hereby renounce, frustrate, and make void all wills by me formerly made and declare and appoint this my last will and testament.

Item.—I will that all those debts I owe in right or conscience to any manner of person whatsoever shall be well and truly paid or caused to be paid.

Item.—I do give and bequeath to Mr. Josiah Chitty one burial ring, and to Captain Henry Harnet one more, and to his wife, Elizabeth Harnet, one more as a legacy.

Item.—I do give and bequeath to Mrs. Elizabeth Harnet, wife of Captain Henry Harnet, my slave girl, named Dianah, during her life.

Item.—I do give and bequeath to my slave, Jubell, in consideration of her true and faithful service, the sum of thirty pagodas, and her freedom, together with the freedom of all the children during their lives.

Item.—I do likewise give to my slave boy, Cesar, his freedom.

Item.—I do likewise give and bequeath to my dearly beloved daughter, Katherine Maxwell, the one-half of my estate, as goods, chattels, or whatever doth or may appertain, and belong to me now, or at anytime hereafter, likewise all my wearing apparel and chamber furniture to her and her heirs for ever.

Item.—I do give and bequeath to my dearly beloved sons Robert, James, and Henry Sinclare, the remaining half of my aforesaid estate, they allowing out of said legacy ten pounds sterling per annum to my dearly beloved mother, Johannah Vixinbridge, during her life, and if in case either of my said sons should die, I will that his share shall be divided amongst the rest.

Item.—I do constitute and ordain my trusted friends, Mr. Jos. Chitty and Captain Henry Harnet, of Calcutta, to be my sole executors, to see this my last will and testament performed, and my will is that they continue my said estate belonging to my sons till they come to the age of 21 in their custody, allowing them what they shall judge necessary, but if in case they shall have occasion of said estate, and my said executors approve and think proper to pay it them, as my executors shall think convenient and most for their advantage. In witness whereof I have hereunto set my hand and seal the day and year above written.

SARAH SINCLARE.   Seal.

Signed, sealed and delivered in the presence of us, where no stamped paper is to be had, being the last will and testament of the subscriber thereof.

SAMUEL BUTCHER.
THOMAS HUBBARD.
ROBERT CARYE.

890.—ZAMINDARI ACCOUNTS FOR MAY.

The accounts of the bazar and the three towns for the month of
July 17th.   May last were brought in and passed, the balance being Rs. 1,045-0-11.

891.—ARRIVAL OF GOVERNOR WELTDEN.

They receive a letter in the evening from the Hon'ble Antony
July 18th.   Weltden, telling them that he had just arrived at
Balasor from England, being sent out by the Company to be Governor and President of the Council, over their affairs in Bengal. The Council sent off a letter in reply at once congratulating him on his safe arrival. The bearer of the letter was one of the Council, Mr. Blount, who was to take down various " conveneinces " and the like for the new President and his family.

In the afternoon some of the Council and several of the Company's
July 19th.   servants went down the river to meet the new Governor.

Z

"This evening arrived the Hon'ble Antony Weltden, Esq., who
was met at his landing by most of the Europeans
in town, and the natives in such crowds that was
difficult to pass to the fort, where he was conducted by the Worshipful
John Russell, and Abraham Adams, Esq., and the Council. The
packet was opened and the commission read. After which the usual
ceremony given on such occasions by firing guns and the keys of the
Fort delivered."

July 20th.

392.—THE NEW GOVERNMENT.

"The President having read his commission, the general letter
was opened, which commission and said letter
did appoint the Government of this place as
follows :—

Thursday, July 20th.

The Hon'ble Antony Weltden, Esq.,[1] President and Governor,
Messrs. Robert Hedges, Ralph Sheldon, John Russell, Abraham
Adams, Edward Pattle, Jos. Chitty, William Bugden and John
Calvert; to be of the Council, and in case of mortality to elect
Messrs. Blount and Love, and after them the next in seniority to
succeed without favour or affection."

"Mr. Sheldon being dead, agreed Mr. Blount be taken into
Council."

"Ordered the two late Chairmen, Messrs. John Russell and Abraham
Adams (it being now late), do deliver to the Hon'ble President the
balance of the Company's running cash to-morrow morning at which
time the Council are agreed to meet again more fully to look over our
Hon'ble Master's orders and instructions."

July 21st.

At this morning's Council there were present—

THE HON. ANT. WELTDEN, ESQ.	EDWT. PATTLE.
	JOS. CHITTY.
JOHN RUSSELL.	JOHN CALVERT.
ABRAHAM ADAMS.	SAMUEL BLOUNT.

The Chairmen delivered up the Company's running cash to the
President, the amount of balance being Rs. 29,469-13-6.

---

[1] Apparently the usage at this time was to give the President alone the title *Esquire*;
the second in Council is styled *Mr.*, or sometimes all the other Members of Council are so
styled. Similarly, the President alone is styled *the Hon'ble*; but the second in Council is
sometimes styled *the Worshipful*. Here the two Joint-Chairmen are called *the Worshipful*.
See also the list of the Old Company's servants on page 17.

"Agreed that the Council be stationed as follows:—

The Hon'ble President and Governor—Cash-keeper.
Mr. Hedges (on his arrival) to be the Chief of Cassimbazar factory.

John Russell	...	Book-keeper.
Abraham Adams	...	Export Warehouse-keeper.
Edward Pattle	...	Import Warehouse-keeper.
Josiah Chitty	...	Buxie.
John Calvert	...	Jemindar.
Samuel Blount	...	Secretary."

393.—FRESH WRITERS.

"The Company's writers which came out on ship *King William Galley* were all sent for and produced their counterpart of their indenture. They were stationed as follows:—

July 24th.

John Barker	...	Assistant to Export Warehouse-keeper.
George Weslyd	...	Buxie's Assistant.
Henry Clare	...	Under the Governor.
Charles Hampton	...	Accompt. Office.
William Spinks	...	Ditto.
James Tokefield	...	Secretary's Office."

394.—THE COURT OF JUSTICE.

"The indisposition of some of the gentlemen belonging to the Court of Justice having prevented their sitting for some time, agreed that others be chosen (viz.) Messrs. Edward Pattle, Josiah Chitty, John Calvert, and that Mr. William Spencer be register."

July 24th.

395.—CLOTH FOR THE SOLDIERS' UNIFORMS.

"Ordered that Mr. Edward Pattle, the Import Warehouse-keeper, deliver Captain Woodville six pieces red and one piece blue broadcloth to clothe the soldiers and that he pay the same."

July 31st.

396.—ZAMÍNDÁRI ACCOUNTS FOR JUNE.

The accounts of the revenues for the bazar and three towns for the month of June last were brought in and passed, the balance being Rs. 1,129.

July 31st.

397.—DEATH OF MR. LOVE.

Mr. Love being ill desires his discharge from the Company's service
and leave to go to England on one of the Com-
August 15th.   pany's vessels; this was granted him, but he
became rapidly worse and could not go, and died at Calcutta on September 2nd.

398.—CLEARING THE GROUND BEFORE THE FORT.

"The Fort being very much choaked up and close set with trees
and small country thatched houses and standing
August 17th.   pools of stinking water, which having maturely
considered, we are of opinion that clearing them away and filling the
holes to level ground will contribute very much to the making of the
town wholesome and healthful."

"Therefore re-order the Buxie to open the way directly before the
Fort, continuing the present walk already made further into the open
field filling up all the holes and cutting small trenches on each side to
carry the water clear from the adjacent places into the large drains."

399.—OLD PLATE.

"There being among the Hon'ble Company's House plate belonging
to this factory, the greatest part very old, broken,
August 17th.   and useless, ordered an exact account be taken of
the weight, and that part of it be melted down and made into more
useful utensils for the service of the table."

400.—SLAVE GIRLS.

"Mr. Isaak Berkley having complained that Captain Payton detained a slave belonging to him, Captain Payton
August 21st.   was sent for and declared that Mr. Berkley had in
like manner had a slave belonging to him; therefore 'tis agreed that
Mr. Berkley deliver Captain Payton his slave by name Barbara, and
that he return Mr. Berkley his slave by name Lucretia."

401.—SELLING OFF OLD RICE.

"There being in the Company's store-house a quantity of rice which
is in a decaying condition, and rice being very
August 24th.   scarce among the inhabitants of this place, order
the Buxie [*Bakhshī*] to dispose thereof at 1 maund 10 seers per rupee,
and when the new rice comes in buy up more for a store and to
upply the coasts."

402.—ARRIVAL OF ROBERT HEDGES.

Mr. Robert Hedges arrived in Calcutta, also five covenant servants,
two merchants and three writers. Mr. Hedges
took his place as second in Council.

August 29th.

403.—RECEIVED AS A WRITER.

Mr. Mathew Delgardno, son of Mr. Alexander Delgardno, is
received as one of the Company's writers; he
is to be employed in the Secretary's office and
to receive the customary salary of five pounds per annum.

September 4th.

404.—COST OF CLEARING THE GROUND.

"Mr. John Calvert, jemindar [*zamīndār*], brought in an account of
the charges of houses pulled, removed, and
pulled down, to clear the new way now making,
amounting to Rs. 109-14. Ordered that the Buxie pay the same. '

September 4th.

405.—VISIT FROM THE FAUJDĀR OF HUGLI.

The Faujdār of Hugli comes to return a former visit. "Resolved
that we treat him with all the respect and civility
due to him on this occasion and prepare a present
for him suitable to his quality."

September 10th and 11th.

406.—ZAMĪNDĀRI ACCOUNTS FOR JULY.

The July accounts of the bazar and the three
towns were passed, the balance being Rs. 1,431-4-5.

September 15th.

407.—LOVE'S HOUSE AND GARDEN.

"Mr. James Love, lately deceased, had a garden and small house,
which lies very convenient for the Company's
use. Resolved we purchase the same for the
Company."

September 15th.

408.—REPAIRS AT HUGLI.

Mr. William Spencer and one of the Company's writers are sent to
Hugli, with orders to repair the Company's house
there and remain in it till further orders from
the Council.

September 25th.

409.—A REBELLIOUS CREW.

The Council decides the case of the officers and men on board one of
their ships who refused to obey their Captain on
account of his brutal treatment of them. The
Council seem to have thought the officers and men in fault; but if

October 2nd.

they were punished and sent away from the ship, it would be impossible to man the ships again in Calcutta. Hence they resolved to compromise the matter. All the officers and men agreed to go on board again if the Captain would give his word to treat them better. The only man who held out was the second mate, who was ordered to be kept a prisoner in the Fort until he could be sent to England.

410.—ESCORT FOR THE PATNA FLEET.

Soldiers are sent up to meet the Patna Fleet and bring it safely to
October 26th.   Calcutta.

411.—A SAR-O-PĀ FROM FARRUKH SIYAR.

"The Governor of Hugli advised us the beginning of last week
November 6th. that he had received a favourable letter from Furuckseer [Farrukhsiyar], the present Emperor's grandson at Rojamahal, with a surpaw [sar-o-pā] for the Hon'ble President, which he desires might be delivered at Hugli. Therefore on Wednesday last the Hon'ble President, accompanied by Messrs. Hedges, Chitty, Blount, and several others, went up and paid the Nabob a visit, and (the President) received the surpaw and letter with a fine horse of Rs. 1,000 value and returned again on Friday."

When the Council had read the letter from the Prince, which was very favourable, they agreed to write to the Prince, and send him a present, as he is the son of the favourite son of the Emperor and might therefore help them procure a farmān.

412.—ZAMĪNDĀRĪ ACCOUNTS FOR AUGUST AND SEPTEMBER.

The accounts for the bazar and the three towns for the months of
November 9th. August and September were brought in and passed, the balance being, August, Rs. 988-5-4, September, Rs. 1,415-11-2.

413.—RELIEF TO THE POOR.

"Mrs. Cary, widow, having made application to us for relief, being
November 23rd. very poor and needy, ordered the Minister and Church Wardens pay her Rs. 30 monthly for her subsistence, and to Mrs. Dorothy King (widow) Rs. 20 per month, and for the future that they shall give no stated allowance or maintenance to any other poor person without the consent of the Hon'ble President and Council."

ADDENDA.

ADDITIONAL EXTRACTS

FROM THE

INDIA OFFICE RECORDS.

---◆---

414.—ADVICE TO THE ROTATION GOVERNMENT. [1]

Consultation.

January 31st, 1703-4.   At a consultation present:—

The Hon'ble John Beard, Esq. ... *Presidt.*

Mr. Ralph Sheldon.

„ John Russell.

„ Edward Pattle.

Messrs. Hedges, Sheldon and Councill for the United Trade signifying their readyness to receive charge of the Garrison and the United Dead-Stock, order'd that it be deliver'd them this morning, and that all the soldiers, servants, and inhabitants be summoned, which was accordingly done, they also signifying their intention to proceed for Hugly to receive the Dead-Stock of that Factory, when done, that they shall acquaint the Moors Government that they are to manage the affairs of the English in Bengall, and if we had anything to offer thereon for the benefit of the Old Company that they were willing to prosecute it, conformable to their orders.   We have therefore thought fit to give them the following Memoir in relation to their making application to the Government, and that they would take particular care of the Old Company's affairs, not to detriment them in anything whatever.

Letter.

To Messrs. Robert Hedges and Ralph Sheldon and the rest of the Councill for the management of the United Trade—

Gentlemen—'Tis our opinion that you be not over-hasty to go to the Government but let each Company's Vacqll. give answer when they

---

[1] Old Company's Diary, 1703-4.

are askt that the two Companys are joyn'd and the business to be done
in Calcutta that all priviledges granted to either party is now become
the United, and the affairs of this shipping is left to the Councills of
both. Expecting a President to be instituted by next shipping which
we expect to arrive in three or four months, and their seal is to be
order'd with the Company's inscription for their dusticks and passports
which shall be sent them with the Vacqll. who is alone to tend the
Durbar, least by other application each affair may be embroiled.

Vera Copia.

JOHN CALVERT, Secy.

415.—TONNAGE AND PASS MONEY. [1]

The Secretary paid into the Right Hon'ble Company's cash, viz.
Charles King for a license to keep a public
12th April, 1704, Wednesday. house of entertainment one hundred and fifty
rupees.

To two-thirds of a pass to ship *St. Martin*, burthen one hundred
tons, belonging to Cojah Matroos, bound for Acheen, Francisco Newins,
master, the sum of ten rupees. To two-thirds of a pass to ship
Romence, burthen two hundred and seventy tons, belonging to Mahmood
Tuckee, bound for Gombroon, the sum of fourteen rupees. To tonnage
of ship *Monsoon*, one hundred and thirty rupees, and two-thirds of a
pass, ten rupees, belonging to the Hon'ble President bound for Gombroon, Captain Child, Commander. To two-thirds of a pass to ship
Tawockall, burthen one hundred and fifty tons, belonging to Allie
Rajah, bound to Persia, ten rupees. To tonnage of ship *Commerce*,
burthen fifty tons, fifty rupees, and two-thirds of a pass, ten rupees,
belonging to the Hon'ble President, Benjn. Hemming, Master, bound
for Madras, in all three hundred eighty-four rupees.

416.—THE PILOT SERVICE. [2]

A List of Pylotts, Masters, Seamen and Lascars, belonging to the
Company's Vessels</i> (viz.)</div>

April 16th, 1704.

				Rs. A. P.	Rs. A. P.
Stephen Shaw	...	...	...	45 0 0	
John Rainbow	...	...	...	45 0 0	
					90 0 0

1 Old Company's Diary, 1704-5.
2 Diary of the United Trade Council, 1704.

Thomas Harris, reserved in pay to send him
    when the season permitts in a sloop for
    Madras

				Rs. A. P.	Rs. A. P
Thomas Harris, reserved in pay to send him when the season permitts in a sloop for Madras				...	30 0 0

London Yacht.

				Rs. A. P.	Rs. A. P
Thomas Morris [Master]	...	...		30 0 0	
Timothy Kissum [Boatswain]	...	...		20 0 0	
Richard Dean	...	...	...	12 0 0	
1 Tindell	...	...		7 0 0	
7 Lascars	...	...		35 0 0	
					104 0 0

Mary Buoyer.

John Mander [Master]	...	...		40 0 0	
Thomas Holbridge [Boatswain]	...	...		30 0 0	
Daniell Wilkinson	...	...	...	22 0 0	
1 Tindell ...	...	...	...	7 0 0	
10 Lascars ...	...	...	...	50 0 0	
					149 0 0

Sloop Kassimbazar.

Josia Townsend [Master]	...	...		35 0 0	
Daniell Holsten [Boatswain]	...	...		20 0 0	
Titus Oakes ...	...	...	...	20 0 0	
1 Tindell ...	...	...	...	7 0 0	
9 Lascars ...	...	...	...	45 0 0	
					127 0 0

Rising Sun, 1 Tindell and 2 Lascars,	½ pay ...	...	6 0 0	
William, Smack, " "	½ " ...	...	6 0 0	
Charles and Betty, " "	½ " ...	...	6 0 0	
Phillip Finch at Rs. 12 per month ...	...	...	12 0 0	
			530 0 0	

417.—MURDER OF RICHARD NICOLLS. [1]

Complaint.

Captain Finch Reddall, Commander of the *Samuel and Anna*, complaining that last night his third mate, William
Harriot, and his cooper, Richard Nicolls, were
assaulted in the highway by some Blackmen, that Harriot got off with
little hurt, but that Nicolls was barbarously mangled, his leg broke and

July 20th, 1704.

---

[1] Diary of the United Trade Council, 1704,

his wound so desparate that his discovery [? recovery] is dispared of, on which we thought necessary to make what enquiry we could into the matter.

Enquiry.

Nathll. Jones, boatswain of the Sloop *William*, Richd. Dean, a sailor aboard the sloops, and James Harris, late a soldier, appeared as witnesses. Harriot declares that about midnight or a little after, he together with Richd. Nicolls were going from King's punch-house, and near James Harris his house, he saw an old man sitting without his door, and they sat down by them to enquire if any of the shipsmen were [?there], but not hearing of any they rose to go away, but had not gone far before they were assaulted by four men, three of which were armed with swords and staves, thus much he said. Nathll. Jones and Richard Dean declare that they were in bed at James Harris his house, they heard a noise of quarrelling in the street, and went to see what the matter was. When they were out they heard Nicolls groan and call out he was murdered; they also saw five men striking at Nicolls as he lay on the ground unable to rise.

They both say Assuria was one that assaulted Nicolls by calling and bidding them strike him, also that Woojolle ['Uj 'Alī] was in company with a club in his hand, but neither of them saw him strike, also that Janno [Jānī], a peon, not taken, was one of them that struck him. Richd. Dean says that Abdullreaheen ['Abdu-r-Rahīm] was among them, and he saw him strike Nicolls as he lay on the ground.

Jeronima says he saw and knew Janne (not yet taken) also Abdullreaheen armed and strike Nicolls; he also saw Woojolle with a staff in his hand, but did not see that struck.

Woojolle testifies that he saw Assuria and Janne strike Nicolls as he lay on the ground.

James Harris declares that he had been abroad, and was returning between twelve and one a clock to his house, but near his own house he mett three men, two of which were armed with clubs, and the other with a lance, but he did not see their faces so as to know them. The man with the lance knockt with the end of his lance at the door of Lollen's [Nalin's] house to call people out, Harris was not long within his doors before he heard the noise of quarrelling, and an English voice call out saying 'O Lord! O Lord! I am murdered,' on which he went to the Banksaul not far from his house to call for assistance. On the arrival of which the assaulters ran severall ways, escaped, leaving Nicolls with a broken leg and very much bound and wounded.

Jones and Dean further say that Janne called for ropes and sayed he would cut Nicolls in pieces, then bind and carry him to the Governor at Hugly.

Jones says that when he saw Nicolls lie on the ground, as he thought he was dead, he desired the fellows rather to strike himself than to add more blows to the man they had so much abused already, and they struck at him, but before Jones got any harm, assistance came from the Banksaul which frighted the rogues, so each man ran a several way and escaped being taken at that time. The old man at whose door Harriot and Nicolls sat down by him is Allabux ['Alī Bakhsh], the father of Abdullreahee, and he was the beginner and fomenter of the assault. Ordered that Allabux, Assuria Abdullreaheen, and Doud [Dāūd] be kept in safe custody.

Examination of Jānī.

Jannee, the peon, yesterday accused of being a principal actor in the
July 21st.
assault of Richd. Nicolls, was last night taken and now brought on his examination. Richard Dean knows him to be one he saw very active in striking Nicolls when down for dead.

Nathll. Jones also knows him, and says he is the man that struck at himself when he endeavoured to perswade him to forbear striking Nicolls.

Woojolle, a Moor, also knows him, and saw him strike Nicolls. Jeronima says he saw Janne strike Nicolls on the breast as if he designed to kill him.

Ordered that Janne, Allabux, Assuria and Abdullreaheen be secured in irons; but Doud be secured without irons.

418.—WILL OF JONATHAN WHITE[1].

Mr. Jonan. White, second of this place, deceased the 23rd January
November 14th, 1704.
last, enquirey was made whither any will was left behind to appoint any person or persons to look after his affairs, and none being found his wife was advised to take letters of administration out of the Court of Admiralty at Fort St. George. But there being a paper wrote with his own hand, as very well known to us, but without date interlin'd nor firm'd or

---

[1] Old Company's Diary, 1703-4.

seal'd, the executors mentioned would not act, however, we thought
fit to have it enter'd next to this consultation.

WILL.

In the name of God, Amen. I, Jonan. White, now residing in
Calcutta in Bengall, Factor to the Rt. Hon'ble. Company of Merchants of London, trading to the East Indies being at the writing
hereof in health of body and sound memory, but considering the
uncertainty of this mortall life doe make this my last will and testament in manner following, revoking all other wills by me heretofore
made. And first and principally I recommed my soul into the hands
of Almighty God, my heavenly father and Jesus Christ His only son,
my blessed saviour and redeemer, trusting by and through his meritts,
death, and passion to obtain everlasting life, my body I commit to the
earth, to be decently buried at the discretion of any executors hereafter
named, and for the worldly estate it has pleased God to bless me with
I give and devise and bequeath the same as follows.

First my will and mind is I doe hereby give and bequeath unto my
brother William White as a legacy the sum of two thousand rupees
currt. of Bengall.

Item.—I give and bequeath unto my sister Elizabeth King the sume
of one hundred current rupees, and to brother John King, her husband,
the adventure sent in his hands to Mocha and the profits thereof.

Item.—I give unto sister Elizabeth Bowridge, her daughter Elizabeth,
and sister Elizabeth Meverell each fifty rupees to buy them rings.

Item.—I give and bequeath unto Mrs. Boyd forty rupees.

Item.—I give and bequeath unto the Hon'ble John Board, Mr.
Ralph Sheldon, Mr. Benjamin Adams, and .Mr. Thomas Wright
of Fort St. George a ring of fifty rupees a piece, and Mr. Samuel
Feake of Bengall one hundred rupees.

Item.—I give and bequeath unto my uncle Abraham Spooner,
couzin Richard Glover, and his lady, couzin John Hungerford, Esq.,
and his lady, each rings of twelve rupees vallue a piece.

Item.—I desire and appoint the Hon'ble John Beard, Presidt.,
and Ralph Sheldon of Councill for the Right Honourable Company's
affairs in Bengall, to be the executors of this my last will and
testament.

Item.—I will and appoint that my body be interr'd near my late wife
in her Father's Toomb, and that a Toombstone of about one yard
square be engraved in the usuall manner and sett up in said toomb.

Item.—I give unto my servants, Killeram, Annuntram Siddo, Chunee, Beatrice, and Maria my former slaves each twenty rupees.

Item.—I give and bequeath unto my wife the other one Third part of all my personall estate that shall be found to remain and appertain unto me after the discharge of my just debts, &c., as above said, including therein the house, household necessarys, plate and jewells and pallankeen that she may be desirous to possess, which shall therefore be estimated by my executors.

Item.—I give, devise, and bequeath unto my daughter two-thirds of all such estate (debts, legacies and funeral charges being deducted) as I shall at the time of my death dye seiz'd or possessed of, interested in or entitled unto.

Item.—If it please God to give my wife a safe delivery of a child my intent and meaning is and I doe hereby devise and bequeath unto the said child one-third part of all my estate, that is to say, the moiety or half part of what bequeathed my daughter Katherine, and if either happen to decease during their minority or nonage the moiety or portion thus bequeathed shall descend to the survivor.

Item.—My will and request is that my daughter Katherine be sent, for England for education with good attendance and provision for soe tender an infant the voyage, and that the executors accept of soe good an opportunity to accompany her aunt Bowridge if she goes for England in two years time, otherwise that the child goe by such good commanders of a ship as my executors shall see fitting, and then if it please God the child arrive in England is to be committed to my couzin Mary Hungerford and my brother, to whose care and guardianship joyntly with my brother William White I recommend the child during her nonage.

Vera Copia.

JOHN CALVERT, *Secty.*

419—DISPUTE IN THE CURGENVEN FAMILY.[1]

Application by John Curgenven.

"Received a letter from Mr. John Curgenven desiring we would write to his sister to suffer him to inspect his deceased brother's books and papers of accounts, etc."

May 17th, 1705.

"Wrote a letter to Mrs. Rachell Curgenven, desiring her to comply with her brother's desire."

---

[1] Diary of the United Trade Council, 1705 —See also pp. 263, 373.

Rachel Curgenven's complaint.

Mrs. Rachell Curgenven, the widdow of |Mr. Thomas Curgenven deceased, making complaint to us about five of the clock of the evening that the house she lives in, and particularly her bed chamber, was forcibly entered and all her clothes and necessaries taken out by Mr. John Curgenven, brother of the deceased Mr. Thoˢ Curgenven, assisted by Mr. John Calvert and Mr. Richard Smith. The complaint first reaching Mr. Ben. Bowcher he went, and quickly after him Mr. Robert Hedges went to Mrs. Curgenven's house, where Mr. John Curgenven, Mr. John Calvert, and Mr. Richard Smith aforesaid were, Mr. Calvert said nothing at that time, but Mr. Curgenven and Mr. Smith stood on the justification of what was done, they lockt and sealed a chamber door in which they said all that Mr. Curgenven had seized was put, and Mr. Hedges ordered two soldiers to wait in the house and see nothing be removed till the Council meet and direct what is to be done. And being now mett, 'tis unanimously agreed and ordered that Mr. John Curgenven, Mr. Jno. Calvert, and Mr. Richᵈ Smith be immediately sent for and examined about the same.

May 23rd.

John Curgenven's statement.

Mr. John Curgenven being first called for says, in justification of himself, that he had applyed himself to us for justice which he thought we delayed, therefore would right himself, which obliges us to insert the application he speaks of and 'tis in substance as follows.—Mr. John Curgenven in a letter dated and deliv'd to us in Councill on Thursday 17th currᵗ, desires his sister may be informed that he has as much power as she and perswaded to have the books of his brother and her deceased husband made up and to give him an account of what she had already disposed of, and that Councill did the same day, in complyance with his request, write to Mrs. Rachell Curgenven, declaring he ought to have the inspection of the books of accounts and all papers whatsoever relating to the estate of her deceased husband, and she ought to give him a satisfactory account of whatsoever goods she had disposed of, of the estate of her deceased husband, which was all he seemed to desire at that time.

We expected an answer from her, but he being impatient, could not wait a day or two longer till her answer came, but violently seiz'd on everything in her possession, as is before related.

Richard Smith's statement.

Mr. Smith being next called in says Mr. Curgenven call'd him to take account of and wittness what he removed, but both Mr. Hedges and Mr. Bowcher do testifie he was very active in councilling Mr. Curgenven; for instance he said he ought to let her have more wearing cloathes out of the chest, but nothing else. Mr. Bowcher also testifies, and so does Mr. Ralph Woodriffe, that they saw Mr. John Curgenven force open the door of Mrs. Curgenven's bed-chamber, which they believe was lock'd being close shut and a spring look on it, but Mr. Smith affirming the contrary, Mr. Hedges caused the door to be lock'd to try if it could be forced open without breaking the door or lock, and was twice forced open without breaking either. Mr. Smith spoke reflectingly on us all, saying we were friends of the widdow and not to justice, but he reflected most on the widdow, telling Mr. Bowcher if he believed her, nobody would believe him, and he called her a notorious lyar with much more such ungenteal expressions. He at last told us he would not answer us to any more questions till we were a full Councill.

John Calvert's statement.

Mr. John Calvert was called in. He says Mr. John Curgenven desired him to go with him to be a witness, but he absolutely refuses to answer further till a full Councill meets.

Let us wait for a full Council.

On the consideration of all which 'tis resolved and unanimously agreed, that Mr. Bowcher and Mr. Edwd Pattle do take Mr. John Curgenven with them, also Mr. James Williamson and Mr. Ralph Emes for witnesses, and in their presence, take an account of all they find of what Mr. Curgenven seized on, and after that account is taken and attested by the witnesses present, they are to deliver to Mrs. Rachell Curgenven, her wearing clothes and such other necessaries as she has present occasion for.

Ordered that further consideration of this matter be deferr'd till the rest of the Councill come from Hugly, or at least till a majority is present.

John Curgenven obstructive.

Messrs. Bowcher and Pattle, as ordered in yesterday's consultation,

May 24th. sent for Mr. Jno. Curgenven and desired him to go along with them to take an account of the

A A

goods he had seized, but he declared he would not permitt them to open the door or take an account of anything.

Full Councill.

Mrs. Curgenven's letter to the Councill being before us, the person, accused were sent for and examined. Their exami-
June 2nd. nations are annexed to this consultation, and consi-
dering that the widdow has been abused, for her present satisfaction 'tis thought fit that Mr. John Curgenven, in the presence of Mr. Ben. Bow-cher and Mr. Edw. Pattle, do deliver the plate and goods taken out of her bed-chamber into the said bed-chamber again, into her possessions according to the list already taken, and that she deliver up the books and all papers relating to Mr. Curgenven's estate, into their possession, to be seal'd up in Mr. Curgenven's scrutore till persons are agreed on and appointed to adjust the said Curgenven's books, by which all things may be cleared and the account of what goods belonging to said Curgenven's estate in said house be taken by them and that she as speedily as possible, do deliver into the Councill an exact account of everything she has dis-posed of belonging to the said Curgenven's estate, that the said account may be delivered John Curgenven for satisfaction according to his former application and that Mrs. Curgenven is askt immediately on deli-very of each chest or scrutore whether she has rec^d the contents of each, and if she makes exceptions, that then they immediately overlook such chest or scrutore, and take a particular account of everything therein, and when the whole is delivered, she is to acknowledge the same for a discharge to said Curgenven, but in the case she makes exceptions of want of anything of value, that she will not give the said Curgenven a discharge for the whole taken away, then the goods are to be kept entire, as they are and not to be deliver'd her till farther order.

Widow Curgenven's letter.

To the Honble Councill for affairs to the United Eng^l East India Comp^y in Fort William, Bengall.

Gentlemen,

I suppose by this time you have all heard the story I am going to relate, but because 'tis fitt you should be acquainted with all the circum-stances of it, and especially from me, who am the sufferer in it, be pleased to take it as follows, viz^d : —

On Wednesday about 4 in the afternoon, being in the house of my deceased husband Mr. Tho. Curgenven, and in my bed-chamber, Mr. Jno.

Curgenven, together with Mr. John Calvert and Richd Smith, came into my said bed-chamber, and then and there the aforesaid John Curgenven demanded of me the keys of all my chests, boxes, scrutories, for that he said he must take an account of all that I had. I knew of no authority that obliged one to satisfy such unreasonable demands, so refused him the keys, upon which Mr. Calvert and Mr. Smith told me they had an order to remove all my goods into my brother's possession; that I must not think it hard, he must have the use and possession of them scince I had enjoyed them so long, so to work they went as fast as they could to remove my goods. I desired them to forbear till I could get Mr. Bowcher or somebody to take an account of what they carried away, but finding nothing would prevail, I made all the resistance I was able. But the aforesaid John Curgenven with a naked sword in his hand pointed to my breast, uttering several horrid oaths, said that if I touch'd or meddled with anything or call'd anybody to my assistance he would stab me, and if Mr. Bowcher came into the house, he would run him through. Upon this I went to Mr. Bowcher and beg'd him for God's sake to come and see how barbarously I was used. By that time I came back, they had conveyed away all my plate, jewels, ready money, bonds, bills, and other writings, to a great amount, almost most part of my other household goods, insomuch that scarce anything was left me in my bedchamber except a chest of drawers in which my clothes lay. Upon Mr. Bowcher coming, my brother and he having some dispute, I got possession of my bed-chamber and lock'd the doors in hopes keeping my wearing apparell, but John Curgenven soon broke open my door and took hold of my chest of drawers, and because I opposed him carrying of it away, laid violent hands on me and gave me such a blow with his fist as almost beat me backwards, at the same time threatening with a horrid imprecation if I touched anything he would beat my brains out; after this they lock'd up the door of my bed-chamber, so that I was forc'd to be beholden to a neighbour for a lodging that night and ever since, otherwise must have lain in the street. Thus I have been robb'd of all I had in the house, and not only so, but have been violently assaulted and put in fear of my life.

Gen^t I have barely related matter of fact, and that I have done without the least aggravation   sev^{ll} gen^t in this place will bear me wittness. These are crimes, gent^l of such a nature and consequence, and call so loudly for justice, that I can't in the least question that you, who by virtue of a charter from the Queen of England, have taken upon you the civill government of this place, will do me the Justice which I have a right too by the laws of our Native Country.

> I am gen^t yor obliged servant,
> RA. CURGENVEN.

Calcutta, May 26th, 1705.

Examination of John Curgenven.

Mr. John Curgenven being examined by Mrs. Ra. Curgenven's letter, his answer thereto is as follows, viz^d :—He acknowledges he demanded the keys (as the widdow mentions) in presence of Calvert & Smith, and she refused them.

He denies that Smith and Calvert spoke to the widdow that they had orders to take her goods and give them into his possession.

He says that he himself, or by his orders the Cooleys, removed the goods out of her bed-chamber into another room. He farther says his sister only said he should not remove them but that she would send for Mr. Bowcher.

He denys that he ever threatened his sister with a naked sword or presented it to her breast, or that he ever threatened Mr. Bowcher to run him through. He acknowledges that he removed some plate, sev^{ll} chests, and any jewels, bonds, or ready money.

He says that after Mr. Bowcher came into the house, she went into the bed-chamber with one slave wench, and he finding the door shutting too, he set his foot against it, and forc't it open, & he acknowledges he took the chest of drawers and sev^{ll} other things and put them into the chamber aforesaid.

He denies that ever he set violent hands on her or struck her a blow, or ever he threatened to beat her brains out, with any horrid Imprecations.

He says he lockt the door within side and went through another chamber and lockt the outward door, but had not the key of her bed-chamber.

Mr. Curgenven was askt the following question, viz^d—

Q.—Who counselled you to remove the goods?

A.—'Twas on my own head and my own act.

Q.—By what authority or by whose instigation did you seize and take away the goods out of your sister's room?

A.—'Twas to secure myself, but had not any authority, nor was I persuaded thereto.

Q.—Were not the books in your possession or where you could come at them when you wrote to the Councill about getting the accounts, ect., adjusted ?

A.—I could come at them then.

Examination of John Calvert.

Mr. John Calvert being examined by Mrs. Ra. Curgenven's letter, his answer thereto is as follows, viz^d : — He says he was not in her bed-chamber when Mr. Curgenven demanded the keys of her chest, ect., but that he heard him demand them and said he came to take an account of all she had, but she denied him the keys.

He denies that ever he told her he had orders to put all her goods into her brother's possession.

He says he never heard her say she desired him or them to stay till Mr. Bowcher came to take an account of what they carried away.

He denies that he ever heard John Curgenven threaten to stab her or saw him present a naked sword at her breast, or that he said if Mr. Bowcher came he would run him through.

He also says he saw no jewels, ready money, bonds, bills, or other writings, carried away, only some plate, chests, ect., contents not known and put them into another room in the same house.

He says he cannot be positive whether the door was lockt or n^{t}t, but Mr. Curgenven hearing the door shutting too, turned abo^t set his foot against it and pushed it open, a slave wench standing behind at the same time.

He also says that he did not see Mr. Curgenven strike her or lay hands on her or use any imprecations, saying he would beat out her brains.

Mr. Jno. Calvert was askt the following questions, viz^d :—

Q.—Why did you go to the house with Mr. Curgenven ?

A.—At his request to witness what past.

Q.—Who took an account of the things that were moved?

A.—I took an account of everything that was taken out for my own satisfaction, being not desired thereto, the chests and scrutores not being then open

Examination of Richard Smith.

Mr. Smith's answer to Mrs. Curgenven's letter :—He says he was in her bed-chamber with Mr. Curgenven and heard him demand the keys of her chests, ect., saying he must take an account of all she had, she at the same time refusing the keys.

He says he never assisted or helped any one to remove any goods out of her bed-chamber or elsewhere.

He never heard her say anything to desire her brother or them to stay till Mr. Bowcher or any one came to know or take an account of what they carried away.

He says Mr. Curgenven did not present a sword at her breast, nor utter any oaths, that if she called in any one to her assistance, he would stab her. Neither did he hear him say that if Mr. Bowcher came into the house, he would run him through. He also says he saw no jewels, ready money, bonds, bills, or other writings. There was only some plate, chests and scrutores being not opened, which were carried out of her bed-chamber and put into another chamber in the same house.

He says that the widdow with her slave wench went into the room after Mr. Bowcher came there, her slave wench shutting the door. Mr. Curgenven sett his foot against the door and forced it open, but he knows not certainly whether the door was lockt or not, but to what he saw he thought it might not be lockt.

He says he never saw Mr. Jno. Curgenven strike her or lay violent hands upon her, or threaten her with any imprecations to beat her brains out if she toucht anything.

Mr. Smith was askt the following questions:—

Q.—Why did you go to the house with Mr. Curgenven ?

A.—It was at his request, that I might see what past that there might be nothing more laid to his charge than he really did.

Q.—Did you take an account of any goods that were removed or attested that an account was taken ?

A.—I took no account myself, but witnessed the account that was taken and saw 'twas right.

Mrs. Curgenven put in possession.

Mr. John Curgenven being called and desired to go with Mr. Bowcher and Mr. Pattle & deliver the goods back into the possession of Mrs. Ra. Curgenven which he irregularly seiz'd and took from her, he seemed resolv'd to stand on his own justification & not deliver back anything. 'Tis therefore unanimously agreed & ordered that Mr. Robᵗ Nightingale and Mr. Edward Pattle do put her in possession as last consultation ordered, tho' Mr. Curgenven should refuse to consent or go with them.

June 4th.

Mr. Robert Nightingale and Mr. Edward Pattle according to order of consultation of this day went to Mrs. Rachell Curgenven's house and sent for Mr. John Curgenven to be present at the delivery of the goods (he had seized) to Mrs. Rachell Curgenven.

John Curgenven still recalcitrant.

Mrs. Rachell Curgenven relict of Mr. Tho⁸ Curgenven, having, 28th ult. sent us the account of goods left in her

July 2nd.

possession by her deceased husband, that is to say, of what she had disposed of and what still remains with her, the account was sent to Mr. John Curgenven, brother of the deceased, by Mr. Pattle, Sect^ry, but Mr. Curgenven refused to look into it, pretending the Councill took the management out of his hands, which we declare we neither did nor intended to do, neither did we any action tending to it, but his pretence arises from our opposing his seizing, without any reasonable pretence, on everything that she had wherever he could find it, not excepting her wearing apparell, and because he might not take the violent course that seemed best in his own conceit, resolves not to trouble himself with any of the accounts & there being sev^ll debts due from the deceased Tho^r Curgenven to the Old Comp^y Mr. John Johnson deceased and others, which are demanded, Mr. John Curgenven was askt whether he would give his consent to the dwelling-house of his deceased brother, ect. goods & chattles might be sold, in order to the payment of the debts, he answered he would have nothing to do, nor give any orders about it, but that we might do as we pleased.

Mrs. Rachell Curgenven having, in a letter delivered to us, 16th of this present July, requested that the dwelling-house

July 19th.

and some merchandize of Mr. Tho⁸ Curgenven's deceased (her late husband), may be sold in order to the payment of debts due from the estate of her deceased husband, she having already desired the concurrance of Mr. John Curgenven (Brother of the deceased) in writing, & his reply to her that he would give her no answer, Mr. John Curgenven was sent for, who, appearing, was askt whether he would consent that the house and merchandize of his said deceased brother be sold in order to the discharging debts, and whether he would take any care to appoint anybody to make up the books, to which he refused to give any answer, only that we had askt him the same question before, and we knew what he answered then, & he would say no more now, which last answer was the second of this last July; in these words, he will have nothing to do nor give any order about it, but that

we might do as we pleased, that Mr. John Curgenven might have time
to consider very well whether he resolves obstinately not to give any
other answer about the disposall of his deceased brother's house, ect.,
goods, resolved that he be sent for again to answer before us next Monday or the first day we meet in consultation.

They dispose of the property in spite of John Curgenven.

Mr. John Curgenven sent for a third time to know his resolution
whether he would do anything in the disposing
of the estate of his deceased brother joyntly with
his sister, to which he answered as before that he would not concern himself with it.   Agreed that since Mr. John Curgenven will not comply
with his sister for the selling of the house, ect., clearing his debts, ect.,
depending accounts belonging to the deceased Thomas Curgenven (notwithstanding our perswations [*sic*] & directions) that we write to Mrs.
Curgenven a letter advising her to sell the house and dispose of the
goods, ect., belonging to her deceased husband, in order to pay the black
merchants and others, adjusting all things in this place relating to said
estate.

July 23rd.

It being ordered the 23rd day that Mrs. Rachell Curgenven may
dispose of the late dwelling-house & other goods
in her possession of her deceased husband, ordered
that Mr. Nightingale and Mr. Pattle do take the seal off the scrutore
containing the writings, which were sealed up by order in a former consultation and deliver the same up to her, that she may be able to have all
accounts relating to the estate of her deceased husband adjusted.

July 30th.

Money from Mr. Gulston Addison of Madras.

A letter from Mrs. Rachell Curgenven, complaining that her brother
John Curgenven had detained the money in Capt
Bolton's possession that came from Mr. Addison at
Madrass.

August 20th.

Wrote a letter to Capt Bolton, Commd^r of the 'Loyall Cook,' to
deliver what money he has brought from Madrass (belonging to the
estate of Mr. Thomas Curgenven, dec^d) to the widdow, Rachel Curgenven."

420—THE BLACK SERVANTS UNDER THE ZAMINDAR.[1]

Mr. Ben. Bowcher having delivered in a paper desiring it may be
entered in the consultation book, ordered it be
entered after this consultation.

July 27th, 1705.

---

[1] Diary of the United Trade Council, 1705.

To the Honble Council for affairs
of the Honble United English
East India Company.

GENTLEMEN,

Since there has been so many abuses proved in the Black Servants
with relation to the Revenues of the three Towns and Buzzar under
my care I should be wanting to myself if I did not say something in
my own justification, be pleas'd therefore to take the following account.
Upon my first coming into the United Councill I was appointed *Jemi-dar* and to take care of the Comp^s Revenues, but being altogether a
stranger to that affair Mr. Sheldon recommended to me two persons, one
as a gen^ll bookeeper and the other as a generall supervisor, and these
two he told me were able and would give me such an account of all
matters as that the Comp^y should not be cheated or imposed upon. I
then took Mr. Sheldon to be my friend, so I accepted of his offer, but
not being an absolute master of the Language for my better information I employed a person as a Linguist and ordered the Black fellows
under me to let him inspect the Books, and be acquainted with all affairs,
tho' at the same time I took a strict account of the rest also; thus the
business to the best of my knowledge went currently and fairly on, and I
had the more reason to think so because the increase of the revenues is considerable more than the proportion arising from the new rents amountts
to; however it seems there have been abuses comitted, and my Linguist
has had a hand in them: but pray gentlemen let us trace this matter
up a little higher, and you will then see if it was in my power to prevent
what has been done, let us examine then upon what terms these two
creatures of Mr. Sheldons were imployed. The bookeeper purchases his
place with a bribe of fifty rupees, and who does not see whither this tends,
this fellow's place could not afford such a bribe unless he was connived
at in his Rogueries, and tis plain he was connived at till the spleen got
uppermost I mean above all consideration of justice and honour,
the other fellow had a task assigned him which looks very odly, he was
to give Mr. Sheldon an account what money the Comp^y was cheated
of, what share he got of it, and how the rest was divided. This fellow
then was originally designed to have a share in the booty, in order to
which he must make it his business to tempt others, and my linguist
among the rest, to be as great rogues as himself, and we are none of us
ignorant how easily any of these black fellows are tempted to play the
rogue, well but pray why is Mr. Sheldon to know of these abuses and
nobody else: why was not the Council acquainted with this matter

sooner ? If the design had been to serve the Company the sooner the
discovery had been made the better, for we all know that when these
black fellows get money into their hands tis a hazard whether
it be recovered again, and truly tis my opinion we had never
known but for what I am going to acquaint you with. The gen^{ll}
bookeeper was grown so impudent as to write letters in my name
without my knowledge, for which I discharged him about six months
ago, and tho' I then enquired of all the people, and perticu'arly of
Nunderam, the gen^{ll} supervisor, whither they knew of anything he had
cheated the Comp^y of that so I might take satisfaction before he
went off, yet I could hear of nothing to charge him with.—The
other fellow, what with the encouragement he had from others,
and what with the power was given him by me to enable him to have
a thorough insight into everything, grew so insolent that I could not
bear with him no longer, so about the begining of this month I discharged him also, and now out comes all the murder, for the next
consultation after turning out the last fellow Mr. Sheldon falls upon
me with all the violence imaginable for having done it without his
leave, and then he tells you that my Linguist, the Cattwall, and the other
two which I turned out, together with the Rent gatherers, had cheated
the Company to the amount of about Rs. 3,000, two hundred whereof
he says the gen^{ll} supervisor had brought him in severals parcells as
he shared it with the rest, and Mr. Sheldon says it is in his possession.
Gentlemen, this is two [*sic*] much money for the Comp^y to loose for want
of timely care to prevent it, and tis to be feared a good part of it will be
lost. I know not what Mr. Sheldon or others may think of this kind of
management, but I fancy that when our Honble Masters come to know
that Mr. Sheldon was all along from the begining acquainted with
those abuses which were carrying on to their prejudice, and never opened
his mouth about [it] till his spleen came to be moved, and that upon
so triviall an occasion as the turning out of a Black servant, they will
give him but little thanks for his pains. If Mr. Sheldon had consulted
either the interest of our Honble Masters or his own reputation he
would have made the Councill privy to those abuses before they were
gone so farr, and then he had fairly acquitted himself in doing what was
reasonable to have been expected from him, but such clandestine practices will sooner or latter leave a blot behind them. I shall not go
about to purge myself from these abuses any further than I have done
it, but I think I have some reason to complain I have been treated as if
I had had a hand in them, upon this discovery Mr. Sheldon desired that

the government of the Black people might be taken out of my hands, then I am excluded from having any share in examining the information; tis true I made no opposition to either of these because I would leave them no room to say that while I was in power none would dare to inform against me, but still these proceedings are to my dishonour, they lessen and disgrace me, and this is all that has been aimed at, for the Comp{ys} interest had been much better provided for by the way of prevention, and I believe if they lose any of the money which they have been cheated of they will charge the fault upon him that delayed the discovery, when he both could and ought to have made it sooner.

Gent., the reason why I have chosen to lay these matters before you in writing is because of the great disorders that are in our consultations, I mean our debatts are not free as they ought to be, particularly for my own part I have seldom or never had a fair hearing among you, so I desire this paper may be entred in the consultation book.

I am,

Gentlemen,

Your most humble servant,

BEN. BOWCHER.

FORT WILLIAM, *the* 26*th July* 1705.

"Mr. Benj. Bowcher wanting a Banian to serve under him in the jemidar's office, agreed that Jagurdass may be employed by him in that service."

August 16th, 1705.

421.—WILLIAM BUGDEN'S WILL.[1]

Mr. John Calvert, one of the Trustees of Mr. William Bugden, deceas'd, presented his last Will and Testament, wittnessed by Thomas Woodvill Richard Acton and Tho. Tymme. Mr. Acton being absent the other two were sent for and swore that they saw Mr. Wm. Bugden signe, seal, and publish his last Will and Testament in their presence, and that they wittnessed the same in the presence of each other.

October 2nd, 1710.

---

[1] Diary of the United Trade Council, 1710.

WILL

In the name of God, Amen. I, William Bugden, in the service of the Honble United English East India Company in Bengal, being of perfect mind and memory, knowing the uncertainty of life and certainty of death, do make this my last will and testament in manner follows.

First I recommend my soul into the hands of the Allmighty God that gave it and for my body to be buried in a Christian and decent manner as my overseers shall think fitt. Touching such wordly concerns were in it has pleased God Almighty to bless me with in this life I give and bequeath as follows. I give to Mrs. Eliz^a Turner, my most Honble Aunt in England, a gold ring of thirty Shillings vallue. I give to Mr. James Hunt and wife in England to each a gold ring of twenty shillings vallue, to Mr. James Taylor a ring of the like, and if married to his wife of the same value. To my brother, Mr. Edw Bugden, to his wife Theophila, and my brother Charles, his widdow, Mrs. Cornelia Bugden, to each a ring of fifteen shillings value and to each of them mourning. The remainder of my estate or what shall be found belonging to me I give to the four children of my dec^d brother, Mr. Chas. Bugden, to be eaqually divided amongst them, or to the survivors, and this to be improved as my trustees shall think fitt for their advantage and not to be paid them untill they come to years of discretion. Lastly I do appoint Mr. John Calvert and Mr. Stephen Shaw to be trustees to this my last Will and Testament, and to each of them I leave fifty rupees as a legacy, in witnness whereof I have hereunto sett my hand and seal. This 11th of March 1709-10.

WILLIAM BUDGEN (Seal).

Signed, sealed, published, and declared by Wm Bugden to be his last Will and Testament in the presence of us,

THO. WOODVILL.
RICH^d ACTON.
THO. TYMME.

I do attest this to be a true copie of the orign^l examined and ent^d by me.

S. BLOUNT.

422.—LETTER FROM CAPTAIN FRANCIS CHILD. [1]

FORT WILLIAM *in Bengala*,

the 5th of January 1709-10.

HON^D SIR,

Upon the recomendations of several persons of quality, members of Parliament who have known me for some years, and also of His Grace the Duke of Beaufort in a particular manner to Sir Thomas Cook I obtained a comison as Lieut^{nt} to comand one of the Companies at Benjar, but upon the news of the distruction of the settlement I was order'd to Bengala with only one serj^t and twenty men. The rest of my Company, consisting of 104 men, were dispers't to all the other factories in India, yet doe not blame any person but my own misfortunes in being obliged to part with above 80 brave men which were turned over to me by my friends in her Maj^s service. On or near the first of May 1708 I was called before their Honn^{rs} at Skinner's Hall, Mr. Bull then in the chair, who assured me of the favour of the Honble Court, and that they had a due regard to my deligence and industry in raising such a number of men, and the care I had in readily obeying all the orders I had from time to time, and that as soon as I arrived at Fort William I should be put at the head of a Company as usual in such cases. The Honble Court exprest themselves so much in my favour that when I was askt if I would if I desire anything more of the Court, I could not make any answer, for the Honble Court had assigned me all that my station could desire; and as a farther mark of their favour presented me with 25 guineas over and above all other equal gratuities, as the Honble Committee of shipping did £60 more in consideration of my raising 64 men over and above the 40 I was obliged to raise. Gentlemen, I must confess I had as much favour from the Honble Court of Managers as I could wish for; which was the maine encouragement I had to proceed soe long and tedious a voyage, not thinking or doubting of anything but the like treatment at Bengall, which I have found to be quite contrary. I know that the Board here (I suppose in it to excuse their ill-treating of me) have characterized me but indifferently; their objections I think to tedious to answer, only in generall that I have had the honour to bear Lieu^{nts} comision in the Queen's service, and think I have had very

---

[1] India Office Records. Unbound Papers (Packet 32.) To go with range 446, Vol. XI October 1715 to May 1716.

hard usuage here from a board of gentlemen, when they have not obeyed the orders and the comision you gave me. Your Honours I hope will pardon my plainesse when I acquaint you that I never had any command of a company since I have been here; therefore of consequence guilty of no fault in my post; and as to my studdying to please any private persons it was never my great care, only in the faithful discharge of my duty and the trust of it reposed in me; and as to my capacity I leave it to the world to judge. I can only acquaint your Honn^{rs} that I am subplanted by those persons that never had any comision before the honour of yours. When I first arived at Fort William the Councill told me that if I had arived before Captⁿ Miners I should have procurred, but as matters were there was but two Companios, and desired me to act as Ensign till they could have other opertunities to give me a company which I could not but resent, when I had your commison as well as your word for the performance of all, which was the occasion of all our future differences; for no person can believe that the Honble United East India Company will trappan or ensnare any gentlemen, but will perform their promisses in everything, and that no Englishman can be so base as to act in such a plot, that has been Ensign Lieut^t and Capt^{rs} in Her Maj^{tys} service, but would rather go to his native country, where he is sure of justice from so many Honourable and Worthy gentlemen. I humbly begg pardon for sending this long letter, and pray your Hon^{rs} to consider my case and to make me full satisfaction for all that I have suffer'd and lost by the Company's not performing their promises, and your orders that I command an entire company for the future, and to take post of every comision if it is not of an older date, I thinking it my right to preceed every other person that never had a command in the army, as is customary in all such cases, even in her Majesty's service. Which if your Honours will please to grant I will serve you faithfully. If your Honn^{rs} think me unreasonable I pray to be put for home by the first shipping.

I am,

your Honn^{rs} most humble and
most obed^t servant,

FR. CHILD.

To the Honble the Court of Managers of the United East India Company at the East India House in London.

SHIPPING LISTS[1]

OF THE

EAST INDIA COMPANY.

SHIPS TAKEN, LOST, BURNT, OR OTHERWISE DESTROYED.

FROM 1702 TO 1710.

Date.	Ship's name.	Tons.	By what means.
1	2	3	4
1702	Queen	320	Taken.
1703	Neptune	275	Lost.
	Dover	180	Taken.
1704	Hester	350	Lost.
	Albemarle ...	320	Lost.
1705	Edw. and Dudley ...	300	Taken.
	Bombay	300	Blown up.
1707	Herbert	210	Taken.
	Dispatch	110	Blown up.
1708	Godolphin	280	Lost.
	New George	400	Taken.
1709	Sherborne	400	Lost.
	Dutchess	430	Taken.
	Phœnix	400	Lost.
1710	Jane	180	Taken.

[1] Reprinted from the *Register of Ships of the East India Company* by Charles Hardy, a rare publication in the India Office Library.

EAST INDIA SHIPS WITH THEIR COMMANDERS, etc.

Season 1708-1709.

Voyage.	Ship's name.		Tonnage.	Commanders.		Consignments.
1	2		3	4		5
4	Godolphin	...	280	S. A. Rice ...	...	Bombay.
4	New George	...	400	James Osborne	...	Surat.
4	Tankerville	...	425	Ch. Newman	...	Surat.
4	Halifax	...	350	Hen. Hudson	...	Coast and Bay.
1	Heathcote	...	400	Joseph Tolson	...	,, ,,
3	Frederick	...	350	Rich. Phrypp	...	,, ,,
3	Loyal Bliss	...	350	Rort. Hudson	...	,, ,,
4	Loyal Cook	...	330	Jonathan Clarke	...	China.
4	Carlton	...	275	Geo. Littleton	...	Bombay and Benc.
2	Nathaniel	...	250	Jonathan Negus	...	Bencoolen.

1709-1710.

1	Blenheim	...	260	Abraham Parrott	...	Mocha.
1	King William	...	400	Nicholas Winter	...	Coast and Bay.
4	Europa	...	300	Humph. Bryant	...	,, ,,
1	Susannah	...	300	Richard Pumell	...	,, ,,
1	Bouverie	...	420	Hugh Raymond	...	,, ,,
1	St. George	...	450	Sam Goodman	...	,, ,,
3	Rochester	...	330	Francis Stames	...	China.
4	Mead	...	310	Daniel Needham	...	St. Hel. and Benc.
1	Sherborne	...	250	Henry Cornwall	...	Bencoolen.
3	Stringer Galley	...	250	Isaac Pyke	...	China and Mocha.
3	Dutchess	...	430	John Blacon	...	Surat and Persia.
1	Catharine	...	450	Edward Godfrey	...	Surat.
1	Phœnix	...	4J.0	Edward Pierson	...	,,

1710-1711.

3	Success	...	180	Thos. Clapham	...	Coast and Bay.
4	Windsor	...	200	Zacp. Tovey	...	Mocha.
1	Hester	...	250	Charles Kefar	...	China.
4	Howland	...	450	George Cooke	...	China and Mocha.
4	London	...	500	William Upton	...	Persia and Bom.
1	Dartmouth	...	440	Thos. Beckford	...	Coast and Bay.
3	Aurengzebe	...	450	Edmund Stacey	...	,, ,,
3	Averilla	...	300	Robert Hurst	...	,, ,,
1	Derby	...	450	Thomas Wotton	...	,, ,,
1	Juno	...	180	John Austin	...	Madras and Benc.
4	Toddington	...	230	Thomas Blow	...	St. Hel. and Benc.
1	Thistleworth	...	250	Daniel Small	...	Ditto.
4	Litchfield	...	400	James Lee	...	Bombay and Surat.
4	Montague	...	375	James Stoakes	...	,, ,,
2	Heathcote	...	400	Joseph Tolson	...	,, ,,

BENGAL

IN

GOVERNOR PITT'S CORRESPONDENCE.

The letter-books of Thomas Pitt[1] have been already extensively used by Sir Henry Yule in his edition of Hedges' Diary. I have however gone through them again, not so much with a view to discover materials for a life of Pitt, as to gain additional light on the history of the English in Bengal. The following is all that I have found worth noting.

1. Writing on the 4th May, 1700, to John Beard, Pitt says:—

"I send your Lady (to whom I give my service) [one p. of China silk mark^d J. B.][2] four potts of tea four jars of China sweetmeats two gammons of bacon and 20 potts of hogsue and if she please at any time to hon^r me wth her command for anything she wants in these parts I shall be very ready to serve her."

2. On the 8th May, 1700, Pitt writes the following letter to Khojah Sarhad :—

"   Fort St. George, May 8th, 1700.

To Cojah Sarade, Merch^t,
        in Bengale

The small acquaintance I have wth yor uncle Calender & you in England having seen you sev^{ll} times at Mr. Ongleys, makes me request yor favour and assistance to Mr. Griffith and Capt Hornett in the *Sedgewick* in which I am concerned, wee designing her for Persia, and hope by yor means to gett a good ffreight, she is a very good ship, and sails excellent well and good defence, she is but small soe must carry none but fine goods and hope there may be enough procured to lade her y^t she may depart in Septemb^r wch will be of great advantage to the freighters getting there early, and carrying soe small a quantity.

---

[1] British Museum, Add. MSS., 22842 to 22853.

[2] The words within square brackets are written in the margin.

I allsoe am sending downe a small ship for Moco when shall write you more att large. If I can serve you in any thing here you may att any time command y^r assured

friend to serve
you T. Pitt."

3. On the 10th April, 1700, Pitt wrote to Captain Alexander Delgardno asking him to pay back the money which he owed. On the 13th March, 1701, he writes to Thomas Curgenven saying that Delgardno is to be seized by the native government at Hugli.

4. On the 20th May, 1701, writing to Beard, he says:—

"If the interest of the Armenians cannot fill a ship for Manilla 'tis a sign that trade is little worth.........Your son is very well but has boils which is a sign of health. A letter from your mother Ivry I here inclose."

5. Writing on the 20th May, 1701, to Curgenven, he says:—

"I wish you may go to Dacca wch I take to be as advantageous a post as most in the Comp$^{a's}$ service."

6. On the 30th June, 1701, he sends a letter to Curgenven by "your brother who came out a soldier on the *Bedford*......I wonder y^r uncle would not send him out under better circumstances."

7. On the 9th July, 1701, to Robert Hedges:—

"Y^r brother Raynes sent me by the adventure from Surat some snuff for you."

8. On the same date to Beard:—

"Y^r mother and son is pretty well tho. uneasy under the present excessive hot weather wee now have & so am I too."

9. On the 26th July, 1702, writing to Beard, Pitt hopes he will "make a tolerable end of that troublesome business," i.e., the quarrel with the Mogul government...." My kinsman Halsey was very much in the wrong when he pressed the giving of money but a man in troubles is like one that is sick take anything for the present case without considering the consequences and that has been the unhappy temper of some of our predecessors and as to what you wrote that if the trade is not opened there may be a trade carried on underhand by the connivance of the Government who will be p^d for it and always ready to create us troubles for that end and doubtless 'twill raise a good

revenue to the Gov' of Hugly if he can have four rup. a chest for ophium and so in proportion for bales."

10.   On the 24th September, 1702, to Curgenven:—

"I recᵈ a letter from yʳ uncle per the *Colchester* in wᶜʰ was two parhs. I now send you in a paper apart. I suppose they are grounded from somewhat yᵗ you wrote the reasons thereof I desire to know yᵗ soe I may justify myselfe for I have reason to fear you have not dealt fairly by me, nor have made such due representation of my repeated kindnesses to you as I have justly deserved."

11.   On the 25th September, 1702, writing to Beard:—

"Your mother Ivory has been out of order some time butt your son is well and lusty."

12.   On the 5th November, 1702, to Beard again:—

"Wee are all beholding to you for the care you have taken in the *Rubies* business. I am glad the management of your ship *Monsoon* is to your satisfaction having done therein as if it had been all my own as alsoe in the sale of your peper & the returns thereof....I observe what you say was said in Bengala by Coja Surhaud about letting out the *Phenix*, & I am of his opinion....Your mother Ivry is indisposed but your son well."

13.   On the 7th November, to Sheldon:—

"The balance of your account with Mr. Whistler is paid to Mr. Affleck as advised.

I observe what you write about your government & 'tis much the same here all matters standing as when I last wrote having not as yet released our goods nor asked for a penny of money & if they do'nt do the former speedily I am thinking to fetch the goods from St. Thomas....Sir Ed. I believe is convinced by this time that there will be a union between the two compᵃˢ. The new Compᵃ nicked it in their uniting for here is a whole catalogue of misfortunes gone home to 'em. I hear that you are the top-gardener in Bengall and I am as well as I can imitating of you here for in our last trouble we extremely wanted garden trade, so am now contriving to have all within ourselves and should be extremely obliged to you if you would yearly furnish me with what seeds your parts afford. Beans, pease &c. they must be new & the best way to send 'em is in bottles well stopped for no manner of seed thrives here if it be the growth of the place, for it dwindles to nothing."

B B 2

14. On the 8th November, to Halsey:—

"I was glad to hear that you & y^r lady had gott clear of the Gov^t who I wish may not make it their practice for the future to seize our persons & estates upon all light pretences soever but now the two Compa.s are united hope they will call 'em to account for the same."

15. On the 8th December, 1702, to Beard:—

" Sir Ed. may talk of a Phirmand, tho. I am pretty sure he'l never get any....Dowd Cawn is come again within 3 leagues of this place designing as is reported to go against some Polligars....The 3rd instant your mother Ivory died.[1] Before when there was no probability of her recovery I enquired whether you had given any orders about your son & found you had to Mr. Affleck otherwise I would have taken charge of him till your further order. I also recommended to Mr. Affleck the care of your mother's concerns & write you fully thereof by this cossed which comes on purpose....I have wrote to Mr. Haynes about the Blunderbusses but to this day have had no answer to it but have lately refreshed his memory with another letter."

16. On the 5th January, 1702-3, to Beard:—

" Mr. Haynes acknowledges that he has had the 11 blunderbusses. ....Dowd Cawn is gone about 12 leagues distance into the country ransacking all where he comes....I should be extremely obliged to you if you w^d send me by all conveyances good store of garden seeds such as pease beans turnips carrets cabages water-melons &c. they must be new & the best way of putting them up is in bottles. The Armenian in the *Johanna* sent me a few, which I believe he had from Patna which proved very good."

17. On the 7th January, 1702-3, to Samuel Ongley, London:—

" My liesure time I generally spend in gardening and planting and making such improvements which I hope will tend to the Compa's advantage and the good of the whole place for that in a little time I hope the place will be able to subsist of itself without much dependance from the country for that in the late long siege we were not a little pinched for provisions."

18. On the 28th January, 1705-6, to Mr. John Affleck, London:—
"You'l hear that there has been a great mortality in Bengal and those escaped hither with their lives look most dismally more parti-

---

[1] The Madras Burial Register gives: "Elizabeth Ivory, buried December 2nd, 1702, by George Lewis."

cularly brother Harris. Poor Stratford died in Bengal. Mr. Boucher & Mr. Redshaw & Mr. Harris that married the widdow dyed here lately. Mr. Wright is married to Mrs. Beard & the other Mr. Wright goeing to marry Mrs. Hart which is all the news I now think of." [1]

19. On the 10th March, 1704-5, to Wm. Dobyns Esqre, Lincoln's Inn, London :—

" Few days past we had the ill news from Bengal of Mr. Curgenven's death who married y^r daughter in law, who as 'tis said have lately met with misfortunes in trade so I fear has left his widdow but in poor circ^s."

20. On the same date to Mr. Curgenven :—

" The *Dutchess* did not sail till Febr^y when I advised you of your nephew's death in Bengall and doe now of your nephew Thomas who died the 25th Dec^r, & as reported his affairs involved by overtrading himself. The other two brothers are n^r Acheen & speedily expected here to whom I will give my utmost assistance as also their brother's affairs to extricate them out of any trouble."

21. On the 27th September, 1705, to Wm. Dobyns of Lincoln's Inn :—

" I rec^d y^{rs} of the 29th Dec. last by the *Fleet* frigate who arrived here the 27th of June & know not how to answer every particular clearly relating to your son's affairs unless Mrs. Curgenven was here whom I expect in a little time. Her husband dying after I wrote you by the last ships copy of wch comes inclosed the account I sent you attested by my accountant is as authentic as if subscribed by myself. I can give you no other account of your son's estate but as it came to my hands for his transactions of it before was unknown to me....I wrote you formerly that the acc^t y^r son sent you was a sham acc^t & so declared by him. I believe his outcry was fair & just, for 'twas sold at the sea gate where those sort of shams can't be practised & I believe if the arrack had been worth a fanam more Germain had not had it. Your son in his sickness was pressed several times to make a will but could never be persuaded to it and I believe the widow delivered up all his effects to which she took her oath as advised in my last letter."

---

[1] The Register of Marriages at Madras in the India Office gives : "January 6th, 1706, Thomes Wright and Mary Beard......February 1st, Robert Wright and Eligabeth Hart."

22. On the 20th January, 1706-7, to John Dolben:—

"Since you went hence we have heard of a very great mortality amongst our Europeans at Bengal when Mr. Sheldon was very near aging wch we believe is the only reason that has prevented his sending us any of yours or our own accounts."

23. On the 1st February, 1708-9, to Robert Hedges, in England:—

"I rec^d the favour of yours of the 5 Jan. 1707-8 by the *Somer* who arrived here the 18th past, ... the *Lichfield* and *Montague* have been very near to falling into the French hand. I am heartily glad that you escaped and arrived safe in England and 'tis reported here that you are hastening out to the Presidency at Bengal, if so I wish you good success.... Shealem[1] wth his army is now at Golconda having killed in two battles two of his brothers & 3 of their sons so have hopes that all now will be quiet but some doubt it fearing there will be speedily fresh troubles between his sons & he'll also meet with trouble from the Rashboots with whom he has broke his word.

Mr. Nightingale will acquaint you with the news of Bengal and those parts where the Gov^t is very troublesome we are sending some persons with a present to the King......."

24. On the 21st October, 1709, to Robert Nightingale, in England:—

"I have by this ship *Heathcote* wherein I take my passage wrote to Sir Stephen Evance & yourself jointly and sent you by the hands of the Cap^n four bulws. of Diamonds am^s to Pag. 3639 : 35 : 40 wherein you are interested Pag. 1069: 2: 42 the ball^ce of .y^r acc^t which I here inclose I shall not enlarge hoping to be with you as soon as this."

---

[1] Shāh 'Ālam.

REPORTS AND LETTERS

CONCERNING THE

COMPANY'S AFFAIRS IN BENGAL.[1]

1661 TO 1685.

CASSIMBAZAR.

Mr. Kenns,[2] etc., advices about Bengall, etc., in the year 1661, being writt from Cassumbuzar.

Goods vendible.

The commodities chiefly vendable in this place are Silver and Gold ; Silver either in Coin or Barrs according to its fineness. The best time of the year to sell it in is in December except the Dutch should have no more silver from Japan, and the best time for sale will be in May. Rialls of $\frac{3}{8}$ are esteemed weighty, when 50 of them w^{as} 120 sicca (which are new Rupees of that year's coin) Rupees. The weight of each sicca is $10\frac{1}{4}$ mass, 8 of which mass is equall to the full weight of a 20^s piece in gold; Gold either in Coin, wedge or sand vendable at all times, there being much less difference in the price than in silver, which rises and falls a great deal more. The first of these three sorts is most vendible to proffit, whether 5, 10, 20, or 22^s ps. or 8 Spanish Doublons, or Venice Chequeens. The next sort vendible is in the Wedge. The sand Gold is in somewhat lower esteem, tho' of the same fineness, the reason is because the coined gold of the sorts abovementioned is generally known as to

---

[1] This forms the ninth and last section of a manuscript volume in the British Museum, (Add. MSS. 34,123) called a *Register of papers relating to the English and Dutch East Indies*, 1632-1735. The volume seems to have belonged to Henry Vansittart, Governor of Bengal. It has fifty pages. The extract here given begins on p. 42. There are other scattered notices of Bengal in the earlier pages.

J. Marshall, a superstitious sailor with an enquiring mind, has also something to say about Bengal at this time in a Journal headed "Laus Deo, Sept. 3 Anno Dmi 1668. An account of some pts. of India and w^t remarkable therein taken by me, J. M." British Museum, Harl. MS. 4254. He, however, speaks rather of the Indian language, religion and science. In Harl. MS. 4253, we have a dialogue beween J. M. and a Brahmin at Cassimbazar. In Harl. MS. 4255 J. M. gives us the Sanscrit alphabet. Harl. MS. 4252 is the journal of the voyage of the Unicorn, 330 tons, leaving Blackwall, 29th December, 1667.

[2] John Kenn was appointed, in 1658, Chief at Cassimbazar, salary £40. See above p. 33, and *Hedges' Diary*, III, pp. 189, 192, 193.

its fineress by all merchants without further tryall than inspection as for its value, that is as the gold is in fineness, yet you may note that a 20 ps., that is weight sells allways from 10 to 10½ rupees, never under nor over. The merchants buy Gold and Plate pay always ready money, when it is weighed to them, then they presently send it up to Rajamaul (where mint is) to be coined, which costs them about 3½ pc. the charges of coining, but if the English send up any it will cost them more. Silver rises and falls generally according as the Batty [batta] goes on Sicca Rupees.

Other Commodities are vendible here, but not in great quantities except Chank [Çaṁkh] or Tinn.

Goods procurable.

Commodities procurable here are silk Taffaties long and short, women's Clouts of silk about 1½ Coveds long and severall sorts of striped Stuffs and Striped Girdles. The silk is bought at the best hands, it must be bought in the Putta [? paṭa], or short skean, which is first wound off from the Bag of the worm, which commonly is worth from 15 to 19 ans. the half Seer, 70 Tolas, each Tola being the just weight of a Rupee making a Seer, in this silk we commonly wind it into above 3 Sorts, Viz^t head, Belly, and foot.[1] When we buy it of them, we buy only the head and belly, and its Customary that we have 5 Seer of the head to every 4 Seer of the Belly.

There is another sort of Silk which is superfine called Puttany [?patani], which is usually worth from 5¼ to 6¼ Rupees per seer. This silk is in short skeans like the Putta.

There is another sort of Silk which the Merchants buy for Agra, called Dolleria [? Dilheria], which is head, belly, and foot mixt together. According as this silk sells in Agra, so the price of silk in Cassumbuzar riseth or falleth. The exchange of money from Cassumbuzar to Pattana and Agra riseth and falleth as the said silk findeth a vent in Pattana or Agra.

The exchange to Patna.

To pay money in Cassumbuzar and receive it in Pattana, upon bill of Exchange a month after date, always yields proffit. I have known it from 1 to 6 per cent., when the silk sells well at Agra, the produce is usually sent to Cassumbuzar in money overland, which is the reason that when great sums of money come from thence the exchange of money to Pattana in one day doth sometimes fall 2½ to 3 p. c.

---

[1] What would now be called, first, second, and third quality silk.

The ordinary Long Taffaties of 20 Cov^{ds} long and 2 broad are always betwixt 4 to 5 Rupees per piece, the short of 10 Cov^{ds} long and 1½ broad from 8 to 23 Rupees per Gorge [Corja].

At Maqṣûdâbâd.

At Muxadavad, above 3 leagues from Cassumbuzar, there are made severall sorts of silver and gold Girdles from 10 Rupees to 60 Rupees each, also fine Taffaties from 9 to 12 Rupees per piece; but none of those goods are near so fine or good as those that come from Persia.

THE MONSOONS.

The Monsoons Serve to Voyage to and from several parts in India as followeth, vizt—

From Bantam to Macassar from October until Aprill.

From Bantam to the Coast of Cormandell all the months of the year, thro' the Straights of Sunda, except September, October, and November, and those 3 months thro' the straights of Mallaca.

From Surat to Bantam in Aprill, and so arrive at Bantam the latter end of May.

From Bantam to Surat in the latter end of August, and so arrive at Surat the end of September.

From Surat to Persia in the months of October, November, and December, and return from Persia to Surat in February and arrive in March.

From Surat to England the best time is in December, and so to fall with the Cape of Good Hope in February or March and arrive at St. Hellena in Aprill, from whence the common passage to England is three months.

From Bantam to Japan in the month of Aprill and May, and so return in November and December.

From the coast of Cormandell to Bantam all the months of the year either by the Streights of Sunda or the Streights of Malacca, except January, February, and March, those being the 3 worst months in the year, the wind lying at S.-E., and so that a ship cannot get off the coast.

No ship can winter upon the coast of India, but if they depart from Surat in Aprill they must either go for Bantam, the Mauritius, or Augustine Bay, which is upon the Island of St Lawrence.

HUGLI.

Hugly the best time to buy Goods in this place is as followeth, vizt—

In March and April, Wheat, Gunneys, and Sugar.

In May and June, Butter, Ginghams, White Cloths, and several sorts of striped stuffs.

In July and August, Rice, Hemp, Flax.

In December and January, Long Pepper, Oyle, and Rice of the second growth.

In September, October, and November all things are very dear, being the time of Shipping, and in which we receive in those goods for which money was given out in the months afore written.

PATNA.[1]

Commodities procurable.

A List of what goods procurable at Pattana and the season when to be had at the best rates, vizt—

Musk—the greatest quantity is bought in the cold, some out, but that not considerable from Buttim [Butān], a Raja's country towards the Coast of China, 3 months' journey from Pattana; it usually comes thither in the month of November. Sooner they cannot come by reason of the heats, which encounters them to their Destruction, from thence its carried to Agra, and so to Persia, Venice, etc., the price usually from Rupees 35 to 40 the Seer, the Seer being 16 pice weight (16 pice is $10\frac{9}{16}$ ounces Troy) Sawjahaun [Shāh Jahān] such as go at Surat and all the King's Dominions. Musk out of the Cold sold by the Tola from rupees 3 to 6 if high price, then its all in small hard Knobs round, if about 3 then dust without them. Ophium to be bought in March, before which Time they'll make no absolute bargain, because they'll see what crop they may expect, and accordingly it governs in price, in the year 58 we had it from Rupees 50 to 60, but since it hath been dearer from 80 to 100 Rupees prime Cost, by reason of a scarcity of it about Guzzarat, for if they have sufficient of their own growth thereabouts, then its cheap with us, but for these 3 years they have had little there, which hath caused the

---

[1] An attempt was made from Surat through Agra to establish the English trade at Patna in 1632. See *Peter Mundy's Travels*, British Museum, Add. MSS., 2286. P. M. left Agra on the 6 Aug. carrying "8 carts laden with Barrels of Quicksilver and parcills of virmillion for the Honble Companies account to bee there sold, and the money to bee there Invested : as alsoe to see the state of the Countrie what hopes of benefitt by tradinge into these parts." He reached Patna the 17 Sept. and left again for Agra, the 16 Nov. 1632. He reports against trading there. It is his opinion "that the sendinge of mee to Pattana with the Companies goods may not only prove to theire losse, but is alsoe against the intent and meaning of the President and Counsell at Suratt." Stewart in his *History of Bengal* (pp. 140,141) records a still earlier attempt made by Hughes and Parker in 1620.

advance in price with us; if you buy in March to receive in 2 or 3 months after for 1 md. they'll allow you but 38 seers, because of its dryings, if you receive it green by wheight, or when first made you may expect to dry 8 seers in each maund, and accordingly make your account.

Tumerick to be had in June if then bought 1½ maund may be had for a Rupee.

Tincall [tinkār] usually from 9 to 11 Rupees per maund.

Gumlack or Sticklack·very dear, from 9 to 11 Rupees.

Drugs great store of all sorts, that come from Buttim or Buttun [Butān], and the Coast of China.

Silver thread, the best procurable Re. 1-1 per Tola, which is 11 mace, called the Agra Tola, when as the other tola is 12 mace, by which all massee silver and gold, amber, etc., are sold by ; Gold Thread Rs. 2-2.

English Cloth sold by the Plush Yard, which is about ⅛ more than the English Yard, so are Taffaties and all other things measurable at Pattana, you may buy in the Bazar anything by the yard vending much by retail.

All manner of Gazratt, Banara, Jehaunpore, etc., commodities are to be had there, as Gold, Sashes, Urney Girdles, Elatches, Remerrys,[1] etc., all sold by weight the 11 mace Tola, and usually about Re. 1-15 to Rs. 2-1 per Tola.

The Staple commodities that come from Buttim [Butān] are Musk and sand gold, whoever goes theither cannot return above twice in 3 years, for he must barter the goods he carrys theither in Iron, Butter, Oyle, Hemp, Corne, etc., before he can attain either Musk or Gold, or other Transportable Commodities not to be had there. At Banares, 12 course from Pattana and Lachore, 16, theres white cloth fitt for Persia to be had called Umbertees and Camcomp,[2] from Re. 1-8 to 3 rupees per piece in which commodities are invested by Armenian and Mogull merchants at least ten hundred thousand rups. per ann. Transported by Land to Surat, and thence by shipping to Persia. Good proffits are made of them from thence to Surat.

There are better Taffaties made at Pattana than Cassumbazar, which are sold from 9 to 10 as. the long yard, but no great quantities, but if followed a good quantitie might be procured.

Measures in use.

The Gold Moor is 10 mace.
The Sicca Rupee 10½ mace.
Great Tola 12 mace.

---

[1] ? *Ūrṇa* girdles, *Altāchas*, and *Reshmīs*.
[2] ? *Amritis* and Kincob.

Agra Tola 11 mace.

70 Sicca Rupees make a seer.

40 King's Pice a seer.

40 Seers a Maund.

304¼ Ounces Troy makes by Calculation Seer 30 of 16 Pice.

The Yard things are sold by retail is almost ⅛ more than the English Yard.

16 Pice is a seer of musk.

There is three weights goods are sold by there, one they call the small weight, which is pice 28 to the seer. The 2 the middle weight, which is pice 36. The 3 the great weight, which is pice 40.

FURTHER ACCOUNT OF HUGLI.

Hugly sugars to be bought at Chandracona and Tania. The best time to give out money in in Xber to merchants that live at Hugly who will undertake to deliver it you there in August following at Rupees 6 to 7 per Bale, the Bale being m^ds 2 and 13 seers the 40 Pice Seer, its much better to contract with them than to send or go ourselves, for we have found it come out cheaper than we could ever make it come out ourselves, tho' we pay no Custome and they do its usually sold in shipping time from 9 to 10 Rupees per bale.

Long Pepper to be bought at said time, it grows about 16 course thence, it may be had at 4 to 5 Rupees per maund, and in the shipping its usually worth 9 to 10 Rupees, but much of it must not be bought because Bulkey, and will not vend.

Butter to be had what quantitie you desire, its to be had in Xber at 4 and 5 Rupees per maund and is old from 8 to 10 Rupees per maund.

Oyle to be bought in Xber at 1¾ to 2 Rup^s and sells at 3 to 4 Rupees p^r maund at Ballasore; since this new King's [Aurangréb's] Government the weights are there as in Pattana formerly somewhat less than £70 English the Maund now £75.[1]

LIST OF CHIEFS IN BENGAL.[2]

Chiefs in Orixa and Bengall since the Company getting there, viz:—

Orixa.

Mr. Cartwright ⎫
Mr. Joyce   ⎬ At Ballasore.[3]
Mr. Yard   ⎭

---

[1] Evidently Kenn's account ends here.

[2] I have put in the dates given by Danvers in *op cit.*

[3] This again confirms Bruton's account of the coming of the English to Bengal, and the foundation of the factories at Hariharpur and Balasor in 1633 by Ralph Cartwright.

Bengall.

Capt. Brukehaven.

Mr. Bridgeman [1650—1653].

Mr. Walgrave [?1653—].

Mr. Gawding [?1658] and Mr. Billingsley.

Agent Treveza [1658—1663].

Mr. Blake   [1663—1669].

Mr. Bridges   [1669, 70] subordinate to the Fort.

Mr. Clavill[1]   [? 1670—1677].

Mr. Vincent   [1677—1682].

Agent Hedges [1682—1684], directly from the Company.

Agent Beard   [1684, 85], subordinate to the Fort.

BALASOR.[2]

Agreement between Masters and the Merchants.

The agreement made between the Agent and Councill for affairs of the Hon[ble] English East India Company upon the Coast of Cormandell and in the Bay of Bengall and the said Comp[y's] Merchants Chimchamsaw, Chittamundsaw and Company at Ballasore, the 3 day of September Anno 1679.

1*st*.—That the Investments for goods to be bought for the Hon[ble] English East India Company in this Factory of Ballasore, being divided into 10 equall parts, shall be subdivided and allotted or proportion'd as follows :—

Four of the 10 parts to Chimchamsaw, Two of the 10 parts to Chittamundsaw, and the other 4 of the Tenn parts to the rest of the Compas. Merchants, such of them and in such proportions as the chief of this Factory and the said Chimchamsaw and Chittamundsaw shall agree from time to time.

2*nd*.—The said Chimchamsaw and Chittamundsaw for and in consideration of their said respective shares in the investments do hereby

---

[1] The list omits Henry Powell who was appointed to succeed Shem Bridge by a letter from the Court dated 7th December 1669. Probably he never succeeded. See Danvers *op cit.* p. 9.

[2] J. Marshall arrived at Balasor, 5 July 1669, "where the English have a factory a little way from the riverside.........Ballasore is a very great straggling town but scarce a house in it but dirt and thatched ones." Marshall went overland with Mr. Bridges to Hugli. On 23 Febr. 1670, at the crossing of the Pipli river they were stopped by the soldiers of a local grandee, in number about sixty or seventy, daubed with turmeric and armed. The Chief, Mr. Bridges, gave them seven rupees.

promise and obleige themselves severally and proportionably to their
said shares to be security and responsible for all the goods, Treasure,
moneys and effects whatsoever which shall be paid and advanced or
delivered unto them, or either of them, or to any of the other merchants
by their consents upon account of the said Investments, that is to say,
Chimchamsaw is responsible for his own four Tenths and 2 thirds of
the four tenths for the merchants, and Chittamundsaw is responsible
for his own two Tenths and for one third of the four Tenths for the
other merchants.

    3rdly.—It is agreed that the full summs which the Investments shall
amount unto shall be yearly paid or delivered to the said Merchants
in Curr^t Money, or in Treasure within one month after the arrivall
of the ships to an anchor in the Road from England and no part of it
before the arrivall of the ships, and if upon making up the accounts
after the ships departure or after the full investments are deliver'd
and sorted, there shall remain any money in arrears in the merchants
hands the said Chimchamsaw and Chittamundsaw do hereby promise
and oblige themselves, according to their proportions beforementioned,
to repay the same within one month after the ships departure within
Tenn days after demand thereof by the chief of the factory, and in
Case of non-payment of such arrears they promise and agree to pay
1½ p. c. per mensem for interest untill payment, and shall forfeit
and loose their, and each of their respective shares and proportions
allotted to them in the Companys investments as aforesaid, if it shall
be thought fitt not to employ them afterwards.

    4thly.—The orders for the investments shall be given to the
merchants, and agreed upon between the Chief and Councill of the
Factory and them some time in the month of March yearly and the
said merchants do promise and agree to provide all such goods as the
Company or the Agent and Councill or the Chief and Councill of the
Bay shall require to be provided at this factory of Ballasore, at as
reasonable and cheap rates and as good goods as any other merchant
can provide or sell to the same, and they promise and oblige themselves
(severally and proportionable to their said shares to be security and
responsible for all the Goods, Treasure, monys, and effects whatsoever
which shall be paid, advanced, or delivered unto them or either of them
or to any of the other merchants by their consents upon account of
the said Investments, that is to say, Chimchamsaw is responsible for
his own four Tenths and for two Thirds of the four Tenths for the
merchants, and Chittamundsaw is responsible for his own two Tenths

and for one Third of the four Tenths for the other merchants) to deliver all the said goods at the Company's house by the 25 day of November yearly, and what goods come in too late to be sent home upon the ships are to be returned upon the merchants.

5thly.—If the said merchants shall desire any of the Company's money before the arrivall of the ships, and the Chief and Councill shall think convenient to pay it to them, the said merchants do agree to allow 1¼ p. c. per mensem for the same, for so long time as it shall remain in their hands before the arrivall of the ships.

6thly.—If any merchant shall fall short of his proportion of the Goods allotted to him to provide, and the Company be thereby dis-apointed of the full return of their investments, that merchant so falling short, shall forfeit and loose his part and share in the invest-ments for ever after, provided it were not caused through trouble and stopage of the goods in the Country.

7thly.—This agreement shall remain and be in force untill the honourable Company from England shall give order for alltering or voiding the same, unless the merchants thro' their default shall cause a breach thereof. In witness whereof the Agent and Councill have sett their hand and the Honble Company's seale to one part, and the said merchants have sett their hands and seales to one other part, which are interchangably delivered in the Company's Factory house in Ballasore the Day and Year first above written.

•

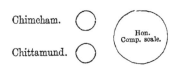

Chimcham.

Chittamund.

Hon. Comp. scale.

STRYENSHAM MASTERS.
RICHARD MOHUN.
RICHARD EDWARDS.

It is declared that Chinchamsaw and Chittamundsaw are jointly responsible for all fresh mony or effects that shall be paid and delivered to the other merchants upon the four Tenths allotted to them as they the said Chimchamsaw and Chittamundsaw, shall underwrite or pass receipts for in the Company's Receipt book, and not otherwise.

STRYENSHAM MASTERS.
RICHARD MOHUN.
RICHARD EDWARDS.

Contract for 1679.

A Contract made by Mr. Masters, etc., at Ballasore, 1679, with the merchants there for the goods following, viz[t]—

1,000 ps. Sannoes, whited and cured 30 Covds. long, 2 do. broad.	1,000 ps. Gingham colour'd 20 Covds. long and 2 do. broad.
Suro Sannoes — Head No. A at 74$\frac{1}{8}$, Belly No. B at 69$\frac{1}{8}$, Foot No. C at 64$\frac{1}{8}$ } Rups. per Corge.	Head No. A at 56, Belly No. B at 51$\frac{1}{4}$, Foot No. C at 45 } Rup. per Corge.
Herapore Sannoes — Head No. A at 67$\frac{1}{2}$, Belly No. B at 62$\frac{1}{4}$, Foot No. C at 57$\frac{1}{2}$ } Rup. per Corge.	1,000 ps. Nillaes 20 Covds. and 2 do broad. Fine ... { Head No. A at 80, Belly No. B at 75 } Rup. per Corge.
Mohunpore Sannoes — Head No. A at 59$\frac{9}{16}$, Belly No. B at 54$\frac{7}{16}$, Foot No. C at 49$\frac{7}{16}$ } Rup. per Corge.	Ordinary { Head No. A at 70, Belly No. B at 64, Foot No. C at 57$\frac{1}{2}$ } Rup. per Corge.

The difference in the prices of these very sorts of Goods bought in Anno 1679, viz[t]—

The Saunoes about 20 p. c. cheaper, the Gingham 12 p. c. and the Nillas about 16 p. c.

AT CASSIMBAZAR.

Advices from Balasor.

Upon reading advices from Ballasore concerning Salt Petre, Romalls, Cossaes, Mulmuls and Hummums, which the merchants there desire to put off to the Hon[ble] Company, it was resolved not to buy any of these goods at that place, better and Cheaper being provided in the other factorys.   •

1679, October.

Fine Taffaties were prised and the prices sett down in the Weavers books at 4 to 5 Rups per piece of 20 Coveds, they arose well.

November.

Rates of Exchange.

Some of the Company's Merchants and Shrofs of this place that have dealt much in buying their silver and gold, haveing been severall days treated with about making a firm and lasting Contract for all the Silver and Gold that should be sold in this Factory, at the last Chittermull was brought to agree to give 210 Rupees Sicca or 212 Peet[1] for 100 Rialls of Eight weighing 240 rupees, and the same price for Silver in Ingots of the same Essay with Rialls, but differing upon the Essay of Ryalls of Eight, which are said to be 6½ Ruttees, and he says but 5½ Ruttees waste in a Rupee weight, the bargain was defer'd, and this evening Essays were made of Rialls of eight Mexico and Sivill and of a

---

[1] Apparently peth, market-rate.

standard silver which came out at 5¾ Ruttees, 6 Ruttees, and 6¼ Ruttees in the Rupee, a Rupee is accounted fine silver and weighs 10¼ mace, the last year Rialls of Eight were sold here at 210 and 209¾ Rups. peet, and this year they were sold at 209 and 208½ Rupees peet, for 240 Rupees weight, and the silver in Ingots was sold last year at 209½ Rupees Peet for 240 rupees weight, and 2 dwt. finer than Standard allowed to make it Equall with the Essay of Rialls of Eight, 1 dwt. being to a pound 2¾ Chaul to a Rupee. The Gold sold last year at 15 rupees per Tola fine the waste upon Standard ¹⁄₈ Mace in a Tola and Pistols at 13¼ Rup. per Tola; this year Pistols sold at 13 Rupees per Tola. Moors last year worth 13 Rup. and this year 12$\frac{14}{16}$ Rup. per ps. the Moor is accounted to be fine Gold and weighs 9¾ mace. Chittermull was brought now to give 13⅛ Rupees per Tola (Peet that is currant money) for Pistols and for Gold of Pistoll Essay the same price, to return Moors at 13 Rups. a piece or to pay mony, and if the price of Moors shall rise, the price of Gold to rise accordingly. Note 8 chaul is a Ruttee, 8 Ruttee is a Mace, and 12 Mace is a Tola, the Charges about 6 p.c.

REGULATIONS FOR THE BAY OF BENGAL.

For the better regulating the affairs of the Honble. Company in the Bay of Bengal that the same may be managed in good order and method in the respective Factorys, it is resolved and ordered.

Books of accounts to be regulary kept.

That the Chief of each respective Factory shall keep a receipt book wherein he shall take receipts for all money paid or issued out, and shall also pass receipts for all money received upon the Companys account: Whereas it was ordered in the regulations made the third of November 1676 at Cassumbazar that the Bills and attestations for mony paid out of the Cash should be read and passed in Councill every week and noted in the Consultation Books, in regard the amount Cash is since orderd to be enterd at the end of every months Diary; it is thought best and ordered that the account Cash be read and passed in Councill the next Councill day, that is upon the next Monday or Thursday after the last day of every month, and the sum of the Ballance or Rest of the Cash sett down in every such consultation, and whereas it was orderd in the foresaid Regulations made at Cassumbazar that in the Book of Accounts each factory should be charged with what was immediately sent or received to or from thence; it is now order'd that for all mony's or goods sent into or received from one Subordinate Factory to another the Subordinate Factory shall credit Hugly Account Curr^t. for the same, in regard it is thought best; and it is hereby order'd that every Subordinate Factory do monthly at the end of their diary and account Cash enter the Accounts of what they have in that month received from or sent into Hugly or any other Factory, in a Leidger account intitled Hugly Account Curr^t. carrying foot or Rest of said Acc^t. from one Acc^ts. to the other monthly, and if the Chief and Councill at Hugly do find that the Acc^ts. from the Factorys do not agree with the Hugly Books, then they are to advise thereof, and to send the Coppy of the said Factorys Account as it stands in Hugly Books, and the Chief, etc., at Hugly are to enter their account Cash, and the Acc^ts. Curr^t. Fort St. George at the end of their Diary, which they are to send to the agent and Councill twice in the year. Columns ruled with red ink for the quantities of all goods and Treasure, the number of parcells and the weights shall be kept in the Leidgers cast up and ballanced as exactly as the outward Column for money, and in Hugly Leidger there shall be a Column for Pagodas, and pounds shillings and pence in the Acc^ts. Fort St. George.

Accounts to be regularly balanced and passed.

And whereas there is an order that the books of accounts shall be read and passed in Councill monthly, it is hereby ordered that if the Books of Accounts, the Warehouse Accounts and the Charges Generall for one month be not read and passed in Councill, the next month following the Chief of each Factory `shall note the reason thereof in the diary, and the person who shall be defective herein shall for the first offence be admonished, for the second forfeit a quarter's sallary, and for the third be suspended the service. And whereas the books of accounts are ordered to be ballanced the 30th Aprill yearly, if the second of any factory shall not have ballanced the books of accounts of the factory where he keeps the same and send the ballance thereof to Hugly by the 31st of May yearly, he shall forfeit a quarter of a year's sallary for such his default; and if the same be not done by the 30th of June he shall forfeit half a year's sallary, and if not by the last day of July he shall be suspended the Honble. Companys service ; and if the second at Hugly shall not have ballanced the generall books within one month after all the ballances of the books of the subordinate factorys are sent theither, he shall forfeit a quarter of a year's sallary for such his default, and if they be not ballanced within two months after he shall forfeit half a year's sallary, and if not in three months he shall be suspended the Honble. Compa^ys. service.

The Charges General Books.

And the Chief and Councill of the Bay are hereby required and impowered to put these orders in execution, advising thereof to the Agent and Councill, and following such further directions as they shall receive from them concerning the same. In the Charges Generall Books at the end of every month the heads and totalls of the several charges are to be sett down and summ'd up, and at the end of the book to make tables with columns for the severall heads or titles used in the Factory Books, summed up for the 12 months that the whole year's expense may appear together, and be the more readily compared with the Factory Books.

Cash balances.

At the balancing of the Books of Accounts the Chiefs of the respective factorys are to examine and see that the remains in specie do agree with the Books of the Factory, and with the cash book and the Warehouse books, and that the debts and credits be adjusted with the persons themselves concerned therein.

Accounts and salaries of the Company's servants.

If any person in the Comps. service do make use of any Goods as broad Cloth, Stuffs, etc., in the Warehouse, it shall not be charged to their accounts in the books, but they shall pay for the same in ready mony to the Warehouse Keeper, who is every month to pay the said mony into Cash in the Chiefs custody. The accounts of sallary is thus to be stated. Every person in the factory where he resides is to be credited for his full sallary by Sallary Generall. He shall be paid twice in the year, that is, at Lady day, and at Michaelmas day in equal halfs what is to be paid by the Honble. Companys order, then he shall be made Dr. to Sallary payable in England for what is short paid here to be paid there. The account of Sallary Generall is to be cleared by charges generall, and sallary payable in England by Account Currant.

Darbar and Port charges.

In the Hugly Books an account must be framed intitled Durbar and Port Charges, to which account shall be charged the Durbar Charges of Dacca, the Charges of the Sloopes, and the extraordinary Charges of Hugly in respect it is the head Factory for governing the rest for which Durbar and Port Charges shall be made Dr. to Charges generall such a summ as the Charge of Hugly exceeds the Charge of Cassumbazar or Ballasore factorys at so much p. °/₀ in the Invoices (besides the factory charges) for which Darbar and Port Charges shall be credited in the Books, and the foot of the Account shall be cleared by proffit and loss as in the foot of Charges Generall.

General letters.

The Coppys of all generall letters from one Subordinate Factory to another shall be sent to Hugly to be entered in the Coppy Books to be kept there and sent for England and the Fort, and in writing of Letters it is to be observed to mention the day upon which the Letters are received. The Letters from the Honble. Comp. and also the letters from the Agent and Councill shall (as soon as they can be coppyed) be sent to all the Factorys for their perusall, and better understanding the Companys business, and the said Letters with all other writings received from, and sent into, England and the Fort shall be coppyed into Books, and kept in the Registers at Hugly.

Office rooms.

In everyone of the Subordinate Factorys there shall be a hansome convenient Room, large, light, and well situated near the Chiefs and seconds Lodgings, which shall be sett apart for the office, and never diverted from that use, in which Room shall be placed Desks or Tables to write upon and presses with Locks and Keys, wherein the Register of the Letters shall be kept and locked up with the accounts and all other writings of the factory, which upon the remove of the Chief are to be deliver'd over by a Roll or List to the succeeding Chiefs, that none may be imbezled, and at Hugly the said Lists are to be kept by the Second in the Accomptants office, and by the Secretary in the Secretarys office.

The public table.

A Publick Table shall be kept as the Honble. Company have appointed, at which all single persons of the Factory are to dyet, and no Dyet mony shall be allowed to single persons, only to those that are married and do desire to dyet apart. Dyet mony is to be paid as the Company have appointed, and the Steward for the charge of the Table at Hugly and at Cassumbazar shall be the employment of one of the young men, a writer or factor, by which they may gain experience, and the third in the others [sic] factorys is to take charge thereof as appointed in Cassumbazar in November 1676.

Establishment charges.

As to the expense of the table and all other charges the Chiefs of the Factorys are to take due care to order the same in the most frugall manner that can be, that no extravagancy be practised, and no more peons or Servants kept than is necessary for the dispatch of the Companys business, and whereas the Company in the 12th section of their Letters of the 3rd January 1676 do order an establishment of charges to be settled, in everyone of the Factorys, which, though it cannot be perfectly done, yet so farr as it can be done conveniently. We do order and appoint as followeth.

The establishment at Hugli.

At Hugly—		Rs. Per mensem.
Servants wages for the Chief	...	12
For the second	...	8
For the Minister	...	6
For the 3rd of Councill	...	5
For the 4th of　do.	...	5
For the Surgeon	...	4
For the Secretary	...	2
For the Steward	...	2

2 Pallankeens, one for the Chief and one for the Second, 7 horses, 2 Cammells, none of which are to be lent by any but the Chief, Gurrials [ghariyāls], Cooks, Mussalls,[1] Washings, Dog-keeper, Barber, etc., Servants, as usual.

The establishment at subordinate factories.

At the Subordinate Factorys—		Rs. Per mensem.
Servants wages for the Chiefs ...	...	6
For the Second	...	4
For the Thirds	...	3
Charges General Keeper	...	2 at Cassumbuzar only.

---

[1] i.e. mash'als, torches. Perhaps here it is used for mash'alchīs, torch bearers.

A Pallankeen for the chief.

3 horses not to be lent out but by the Chief.

3 Gurrials.

1 Cooke and a Mate [assistant].

2 Mussallches [*mash'alchis*].

For Barber 2 Rupees per month.

For Washing what it costs for all the Factory.

No Dog keeper, nor dogs at the Company's charge.

No Candle nor bottle to be allowed as hath been used under the denomination of settlement Charges. Candles are only allowed to the Chiefs, and to those of the Councill in the respective factorys, to the Chaplain, and to the Chyrurgeon.

Lamps are allowed to every chamber.

The responsibility of Chiefs of Subordinate Factories.

No Chief of a Subordinate Factory is to remove from thence to any other Factory without leave first had from the Chief and Councill of the Bay under the penalty which the Hon. Comp. have appointed, and when a Chief doth remove from the Factory he shall first see that the Books of Accounts be brought up to the day, that the remains of the Warehouse and other accounts do agree with the books and the rest of cash he is to deliver up to the second and third, and if these things be not done, he is not to remove, neither the Chief of •Hugly nor of a Subordinate Factory, notwithstanding the licence from the Chief and Councill of the Bay upon pain of being suspended the Hon. Comp. Service, and when upon the removall of the Chief to another Factory, there is occasion of leaving orders in the business of the Factory, the aid orders and directions shall be made in consultation, and not of the Chiefs single authority.

The Chief and Council at Hugli to exercise general control over the trade.

The Chief and Councill at Hugly must appoint the investments to each factory and summ up the whole together in one consultation every year that it may appear how and where the severall goods are to be provided, which the Hon. Company do in order. The price of all goods provided for the Hon. Comp. shall be agreed upon by Musters, and the goods Sorted by those Musters, and in such

Factorys where there's no mony to to be given out upon dadnee[1] or impress upon goods, there the Chief and Councill shall take care to agree with the Merchants for such Goods (or some part of them) as the Hon[ble.] Company require in the months of February, March or Aprill, and that the mony shall be paid upon bringing in the goods in September or October following.

The Company's treasure.

And in regard the Companys Treasure is a long time converting into currant mony so that they are at the charge of interest mony taken up to carry on their investments, therefore 'tis thought fitt and orderd to be observed in all the Factorys that upon all Peet or Currant Rupees which shall be paid to the Merchants upon the Investments or Dadnee[1] or afterwards, they shall allow $1\frac{1}{4}$ p. c. upon Sicca Rupees never less than 2 p. c. and as much more as the batta shall hereafter rise above 1 p. c. and upon gold mohars two annas and an half a pice more than the bazar rate.

Special contracts with native merchants.

Whereas there is a contract made by the Agent and Councill with Chittermulsaw at Cassumbazar for all the Silver and Gold, which shall be sent to be sold in that Factory, and there is a contract made with Chimchamsaw and Chittamundsaw at Ballasore by the Agent and Councill that they shall be paid the full summ for that investment in treasure one month after the arrival of the English Ships, but at no certain rate, for the Treasure, therefore, it is to be observed that the Rialls of eight must be paid to Chimchamsaw, etc., at Ballasore not under 212 Rups. p. % Rials $\frac{6}{8}$ and the gold pistols not under 2 ans. per Tola, above the Bazar rate for gold Mohars, and the allowing that rate the $1\frac{1}{4}$ p. % upon mony paid on the investments is not to be charged on them in respect it will require a month's time or more to convert the treasure into mony, and notwithstanding the agreement made with Chittermulsaw it will be convenient to try what more can be made of the treasure in other Factorys, as at Pattana, and at Maulda, when that Factory is settled, being near the mint at Rajamaul; there being sometimes difference of 1 or 2 p. % between the mony of Cassumbazar, Hugly and Balasore, care is to be taken in remitting mony by exchange or in specie, and also in paym[ts.] in specie to allow the Comp. the Batta that shall arise thereby in every one of the Factorys.

---

[1] dādnī, an advance made to the weaver or craftsman.

No old merchant to be dismissed without a special order in Consultation.

And it is to be observed to keep the Compaˢ⁺ old merchants employed in providing their goods so long as they do well that the Hon'ble Company may upon enquiry be satisfied in their dealings, therefore no old merchant shall be put out of employment nor any new man employed without order in Consultation, and the reasons expressed therein for so doing, but if any old merchant fail in bringing in his goods in Time or not according to Muster, he ought to be discharged, and the Merchants Accounts must be adjusted once a year without fail.

The Company's native servants.

The like is to be observed in the house servants, especially the Vackeels, Banians, and writers, that none of them be turned off or removed, nor new ones taken in without order of Councill signifying the reason for the discharge, being observed to be of bad consequence to turn off old Servants, and the Vackeels, Banians, Mutsuddys, Tagadgeers and Podars shall from this time forward be allowed no monthly wages, but they shall be content with the Dustore of a quarter of an Anna upon a rupee, which the Merchants do allow them, and they are not to take nor the Merchants allow anything more upon pain of being discharged the employment, both the payer and receiver, and the said Dustore mony shall be divided by the Chief and Councill of the respective Factorys to the said house Banians, Writers, Podars, Tagadgeers and Vackeels, if they do not agree it among themselves, except at Dacca, where there being occasion of great expence for a Vackeel the chief Vackeel there shall be allowed what the Chief and the Councill of the Bay shall judge convenient in case the Dustore mony on that investment be not sufficient for his maintenance.

Saltpetre.

The Saltpetre provided at Pattna is to be dryed before weighed off from the Merchants, and not to take moist with allowance for it, and it is to be sent down as it comes in by 3 or 4 boats Loaden at a time, and not at all kept to the last, which hath proved very prejudiciall, the like to be observed in sending the goods from other Factorys, that all be not kept to the last, but sent away as soon as they are packed to prevent the ill consequence of a stop or any loss of time upon the dispatch of the ships.

Packing and packing stuff.

The packing stuff is in all the Factorys to be bought at the Cheapest to hand with the Compa⁸ mony, the account thereof to be kept as appointed in the orders of the 3rd November 1676, and neither the Warehouse Keeper or any other is to have any advantage thereby. The tickets put into the bales by the Warehouse Keepers are to be attested by such persons as are in the Factorys that can be spared to see that the quantitie therein packed be according to the ticket.

The river sloops.

The sloops and the vessells that bring up the treasure from the ships are to be orderd not to sail in the river in the night time when there is treasure on board of them.

Regulations for Civil Servants.

It being necessary to settle and appoint orders for the Civill Government of the Factorys a paper of such orders as are made at the Fort [*i.e.*, Madras] to be observed by people in civill employments there is now with some alterations agreed upon as enterd hereafter and orderd to be observed in all the Factorys in the Bay under the pains and penaltys therein expressed, with orders signed by the Agent and · Councill, are to be sent to the respective factorys enterd in the Con sultation Books affixed up in the offices there, and in the Chappell here.[1]

The places, stations and employments of all the Comps. servants in the severall factorys in the Bay being debated, is agreed and orderd as in the List to be enterd hereunder, and every person that is not now in the employment as is therein appointed is to be order'd to remove and take charge of the same immediately after the departure of the ships and within the month of January next.

Copies of these regulations to be sent to out-stations.

The Regulations and orders are to be coppyed and sent to there respective Factorys for their punctuall observation and complyance therewith, and it is to be observed that these orders are not intended to invalidate those regulations made at Cassumbazar in November 1676 otherwise than is expressed here, and these orders with those made at Cassumbazar 1676 if not allready done are to be enter'd in the diarys of the respective Factorys.

---

[1] *i.e.* in Hugli. For these regulations, see *ante* pp. 68, 69.

FURTHER REGULATIONS FOR THE BAY OF BENGAL.

At a consultation held in Cassumbazar, December 2nd, 1679.

Silk of "Europe" dye.

For the regulating the Honble. Companys affairs in this factory it is resolved and order'd that the books kept for the Account Silk of Europe dye shall be so kept no longer, but that the accounts thereof be included in the books of accounts kept for the factory except the mony given on Dadnee to the Weavers, the particular account of which shall be kept in the Weavers books.

The second in the Cassimbazar factory to keep the silk accounts.

That the second of the Factory shall keep the books wherein the accounts of the Weavers and Silk Merchants are distinctly kept (as well as the Factory Books) and ballance the same yearly, at the same time the factory books are ballanced, and one journall of the said Weavers books shall be copyed every year and sent to Hugly to be sent to England.

The third at Cassimbazar to be warehouse keeper.

That the third of the factory shall keep all the warehouses and have all goods under his care and charge as well as the taffaties and silks, etc., relating to Europe dye as all other goods, and that in the Warehouse Books he do sett down the Rates and prices of all goods received and delivered, and summ up the same except the prises of taffaties which are sett down in the journall of the weavers' books. That the prices of the taffaties shall be written on every piece by the warehouse keeper (if he be otherwise employed) by some other) as the Chief prises them, that thereby he may gain experience in that affair and the Honble. Company be fully informed of the price paid for those goods, and that the price may not be known to others the figures of the annas may be placed first and the figures for the Rupees last and some alterations made afterwards, as shall be thought fit, or as the Honble. Company may advice.

Pricing raw silk.

That the raw silk brought in by the Picars shall be sorted in the Factory before it be prized, and at the prizing thereof, which is allways to be done by the Chief, second and third, the warehouse keeper shall look well to the putting of it back into the baggs, and to write upon the bags the number of the sortment, and the name of the Merchant that so the weight of each sort as received in and deliver'd out may agree, and the warehouse keeper shall keep columns of the weight of each sort in the Leidger.

Entrance to the warehouse.

That the warehouse keeper shall suffer none to go into the warehouse where the raw silk is kept, but such as are in the Company's service, and no natives to go in there at any time without an Englishman, and no more of the Merchants' servants than one at a time whose silk is weighed off to prevent theft, and also deceit in changing and mixing the severall sorts of silk, the course with the fine, and therefore in shifting the bags before it is weighed, but one sort must be open'd at one time.

Weighing raw silk.

That the Raw Silk shall be weighed out and packed for England at the same weight it is received in, that is at 71 Rups. sicca per seer, and that some English of the Factory do assist at the weighing of the silk in and out, and of all other fine goods.

Packing.

That all the packing stuffs and materials for packing the Hon'ble Company's goods shall be bought with the Companys mony, and charged at the true price and an account of packing stuff be kept in the Books as was orderd in the regulations made the 3rd November 1676, and neither the Warehouse Keeper (although he hath disbursed his own mony for such things, nor any other) shall have any advantage therein either this year or hereafter. An account of packing of 65 Xts [?] [1] Taffaties amounting to Rs. 238-7, and 490 Bales of Silk amounting to Rs. 1,262-13-7 and 1 Bale raw Taffaties Rs. 5-12-9 for this year being now examined is approved.

Deductions on payments in current coin.

In regard the Hon'ble Companys Treasure is a long time coining and they are in the intrim at the charge of interest for mony to carry on their investments, therefore to save the said charge it is resolved and ordered that upon all Peet (or currant mony) Rups. which shall be paid either upon Dadnee, or afterwards out to the Silk Merchants or to the

---

[1] Probably the word intended is "bales."

Weavers in full of Accounts shall be deducted R. 1 an. $\frac{1}{4}$ out of every 100 Rupees at the time of the said payment, upon Sicca Rupees shall be deducted 2 Rups. per cent. and as much more as the Batta shall hereafter rise above 1 p. c., and gold mohars shall be charged $2\frac{1}{2}$ ans. a piece more than the Bazar rates.

And in regard its fitt to settle the summs to be impress'd or given for Dadnee upon goods it is order'd that for the first Dadnee upon every Bale of silk of 80 seer shall be given out 200 Rups. upon every Bale of Mucta [mogtà] 100 Rups. and upon every ps. of fine Taffatie 4 Rupees, and no new Dadnee to be given before the former be brought in by the person indebted, and if any merchant or weaver that hath received the Company's dadnee shall deliver his goods to any other he shall not be further employed.

Payment of native agents.

It is also order'd that the Vackeels, the Mustuddys or writers, and the Tagadgeers, Dunneers or Overseers of the Weavers, and Picars and Podars[1] shall from this day forward have no Monthly wages paid them upon the Honble Company's account, but they shall be contented with the Dustore mony of a quarter of an anna upon a Rupee which the merchants and weavers are to allow them, and they shall not allow anything more upon any pretence whatsoever, and the said Dustore mony shall be divided every year twice or oftener by the Chief and Councill of the Factory amongst the said writers, Tagadgeers, Podars and Vackeels, and there shall be kept 5 or 6 writers, one to write and keep the Charges, a Taffatie measurer and weigher, two podars, four or five Tagadgeers, besides Poons imployed therein, one Vackeel for Persia writing, and one to go to and fro of messages upon occasion, and these and others more or less as shall be found necessary by the Chief, etc., are to be paid out of the Dustore mony.

Information of these regulations to be given to the native agents.

And that the Merchants, etc., may know what to trust to and not surprised or think they are imposed on by the Chief of the Factory, when they shall come to receive the Dadnee, it is thought fit to send for such of the Merchants, Weavers, Writers, etc., as are in and about the Factory and acquaint them with what herein concerns them, and that

---

[1] i.e., vakīls, mutasaddīs, and the tagādāgīrs, and paikārs and podārs. The rigin of the word dunneer or dumier is obscure.

from this day forward these orders are to be observed in this Factory, which was done accordingly.

New Buildings.

The throwing House being made of mud walls and coverd with Thatch is falling down although but lately set up, and there being many other buildings about the factory of mud and thatch which put the Company to continual great Charge of repairs often falling and oftener burning down, and endanger the goods and whole buildings, it is order'd that the throwing house and the Weaving house be built of brick within the compound of the Factory, and not at such a distance as the further end of the garden, that the Factory be walled about with a brick wall, and the Kitchen, and as many small outhouses as are necessary for the accomodation of married People be built of bricks, which are now cheap, and that convenient room be sett apart for an office for writing business in which books and papers are to be carefully laid up in presses made for that purpose, and the said room is never to be diverted to any other use.

Measures for Cassumbazar silk.

The Weights of Cassumbazar the Company buys silk by are vizt.— By the Seer which is 71 Sicca Rups. and 40 Seers in that weight, as well as in all other makes a maund, but the silk called Bunga, which is bought by the Surat merchants, is bought by the Seer 77 Tolas or Sicca Rups. The sort of silk bought by the Comp. is called Tanna [? *Tassar*].

At Cassumbazar they have 3 crops or Bunds which are in November, March, and July.

Note, the June or July Bund for raw Silk is allways course.

Note, that most or all the Silks in Cassumbazar, that is, all the Taffaties are bought by the piece of 20 Coveds long and 2 broad, and the first sort to weigh 48 to 50 Sicca Rups. and so they go, declining about 2 or 3 Sicca Rupees in a sort for 5 or 6 sorts.

EXPORTS FROM BENGAL.

From Bengal.[1]

Rice, Oyl, Butter, Cassumber, Cummin seeds, white.

1 Bambo for 8 ms. is accounted dear, when ships come from Surat may yield 3 ms. [mace] this place may spend 40 Bahar.[2]

---

[1] British Museum, Add. MSS. 34, 123, p. 29.

[2] *i.e.*, *bahār*, a load.

Quentry, Metty, Saffron, dry, worth 3 bamboos per 1 mace.

? Herba Doce 10 Behar.[1]

Dry Ginger worth 1 Bamboo per mace.

? Collonghee worth 3 „ per mace.

? Adjevan, 8 Bamboos per mace.

Mustard 4 „ per ms.

Cotton 1 ms. per Bamboo.

Lack worth 3 Tale[2] per Bahar when plenty.

Iron 2½ Tale per Bahar.

Cossaes 1 yd. and 4 fingers broad fine and ordinary 50 Corge May vend.

Elatches 40 or 50 Corge.

Taffates, red, most esteemd 20 Covds. long and as broad as Cossaes 150 Corge or 200 Corge.

Chucklaes about 50 Corge.

Doreas about 15 Corge.

Hummums of all sorts, if [you] sell 30 Corge, [it] is much.

Sannoes, fine, etc., about 36 Corge.

Ophium when no ships go from Bengall to Malacca. Sells well.

Gingerlee [*jinjali*] Oyl[3] more esteemed than Mustard seed.

Soosies from 15 to 20 Tale per Corge.

Romalls 60 or 70 Corge, ordinary sort best.

Raw silk, white, 125 Tale per Bahar, about 2 Bahars may sell.   •

Goods from Bengall proper for the Coast of Cormandell.[4]

Anno 1684.

				Rs.	As.	
Ophium Cost	...	...	...	80	0	per md.
Canch	...	...	...	2	8	„ „
Bees' Wax	...	...	...	19	0	„ „
? Elgaram	...	...	...	12	0	„ „
Cummin seeds	...	...	...	2	8	„ „
Black Cummin seeds		...	...	1	0	„ „
Dry ginger	...	...	...	2	0	„ „
Turmerick	...	...	...	1	0	„ „
Wheat	...	...	...	0	8	„ „
Taffiteas 20 Covds. long and 2 do. broad				6	0	„ piece.
Ditto ordinary 18 Covds. long and 1¾ do. broad	...	...	...	4	8	„ „

[1] I do not understand this passage.

[2] *Tael*, the Chinese ounce, also a coin which was once worth 6s. 8d.

[3] Oil of the *sesamum indicum*.

[4] Add. MSS. 34, 123, pp. 36, 37.

Anno 1684.	Rs.	As.		
Gold flower'd Jemmewars	12	0	per piece.	
Silver flower'd ditto	10	0	,,	,,
Silver Rasters 8 Covds. long 3 do. broad	4	8	,,	,,
Gold Rasters 8 Covds. long 3 do. broad	5	8	,,	,,
Silver Rasters 2½ Covds. broad and 8 long	3	8	,,	,,
Gold Rasters	4	0	,,	,,
Atlasses Striped 1½ Cov. broad 14				
Cov. long	2	8	,,	,,
Birds' Eye Atlass 9 Cov. long 1¼ broad...	1	4	,,	,,
Butter	7	0	,, maund.	
Oyle of Mustard seed	3	0	,,	,,
Pittumbers 15 Cov. long and 2 do. broad	40	0	,, corge.	
Chunder bannies, 1½ Co. broad and 10 Co.				
long	20	0	,,	,,
Pittumbers, 10 Cov. long and 1½ broad ...	22	0	,,	,,
Chunder bannies, 14, Co. long, 1¾ broad...	36	0	,,	,,
Drys, 14 Co. long and 2 do. broad ...	35	0	,,	,,
Pegu Clouts, Spotted	80	0	,,	,,
Silk Lungees	20	0	,,	,,
Boys' Sashes, 5 Co. long, ¾ Co. broad ...	12	0	,,	,,
Do. ,, 4 ,, ,, ½ ,, ,, ...	5	0	,,	,,
Drys, 10 Co. long, 1¼ broad	25	0	,,	,,
Rudder bannes Clouts, 14 Co. long, 2				
do. broad	40	0	,,	,,
Lunge[e] Elatches				
Floretta Yarn or Mucta [mogta] first sort	5	8	per seer.	
Second Sort ditto	4	12	,,	,,
Punga Silk, Head and Belly	2	14	,,	,,
Mugga Silk (will not do.)	1	8	,,	,,

Goods proper to send from the Bay of Bengall to the Coast of Cormandel, Anno 1684.[1]

Raw Silk is a staple commodity all along the Coast; 300 bales of 2 maunds each may vend yearly.

Sugar Tissindy[2] 3,000 bales of 2 maunds 5 seer will vend yearly.

Long Pepper 7,000 maunds per ann.

Salt Petre 2,000 to 3,000 maunds per ann.

Tumerick 1,500 maunds per ann.

Cotch,[3] a commodity which seldom fails, 400 maunds per ann.

---

[1] Add. MSS. 34, 123, p. 37, reverse.

[2] Tissinda or fine sugar.

[3] Apparently the *costus* or putchock, a fragrant root exported to Malay countries and China where it is used to make jostics.

Dammer or Pitch 400 maunds per ann.

Ophium 50 to 60 maunds.

Several sorts of piece-goods from Cassumbazar, *i.e.*—

Petambers.	Taramandes.
Deryeyes.	Several sorts of Silk.
Chamborbannes.	Girdles.
Taffiteas of several sorts.	Soosies, a few.
Flowerd Lungees.	Elatches, a few.

IMPORTS TO BENGAL.

Goods proper for the Bay from the Coast. Anno 1684, viz.—

Copper, Tutanague,[1] Tyn in Pigs and Gants.[2]

Chank [*Camkh*], a vast quantity will sell.

Betle nut.

Peper.

Some sorts of Chints.

Girdles and Sashes of Maslopatam.

The first Dutch ships arrive in the Bay about the latter end of June. They come from Batavia with Spices, Copper, Tutanague, Tinn, and Sandalwood, and are dispatch'd in October to Batavia with goods proper for Europe to send on other ships.

The second fleet comes in September from Batavia and Zelone. Those from Zelone with Chank, Beetlenut, and Cinamon; they are dispatch'd the latter end of November and December, partly with the remaining goods of that year's investments, and to compleat the rest of their loading with Rice, Wheat, Butter, Oyl, Gram[3] and several sorts of Grain, and Hoggs, etc., for their Garrisons.

The third fleet comes through the Straights of Malacca and arrive in January. These come comonly from Jappan and load back with provisions for their garrisons.

---

[1] Port *tutenaga*, used to mean Chinese "white copper," also to mean zinc or pewter.

[2] *Ganza*, fr. Malay *gangsa*, fr. Sansk. *kansa*, bell-metal. The metal which constituted the inferior currency in Pegu, which some call lead and others a mixed metal.

[3] Port *grão*, grain. In India it is used to mean the kind of vetch which is the common grain-food of horses.

Buildings in Bengall.[1]

At Bengall they want builders, not having near so good as upon the Coast, they want here good planks, but have good knee timber and indifferent good iron.

BARON'S ACCOUNT OF BENGAL AND MADRAS.[2]

"*Fort St. George, June* 1695."

The presidency of Fort St. George (including Bengall) is at present the most considerable to the English nation of all their Settlements in India, whether we respect it in reference to the trade to and from Europe, or the Commerce from one part of India to the other. The usual Cargo from China is Tutanague, Sugar, Sugar Candy, China Root, Quick Silver, China Ware, Copper, Gold, Allom, Some few Silks, and Toys. Their price in Madras this year, viz.—Tutanague 24 to 25 pag[s.] per Candy,[3] Copper 60 to 62 pags per Candy, China Root 12 to 18 pag[s.] per Can[y.], last year worth 30 to 40 do., Sugar 12½ to 13 pag' per Can[y.], Sugar Candy 21 to 22 pags per Can[y.], Allom Nankeen 10 pag to 12 do., Amoy 8 to 10 pags per Candy, Quick Silver 60 to 65 pags per pecull.[4] The Coast and Bay are so well provided with China goods that I believe upon the arrival of next ships they will hardly yield so much by 10 p. cent., for which I ascribe the following reasons, viz.—That Bengall is glutted with metalls of all sorts, that the last troubles and famine on the Coast of Gingerlee discourages sending any down thither, and that the continuing devastations committed daily by the Moors and Morattaes hinder their free passage into the Inland Countrys on this side. The usual freight from China, viz., Sugar, Allom, Sugar Candy, Gallingal, China Root, Cubebs,[5] Anniseeds, &c., are accounted Gross goods and pay 25 p. c., Tutanague and Copper 20 p. c. Raw and wrought silk, Quicksilver, Vermilion, Musk, and Camphor are fine goods and pay 15 p. c. and Gold 7 or 8 p. c.

The scarcity of rain hath increased the trade to Bengal, but the plentifull season of rain will (its hoped) put a stop thereto, for surely there can be no advantage more uncomfortable than that which arrises

---

[1] Add. MSS. 34,123, p. 39, reverse.

[2] *Ib*, p. 40, reverse.

[3] Candy, a weight equal to about 500 lbs., fr. Mar. *khaṇḍī.*

[4] *Pikul,* a man's load.

[5] The fruit of the *piper cubeba* used as a spice.

from the poverty and misery of the poor, tho it may be as well charity as interest to deal therein at some time.

The usual freight and price of Bengall goods, viz.—Fine Piece Goods, which are Mulmuls, Tanjebs, Cossaes, Doreas, Taffiteas, Jemewars, Soosees, Sanoes &c., pay 4 and 4½ p. c. freight, and seldom gain above 10 p. c. clear of charges, many times not that. Gurrahs, Sailcloth, and Cambays pay 8 p. c. This year Sailcloth sold for pags 13 per Corge, Gurrahs of 36 Coveds Pagodas 15½ to 16. Taffiteas of 18 Coveds 32 to 35 pag per Corge, ditto of 20 Coveds 37 to 38. Soosees of 50 Coveds from 50 to 55 (the last year worth 60), but no man can proportion these which rise and fall according to fancy and use, but the most rational and probable method is judging by the foregoing rate as a medium. Sugar pays ¾ Pagoda freight per bale. Butter and Oyl pag^a. 1, and sometimes 1¼ per jar. The camp in our neighbourhood and countries adjoining alters the price of goods very much. But should there be brought up any large quantity of goods of sugar this year, upon the arrival of the expected ships from China, the market would be glutted so as to occasion the sending a vessel or two to Persia in September, which indeed often proves a happy necessity; for being the first that can arrive by two months, they have a double advantage in the sale of their goods there and the return hither. Because the sugar in Bengall coming from the country so late as November prevents an early dispatch and cannot in any wise disappoint those that go immediately from Madrass.

Freight of goods from Madrass to Persia, viz., Tissinda or fine Bengall sugar and Sugar Candy 18 p. cent. China and Java Sugars 20 p. c. and all Bussora or Course Bengall Sugars 23 p. c. Romalls, Cossaes, etc. Fine goods 7 to 10 p. c. Pegu stick laque yields a great price, but cannot be permitted on freight being so extremely bulky. The returns, viz., Gold (being either Chequeens, Goldbars, Ibrains [?]) pay freight   per cent. Syrash wine of Abassees per chest. Fruit of abassees per matt bagg each qt. 38 Mds. Tabrees, each Md. Tabrees being 6¾ lb. and where it exceeds to allow per rate. The general custom is to pay the said freight in Persia.

Our correspondence with Acheen is in a manner broke of, for since the scarcity of rice first, and now of slaves, the dearness of cotton and the manufactures of this country (that place being supplyd from Surat at much cheaper rates than can be afforded from hence) its accidental that any vessel goes from this coast thither; except when having had arge quantitys of ophium from Bengal and worth but 12 or 13 pags

per md., it may be adventured, tho it is a very uncertain commodity.
The great gains or disappointment depending upon the Java fleet's
arrival and the quantity they shall have occasion to buy up to carry with
them to their respective ports.

From Fort St. David and this place have gone two or three small
vessels to Queda, carrying blew commissees, morees, and long cloth and
some of each sort white with a small parcel of ophium, tho I
believe they'll make but a poor voyage, considerng that the staple
commodity of the port, tin, is hardly worth 28 pags per Candy and
for dammer, rattans, etc., notwithstanding the profit is great, yet in
respect of the small value and bulkiness of these goods are hardly worth
the bringing.

The trade to Pegu is not very great, the chief design of sending
ships thither being to repair them, though the goods they carry many
times turn to account; but on the returns if the merchant can save
himself he fares very well. Thin Betteelaes, commonly call'd Pegu
Batteelaes, are the proper commoditys for that country, as are likewise
Madrass paintings, the price differing according to the fineness and
goodness of their several sorts, of the Bettelaes we commonly
proportion three, the first 20 to 22 pag. per corge, the second or
middle 13 to 14, and the ordinary course sort 8 to 10 pag per corge.
Of the paintings are various sorts and fineness, the ordinary clouts
are double chequer'd Cambays and popleys being either red or mixt
red black or blow, and cost from 18 to 20 pag. per corge. The better
sort are good [?] dray or colours on fine longcloth, Morees, or Percollaes,
and we proportion them at 1 and 1½ more than the value of their respective cloth when brown, and cleared from the choulky, according to
the notes received from thence. Freight paid out and home is
generally 5 p.c., and returns this year yielded viz. Tyn 27 pags per
Candy, Elephant's teeth small 45 pag per Candy, from 30 to 20 teeth
to the Candy, 50 pags, of 16 to 20 teeth 60 pags, from 16 to 10
teeth, 65 pags., and under that number 70 to 75 pagodas per Candy.
Hartoll[1] or arsenick 32 pagodas gants of the best sort 13, do. ordinary
7, and lead 6. The gants as being the country money is prohibited
exportation under severe penaltys, therefore very seldom in any
quantitys brought away. How be it this year there was found a
contrivance to run and conveigh so much as never was known before
to come over in one season.

---

[1] *Hartāl* or *harital*, yellow arsenic.

I have little occasion to speak of the trade on the west coast of
Sumatra, where you are far better acquainted than I can pretend to;
therefore shall only offer that prosperous voyages may be made thither
both from Surat and hence as well by the manufacture of both places
sold there as the returns in pepper, gold, Benjamin,[1] camphir, etc.

SAMUELL BARON.

---

[1] A kind of incense got from the resin of the *styrax benzoin*.

Reg. No. 818J—500—28-11-95.

INDEX.

A.

Abassees, 402.
'Abdu-l Faẓl, 298.
'Abdu-l Gani, 96, 97.
'Abdu-r-Rahīm, 348, 349.
Abū-l Faẓl, 4.
Accountant, 62, 305.
Accounts, 385, 386.
———— of the Company's servants, 387.
———— of English Company, 220, 227, 229, 231.
———— of Old Company, 219, 226, 229, 231.
Acheen, 346, 402.
Achilles, 100.
Acton, Richard, 330, 363, 364.
Adams, Abr., 186, 191, 240, 275, 279, 288, 289, 290, 292, 299, 301, 302, 306, 307, 310, 324.
Adams, Rev. Ben., 200, 201, 202, 204, 214, 215, 229, 235, 256, 258, 262, 263, 272, 274, 275, 277, 350.
Adams, Wm., 311, 321.
Addison, Gulston, 325, 360.
Adi Gangā, 129, 130, 133, 134, 135.
'Abdu-s Samad, 108, 110, 114.
Admiral, 329.
Agamemnon, 100.
Agarpāṛā, 133.
Affleck, 371, 372.
Afghans, 147, 148, 149.
Āghā Muḥammad Zamān, 7, 8, 241.
Agra, 23, 172, 173, 178, 287, 376, 378, 379, 380.
Ahmadnagar, 171.
Aïn-i-Akbarī, 4, 137.
Akbar, 134, 135.
Akhbārnavīs, news-writer, 259.
Ākhūnd, teacher, instructor, 300, 301, 307, 315, 317.
Aknā, 131.
'Alam Shāh: see Shah 'Ālam, 290.
Albermarle Ship, 367.
'Ali Bakhsh, 349.
'Ali Raẓa, 242, 346.
Allahabad, 80.
Alleja or Alācha, silk cloth from Turkestan, with a wavy line pattern down either side, 17, 398, 400.
Alley, Capt., 74.
Allowances, 239, 249.
Alum, 401.
Alvānī, shawl cloth, 255.
Amber, 379.
Ambua, 130.
Amethyst trade, 125.
Amen Corner, 330.
Amīru-l-Umarā, premier prince, 241.
Amoy, 401.

Amusements, 64.
Anantarāma, the Company's broker, 55, 85.
Anantarāma, a slave, 351.
Anderson, Rev. Wm., 214, 215, 256, 257, 258, 274, 317, 318.
Anna Ketch, 239.
Anna Ship, 308.
Anniseed, 401.
Antelope Ship, 154.
Arabia, 123, 140.
Aracanese, 18.
Arreanes, 53.
Arakān, 34, 49, 54, 119, 121, 122, 134.
Arbuthnot, Capt., 96.
Ariadaha, 131.
Armagaon, 20.
Armenians, 125, 137, 144, 150, 205, 370, 379.
Arrack, 17, 66, 146, 256, 276.
Asad Khān, 125, 172, 241, 281.
Asālat Khān, 23.
Ash, Mrs. Domingo, 146, 207, 256, 276, 295, 301.
Ashāṛi, money due in the month of Ashāṛ or July, 221, 222.
Ashby, Capt. Steph., 115.
Ashe, Sir Joseph, 67.
Assam, 8, 35.
Assuria, 348, 349.
Atlas, satin, 399.
Auṣ, early rice, 285.
Augustine Bay, 377.
Augustinians, 143.
Aurangabad, 174, 184.
Aurangzēb, 8, 34, 48, 78, 90, 93, 99, 101, 107, 122, 139, 140, 141, 148, 153, 160, 168, 171, 180, 184, 212, 232, 241, 280, 281, 380.
Aurungzebe Ship, 368.
Austin, John, 368.
Austin, W., 16.
Averilla Ship, 368.
A'zam, 78.
A'zam Shāh, 171, 172, 173, 174, 177, 178, 241, 281, 287.
'Aẓīmu-sh-Shān, 148, 149, 150, 161, 168, 172, 177, 178, 180, 181, 182, 186, 190, 200, 233, 240, 282, 296, 297, 298, 299, 300, 301, 307, 309, 320, 329, 342.

B.

Bad language fined, 265.
Bāfta, woven, a kind of fine calico, 255.
Bahādur Khān, 105, 118, 119, 121, 122, 123.
Bahār, a load, 397, 398.
Bakhshbandar, Happy Harbour, a name for the port of Hugli, 259.
Bakhshī, military paymaster, 236, 238, 247, 275, 279, 299, 329, 332, 340.
Bakuya, 137.

Milton Keynes UK
Ingram Content Group UK Ltd.
UKHW020641070923
428220UK00006B/245